TCHAIKOVSKY

The Man behind the Music

Also by Lawrence and Elisabeth Hanson

THE FOUR BRONTES

NECESSARY EVIL: THE LIFE OF JANE WELSH CARLYLE

MARIAN EVANS AND GEORGE ELIOT

CHINESE GORDON: THE STORY OF A HERO

NOBLE SAVAGE: THE LIFE OF PAUL GAUGUIN

PASSIONATE PILGRIM: THE LIFE OF VINCENT VAN GOGH

THE TRAGIC LIFE OF TOULOUSE LAUTREC

VERLAINE: FOOL OF GOD

IMPRESSIONISM

THE SEEKERS: GAUGUIN, VAN GOGH, CEZANNE

PROKOFIEV

TCHAIKOVSKY

The Man behind the Music

by

Lawrence and Elisabeth Hanson

ILLUSTRATED WITH PHOTOGRAPHS

DODD, MEAD & COMPANY

NEW YORK

Library of Congress Catalog Card Number: 66-13606

Printed in the United States of America
by The Cornwall Press, Inc., Cornwall, N. Y.

Preface

SOME TIME AGO the English musicologist David Lloyd-Jones broadcast a most interesting talk on Tchaikovsky. The substance of his
talk was that Tchaikovsky was not the namby-pamby neurotic
recent biographers have made him out to be and that a great deal
of his unplayed music ought to be heard regularly. In short, as
man and composer Tchaikovsky has been misunderstood and un-
derrated. Mr. Lloyd-Jones called for a definitive biography which
would establish the composer as he really was.

When this broadcast was made we were in fact hard at work on
just such a biography, as we told Mr. Lloyd-Jones, with the reservation that we did not aim at a definitive one.

We have written on Tchaikovsky because we admire him and
his work, because we think it high time that he was looked at
afresh, and because we believe the very large amount of new
material—letters and reminiscences chiefly—made available in the
Soviet Union within the past few years helps the new biographer
to present a more rounded and more accurate picture.

At the risk of boring those who know the past history of Tchaikovsky studies we give a brief résumé, for those who do not know
how the present widespread impression of him came into existence. It began with a large biography (translated into English
in part only) by Modest, the composer's brother. Modest was the

family black sheep, charming, silly, and a poor writer. That he intended to do honor to his dead brother is certain but he fell into the trap awaiting all biographers—instead of identifying himself with his subject he identified the subject with himself. This biography, which has set the standard for all others, is in essence a biography of Modest Tchaikovsky as he would have been had he possessed his brother's gifts. In spite of its great length—three volumes—Modest was obliged to select from a mass of material (Tchaikovsky was a prodigious letter writer) and his selection was, unconsciously no doubt, made to show the composer as Modest preferred to think of him, a man much like himself. The Tchaikovsky radically opposed to Modest—the vigorous, plainspoken lover of the good things of life—was soft-pedalled almost out of existence. The text of letters was tampered with to this end, and the biographer's commentary all pointed in one way.

Naturally such a book by a man who knew Tchaikovsky so well had a decisive effect on public opinion. More harm was done—again unconsciously—when Rosa Newmarch published a shortened version of Modest's book in English. She went even further than Modest and bowdlerized the long quotes from Tchaikovsky letters so as to make him appear the gentle, nervous creature, feminine to a degree, that, following Modest, she believed him to be.

Then came the era of "freedom" in the West when discussion of sex was all the rage. The trend was expressed in biography too, and later biographers of Tchaikovsky drew the conclusion that he was homosexual, and, in line with the tendency of the age, came out with it as a fact suppressed by Modest and the early biographers who followed him. What they did not do was to relate this belief (at that time it was no more) to the man and his music, at once so introversive and so masculine. Admittedly they lacked much of the evidence now available, yet the most cursory study of his work must surely have shown that he could not have been the caricature of a man which the term homosexual often suggests. As it was, they took the superficial way out, painting Tchaikovsky as a moral and physical weakling, which has bewildered those unable to reconcile such a picture with the music. Our conclusions, based on a study of all known material, show him in a different light, as the kind of man who would have written the kind of music we all know.

The misconception about him seems to have arisen from the emphasis placed on his sex life by recent writers and from the fact that he was both a deeply feeling man and a man of his age to whom the shedding of tears was as natural as our modern restraint is unnatural. Likewise with his music; to think of a man as neurotic and self-tortured is to find those elements predominating in his work. The vigor, liveliness, fun, elegance, and complete command of the grand manner just as typical of Tchaikovsky are not so much overlooked as put into the back of the mind because the picture of the man does not square with such music.

We have gone back to the sources and present as clearly and as fairly as we are able a picture of a great man as he reveals himself. Biographers are usually faced with incomplete material and this confronts them in turn with a dilemma; if they attempt to use their imagination, based on a study of what material exists, to fill in the gaps, they are liable to be written off as nonserious romancers; if they sit on the fence they are called dull and cowardly; if they simply state the bare facts as they know them they are called lazy. But with Tchaikovsky the position is reversed. The Russians have surpassed themselves in thoroughness. His letters and letters to him (thousands in all) have been printed. His diaries have been printed. All his writings, including many recently discovered letters, are being printed—as we write, seven out of ten volumes have appeared. A small host of reminiscences by his contemporaries have been printed—again, many recently—and a number of manuscripts have been collected in libraries as shown in the Bibliography. And as if this were not enough, the indefatigable Soviet authorities have published a book in which Tchaikovsky's movements for almost every day of his adult life have been carefully noted.

The gratified but rather stunned biographer, faced with this plethora of material, is also puzzled. If a Western reader were presented with all Tchaikovsky's letters (still mostly untranslated) he would have to struggle through many volumes—struggle is the operative word, for Tchaikovsky was no great letter writer—and if he ever reached the end of them he would still only know Tchaikovsky as he saw himself, which is not at all the Tchaikovsky seen by others, let alone the sum of the man, which no one saw. The reminiscences (also mostly untranslated) are very valuable, but like all reminiscences, they are written from the point of view of the author who has been presented with one side of Tchaikovsky.

All this material, including hundreds of not very exhilarating reviews written by Tchaikovsky, has to be studied by the biographer who really wants to get at the truth, and long before he has finished he is wondering whether it might not be a good idea to advise the reader simply to listen to Tchaikovsky's music. Not just the music usually played but all the music he wrote. If he were able to study this over a substantial period he might get to the real man. Unfortunately this is not possible; neither broadcasts nor concert performances nor recordings cover more than a low percentage of Tchaikovsky's complete output. We therefore offer the present study as a stopgap. We include new material— that is, material formerly unprinted or untranslated—not just because it is new but only if in our opinion it gives body to the picture of the man. The translations are our own. We have also discussed in simple terms some of the many unjustly neglected works of Tchaikovsky.

The emphasis in this book is on the man who wrote the music and not on the music that man wrote—this in the belief that the more one can understand Tchaikovsky the more one will understand and love his music. And that is why, when the music is discussed here, it is discussed in the simplest possible terms. Like every other great composer, Tchaikovsky did not write for the critic, the commentator or for an academic clique. He wrote for men and women like ourselves who simply love music and love it simply. We have tried to follow his lead.

Because of the dissimilarity of the English and Russian alphabets, it is not always possible to make an entirely satisfactory transliteration. In general, we have tried to follow the accepted American practice, using the spelling of names, for example, which would be most familiar to American readers.

Our thanks for many and various favours must go to the staffs of the Soviet Embassy in London and the British Embassy in Moscow (in particular Mr. N. Kiasashvili and Mr. A. Brooke-Turner); to the curator of the Klin Museum, the librarians of the CSALA and the GCMMC in Moscow; the Music Library, the Reid Library, and the National Library in Edinburgh; the British Museum and the Central Music Library; to Professor Dennis Ward of Edinburgh University, who helped us to translate a particularly badly scrawled autograph letter; to Mr. Lloyd-Jones for his generous assistance in many directions; to the Librarian of the Library of Congress, Washington; and to Dr. Kurt Eulenburg of Ernst Eulenburg Ltd. for his interest and provision of scores. And a special word of grateful thanks is due to Miss B. Carpenter who typed and retyped this long book from abominably maltreated scripts, and did it all at great speed and without complaint.

We would like to end with a word of gratitude and esteem to Herbert Weinstock whose biography of Tchaikovsky was the first modern study of the composer. Mr. Weinstock's book set a high standard in musical biography that we have tried to live up to; we owe a great deal to this work and hope that we may allowed to pay this respectful and admiring tribute.

Two final notes. First, all quotations from Modest Tchaikovsky in our book are taken from his autobiography—in our opinion by far his best work—he died before he could finish or "improve" it. Second, the now almost completed Russian edition of the Tchaikovsky letters contains a number of omissions, denoted in every case by asterisks. We have satisfied ourselves that the editors have been justified in making these omissions which consist without

exception of references to homosexuality. Students in a position
to consult the autographs in the Klin and Glinka museums can
check these passages for themselves.

L. H.

E. H.

Contents

Illustrations

Unless otherwise noted, all illustrations are from the Tchaikovsky Museum, Klin

Part One

PRELIMINARY

CHAPTER 1

The Tchaikovskys
1840-1844

"I AM RUSSIAN, RUSSIAN, RUSSIAN!" Tchaikovsky wrote in a fury when he heard that he and his music were being traced to Polish sources. He did not mean that he had no Polish blood in his veins, on the contrary he admitted ruefully that he probably was of Polish descent; he meant that he personally loved Russia with a passion and that his music expressed Russia.

This acknowledged, he did not care one kopeck where he came from. When he became famous, some members of his family busied themselves by unearthing equally famous ancestors. He laughed at them; it was much more likely, he said, that the Tchaikovsky advertising a corn cure in a Moscow newspaper was a distant relative; it was a fairly common name in Russia and even commoner in Poland.

It will be gathered from this that genealogies did not interest him; he was concerned wholly with his own sympathies. Yet as far as can be seen, which is admittedly not very far, his ancestors seem to have been as Russian as his music.

The first definitely placed Tchaikovsky was Fyodor Afanasye-vich, lieutenant in the Cossacks. He was mortally wounded in the service of Peter the Great in a battle which led directly to the rise of Russia as a great European power (and, much more important, as a strong cultural influence in the world), the battle of Poltava against the Swedes. His father-in-law was wholly Russian too and spent his adult life in a very Russian occupation; he was one of the deacons in a Petersburg church.

The son of Fyodor Afanasyevich, Pyotr Fyodorovich, entered government service and became Chief of Police, first at Slobodsk, then at Glazov, in the province of Vyatka. He seems to have been a versatile man, for he won a local reputation as a healer of the sick. It is a curious coincidence, when one considers the enormous size of Russia, that this grandfather of the composer held office within fifty miles of the town in which Tchaikovsky was born. Vyatka, halfway to Siberia, had no special connection with the Tchaikovsky family and certainly did not attract them—it was remote, primitive, unlovely; sheer chance was to bring Tchaikovsky's father back to it many years later.

On the maternal side the patriotic note is repeated as well as the connection with the Cossacks. The woman Pyotr Fyodorovich married, Anastasia Posokhova, was a daughter of one of the many officers in the army of Catherine II who were slaughtered by the famous Cossack rebel Pugachev while trying to hold outlying frontier posts for the empress. The couple had many children and the youngest, Ilya Petrovich, born in 1795, was the composer's father.

Ilya Petrovich Tchaikovsky was a brown-haired, blue-eyed man of medium height with a fine forehead and strong nose. His appearance was not remarkable—the most noteworthy thing about it was the pompadour into which he brushed his hair. This gave him an aggressive air, misleadingly, for he was the mildest of men, good-natured and extremely sociable. He has been harshly treated by the biographers of his famous son and for this, as for more serious errors of judgment, one has to look no further than the biography by Modest Tchaikovsky. In this book on which succeeding writers have relied heavily and too often uncritically, Modest says his father worked hard and efficiently but sneers at his slow progress: "It took him twenty years to attain the rank of lieutenant colonel." The book only needed a reference to Ilya

Petrovich's failure to master the flute in his youth to put the unfortunate man firmly into the category of unworthy sires of genius.

It is clear that he had few cultural interests; apart from the abortive attempt to learn the flute, he knew and relished a good tune and read the romantic novels of his day with great enjoyment, and that was about all the concern for the arts that he could claim. However, to be weak in musical appreciation and to have a mediocre taste in books is not necessarily to be a nonentity, nor does it follow that Ilya Petrovich had nothing to hand on to his son.

Apparently he did not distinguish himself as a student in the School of Mining from which he emerged at twenty with a diploma in engineering. This was in 1815. Not until 1837 was he promoted to the rank of lieutenant colonel and appointed chief inspector of the government mines and factories at Votkinsk.

There is no dispute about these facts; what is in dispute is the conclusion drawn from them. To get your first important appointment at the age of forty-two is, in the eyes of Modest and his followers, to confess yourself a failure. But there is another interpretation of the facts that leaves Ilya Petrovich as one of the most remarkable civil servants in his country; his leisurely advancement was not due to inefficiency or laziness but to honesty. He did not curry favor, he would not lobby, he neither offered nor accepted bribes. He was that rarity, a sanguine and amiable man with strong principles. No wonder that he took twenty-two years to become a lieutenant colonel; the wonder is, in the Russia of that time, that he ever arrived at such a rank.

It is doubtful whether anyone, least of all his own children, has done him justice; persistent amiability is a heavy handicap. Tchaikovsky was to owe most of his considerable social success to his father. In his turn he was to be esteemed as a man of honor and, in his later years particularly, as a much-prized guest at any social gathering—and not simply on account of his fame but because of his invincible good nature.

When Ilya Petrovich was posted to Votkinsk in 1837 he at once came into his own. This town was on the border of the provinces of Vyatka and Perm. The iron from its mines was made on the spot into locomotives and wagons for the newly-planned trans-Siberian railroad (due to run one hundred miles north of Votkinsk) and into ships for the Kama, the Volga, and the great Caspian canal. Votkinsk was a busy and flourishing place, a typical product of the industrial revolution then beginning to show its first signs in backward Russia, and its new chief of mines took control of business and social life. He became the most important citizen of Votkinsk, having his special police powers, his seat on the bench and his own Cossack guard, and his house became the social center of the town. There the latest music from Petersburg or Moscow was heard, there one found the best whist players, the best food, the best wine, and the liveliest conversation. It became a little haven of civilization and good living. People competed for the honor of an invitation.

Ilya Petrovich was the life and soul of the Tchaikovsky parties as he was the driving force of the state mines. By the time he arrived in Votkinsk, his brown hair was greying and he had developed a heavy moustache, but his blue eyes were as gay as ever and his gift for entertaining had never been so obvious; cheerful, friendly, a born good mixer, he was in his element in this semi-barbarous town on the edge of nowhere. He did not attempt to promote the cultural side of these gatherings of Votkinsk notables. This was left to Alexandra Andreyevna.

Alexandra Andreyevna was not his first wife. In 1827, when he was thirty-two, he had married a Russian of German descent, Maria Karlovna Keiser. She died two years later, soon after the birth of her only child, Zinaida; and Ilya Petrovich married again four years later. No doubt he wished to provide a home for his little daughter but he was, besides, a domesticated man and a lover of women. His second choice went to the other extreme; this time he chose a Russian of French descent.

Alexandra's father, the Marquis André d'Assier, had fled from France during the Revolution and, marrying a Russian, decided to make his home in Russia. He was a man of taste and learning with a passion for the arts and brought up his two girls in this atmosphere of culture. His brother, who left France with him, shared his tastes and was a gifted singer. D'Assier's sensibility seems to have run to excess at times—he was a victim of occasional attacks of epilepsy—but his children escaped the malady and one of them, at least, the sensibility too. Yekaterina Andreyevna had a real gift and, as Madame Schobert, had become well known in Petersburg as an operatic singer. Her sister, Alexandra Andreyevna, showed her upbringing in more conventional fashion; she sang and played the pianoforte adequately, as every Petersburg society girl was honor-bound to do but without any sense of a vocation and, it appears, without much feeling.

In the Tchaikovsky house at Votkinsk, however, she had next to no competition and what she lacked in technique and fire she made up for in grandeur. If Ilya Petrovich made his parties successful, his wife gave them the cachet which made the townsfolk eager to be invited. She was an imposing woman of twenty-four when they settled at Votkinsk in 1837, not so much good-looking as overwhelming—tall, full-bosomed, with a regal carriage, dark hair piled high and large dark eyes under heavy brows.

It is not surprising if the guests failed to notice that these eyes lacked expressiveness, like their hostess's piano playing; she had a distinguished manner, was gracious, and brought to the town an appearance and clothes of a kind it rarely saw. Her performance at the piano was commonly the climax of the evening's entertainment and she was much sought-after as an accompanist. Her real beauty seems to have escaped everyone except her second son, for though compliments on her playing and singing abounded, only he stared fascinated at the keyboard the whole time she was playing. "I couldn't even begin to imagine hands which would compare with my mother's," he used to say years later.

It might reasonably be expected that children of the capable, kind, and lively Ilya Petrovich and the majestically musical Alexandra Andreyevna, brought up in the midst of a whirl of musical and literary gatherings, would show signs of distinction. The first surviving child (a girl had died at birth) by no means lived up to his parents; Nikolai Ilyich, born the year after the arrival at Votkinsk, was a stolid, lazy boy without a spark of his father's bonhomie or his mother's dignity. He seemed to have no special gift. He was not malicious and that is all that can be said for him as a child.

The second child, born two years later, on May 7, 1840, was a different proposition. Pyotr Ilyich (Petya), his parents (and indeed everybody in the house but one) thought, had altogether too much sensibility, but there was no denying that he was gifted.

The one who thought differently was the third child, Alexandra Ilyinishna (Sasha), born two years after Pyotr Ilyich. She, the only living daughter, worshipped Petya and could see no wrong in him. The relationship between brother and sister was to last until death and is one of the most striking examples of its kind. Alexandra Ilyinishna, more level-headed than her brother, was to spend much of her adult life trying to restrain and soothe the self-reproaches he insisted on directing at himself; their correspondence is always moving, even when the reader cannot help smiling at the brother's exaggerations, because of the love and faith on both sides, feelings which faltered once only in fifty years of intimacy.

At Votkinsk the relationship was in its infancy in every respect; little Sasha regarded Petya with awe as well as devotion and was too young to understand that her god could have weaknesses. What she saw clearly enough was that she had a rival (though she would not have put it in those terms) and that the rival was supreme; the greater part of Petya's love was given to his mother. He had plenty left for his father and brothers and sister—never was there a child with such a capacity for affection—but Alexandra Andreyevna was the human mainspring of his life from the moment he drew breath. Sasha was too young and the Tchaikovsky family loyalty too strong to perceive that her adored brother was worshipping before a graven image, but, love being what it is, perhaps neither he nor she would have acted otherwise even had they been gifted with adult insight. Alexandra Andreyevna was a cold woman and accepted the devotion of everyone in the house with composure. To the impetuous, fiery Petya this composure could be chilling; his mother did not care for warm hugs if a gown was in danger, and spent much of her limited time with the children repressing Petya's ardor. Fortunately for him, as for all warm-hearted people, to love was almost enough and the occasional response kept him happy for days.

He had, besides, another love—passion would be the more correct word—which was to govern his life, the love of music. Yet in his early years even this was connected indissolubly with his mother. It is a little ironic to reflect that the tepid piano playing of Alexandra Andreyevna and her correct but lifeless rendering of the sentimental ballads of the day could rouse a genuine musician to a frenzy of admiration. Wherever Petya got his genius it was certainly not from her, yet she, unknowingly and unwillingly (she often reproved him for his extravagance as she called it), fostered the genius in him. She accepted with dignity her reputation as the town's leading musician. Only little Petya's reactions displeased her. Perhaps she knew in her heart that she was not what he thought. It may be that she was worried by his sincerity. In any case, destiny was too much for her; in her dull, stately way she was to be the harbinger of greatness.

She, of course, was chiefly concerned to see that he, like the rest of her children, behaved well—that is, did not bother or embarrass her—and fitted himself for the civilization of Moscow or Petersburg (return to which was one of her chief concerns) by mastering his lessons and learning the even more important rules governing the man who was *comme il faut* in the best society.

Her reactions could scarcely have differed more from her daughter's. Sasha was not particularly musical and considered Petya's feats on the piano with the almost indifference of the loyal subject who knows that her king will excel at anything he chooses to take up. What she loved about this brother was his loving kind-

ness; his hatred of cruelty, his wish to see good in all, his immediate response to affection whether from her, his mother, his nurse,
the cook, or any of the serfs who worked on the estate. In his
small electric body he was, to her, love personified. That, too,
would have been Ilya Petrovich's view, given with a genial laugh,
for it was the father in the boy, a hundred times sensitized, that
young Sasha worshipped.

The Tchaikovsky family was enlarged by the birth of another
boy, Ippolit Ilyich, in 1843, one year after Alexandra, and not
very long afterwards the whole family was photographed. The
photograph is instructive, as so many were in those days of true
artists behind the camera. On the right (the left facing the camera) is Ilya Petrovich, left hand on thigh, right hand pressing his
latest born close to him. His quiff has turned grey, and a large
greying moustache droops below his lower lip. Ippolit is little
more than a pair of wondering eyes, but Nikolai, standing next
to him, is seen in the round. His pleasant but rather blank face
conveys next to nothing of the person, which was right enough,
because then and for some time afterward he did not amount to
much. Beside him, five or six inches taller, stands the half-sister
Zinaida with an arm round her stepmother's shoulder. Zinaida
shows signs of self-possession (she was then well into her teens)
and a certain air of superciliousness. Her dark hair is parted in
the center in the fashion of that time.

Sitting on a stool below her, with an elbow resting on her
mother's knee, is Alexandra Ilyinishna. As one hand is pressed
against her cheek, Sasha's face is a little distorted. The widely
spaced eyes are a feature of her face even then and she is looking
at the photographer with some apprehension. Alexandra Andreyevna, sitting in the seat of honor, has what is known as the Florence Nightingale hair style, her black hair pressed down over the
ears under a lace cap. The fine eyes are there for all to see, as is
the strong nose and somewhat discontented mouth. But the general impression of her face is of a placidity which owes nothing
to the resolution of inward struggles and almost everything to

self-satisfaction. Her large build and the well-shaped hands are also evident.

The group is completed by the subject of this book. He stands on the right of his mother with one arm crooked round hers. His long hair looks darker than it really is and has been swept off the forehead. The mouth is wide and, like the mouths of all painfully sensitive people, looks indeterminate, accentuating the other features—the strong nose, the brilliant wide-spaced eyes, and above all, the massive forehead. He was then only eight years old and anything but handsome. Yet one glance at the photograph is enough; of the seven faces his is the only outstanding one; the Tchaikovsky swan stands out from the geese. That he is exceptionally intelligent and also pitifully vulnerable to all the assaults of feeling is plain enough.

CHAPTER 2

Fanny Durbach
1844-1848

IT IS NOW NECESSARY to go back a year or two to introduce a young woman who is notable in the history of Tchaikovsky in two important respects: she was to influence the little boy profoundly in his formative years, and her reminiscences give a clear picture of the Tchaikovsky household, and specially of Petya, at this time. Apart from the occasional recollections of Nikolai Ilyich, Alexandra Ilyinishna, Ilya Petrovich, and Tchaikovsky himself passed on in later years to Modest and "brushed up" by him, these reminiscences are the only trustworthy record of the composer as a child.

In the late summer of 1844 Alexandra Andreyevna went on a visit to Petersburg. This time she had another purpose besides the wish to stay with her sister and enjoy a few weeks of the civilized life she had been brought up in; she was looking for a governess. There was no school in Votkinsk to which she could send the children without loss of face, and as the birth of Ippolit was only a few months away, Alexandra Andreyevna dismissed the last vague thoughts of trying her hand at educating the six-year-old Nikolai.

The girl she found was, of course, French. Fanny Durbach came from Montbéliard, on the border of Alsace and Franche-Comté. She was twenty-two and was typical of her nation—efficient, sensible, cool, with romantic leanings well under control.

She needed all the sangfroid she could muster as the journey to Votkinsk spun out its dreary and uncomfortable weeks for the greater part of a thousand miles east of Petersburg. During this apparently interminable procession of alarming ferries across huge rivers, of post houses with their fleas and prolonged waits in smoky rooms for fresh horses, Alexandra Andreyevna may well have told Fanny with a smile of the letter she had had from her husband informing her that Sasha and Petya had between them composed a song in her honor called "Our Mama in Petersburg." Petya was then four and a half and Sasha not quite two, so her contribution must have been on the slender side. The children were waiting feverishly to sing the composition to their mother as a kind of hymn of thanksgiving for her arrival home.

It is doubtful whether this significant feat—the first mention we have of Petya as composer—would have stirred Fanny Durbach. She was not musical, and Petya was not supposed to be her pupil. In any case she must have been busy fighting her dismay as she found herself jerked inexorably mile by mile into what appeared to be a savage wilderness of forest, river, and plain. Votkinsk, when they at last came to the end of their twenty-two-day journey, did not please her; it was noisy, dirty and, as far as the workers went, drunken; there was scarcely a decent building in the town, the streets were rivers of mud, the shops pitiful.

The Tchaikovsky house reassured her a little. It was one of the few stone houses in Votkinsk, with an impressive pedimented first floor gable and the then extraordinary luxury in the far provinces of second floor rooms. The main apartments were large and comfortably furnished—or overfurnished, as the habit then was in well-to-do families—and life lived in them was, in the eyes of the governess, absolute bliss, with an abundance of food and wine served by a large staff of serfs. The garden seems not to have been in any way extraordinary—Votkinsk was a comparatively treeless place and as flat as a board—but had water and arbors and flower gardens bounded by vegetable gardens, orchards, and pastures.

By Russian standards it was uninteresting, by Votkinsk standards almost paradisal.

Alexandra Andreyevna was too lazy and too much of a fine lady to concern herself much with the running of the house or with the people living in it. She had her daily half hours with the children dutifully grouped round her, she devoured novels and sweetmeats, she spent day after day like the squire's wife in Gogol's *The Carriage* who would glance in the mirror for a moment and was still gazing a couple of hours later. Only in the evenings did she come to life. At the inevitable party she would speak with calm authority on the most recent works of the popular poets and novelists and would climax the entertainment by complying graciously with insistent requests for a song or pianoforte piece.

Such a mistress gave the new arrival great scope, and the strong-minded Fanny took her chance. She was soon mistress in most practical senses of the word and earned Alexandra Andreyevna's gratitude by taking the children off her hands. She had been engaged to teach Nikolai and a niece of Ilya Petrovich, Lidia Vladimirovna Tchaikovskaya (who after the manner of those days had come to visit and was staying more or less indefinitely), but soon attracted Petya and even the tiny Sasha. These two competed for the honor of being included with the older children—or, it would be truer to say, whatever Petya did Sasha must copy—and it was not long before Petya had wormed his way insidiously into the classes.

Fanny remained stern but was secretly very glad of him; Nikolai was lazy and dull, Lidia "difficult," but this younger child was quite another matter. Indeed, Fanny's first reaction to Petya was dismay because he was so sensitive. Yet he was obviously gifted as the others were not, and all the pedagogue in her rose up in determination to save these gifts from their almost certain destruction by hypersensitiveness.

She gave way to his importunities, in themselves absurdly exaggerated, she thought, in the form of a rescuer, and saw herself as the savior of high gifts, perhaps even of genius. At first she had no idea what she was taking on, and tried to treat him like the others. Only for a short time, as she reports. "One day the two brothers failed to resolve a problem I had set them. I reproached them vigorously, drawing a picture of their unhappy father forced to sacrifice himself to make it possible for his sons to have a good education, and so on. Nikolai heard me out to the end with complete indifference, then went on with his games as if nothing had happened. Petya remained sombre until supper. When he was undressing for bed and I had forgotten all about the incident he suddenly burst into tears, began to insist that he loved his father deeply, that he was filled with gratitude towards both parents, and reproached me for injustice. I had the greatest difficulty in calming him, for his sensibility in everything passed all bounds of the imagination. . . . He was truly *un enfant de verre*."

This judgment too she had to revise soon afterwards. Her porcelain child who needed protection from the world was missing one day. He was not in the house, not in the garden. There was a hue and cry round the town. Eventually he was found smilingly returning from the poorer quarter of Votkinsk. Questioned angrily, he explained. In the kitchen where he liked to pass some part of each day (and where he was truly welcome as the rare "little Master" who treated the serfs as human beings) he heard about a cat who had just kittened. Every kitten but one had found a home. That one was to be destroyed. He snatched up the kitten in his arms and ran off. He toured the neighborhood, calling at every house. At last he found someone to take it and came back triumphant.

This showed Fanny that she was dealing with that rare case, a sensitive child who had the courage of his convictions and would master even his paralyzing shyness when need arose. And what a need! In the Russia of that day the lives of human beings were regarded by almost everyone with complaisance. Landowners punished their serfs savagely for the lightest offense or for no offense at all without a flicker of conscience. Imprisonment and exile to the death in life in Siberia did not cause a raised eyebrow; death from floggings was a common event. And here was a little boy who could not bear cruelty to anything and still less the taking of life, even the life of a kitten.

From that time Fanny treated him with particular care. As she was the kind of woman who could not endure unreason, she looked for the cause of his abnormal sensitiveness and found it in his passion for music. From the moment she arrived, even before he became her pupil officially, she had watched him, unwillingly fascinated by what she saw as his obsession. He would stand by the piano absolutely silent while his mother played, and the moment she stopped would beg to be lifted on to the stool. Once there, he would pick out the notes of the pieces she had been playing and would stay there as long as his playing was suffered.

But to Fanny the greatest enemy to the development of the reasonable in Petya was the orchestrion. This was a superior type of musical box, with stops which created varied orchestral effects. The Tchaikovsky orchestrion spent most of its time in the children's room and was seldom silent; an entranced Petya had to be dragged away and Fanny was soon practically at screaming point. The repertoire included airs from Bellini, Donizetti, and Rossini and from *Don Giovanni,* and opened a new world of music to him. Frantically excited, he would dash from orchestrion to piano, trying to reproduce on the keyboard the tunes and something of the orchestral harmonies. He said long afterwards that the orchestrion drew him irrevocably to opera and that his overmastering devotion to Mozart began with it.

Fanny thought it not only a bore but a threat to the mental stability of a promising child. She did what she could to discourage him, but he had always finished his lessons long before the elder couple and was quick to take advantage of the slightest opportunity to make music. She had only to turn her head or leave the room for a moment and he was off his chair and at the piano or orchestrion.

At last she forbade him absolutely to play during the hour after supper when he, Nikolai, Lidia, and Sasha gathered to tell her what they had done since lesson time and then listened to some edifying tale. This particular ban was unbearably frustrating to him because darkness seemed to brighten his imagination, and he had begun to improvise on the piano, to invent new and gorgeous harmonies and tunes of every description.

The sequel might have suggested to a less determined young woman that she was wasting her time. Petya could not play the piano after supper but nothing on earth short of binding his hands would prevent him from playing music; he could do without the piano at a pinch, for the notes were in his head. Confined to his chair, he played with his fingers on any smooth surface nearby; that, he thought, could annoy no one, since no one except him would hear anything.

But what music he heard, what superb chords, what magnificent harmonies! Intoxicated, he saw nothing, he was all sound, ravished away from the mundane playroom. When the smooth surface was a table no harm could come of his disobedience except an occasional reproof for inattention when he failed to answer a question. But one day his chair happened to be next a window. As there was nothing else within reach he began to play on the window. At first he drummed lightly, then, as the imagined music swelled to a great climax, the drumming rose to a clatter, the clatter to a ferocious pounding. Before Fanny could call out the inevitable happened, the glass broke, his hand plunged through, and in a second he was a badly frightened child holding out a hand streaming with blood.

For a time the shock kept him obedient. Then his parents staged a special musical evening in honor of a Polish pianist, Mashovsky, who was visiting the town. Mashovsky of course played Chopin, and Petya, carried away, imitated him in two mazurkas. He played the unknown pieces with such brio—his ability even so early to reproduce music on a first hearing was startling —that the honored visitor embraced him publicly and hailed him as a musician of great promise.

The piano was scarcely silent all that evening until late, but the boy went out long before the end. Fanny, seeing him go, thought with pleasure that he had more sense than she had given him credit for; she had been prepared for strenuous pleas to be allowed to stay. Two hours later she went up to bed. Looking into Petya's room as usual she was amazed to find him still dressed. He was sitting on his bed weeping heartbrokenly.

"What is the matter, Petya?" she asked in alarm.

"Oh, the music, the music!" was all she could hear through the sobs.

She persevered, and at last he cried, clinging to her, "Save me from it, Mademoiselle Fanny, save me! It won't leave me alone. It's here . . . here!" And he struck his forehead with one hand.

Fanny was not one to ignore an appeal of this kind. She herself went as far as to imagine her little favorite losing his mind because his head was filled with sound. But she had learned wisdom; she no longer forbade him to play or tried to belittle music. On the contrary, she encouraged his parents to regularize the passion by employing a local teacher—whether she was astute enough to realize that such a teacher could not compare with herself one does not know—and she tried to get her way by flattery and tact.

Her ruse succeded. The music teacher, Maria Markovna Palchikova, a freed serf who gave lessons as much out of gratitude to Ilya Petrovich as anything else, was a pleasant young woman and a hard worker, but her knowledge of music was slender and her ability even more restricted—Tchaikovsky afterwards said that he could not remember her being able to play anything through. And when, inevitably, she was obliged to sight-read she made such heavy weather of it that Petya used to take her place on the stool and read the piece for her.

Naturally, the lessons became rather farcical—more a case of Petya teaching Maria Markovna than the other way round—but though set hours for lessons and practice did not entirely stem his wish to play music all day long, they did have the reassuring effect Fanny had hoped for. To have what was virtually a grownup pupil on his hands steadied him (for though he sometimes made fun of Maria Markovna he was too affectionate to go far) and the changed status of music calmed him too. It ceased to be a forbidden pleasure, frowned on by his beloved Mademoiselle Fanny, and by degrees the hysterical element went out of his regard for it and his true feeling took charge.

Rival studies had also appeared. For all her level-headedness Fanny was a woman of her age; she had a weakness for the romantic poets and novelists. She soon cast Petya for the part of poet. Except for his very healthy appetite and liveliness he looked and behaved like the popular idea of the poet; he was extremely untidy, not at all keen on washing himself, and had never been known to brush his hair; above all, he was incurably romantic. She did all she could to encourage an ambition to write.

Within a year or two of her arrival Petya was a fair French scholar and not a bad German one (she was bilingual), outdistancing the sluggish Nikolai, and had been introduced to all the romantics whom he read and copied voraciously. Another year, and he was writing essays, mainly on French subjects though stubbornly refusing to acknowledge that the French could be in any way superior to the Russians, and eventually breaking into verse. Already his patriotism had reached a pitch of fervor. Fanny one day came across him with an atlas before him. It was open at the map of Europe and he was busy alternately kissing the large splash of color denoting Russia and spitting on the other colors to the west of it.

She reproached him; knowing that he could always be led through the affections, was indeed wholly governed by them, she pretended to be hurt: if he spat on the map of France, she said, he was spitting on his Fanny; he ought to be ashamed of himself.

He had an answer: "Don't scold me, Fanny. There's no need. Can't you see my left arm is covering France?"

His first efforts at verse were on one of Fanny's goddesses, Saint Joan, and on the lost Dauphin of the Temple. Behind them came a string of romantic themes interspersed with intensely patriotic poems.

When a young woman like Fanny drew tempting pictures of him as the poet Russia was waiting for, a modern Pushkin, or, if he failed in that, at least one of the great modern essayists and critics, no child, not even a Tchaikovsky, could belittle them. He dashed at writing as he dashed at everything, full of ardor. Yet this outburst of literature at Votkinsk no more than toned down the passion for music, and even if Fanny had been left to carry on her propaganda to the end of Petya's childhood as he and she both expected, one can scarcely doubt that she had met her match. As it happened she was not given the chance to make a real fight of it; soon after Petya's eighth birthday came a sudden, horrid parting.

Fanny had not taken his mother's place—there was room in this child's heart for innumerable loves—curiously enough, her coming had innocently elevated it. The more Alexandra Andreyevna retired placidly from her children's affairs, the more Petya yearned after her. Cold people sometimes have the advantage over warm people, as Alexandra Andreyevna proved at Votkinsk by having less and less to do with Petya. Since the coming of Fanny she had become the great unattainable and her unearned reward was an adoring son.

But though forced to play second fiddle to his mother, Fanny had established her niche and a very powerful one it was, compounded of fear, respect, admiration, and the sheer animal love of a small boy for an attractive young woman. Life without her seemed inconceivable. Then, abruptly, she was gone, and his secure, ordered life dissolved into chaos.

CHAPTER 3

Child
1848-1850

FANNY DURBACH HAD DONE Petya a great service; how great can be seen if the true meaning of her "porcelain child" is understood. He was at the opposite pole from the sensitive child of so many modern biographies. He loved to eat, to walk, to play games, to get dirty. He loved nature, not by brooding over it, but by energetically using what it offers a child. He planted flowers, and liked the look and smell of them; he romped with animals, and sat quietly with them. He was, in short, what is known rather absurdly as the normal child.

Where he differed sharply from this hypothetical creature was in his reactions to art and specially to music. In this he was what the world calls unbalanced, and Fanny's alarm is understandable. Had he been left to himself during these vital years from four to eight, or to the not very tender mercies of an indifferent or stupid governess he might have echoed the history of the man he so obviously resembled, his epileptic maternal grandfather. Luckily for himself and the world he met Fanny. She could not change his nature but she could and did steady him, and the threat of epilepsy disappeared for ever.

As things turned out, the next four years seemed to put him back where he began, but in spite of their miseries he managed to come out of them sane and healthy, though with shaken confidence, and livelier than ever. For this he had to thank the years with Fanny and correspondence with her afterwards.

The trouble began with his father. Ilya Petrovich had the faults of his virtues. The borderline between trustfulness and credulity is hard to place, and his optimism, which made him so likable, more than once landed him and his family in difficulties, as in 1848. A Moscow friend urged him to retire from government service and promised him an excellent post in the capital. Alexandra Andreyevna and Zinaida Ilyinishna (who had joined the family at Votkinsk) were both more than anxious to return to civilization, so the good-natured Ilya Petrovich took his friend at his word, resigned his position with the rank of major-general and, in autumn, packed up and left.

The entire family with its bulky belongings traipsed the six hundred miles or so to Moscow only to find that the friend had had second thoughts, had taken the job himself, and would not budge from it.

To Petya by far the worst aspect of this calamity was what it led to—the loss of Fanny. The Tchaikovsky parents had intended to send their boys to a Moscow school. Sasha and Ippolit would still have needed a governess but the false friend deprived them of one and Petya of his best friend; money immediately became short and Fanny left to join a family of noble rank.

The Tchaikovskys' unhappy situation was aggravated almost immediately by a cholera scare. Because of the wretched hygienic conditions in the cities, cholera was the deadliest of all diseases in Russia then and for long afterwards. Tens of thousands died from it every year. When a servant was smitten in the temporary apartment the Tchaikovskys had taken, Alexandra Andreyevna panicked and insisted that they move to Petersburg, which they did. Ilya Petrovich rented a house on Vasilyevsky Ostrov and was prepared cheerfully to find another post; the possibility of failure did not occur to him.

This search for work, added to the general chaos in the home after two rapid moves, had a further unhappy effect on Petya.

His only powerful anodyne to the loss of Fanny was his mother. But Alexandra Andreyevna was preoccupied by one thing after another: the moves, the setting up of a new home in Petersburg, and finally the use of her charm and social influence to help her husband meet men of consequence or, when he had brought them to the house, to entertain them attractively. It was not a work for which Ilya Petrovich had any aptitude. His wife, more worldly than he, possessed a fairly large circle of acquaintances who she hurriedly took up again. She visited much and entertained much, understanding better than her husband that the secret of getting a good post is to appear not to be in need of it.

All this, with a natural laziness and the effect of four years of freedom from intimate contact with her children, made her almost unapproachable. She consigned them to the care of Zinaida.

This half-sister was no friend to Petya. She had joined them two years earlier, after graduating from the Yekaterinsky Institute at Petersburg. Even more than her stepmother she took a very dim view of Votkinsk; for a seventeen-year-old girl just looking forward to the bustle and parties of Petersburg, it must have seemed the most savage of backwaters, without a presentable, to say nothing of a marriageable man in it. Apparently she had not even the mediocre musical gifts of her stepmother to help her to shine in what society there was, or perhaps Alexandra Andreyevna, only sixteen years older, made sure that she had no rival inside the family: the dress Zinaida is wearing in the family photograph of 1848 suggests that she was being kept younger than her age.

There was no possibility that a disgruntled Zinaida would look kindly either on Fanny or Fanny's pride and joy. She would see him as a spoiled and boring little prig and his French and German and music triumphs as material for sarcasm. Her rejection of his instinctive offer of affection must have been a considerable shock to a child whose impulse was to love everyone.

Little is known about Zinaida but, with every allowance made for her position at Votkinsk and again at Petersburg, what she was can be deduced with fair assurance from the fact that Tchaikovsky never spoke or wrote of her or attempted to see her in later years.

Her method of caring for the children in Petersburg can be imagined. By the time Petya was sent to school with Nikolai, late in 1848, he was reduced to despair as his letters to Fanny demonstrate. They are what are known as exaggerated—a description which usually means that the reader declines to use his imagination—but though passionate children do not die of grief as they think they will, they suffer. Petya suffered them; it was his first experience of coldness except for the version he could not recognize, his mother's calm refusal to allow the hugs he longed to give her.

The Schmelling Boarding School proved that a worse fate than supervision by an unloving Zinaida existed only a few streets away. Petya was utterly wretched. He and Nikolai were mocked by the other boys as country hicks—in clothing, manners, and attainments. Nikolai took the bullying stolidly, Petya collapsed as he was always to collapse in the face of motiveless hatred.

In certain directions he could normally have held his own with the boys; though younger than most, his French was excellent, his knowledge of history and German good, and his gift for essay writing considerable. But all these gifts vanished in the face of malice and he stood confessed as a dunce and a weakling. Bad marks led to homework—the brothers attended as day boys—of fantastic length; often he had to work until after midnight, only to be on his way to school again at half-past seven the next morning.

He had one substantial compensation for this run of misfortune; his parents engaged a music teacher for him. This man, Filippov, was a professor of music, though of no particular eminence, and Petya began to forge ahead. It was, after all, the first professional attention he had had in his life, a short life in years but more than half of it devoted to music.

As a counterpoise to the savagery of Russian school life at that time, contact with a civilized man was absolute heaven. Had he been allowed to continue his lessons with Filippov he could have fought all his troubles; school, Zinaida, and his mother's withdrawal. But it was not to be; bad luck pursued him; he and Nikolai both caught measles and he could not throw it off. The puzzled doctor, who had no conception of what his little patient had been through since leaving Votkinsk, recommended a complete break from work, and the Tchaikovsky parents took the advice so literally that they stopped music lessons too.

Petya's feelings are best not lingered on. His mother complained to Fanny that nothing could be done with the child and blamed him for malingering. Stupidity could scarcely go further, nor could un-Russianness.

In May, 1849, Ilya Petrovich managed to get a post; it was a good one, the management of iron works, but once again it took him and his family into the wilds, this time to Alapayevsk in Perm province. Alapayevsk was 300 miles further east than Votkinsk and on the Asiatic side of the Urals, but to Petya the move was a blessing; he could once more get into the countryside he loved, he had books (Fanny was still propelling him enthusiastically by post through French literature and he was exploring the Russians for himself, Gogol specially), and he had a piano. He also had Zinaida, who was furious that she had been dragged into a social desert for the second time, but he found an ally in that typically Russian phenomenon, a dependent relative. This was Anastasia Vasilyevna Popova, daughter of Ilya Petrovich's sister, come to help Zinaida run the house until Alexandra Andreyevna, who was pregnant, felt able to take charge again.

Anastasia Vasilyevna was an old ally of Petya though by no means a blind one. "When we received your letter, dear Fanny," she wrote, "Petyenka read it aloud and cried a lot. He loves you very much but now that his health has improved his moods are a thing of the past." Alexandra Andreyevna had withdrawn from all but the lightest of contacts with duty but occasionally permitted Petya to accompany her in songs. He remembered one of them, "The Nightingale," learned with Filippov, to the end of his life as marking moments when he and his mother became as nearly as possible one person. For the most part, however, she left him and the other two (Nikolai had been put into the School of Mining in Petersburg) to the care of Zinaida.

It was a dull life for Zinaida. As at Votkinsk the Tchaikovsky house quickly became the focal point for musical evenings but attractive and eligible young men were few and far between. She tended to work off her irritation on the three children, Petya, Sasha, and Polya, and some part of Petya's black moods can be traced to this mild tyranny.

Eventually a fairly obvious solution occurred to Alexandra Andreyevna and then only because of Zinaida's complaints. There was talk of a governess. In the Tchaikovsky household things either happened at breathless speed—as when Ilya Petrovich decided to give up his post—or at the pace of a snail. The governess question, which affected neither parent immediately, was in the latter category. Not until the last month of the year did Nastasya Petrovna Petrova arrive to free Zinaida.

Two vital facts about this new governess emerge from Petya's letters to Fanny: she was affectionate and she liked music. At once he cheered up. He did not forget Fanny or the rare sights of his mother, but instead of glooming in the garden or in a chair when fits of melancholy came over him (Anastasia Vasilyevna was optimistic in thinking them "a thing of the past"), he played them off on the piano. It was a form of indulgence which Fanny would have put down firmly. The new governess had neither the will nor the wish; sooner or later the piano charmed her pupil from moodiness into the joy of making music, and he was then sunshine itself.

His devotion to the piano, and the efforts of Sasha and Polya to emulate him, at last moved the Tchaikovsky parents to another bout of action. They sent for Maria Markovna from Votkinsk. This diverted Petya but no more; this time there was not even a pretense that he would benefit. "Sasha and Polya are to learn music," Anastasia Vasilyevna told Fanny, "but as Petyenka had lessons with the best teachers in Petersburg there is nothing she can teach him."

It was perhaps as well for him that eight days before his tenth birthday his mother bore twins, Anatoly Ilyich and Modest Ilyich. Their arrival revealed an aspect of him—his complete absence of envy or spite—which was to make the adult Tchaikovsky such a lovable man. There was every reason why he should resent the twins; he knew that he had seen so little of his mother during the previous months because of them. He knew that twins would keep her attention away from him even more than one baby. Yet instead of the fits of jealousy shown by most elder children he begged to be allowed to see the twins, hung over their cradles with a kind of adoration, and wrote ecstatically to Fanny that the more he saw of them the more angelic they seemed to him to be. He could scarcely believe, he said, that they were not angels come down to earth.

He was not allowed to see much of them; his parents decided that he must follow Nikolai to Petersburg and school; not the School of Mining, but the Law School. They took no account of the difference in temperament between him and Nikolai; as the eldest boy was doing well at his school they assumed that Petya would do well at his.

Like most parents they wanted to toughen him so that he would become like all the other little savages; they saw his extreme sensitiveness as a blemish that contact with ordinary boys would rub off. The history of the Schmelling School went for nothing.

Alexandra Andreyevna thought she would help herself to recover from a severe lying-in and encourage Petya to accept the break with family life by taking him to Petersburg. By September, 1850, they were there and a few weeks later he matriculated; spurred by his mother's presence he passed his entrance examinations with misleading ease.

Alexandra's praise was an oasis in a desert; this period in Petersburg was almost wholly an agony to Petya for he knew that she would go back to Alapayevsk and could neither bear to contemplate the break nor persuade himself not to. Every thought was blackened by the future except for one unforgettable excursion. His mother took him to the Maryinsky Theater to hear Glinka's opera, *A Life for the Tsar.*

If Tchaikovsky ever felt like criticizing Alexandra Andreyevna in later years—and there is no sign that he did—he would have forgiven every selfish act for this one favor. Few children can resist the magic of a great theater at night; the feelings of the highly impressionable Petya can be imagined as he and his mother walked up the flights of steps between the tall pillars, entered the brilliantly lit foyer, and climbed to their box. The view from the box of the beautiful blue and silver auditorium must have taken his breath away.

All this and a supreme musical experience to follow. "We all come from Glinka," he was to say, and the birth of this profound conviction was that final evening with his mother.

The next morning her carriage was ordered. They were staying with Ilya Petrovich's friend Modest Alexeyevich Vakar, in whose honor one of the twins had been named. The Vakars promised to act as Petya's guardians and to invite him every weekend to their house. He was very fond of them and of their little boy but they could do nothing with him that morning. As the minutes ticked away he alarmed everyone; he could not control himself.

At the last when all farewells had been made, when his mother was sitting in the carriage and the door was closed, he refused to let go of the handle. He was dragged back to the door of the house. The coachman whipped up his horses, the carriage began to move. Petya wrenched himself free, ran to the street, and flung himself at the rear wheel. He caught one of the spokes and clung to it, trying to hold the carriage back. Then he was shaken off and fell, muddy, bruised, half-unconscious on the pavement.

CHAPTER 4

Schoolboy
1850-1854

IT MIGHT REASONABLY BE EXPECTED that the experience of this passionate farewell, which was to make the adult Tchaikovsky feel ill whenever he thought of it, would prostrate the young Petya. If he had been the hopelessly morbid creature so many biographers have portrayed, he would have collapsed then. But he did not; he surprised everyone by a determined effort to please his parents by doing well at school.

No doubt some part of his stand against loneliness and the rigors of school was due to the Vakars. Modest Alexeyevich was a good man as he was soon to demonstrate. But in less dramatic fashion he demonstrated it from the beginning; he and his wife quickly became very fond of Petya, as almost everyone did who knew him, and this was quite enough to make him wish to be worthy of their affection.

But there remained the Petersburg school of 1850 filled with young toughs contemptuous of the country boy and eager to teach the apparent softy what it is to be virile. Petya had to spend six days out of every seven in this atmosphere, with his family more than a thousand miles away—so far as to be in another world. His sufferings at night, specially—for the dormitory hazing was savageness itself—defy the imagination.

It was then that he showed his spirit. He taught the boys that

a child can be loving and devoted to art and yet take on the philistine at his own game. Not every boy can or would dare fling
himself at a moving carriage wheel and be up and about again
the same day. Ten years of country air, good food and long walks
had made him physically stronger than many a scrawny city boy.
He had no wish to fight but when he did he held his own. After
a few weeks the bullies began to respect him and leave him alone.
His natural charm and liveliness did the rest.

By that time he had begun to show himself in another sphere
more than the equal of most of his schoolmates; his natural intelligence and Fanny's teaching paid handsome dividends. He was
soon high in his class and stayed there, but more by fits and starts
than steady application. His letters home veer between triumph—
"I have received full marks in the examinations in every subject
but Latin and Scripture"—and remarkable frankness: "I haven't
even tried to learn my lessons this week, so I have been given
three black marks and shall have to stay in all next Sunday." To
which he appended the usual heartfelt "Do please try to forgive
me and I'll try not to learn so badly that I cause you pain. I know
that I shall make you weep with this news. I have wept too but
this won't help my dear angels of a mother and father—not at all."

It is generally assumed that during this period at school in
which he distinguished himself so unexpectedly Petya virtually
dropped music, thus justifying all the arguments of Fanny at Votkinsk. Biographers have based this assumption on the fact that
he rarely mentions music in his letters to her.

The truth is simple; he did not mention music to Fanny more
often than he could help because he knew he would worry her.
What she wanted to hear was talk of the books he had read and
his own writings. There were no opportunities to use the piano
at school as far as is known, but at weekends and on the many
saints' days it was another matter; the Vakars were musical, and
he not only heard music when they took him to opera or a rare
concert but made music himself, alone and with them.

Nothing was easier for him than to become fond of people—

they had only to behave decently—and he was soon like another son to the Vakars and an elder brother to their eldest child. He was too much a grandson of the Marquis d'Assier to avoid fits of melancholy when he thought of his faraway family. But with that reservation he passed many satisfactory weeks in the winter of 1850. He was proud of his progress at school, not so much for himself as for his parents who had been unwise and unkind enough a year earlier to compare him unfavorably with the steady Nikolai. He was hearing music, not on the orchestrion but in the opera house. He was always hopeful that the family would move back to Petersburg—the comments of his mother and Zinaida suggested it.

It seems that whenever Tchaikovsky, man or boy, reached a tolerably peaceful state he was destined to be torn out of it. Lesser people know this apparent law of providence, but he was so much the more sensitive and his shocks so much the more brutal that one cannot be surprised by his preoccupation with the workings of fate in human lives. Towards the end of the year, when he was looking forward to Christmas with the Vakars, an epidemic of scarletina spread through the school. Vakar at once brought him home to save him from school quarantine. Petya caught the infection but quickly recovered. He had no sooner done so than the eldest Vakar child, a boy of five, came down with it and died.

Knowing Petya's acute moral sensitiveness, the Vakars tried to conceal the cause of their son's death. In vain. He fell into a fury of guilt, accused himself of a "terrible breach of friendship" and went about the house half-demented, demanding that he too die. He could never bear to be disliked even when he had done no harm and lashed himself into self-hatred; he tried to avoid the Vakars, declaring that they must loathe the sight of him. He wrote letter after letter to his mother begging to be taken away from people he had treated so abominably.

He was in fact taken away later; Alexandra Andreyevna was hard to persuade that he could be serious. But before then, as if to illustrate another side of fate, he had an experience that was all joy and which marked the second crucial stage in his musical life. Neither Vakar nor his wife could endure Petya's sufferings and one evening Vakar carried him off to the Maryinsky, believing that this was the only chance of turning his mind from the tragedy.

They were playing *Don Giovanni* that night. Petya had almost to be dragged into the theater but once the opera began he forgot everything but the music. The excerpts on the orchestrion had already given him a special love of Mozart; now he heard the whole opera.

"The music of *Don Giovanni* was the first to conquer me completely," he was to write. "It awoke an ecstasy in me of which the consequences are known. It gave me the key to the spheres of pure beauty in which the greatest geniuses soar. Up to then I had only known Italian opera. That I vowed myself to music is due to *Don Giovanni*. . . . In this opera Mozart has put on stage an objectively tragic character, the most powerful and the most hallucinatory music ever created—Donna Anna. I simply cannot express what I felt when I saw this proud beauty appear, tragic and vengeful. When she at last discovers Don Juan, the murderer of her father and her seducer, when her anger flares out in a recitative of genius followed by a sublime aria, when her fury and pride are reflected in the slightest chord, the slightest whisper of the orchestra, I shiver with horror, I want to cry aloud, to weep, to throw myself about, overcome by the strength of the impression given by the Master."

So within a few months the boy heard on stage his great Russian predecessor and his great god of music since childhood. The two events were to be decisive yet there was no sign of it in these last days of 1850 or the months ahead. He went back to his school and worked hard for the next six months. He was the youngest boy in his class but easily kept abreast of them. With the breaking of the link with the Vakars (he did not go back to them for the Easter holidays of 1851), music was difficult to play but not at all difficult to think about, and he relieved his feelings slightly in letters to his mother. He did not forget it or his hopes for one instant, and when the summer holidays arrived he divided his time between the piano and long walks. There was no rivalry here; already he thought of expressing his love of nature by means of music, a music that would be wholly Russian just as the lakes and forests and gardens he saw outside the city could only have been found in his country. He loved them all passionately.

As though in reward for this prolonged attempt to get the better of his temperament, Petya found his father waiting for him when he got back to Petersburg one day. Ilya Petrovich had good news; he was hoping to get a Petersburg post and to bring the family back there, and six months later, in May, 1852, Petya had the happiest of twelfth birthdays, reunited with them all. He had proud news for them too; he was sure to graduate that summer from the preparatory Law School. As he did, his youth notwithstanding, and he went off gaily for a summer holiday with them all knowing that he was now a senior student of the Law School.

2

The next two years, from his twelfth to fourteenth birthdays, were by Petya's standards blissful ones. He forged ahead in school, he re-established contact with his family, coming closer in sympathy to the fast-growing Sasha, he made great strides in music, and he finally got rid of Zinaida; she was married early in 1854 to Yevgeny Ivanovich Olkhovsky with a pomp which was to impoverish Ilya Petrovich for some time afterwards. She was followed into matrimony by Nikolai's old reluctant companion in education, cousin Lidia (with a widowed Aunt Lisa she had remained a permanent member of the Tchaikovsky family for years), who to Petya's intense interest proved the adage that one marriage led to another: "Lidia has married Colonel Olkhovsky, brother of Zina's husband, an admirable man who adores her." The "difficult" girl of Votkinsk had disappeared. "Lidia seems like another person," he told Fanny. "Now she is a splendid girl physically and morally." Ilya Petrovich thought so too, it is to be hoped; he again paid gaily for a wedding reception he could not afford and continued to live handsomely on credit.

Most important, in Petya's eyes only, was the music. These two years began, musically, with a prolonged treat, a summer holiday at Chornaya Ryechka where his aunt, Yekaterina Andreyevna, set herself to tutor this obviously gifted boy. When he spoke of the performance of *Don Giovanni* she found a score and went through it with him, bar by bar, with illustrations on the piano. And when she discovered that he had a rather good voice she sang a duet from *Semiramide* with him and praised his command of the trills Rossini demanded so liberally.

From that moment he and she were inseparable while the holiday lasted, and he came back to Petersburg and senior school in the curious but not unprecedented position (Stravinsky and Cherepnin, for instance, were to follow a similar pattern) that, outwardly vowed to the law, every instinct tied him to music. Had he lived in a different age the Law School might have continued without him. As it was, neither father nor mother thought of music as anything but a spare time pleasure and they were supported by the trend of the time. The professional musician was socially as well as legally beyond the pale—most of them were imported from Germany and Italy because Russians refused to take up a vocation undignified by legal standing. Even the virtuoso career was not considered—men and women would pay high prices to hear famous opera singers, for example, but would never dream of permitting a child of theirs to follow such a profession, doubtful financially and damning socially. In the Russia of those days the good musician of good family remained an amateur, like Petya's aunt.

So to school he went (college would be the better word) and after the usual painful readjustments because he remained well under the average age of his class, discovered a considerable difference between preparatory school and school proper. In the latter, music had a strong hold, literature an even stronger hold, and the general atmosphere was civilized as might be expected from boys in their middle and later teens preparing for a career in law. He was soon drafted into the school choir and, much more satisfactory, could talk music. He made friends, good ones, and his loneliness disappeared.

At home was the piano and his mother's playing and singing. There too was a governess who encouraged him to play and talk of music, and Sasha, a willing confidante and steady admirer. There were also the twins. His affection for the little boys did not grow less; he developed an almost parental attitude towards them. That this was a commentary on the Tchaikovsky parents he was never to see; his mind did not work in that way.

In every direction he was being fortified against the next blow, by new interests, new friends, a renewal of old interests and, best of all for such a domesticated boy, the knowledge of a loving home nearby even when he was not in it.

Then fate struck again. On June 25, 1854, Alexandra Andreyevna died suddenly from cholera. The shock for everyone was the greater because she seemed to be recovering. Then came an abrupt relapse. She died in the bath of hot water reserved as a last remedy. She was forty-one.

The death of Alexandra Andreyevna has given the denigrators of Tchaikovsky an opportunity they have taken full advantage of. They use it to "prove" that Tchaikovsky was an unhealthy invertebrate and, in the absence of the relevant documents in full, their version of the great composer has been allowed to go unchallenged.

These "proofs" boil down to two items. One is a highly colored description of Petya's sufferings written many years later by Modest Tchaikovsky—four years old at the time. Modest's work—his opera libretti specially—is not merely bad in itself but reveals the true source of the "morbid Tchaikovsky" legend; in his account of his brother he is in fact describing himself.

This is a common failing which the most conscientious biographer has to guard against constantly. Modest is a depressing example of the process at its worst, and the embroiderers of the legend have enlarged on him with gusto. But their crowning argument is that Petya could not bring himself to announce the death of his mother to Fanny for two and a half years.

What these biographers have overlooked is that there was another reason for the long gap between event and announcement. A very simple reason; the warm and confiding correspondence between the boy and his governess was coming to an end.

This decline had begun two years earlier, when the Tchaikovsky family returned to Petersburg. With them came the governess Nastasya Petrovna. She was Russian and musical. She counteracted the French education and outlook of Fanny with startling effect.

Petya did not forget Fanny but he was young and impressionable; all the signs point to the growth of a typical passion of a romantic boy in his early teens for the sympathetic Nastasya Petrovna, and he was soon to give open proof of it. So the correspondence with Fanny (herself increasingly absorbed by other interests) began to dwindle until it almost came to a stop. The death of Alexandra Andreyevna completed the process. Few boys would wish to write "My mother is dead" if they could avoid it and Petya had the best of excuses, that Fanny was not particularly expecting to hear from him in any case.

If every boy who sincerely believed himself heartbroken when his mother dies were written off as a neurotic, the masculine half of the world would consist almost exclusively of them. Petya no doubt believed himself inconsolable, not because he had fallen into homosexual habits in school but because he was an artist and deeply feeling. For all the shock, what he was to remember with horror for the rest of his life was not his mother's death but the day, four years earlier, when she left him to the mercies of the preparatory school. It was then he fought his fight with himself and began to grow up. After that nothing could be so terrible.

To a sensitive child there is not a great difference between absence and death; both mean the one thing, that the loved person is not present, cannot be touched or spoken to or heard. In Petya's day death was not a vague word to a child, it was a believable reality. Most children a hundred years or more ago had lost a brother or sister or both and had seen the loss accepted as inevitable, as the natural course of nature. The serfs in house and estate died like flies. Parents were considered long-lived if they reached fifty. To get a prevalent disease like cholera, for example, was as good as a death sentence. On every side was death, early death, and resignation.

To say that Petya did not resign himself without a fight after his mother's death is to say the obvious. Certainly he never forgot her—why should he? But if we go by his actions, as we must, and by his later comments, it becomes clear that he overcame this shattering loss courageously.

Take the comment first. It is 1891 and his sister has just died suddenly. He is worried about her son Vladimir, one of his great favorites. Then he recalls his own mother's death and feels less worried. "I know from my own experience," he says, "that one gets over such shocks with fair ease at his age."

As for his actions in 1854, he continued his work at school without perceptible break and continued to do well in classes. His friendships deepened. At home his consolations were many—the love and faith of Sasha, the company and affection of the governess, and the devotion of the twins. From the last he soon had what almost amounted to the trust and love given to a mother, and he vowed there and then to look after them as he imagined she would have done.

Then, above all, there was music and his instinct to express feeling through it. How instinctive this was in him is shown by a simple but significant happening. His father caught cholera soon after Alexandra Andreyevna's death but was one of the few fortunate; he recovered. As soon as he was fit to travel he took the family off to Oranienbaum on the Gulf of Finland for a change of air and scene. At this holiday resort Petya wrote his first composition ("Our Mama in Petersburg" excepted) that has been recorded. It was not a lament for his mother; it was, prophetically, a cheerful waltz and was dedicated to Nastasya Petrovna.

CHAPTER 5

Government Clerk
1854-1862

PYOTR ILYICH, as Petya was now called, spent five more years at the Law School and, against all the odds of the character that has been foisted on him since his death, this period was predominantly happy. It could, as a matter of fact, have been forecast that as such a sensitive boy had weathered the first two years he would soar through the rest; and so it proved.

The Director of the school was an ex-army martinet by the name of Yazykov. He regarded the students as yet another battalion to be licked into shape; military parades were the order of the day; the students were housed in barracks style and slept, if they were lucky, on the hardest of mattresses after the manner of Nicholas I; discipline was ferocious; food plain; art a word not acknowledged. It is difficult to imagine the Tchaikovsky boy surviving such a life, and still more so when it is remembered that his first year was spent under the eagle eye of a master fanatically determined to enforce the Director's precepts. From Yazykov's point of view Pyotr Ilyich was not a promising pupil. He was little more addicted to soap and water in his teens than in his childhood, he remained desperately untidy, his idea of time was hazy, he was plainly that worst of time-wasters, a dreamer.

Yet he survived and even flourished, thanks to the friendships he quickly struck up, thanks also too to a physical toughness out of all proportion to his lackadaisical air and a dignity which demanded respect. And when, in his second year, his class master retired in favor of a Frenchman, Edgar Prosper De Baccarat, he settled down and, in a year or two, became a distinguished member of school.

It is a pity that more is not known about De Baccarat, for he had a beneficial effect on Pyotr Ilyich. He may not have been particularly interested in music but he was a civilized man and encouraged his pupils to develop their talents far beyond the rigid schedule of the law classes. His forte was literature and, like Fanny, his gods were the French romantics. The little group of which Pyotr Ilyich was one of the most enthusiastic was soon declaiming De Musset, Lamartine, Byron, and the rest of the romantics and trying their best to imitate them.

Pyotr Ilyich did not shine as a poet, yet strangely—strange because he was retiring—he was chosen as editor of the school magazine *The School Messenger* which De Baccarat founded. The little magazine is of no importance; its young editor's success is. He was appointed over the heads of many more gifted boys yet justified the master completely—a master probably swayed by the fact that Tchaikovsky's mother was French like himself. Tchaikovsky displayed all the qualities needed to be a good editor: frankness softened by charm, breeding, good humor, and above all, authority.

The main contributors to the magazine were also his best friends but they had to earn their place just the same. They did so because his friends were naturally artistic boys. Less than halfway through his schooldays—in 1855—Nicholas I died and was succeeded by the liberal-minded Alexander II who relaxed the rigid censorship of the arts and, among other benefits, reformed the law courts. This encouraged some of the best minds in the country to read for the bar and led to a sparkling era which has been called the era of the Literary Lawyers. The sons of some of the noblest families were just beginning to attend the law school in Tchaikovsky's time and were to enrich the literary and social scene by brilliant speeches, first-rate literary criticism, some original writing, and some rather less good poetry.

Four of the earliest of the Literary Lawyers were boyhood friends of Pyotr Ilyich and his chief contributors to the magazine. They were Apukhtin, Ertel, Gerard, and Maslov. Only A. N. Apukhtin was to make more than an ephemeral name in literature, and he had considerable influence on Pyotr Ilyich. He was one year his junior, a well-endowed aristocrat who incongruously swathed a naturally rotund body in a black cloak, sported disordered hair, and tried to force a plump-cheeked face into haggard hollows—all after Byron in particular and the romantic conception in general. He wrote verses which were to make him one of the most popular poets in Petersburg. In these poems he yearned after lost purity, created soulful maidens to resurrect knightly behavior, but the basic element in all was indulgence and consequent despair. After he left school Apukhtin was to live up to the prevailing tone of his poetry; at school his work merely echoed his romantic masters, though with a certain art.

There is nothing more catching than Romanticism and Pyotr Ilyich was never to throw it off; he found it only too easy to see himself as a deplorable character, weak, sinful, self-indulgent. The game was to change its nature, but at school he managed to enjoy himself in his poems and letters as thoroughly as the would-be masochistic Apukhtin. They were a happy band of friends, deliciously united in melancholy.

Although literature occupied much of his spare time—he was meanwhile rising from class to class without undue effort or enthusiasm—music soon had powerful supports. His best friend did not belong to the littérateurs; he was a boy who represented the best element in the civilized lawyer class then being built up despite the barbarically militaristic Yazykov.

Vladimir Stepanovich Adamov was solemn, earnest, and appropriately melancholy. Unlike most of his schoolfellows he was really devoted to law and had a fine legal mind. But he believed that one who was to interpret his country's laws must be a cultural leader too as befitting a man looked up to far and wide. He cultivated music; he loved it, not with the instinctive passion of Pyotr Ilyich, but with the joy of one who found in it a challenge and satisfaction to the subtle, disciplined legal mind. Like law it was civilized, intricate, unending in its intellectual satisfactions.

Obviously such a boy would find his ideal counterpart in Pyotr Ilyich. Their arguments were endless and inconclusive but never fatal to friendship because each in his way truly loved music. The passionate Pyotr Ilyich leavened the calculating Adamov slightly; Adamov put a brake on Pyotr Ilyich's extravagances. They went well together and lived music evening after evening, going to all the concerts and ballets and operas at weekends, discussing them, playing them over. Their taste was catholic but Pyotr Ilyich began to acquire the rudiments of an analytical sense.

At the same time as he benefitted from Adamov's soberly encouraging enthusiasm, Pyotr Ilyich was making his mark in the school choir, taking private singing lessons with G. A. Lomakhin and outstriding the school piano teacher, Bekker, with whom he had begun lessons as soon as he entered the senior school. Bekker was soon as hopelessly outplayed as Maria Markovna at Votkinsk. Becoming impatient with the man's incompetence, Pyotr Ilyich asked his father if he could have private lessons from a teacher of repute.

By this time—it was the year of Alexandra II's accession—a considerable change had taken place in the Tchaikovsky household. The retired Ilya Petrovich joined forces with his elder brother, Pyotr Petrovich, after whom Pyotr Ilyich had been named. Pyotr Petrovich had been seized with religious fervor after retiring from the army and kept to his own rooms in which he spent most of his time composing religious tracts.

The jovial (and indigent) Ilya Petrovich put his head together with his brother's wife, by no means of her husband's inclinations and persuaded his sister-in-law Yekaterina Andreyevna and her family to follow him. The results were satisfactory: one party after another and much music.

Yekaterina Andreyevna brought with her an ancient retainer in the shape of an ex-opera singer from Naples who had earned a wretched livelihood in Petersburg by giving singing lessons until the Schoberts took him up. Piccioli was a character, a rouged and dyed dandy with very decided views guaranteed to liven every musical party. He was naturally a hundred per cent in favor of Italian opera. He demolished the Germans and preached the virtues of the young Verdi, then almost unknown in Russia.

When Pyotr Ilyich arrived for his weekends at this new home on the Kadetsky Line he leaped straight into the general lively mood. Leaped is the *mot juste*. This supposedly morbid and brokenhearted boy (he was then in his mid-teens) showed himself a thorough madcap. The twins were ravished, two fanatical worshippers; they waited all week for him and had eyes for nobody else when he was there. They were well rewarded: "He radiated *joie de vivre*," said Modest, looking back on those halcyon days, "he was like a never-ending hymn of joy. Like the birds in Spring who make senseless songs just for sheer joy of living so he made senseless jokes and made them so supremely well that he managed to color them with a sort of fascination—how did he think it all up on the spur of the moment?"

He gives an example: "Beckoning to me, he'd make me say 'Pita, Pita, Pito, Piye, Pyetu, Petrushka!' before he allowed me to kiss him." This declension of his name (which varied every time) never failed to bring gales of laughter from the two small boys: "Nothing could have seemed wittier or happier to us."

As an inventor of games he was, they thought, incomparable: "I've never met anything like them. He didn't 'condescend' to play with us, he became like one of us, improvised and created one game after another in the gayest of moods, all originating in his strange and magically charming nature."

Sentimental exaggeration, one might think, from children overcome by such attention from a ten-years-older brother. Yet Modest's words were to be borne out through Pyotr Ilyich's life; men and women were to be almost literally bewitched by him, by the kind expression in his eyes, his grace, and, for the greater part of his life, by this spirit of original fun which enlivened party after party. Even in his last years he could reduce his friends to near hysterics and he was never to lose his rare gift with children.

In these middle 1850's the boy carried his gaiety with him when he gave the twins their goodnight kiss and ran downstairs to the elders. Piccioli was a joy to him and he to Piccioli. He not only had all the music he could wish for but learned via this new friend to appreciate Verdi and was soon being driven to shift his defense of the beloved Mozart—who was, he came to agree, in every true sense of the word an Italian composer. His devotion to Rossini, Bellini, and Donizetti was encouraged by Piccioli who, finding eager talent on his doorstep, quickly monopolized the young student and paid him the compliment of passing on his knowledge of opera. In later years Tchaikovsky was to recall these talks with gratitude, and placed them alongside the orchestrion of his childhood, the never-to-be-forgotten Glinka and Mozart operas at the Maryinsky, and the summer holiday with his aunt as among the seminal forces in his career.

Piccioli in fact continued that long-past summer's instruction by Yekaterina Andreyevna (which he had largely imparted to her in the first place) and left the young Pyotr Ilyich with a fairly strong grasp of the requirements for writing a singable opera—how the composer chose his libretto, how he built up an opera, how he wrote arias which made the most of the soloist's voice without asking for the impossible or the ludicrous, how he blended singer and orchestra to best effect.

The Italian also encouraged the boy to take up composition again. This time, naturally, the composition was a song, set to the Italian translation of a Russian poem by Fet, which shows how Italianate the impressionable Pyotr Ilyich had become. Not content with writing the song, "Mezzanotte," he went to the length of having it privately printed. It was not a very good song but the event was a milestone and helped to put him still further out of sympathy with the idea of a legal career.

In view of this outburst of music in the new Tchaikovsky home it is no wonder that the different Pyotr Ilyich worked up enough courage to speak to his father about a good music teacher.

Ilya Petrovich agreed. It may be that he would have agreed in any case through sheer good humor, though this insistence on music by a law student must have struck him as odd. But events were in his son's favor; the nightly parties were draining Ilya Petrovich's purse and his response was to begin to play the markets under the guidance of a friend with "inside information."

Ilya Petrovich was an optimist but he also had a conscience. He knew that he was taking an unjustifiable risk when all six children except Nikolai were far from earning a living and two of them were little boys. His response to the prick of conscience was in character; within reason he granted all their wishes. This cost still more money but eased his mind which worked on the principle, if I throw my money about, let them all have a share of it. He may even have dealt with an unimaginable possibility: if disaster came, the children would at least have had a slight picking before everything disappeared.

However this may be, there was a rash of happenings in the Tchaikovsky family: Ippolit Ilyich went off to the Navy as a very well provided for midshipman in time to see the end of the scandalous war which England and France had forced on Russia; Alexandra Ilyinishna was sent to the exclusive Smolny Institute for young ladies; Nikolai Ilyich was given enough financial backing to get him a good first appointment after graduating from his School of Mining; and Pyotr Ilyich was granted his much more modest request, to have a good piano teacher.

Rudolf Vasilyevich Kundinger has not gone down in history as a great teacher of the pianoforte and in fact he was not a great teacher. His place in the memories of men is probably unique, for he is the only known example of a human being who taught genius and, in after years, did not claim to have recognized and fostered that genius from the first. Kundinger, with superlative

honesty, declared long afterwards that he found no genius whatever in the young Tchaikovsky.

"If I could have dreamed what Pyotr Ilyich was to become I
should have kept a record of our lessons," he said. "But I must admit, to my great confusion, that at no time did the idea enter my
head that Tchaikovsky had the makings of a musician." He continued, even more courageously: "Of course he was gifted. He
had a fine ear, a good memory, and splendid hands, but beyond
this nothing, absolutely nothing which could foretell the rise of
a composer or even of an outstanding instrumentalist—nothing
special, nothing phenomenal."

The years with Kundinger naturally did not convince his pupil
that it was his bounden duty to take up music. Kundinger's tepid
praise banked down a fire ready at any moment to burst into a
blaze. Pyotr Ilyich still regarded a career in law—even the reformed law—with a sort of incredulity, and waited hopefully for
his father to make the expected millions before declaring himself
quit of the farce.

What actually happened was, as might be expected, that, a year
before his son was due to graduate, Ilya Petrovich lost every ruble
and was forced to find another job. He did find one—he was appointed Director of the Institute of Technology after an agonizing search—but the harm had been done; Pyotr Ilyich could not
be sure that his father, sixty-four by that time, could hold the
position. His strong family sense was stronger than his distaste
for government service. Nikolai was launched and was to follow
his father, though at a safe jog-trot; Ippolit was obviously taking
to naval life; Alexandra had met Lyov Vasilyevich Davidov and
a marriage was being talked about; but the twins were still some
way from their teens. In the spirit of his self-imposed role as guard-
ian, Pyotr Ilyich sacrificed music to ensure them a fair chance of
a good education and a carefree childhood. When he graduated,
in May, 1859, thirteenth in his class of more than fifty, he applied
for a post in the First Division of the Ministry of Justice. He was
appointed.

2

The next three years or so, from the age of nineteen to twenty-two, consisted of almost nothing important. Pyotr Ilyich's career in the Ministry of Justice followed the course of any intelligent young man who took no interest in his work. Because he was intelligent and the work was simple he could scarcely avoid occasional demonstration of ability: he received regular promotions and in less than a year had become senior assistant to the chief clerk. Because he was good-natured, charming and wellborn, his frequent lapses of memory—he had a queer habit when in a daydream of chewing documents to pieces—were overlooked. Like his father he was a good mixer. Interested he was not. His invariable politeness may have given the impression that he was, but as a government career was understood to be a social and financial necessity for most wellborn Russians, too much interest or attention to duty would have been considered bad form. By four o'clock every afternoon he could be seen with a hundred other government clerks taking the air on the Nevsky Prospekt, preening himself in his uniform and taking note of the young women promenading by the river at the fashionable hour.

For he had become a dandy. In November, 1860, Alexandra Ilyinishna married the young Davidov and left for the Davidov estate in the Ukraine, and the withdrawal of her steadying influence caused this much loved brother to lose hope. This has been held against him as appalling weakness of character. Such a judgment takes no account of the feelings of a highly gifted young man of twenty immured in a government office day by day when all he wanted to do was to make music, and of an extraordinarily affectionate young man who has lost his best companion, friend, sister, and mother all in one.

He knew what he was doing; his letters to Alexandra Davidova, which were to continue for the rest of her life, were filled with self-reproaches. These were so violent that the reader who examines his life at this time is perplexed to find his sins so white.

He became a dandy and led the life of one—that was his chief weakness. He joined the group of young officials in their life of pleasure, grew the *à la mode* little beard, was always faultlessly turned out, smoked furiously, drank more than was good for him, flirted with young men and girls indiscriminately, and was usually to be found at one of the smart restaurants and cabarets. He was in great demand at musical soirées and dances, not so much for his voice or his abilities as a dancing partner as for his willingness to pound out a waltz or muzurka almost indefinitely so that his companions might dance their way through the night. He attended all the operas, operettas, and ballets and duly fell in love with the reigning soprano and ballerina.

Indeed love was the motif of these years—it was the fashion in his set—and his letters to Alexandra Ilyinishna drew the picture of a would-be Lothario. This merely succeeded in making her laugh, but her smile must have become sad when he ended as almost always by promising reform; she needed no telling that as long as he continued to pass his daytime hours stupidly he would be likely to pass the nights stupidly too.

He did not tell her of his dabblings in homosexuality—a relic of the school years—but there is not the slightest indication that he worried about it; he would marry and the habit would die a natural death—that was his not unreasonable argument when he bothered to argue.

His old friends were little help, and the one he saw most of, Apukhtin, no help at all. Apukhtin, now busily practicing what he had preached at school, urged Pyotr Ilyich in one breath to devote his life to poetry and the next moment was carrying him off to a brothel or a cabaret which was little better. He was leading a rakish life and making good poetry out of it; such a gift was beyond his friend.

Adamov, it seems, Pyotr Ilyich fought shy of. No doubt he was ashamed of himself and could not often face the earnest lawyer-musician his friend had become.

There were aspects of this lighthearted existence which display the dandy in a different light. Pyotr Ilyich was always at his best at home; the twins still found him marvelous and no wonder; he spent at lot of time with them and they always felt the better for it. One of their great joys was to sit him at the piano and join in the latest popular songs he played with abandon. An even greater joy was to watch him imitate the ballet dancers he was following assiduously at the Maryinsky.

This second pleasure was a little marred for Modest who had similar aspirations and nursed the sense of injustice which the younger so often feel towards the elder. "Petya could always turn the blamable (for me) into the permissible (for him). He was passionately fond of imitating ballerinas and all their special mannerisms. I wanted to do this too. But when I tried it everyone mocked me and told me to stop clowning. Petya on the contrary fascinated everyone so much—children and grownups alike—that he used to give entire performances of this ballet-baiting in the evening, usually near the dacha in the broad ditch separating the New Place from the English Park. No one thought the performance unfitting; all applauded and youths of his own age used to jump into the ditch, fired with the wish to emulate him, and throw themselves into similar clever caricatures of the dance."

Ilya Petrovich first put the brake on this frivolous life. Not for moral reasons but in a fit of conscience. He had settled into his post, his monetary affairs were as stable as they were ever likely to be, and he saw with uneasiness his son wasting his time at the Ministry. He knew well enough why Pyotr Ilyich was there. Eventually he asked him whether he ought not to take up music seriously.

This was the first time any member of the young man's family had so much as recognized the obvious, but by the time the suggestion was made, Pyotr Ilyich had worked himself into such a state of self-disgust that he could not even begin to consider acceptance; he had lost faith in himself as a musician as well as man.

The idea stuck nevertheless. The crucial moment came a few months later, in the summer of 1861, when he went off with a friend for the time-honored European tour. The tour produced no notable reactions from the twenty-one-year-old traveler. He did not care for Berlin, liked nothing about London, not even the singing of Patti, and considered Paris (which entranced him) in most ways inferior to Petersburg.

The value of the trip lay in his meditations when left to himself. He returned to write a particularly extravagant letter to his sister, blaming himself for throwing money away the moment he had it, and very foolishly too. He was still doing it, he assured her, which proved his weakness fully. And to make matters worse, without even the result vanity might hope for: "I am having no luck at all in love." This meant that the Apukhtin remedy for sowing wild oats, to marry a pure girl, had failed.

Then, having spent himself, came the historic announcement which must have made Alexandra radiant with pleasure. This time he did not end with the usual flood of promises to do better but with a piece of hard news. It was a scribbled postscript: "I am studying thorough bass and am doing quite well." Followed by an even more acceptable: "Perhaps in three years or so you'll be hearing one of my operas or, better still, singing the arias from it. Who can tell?"

3

When Tchaikovsky cried "I am Russian, Russian, Russian!" he was, unknowingly, warning all non-Russians not to equate the Russian temperament with the Western and judge a Russian as if he were one of themselves. Anyone who knows the Russians will be familiar with two outstanding characteristics common to the entire nation: they are a feeling people and they are subject to fits of sloth or what could be called paralysis of the will to action. These characteristics merge time after time when the Russian, regarding this period of sloth, cries to heaven that he is the most contemptible of men, that he makes resolutions only to break them, that he is unworthy to exist, that his faculties rust and decay because of his appalling weakness. And so on, at length and in the most impassioned terms.

The Westerner, reading or hearing this, accepts it at face value and pities or scorns according to his nature. What he rarely understands is that the difference between him and a Russian is not that the one is lazy and unrestrained and the other businesslike and sensible, but that the one feels so deeply that he says exactly what he feels while the other has been schooled to govern and conceal his feelings. The Russian tells the exact truth about himself, the Westerner does not. The amount of work done by both is, in fact, very similar in the long run, for the Russian, spurred by guilt, works at a rate and with a fury of concentration that the Westerner knows little of.

If a reader allows for this when he reads Tchaikovsky's letters he will understand him much better. Everyone has moments of guilt, not to speak of the myriads of neurotic fancies which oppress humanity, and the fact that the Westerner keeps his guilt-feelings to himself is not necessarily the merit he often claims. The difference between Tchaikovsky and most of his fellow countrymen is that, being a great artist, he is even more frank and even more self-abusive. He meant what he said, every word of it, at the moment of writing, but half an hour after posting his letter he was as likely as not to be found working. And how he worked! He was often to perform miracles—such as the lightning composition of the *Sleeping Beauty* score—but even in his earliest years he threw himself into everything musical with a fervor quite incongruous with the drawling, leisurely dandy.

Perhaps the best proof that the young Pyotr Ilyich must not be judged so harshly as he judged himself is the passivity of his sister. Alexandra loved him with a selfless passion rarely found in brother and sister. She heard all his news and shared all his feelings. If she had been a Western woman she would have rushed up to Petersburg from Kamenka the moment she read almost any one of his youthful letters, they were so despairing, so denunciatory of all he was and was likely to be. But she did not move. She knew Russians, she knew her brother.

Pyotr Ilyich's decision to prepare himself for a career in music—

for this was at the back of his mind when he began lessons in thorough bass with Nikolai Ivanovich Zaremba in 1861—justified his sister's faith. He was not only the most Russian of Russians, he was a young man of twenty-one having a very good time in one of the gayest cities in the world. His charm and good nature and excellent manners made him welcome to the bright young things who were dancing and drinking the nights away. Women liked him because he flirted with an air and made a most obliging cavalier; men liked him because he was open-handed, a loyal friend and without a tinge of malice in his make-up. Even the boring hours in the Ministry were made more acceptable because of his widespread popularity; he treated the old clerks with consideration instead of the usual insolence and his manner with his superiors was so easy that they excused even the nibbling of documents and the spells of forgetfulness when he would daydream for hours at a time.

There was every reason why this young man with his fair share of native indolence should be spoiled and flattered out of all thought of music. He could so easily have relegated his part in it to the role of appreciative listener at the opera and performer of the latest ballads and gypsy dance tunes. And when, stirred by a wish to follow the opera libretti, he took up the study of Italian, he might well have considered this as paying sufficient tribute to conscience after office hours.

In spite of all this, temperament, temptation, flattery, and the natural wish of the young to enjoy themselves, he voluntarily persuaded Zaremba to accept him as a pupil. This shows not only the power of music but a strength of purpose with which he has never been credited outside his own country.

4

He had to persuade Zaremba to take him on because Zaremba was a teacher of some distinction in the Petersburg musical world. He had a greater distinction; he was the first musician of any con-

sequence to tutor the future great composer. His effect on Tchaikovsky's career was important. He came into his life when Pyotr
Ilyich made his first serious effort to take up music as a profession.
The counter attractions to music being what they were, much
responsibility devolved on the man he asked to teach him. Zaremba was equal to it. His theory was rigid—he had studied harmony under Marx—but in his inelastic way he loved music and
had no serious thoughts of anything outside it. To work under
such a man was to live with a calm, unspoken acceptance of the
supremacy of the arts and of music specially which reinforced
Pyotr Ilyich's decision at precisely the right moment; he felt that
he had chosen rightly and inevitably. There were backslidings in
the sense of doubts about his own ability—Zaremba was a harsh
critic—but they were not long-lasting.

Zaremba, moreover, represented to Pyotr Ilyich much more
than a solitary professor of repute; he stood for a new spirit in
Russian music. This spirit had first shown itself publicly two
years earlier, when Anton Rubinstein, powerfully supported by
the Tsar's aunt, the Grand Duchess Yelena Pavlovna, launched
the Russian Musical Society with royal approval. That winter the
Society began to give its own concerts which Pyotr Ilyich attended
enthusiastically, and sadly too, for the formation of the Society
coincided with his entry into the civil service.

The Society also began to hold classes for students. It collected
a notable staff including, besides Zaremba, two Poles, Henri Wien-
iavsky and Theodor Leschetizky, the cellist-composer Karl U.
Davidov, and Pyotr Ilyich's singing teacher of school days, Lomakhin. The classes were held at the Grand Duchess' Mikhailovsky
Palace where Pyotr Ilyich first took harmony lessons from Zaremba.

For Rubinstein and his supporters this was only a beginning;
they felt that the Society deserved its own home and must have
one if it was to gain enough prestige to force a change in the
status of the Russian musician. Rubinstein often told the story
of the registration which, as a baptized Jew, he had to carry out

every three years. When asked his profession he replied: Musician. The clerk refused the explanation, saying that there was no such thing according to Russian law. Not until Rubinstein gave details of his father was he allowed to go. He was described in the register as son of a merchant of the second guild.

It was this attitude he was now fighting, and three years after the establishment of the Society he succeeded; the Tsar agreed to finance him, and what came to be known as the St. Petersburg Conservatoire was given its own splendid quarters facing the Neva. This was one year after Pyotr Ilyich began lessons with Zaremba.

The sequel shows how closely the young man had been following Rubinstein's efforts. His year with Zaremba was unenlivened by a single motion of lightness—musical theory is a sobering subject at the best of times and when taught by a stiff-necked Russian who has learned his theory from a German it becomes fearsome. But the supposed butterfly Pyotr Ilyich went diligently and methodically through it and his hours of practice at home raised protesting moans from the twins, accustomed to much lighter fare. In vain; he stuck grimly—and happily—to it.

The Conservatoire opened its doors on September 20, 1862, and one of its first students—he had put himself down for the matriculation examination as soon as he heard the news—was Pyotr Ilyich.

Part Two

APPRENTICESHIP

CHAPTER 6

Musician
1862-1866

NOT FOR ANOTHER SIX MONTHS did Pyotr Ilyich formally give up the Ministry farce, but his entry to the Conservatoire in the autumn of 1862 marked the real decision to devote his life to music. With this decision comes the need for a summary of the state of Russian music at that time—music that the new recruit was to do so much, perhaps more than any other man, to make world-famous.

It would be more correct to say, a picture of the state of music in Russia, because there was virtually no Russian music. Centuries earlier, Russian church music had been the finest and richest in the world and Russian folk songs (partly adopted by the peasants from the church music, partly pagan in origin) were incomparable in number and variety. That day had long passed. Folk music still existed but the only composer who had tried to make use of it was scarcely ever heard; church music had gone into decline owing mainly to the rise to power of zealots who abolished all but the simplest and oldest of Byzantine chants and even tried to proscribe the use of musical instruments throughout the country.

When this iron rule of the Church was at last relaxed there were practically no professional Russian musicians left and no recognized Russian music. Folk songs flourished in the villages but were despised in Moscow and Petersburg as barbaric. These

were the days which followed Peter the Great and his Westerniz-
ing policy. One of his most effective methods was to invite foreign
musicians, singers, and actors to his chief cities, and his successors,
Anne, Elizabeth, and Catherine improved on this; they established
foreign opera and ballet companies in Moscow and Petersburg
under resident composers and ballet masters—almost all Italian—
and patronized them lavishly. All the influential nobility followed
the standard set by the Court until by 1800 it could be said that
the only recognized music in the two capitals was Italian. When
Alexander I came to the throne at the beginning of the century
he changed this trend slightly but, from the point of view of the
Russian composer or musician, it was a case of *plus ça change, plus
c'est la même chose;* he encouraged French and German composers and artists instead of Italian.

By a curious mental quirk, Russians in positions of authority,
although they made much of foreign performers and composers,
did not consider these careers suitable for Russians. Not only the
capitals but all the great country houses of Russia had orchestras
and many miniature opera houses and theaters, but Russian performers were seldom employed. When Petya was born, Russian
actors had not long been permitted an official existence; when he
entered the Petersburg Conservatoire twenty-two years later, Russian musicians remained pariahs, with no status. Except for one
man, the few Russian composers obtained a hearing only by diligently copying the Italians or French. A conductor had to speak
Italian or German if he wanted to control his orchestra, largely
composed of foreigners who would not demean themselves by
learning the despised Russian. In Court and society circles French
was *de rigueur*—the mother tongue was considered a language
for peasants, coarse like Russian music.

The exception among Russian composers was, of course, Glinka.
Unlike his few predecessors he had genius and what goes with it,
moral courage. He had one aim, to write music which could only
have been written by a Russian; he chose Russian subjects for his
operas and went to the Russian folk song for his music, sometimes

genuine folk songs, sometimes created by himself from folk song material.

Glinka was far from being a chauvinist; he was a traveled, cultured, wellborn European who fully understood that he could not neglect foreign music which had freely developed through the centuries when Russian art was suppressed. Models were necessary if he were to create a national music and these models were not to be found in Russia. Italy was the natural model, but though his first opera *A Life for the Tsar* is Italianate in construction it is filled with melodies taken straight from Russian life, even to a pizzicato use of the strings to suggest balalaikas. It also introduces the leitmotiv which Wagner was to use with German thoroughness; Glinka carries out the idea with characteristic deftness and lightness.

A Life for the Tsar was first performed in 1836, four years before Tchaikovsky's birth. It was received enthusiastically and remained in the repertory—that was why the ten-year-old Petya was able to see it at the Maryinsky—but a great deal of its popularity was due to the very patriotic libretto of a heroic Russian peasant giving his life for country and Tsar. Glinka's innovations were not appreciated in the circles which counted. Most of his aristocratic audiences did not even notice them and the few intellectuals who did, dismissed them with a sneer as "cabmen's music"—this because Glinka had used a well-known cabmen's song in the first act. The prejudice was as powerful as ever, that it was beneath Russian dignity to write for the public and that, since no decent Russian would do it, all existing Russian music was therefore unworthy of an opera stage.

In *A Life for the Tsar,* Glinka wanted to write "a Russian opera in which my beloved countrymen would feel at home. . . . a big work absolutely national, not only the subject but the music." He had only succeeded in part. He was at once recognized as the first important Russian composer but was not recognized at all as a national composer. Ironically enough his success was due largely to the opera's Italian framework.

Realizing this, he discarded the framework in his second opera; *Russlan and Ludmilla* is wholly Russian. For a man beginning virtually from scratch it is an astounding piece of work. It consists of a medley of influences, not all Russian, but blended with such genius that the most satisfactory test, the opinion of the man in the street, always has the same result: he says "Russian music."

At one stroke Glinka created the idiom which was more and more to conquer the world—that powerful, supple music, as lively and unjaded as though Russia was a newborn country, as in the most important sense she was, for Glinka, Pushkin, and Gogol were recreating her artistically. Like the Sleeping Beauty, Russia awakened fresh and youthful from her centuries-long sleep and her art combined all the advantages of tradition and novelty. If she had missed the development of other European countries, she also missed the after-staleness. Tchaikovsky was to describe the music of Wagner as a sunset. The music of Glinka was a sunrise.

When he joined the Conservatoire, Pyotr Ilyich had not heard a performance of *Russlan and Ludmilla* (then twenty years old) because it had never been repeated. There was nothing obviously patriotic about Pushkin's fairy tale, the libretto had been unhappily mangled, and the Russianness of the music merely struck its first hearers as barbaric. The aristocratic first-night audience particularly objected to the Oriental note in so much of the opera; they thought this retrograde when all intelligent Russians should look to the West for their culture. The Church objected to the story being set in pagan days.

The opera failed dismally and was hissed off the stage. It broke the spirit of Glinka—only thirty-nine at the time—and was partly responsible for his early death. He never wrote another opera and never forgave his country; before leaving Russia for good he spat on the ground. "It may be recognized in a hundred years," he said bitterly of *Russlan and Ludmilla;* and his estimate was not far wrong.

2

Pyotr Ilyich's enthusiasm for *A Life for the Tsar* and Glinka's smaller works, specially the symphonic work "Kamarinskaya," had long since penetrated the Tchaikovsky family to such a degree that when he decided to give up the Ministry in the spring of 1863, his elder brother Nikolai Ilyich, by that time an up-and-coming mining official in the provinces, protested at this waste of civil service talent in a sneer which has become notorious. "I can't see you becoming another Glinka."

His brother's reply has also gone down into history: "I may not become another Glinka but sooner or later you will be proud of me." In fact he was to become another Glinka, doing for Russia in orchestral works what Glinka had done in opera.

In the Conservatoire he heard nothing about Glinka or that other remarkable Russian composer, Dargomijsky, whose opera *Russalka* attempted to popularize Russian folk songs and who was at that moment working on his most original opera *The Stone Guest*. To be precise, if they were mentioned in the Conservatoire it would be disparagingly. Nikolai Ilyich represented the official attitude exactly.

Anton Rubinstein was no lover of Russian music. He was proud of being a Russian and would no doubt have described himself as a Russian composer—he was to leave much music behind him, all moribund—but, perhaps because of his German mother, his sympathies were entirely German. His own work was a poor copy of German music and he followed the Germans in everything, the early Germans at that. He worshipped Beethoven, permitted occasional glances at the not too daring works of Mendelssohn and Schumann and that was his limit.

His renown was won in the battle he fought for the Russian musician. What he wanted—and what he did—was to destroy the attitude symbolized by the official who had told him that he could not register as a musician because in Russian law there was no such thing. But the last thing in his mind was to establish the status of Russian musicians so that they could play Russian music; his aim was to turn them into respected and well-paid performers of music composed outside his own country. In this he was at one with men he despised, the serf owners who had jeered at *Russlan and Ludmilla*. He openly rejoiced at its failure, pointing to it as a warning to his students to reject what he called "barbaric theories."

Pyotr Ilyich's enthusiasm for Glinka therefore received rough handling in the Conservatoire, but there was a place in Petersburg where it would have been surpassed. This was the apartment of Mily Balakirev. Balakirev, three years older than Pyotr Ilyich, was a gifted pianist and musical thinker whose future was decided by a meeting with Glinka. A self-educated composer, he wrote at eighteen a fantasy on themes from *A Life for the Tsar* and, more important, already appreciated the originality of *Russlan and Ludmilla*. When he met his hero that same year, 1855, Glinka praised his pianoforte playing, praised his "Fantasy," paid him the honor of a gift of two themes from his notebook to form the basis of another fantasy, and agreed with his strictures on the study of counterpoint. Glinka, like this young admirer, had not studied very seriously, though for different reasons, and said "Who knows? Maybe it was for the best after all. The strict German counterpoint isn't always good for the free imagination."

In one way and another he was charmed and impressed, and wrote to his sister and chief supporter, Ludmilla Ivanovna Shestakova, "He is the first man I have ever met whose views on music correspond to mine exactly. . . . I believe that in time he'll become a second Glinka."

He did not say this to Balakirev but plainly implied it in his attitude. From that moment the young man's life work was clear, to support Glinka fully and do all he could to make his music appreciated throughout Russia and the world. He thought of himself as an immature disciple but within a few months his hero had died abroad and his role abruptly changed to that of a leader.

He rose to the challenge. He settled in Petersburg and with the help of Vladimir Stasov, to whom Glinka had introduced him before leaving Russia, he set about forming a nationalist school.

Stasov was like Adamov but much cleverer. Educated in the Law School, he became a brilliant speaker and writer, with a keen, incisive wit and a formidable power of analysis. He was deeply interested in all the arts, in music specially, and was no mean performer on the piano, but he had no wish to take up music as a career; his wish was to forward the nationalist cause of Glinka by propaganda and education. Although he wrote no music, this tall, massively bearded man was to make a contribution to Russian music which can scarcely be overestimated. He spanned all that period of the rebirth of Russian music from Glinka to Moussorgsky and throughout it his influence was deeply felt. He was autocratic, overbearing, prolix, often unlikable, but without him Balakirev could not have accomplished the revolution that now stands to his name.

The two men, Stasov and Balakirev, formed a whole, the one intellectually dominant, the other dominating by deep feeling and instinctive artistry. All the worthwhile intellectuals of Petersburg met at Stasov's house; he introduced the unknown Balakirev to them, provided him with pupils and recital engagements, and when they were together discussed and amplified their plans to carry on the nationalist movement. He, it was agreed, would take on the public exposition of these aims; Balakirev would look about for disciples.

He soon found them. In 1857, the year after Glinka's death, he met and fascinated César Cui, an officer in the Engineers who had leanings towards composition and journalism. Cui brought a second recruit in another young officer, Modest Moussorgsky, already an excellent pianist, whom he met at Dargomijsky's house. In 1860 the three became four with the addition of Nikolai Rimsky-Korsakov, a midshipman. Two years later the fifth and last great name was added to the group in Alexander Borodin who worked in the Academy of Medicine.

All the young men took lessons from Balakirev, played four-hand arrangements with him, and fell completely under the spell of his remarkable gifts—he could sight-read and improvise with startling ease—his still more remarkable personality, and his inspired love of Russian music. The lessons were unorthodox. There was no textbook instruction in harmony and counterpoint —Balakirev's grasp of music was purely instinctive—but an endless study of the work of the great masters and a relentless dissection of the work of lesser men. His invariable method was to play over a work, then criticize it, then improvise it as it ought to have been written. Everything his pupils wrote was subjected to this discipline—a discipline made palatable by the teacher's delightful sense of humor and his obvious belief that the criticized pupil loved music as much as he and would be satisfied with nothing short of perfection.

Like Glinka, Balakirev and Stasov were not crudely nationalistic in the sense of rejecting all Western forms of music. Their aim was to make full use of the great wealth of Russian music embedded in the folk tunes of every province but on the basis of a study of the advanced Western composers, Schumann, Chopin, Liszt, Berlioz. They refused to be bound by strict counterpoint or by eighteenth-century forms such as the sonata governing all composition, and they were determined to bring realism into operatic writing (after the manner of *The Stone Guest* which Dargomijsky was then beginning and of Moussorgsky's *Boris Godunov* which was yet to be conceived) instead of following the Italian pattern of a vehicle for displays of vocal pyrotechnics. Their aims were summed up by Cui, who was often to speak for the group, as "to exploit all the seductive elements in music—the charm of harmony, the richness of polyphony and orchestral color" —to which was added, naturally, the popularization of music specifically Russian.

The first task, as Balakirev and Stasov saw it, was to fight the traitor within the gates. The traitor was Rubinstein. To them the Russian Musical Society which Rubinstein founded the year the Balakirev group gained its first adherents, was wholly bad; its aim of liberating the Russian musician was proving worse in the long run than allowing him to stay as he was. They argued that if Rubinstein had his way the opera houses and concert halls would be filled with Russian musicians who had been taught to revere German music and despise that of their own country. When the Conservatoire was opened—it coincided with the completion of the Balakirev group—they jeered at it as "a hive of professors" and a Germanic organization with "not one Russian in the whole outfit"—a jibe near enough to the truth to hurt.

But it was not enough to jeer. Balakirev was not a man to sit down and await events; he made them. Long before Borodin completed the Mighty Handful, as the group was to be nicknamed, its leader had acted. Supported financially by Glinka's sister and Stasov and his influential friends and given plenty of newspaper publicity by Stasov and Cui, he opened the Free Music School in opposition to the R.M.S. He offered free tuition to anyone, man or woman, interested in music, and introduced evening classes for day workers. Far from insisting on a grounding in musical theory, he and his associates based their teaching on analysis of major works. And though, as the response was great, he had to teach by class, he made a point of individual tuition for promising students—again in contrast to the Rubinstein principle.

To popularize the school and bring in funds he organized concerts in opposition to the R.M.S. concerts. The programs were advanced—mostly Liszt, Schumann, Berlioz, Glinka, and Dargomijsky—and as soon as the Mighty Handful produced compositions of their own, he used the concerts to provide his disciples with a platform for public performance and to introduce his large audiences to up-to-date nationalist music written by himself and his group.

3

When Pyotr Ilyich entered the Conservatoire, therefore, he found two rival parties in the city with both of which he felt considerable sympathy.

The question has often been posed: What would have happened to him if he had thrown in his lot with Balakirev? That he would have developed more quickly is certain, proved by the historical fact that he was not to write his first wholly individual work until he met Balakirev and had been guided and inspired by him on a theme chosen by the older man.

On the other hand, he was to owe his greatest strength—as one of the world's greatest orchestrators—to the thorough grounding in counterpoint and harmony and the theory of music he received at the Conservatoire. Years later, when they knew one another, Balakirev wrote to him, "The classics can never teach you independence of form. They give you what you learned from Zaremba when you listened respectfully to his profound lessons on 'the correspondence between the form of the Rondo and the fall of the first man'!" It is easy to make fun of the traditionalists, but dangerous to ignore all they have to say, however pedantically they say it. It goes against the grain to criticize Balakirev, who did so much for Russian music and has rarely been given his due, but it must be said that had he been able to learn music from the bottom upwards he would have been a more resourceful orchestrator and his works would now be played everywhere. It is a question whether, if Tchaikovsky had come under his influence in 1862, he could have written the works which have made him loved all over the world.

As it was, Balakirev, unknowingly, had missed a disciple after his own heart, and Pyotr Ilyich followed Zaremba into the Conservatoire without a second thought—it was as simple as that. Balakirev attacked musical conservatism because it might stifle genius, but if the history of Tchaikovsky is any guide, the only thing the pedagogues can stifle is mediocrity; the genius sooner or later will assert itself. In 1862 Pyotr Ilyich did not know that he had declared for the conservatives and anti-Russians. When he did understand it he showed that not even a Conservatoire directed by Anton Rubinstein could hold him down indefinitely.

In 1862 nothing of this was within the bounds of his imagination; he was a student trying to nerve himself to the plunge of resignation from the Ministry. This had suddenly become an economic matter as well as a spiritual one; Ilya Petrovich, tiring of his post, resigned on a small pension and withdrew to a fairly humble apartment with the twins. He could support and educate them; he could not spare a ruble for Pyotr Ilyich, only a bedroom.

How to live on music? That was immediately the problem, but typically the student did not wait for it to be resolved; he resigned his post; six months at the Conservatoire had shown him clearly the way he had to go.

He was helped, generously helped, by Zaremba, Rubinstein, and the other professors he worked under. This shows better than words the good impression he had made in six months. Pupils were directed to him, engagements as accompanist at concerts were found, he was employed as copyist, doing this dreary job into the early hours of the morning. He managed to live, though on a scale so beggarly that one wonders how a young man who had cut such a figure in society, took cabs everywhere, ate the best food and drank the best wines and put his hand in his pocket at the slightest hint of a loan, could endure the pinch without a moan. But there were no moans; he was doing what he wanted to do and that was worth every luxury he had been used to.

The change from the government clerk of 1862 to the dedicated musician of 1863 was surprising. In 1862 Pyotr Ilyich was still the dandy though he has shaved the beard; his morning coat was faultless, the hair carefully drawn back from the forehead, the gloves still in the hand, the cane ready for the careless swing as he strode the Nevsky Prospekt. The face was immature too. It resembled the photograph of the small boy leaning against his mother, the mouth so sensitive, the cheeks not yet free from puppy fat. At the same time there was the noble forehead and the dreamy, deep eyes which were to be characteristic of him throughout his life.

Towards the end of 1863 comes the fledged musician. The clothes are shabby, the hair lank and overlong, the whole impression rather seedy. But the face is taking on strength of purpose, the slightly puffy cheeks have begun to sink into hollows and the beard that has come back is no longer the neatly trimmed little matter demanded by young Petersburghers but a sprawling collection that shows its owner could not care less what is thought of it—the beard of a man who is too busy with higher matters to be bothered with a razor.

Something of this, it must be said, was due to Apukhtin who supported the apparent change to bohemianism. He preferred that his friend should be a bohemian in art rather than a self-consciously rakish government clerk. He was to be disappointed about the bohemianism which went no further than appearance; Pyotr Ilyich, he found with a shock, really intended to work and was merely neglecting his appearance because he got more work done that way.

All other friends except the steady Adamov, quietly pleased, had dropped off. No more loans, no more wit, no more silliness: they became bored with the serious Pyotr Ilyich and gave him a wide berth. They did him a service; the last temptation disappeared.

He worked hard. How hard, the one famous recollection of Rubinstein will prove. He had been taken into the great man's classes in composition. One day Rubinstein asked him to write a series of contrapuntal variations on a given theme. "I expected that he would present me with about a dozen," said Rubinstein; a dozen being regarded as a fair test of a student's ability. "But Tchaikovsky turned up the next class day with more than two hundred!" Rubinstein soon thought so highly of him that he took the unheard-of step of excusing him from the compulsory pianoforte class so that he could concentrate on theory and composition. The compliment here was double-edged, both to the excellence of his piano playing and to his prospects as a composer. Those two hundred variations were significant and the Director took the hint.

What Pyotr Ilyich thought of his Director could be gauged by the increasing length of his hair as the years passed. There were two massive heads of hair in the Conservatoire. The first was owned by Leschetizky, the professor in pianoforte, then in the first stages of a career as world-famed virtuoso, now remembered when at all by the curious fact that he was to marry four times, each time to a distinguished musician. But Anton Rubinstein had set the fashion which the Pole merely followed; his hair approached the fantastic, a great bob to the neck, and Pyotr Ilyich did his best to emulate him.

His worship of Rubinstein was understandable. The entire Conservatoire worshipped him, these and a host of concertgoers. He remains to this day something of an enigma. In his piano-thumping mood (he once broke one and for ever after had two pianos on the platform at concerts) he could seem to a modern audience simply a charlatan. Yet he loved music and was a true musician and, at times, would play the piano in such a way as to enrapture everyone who heard him. The pedal is the soul of the piano, he used to tell his students, and no man has ever used the pedal with such supreme artistry—from Tchaikovsky to Rachmaninov one witness after another testifies to this. And the peculiar singing tone he used to draw from the instrument has died with him; only reports from admiring listeners remain.

Tchaikovsky, it is clear, saw nothing of the exhibitionist in Anton Rubinstein; he saw the great artist at work. And when Rubinstein exchanged the piano stool for the conductor's podium, the student's reaction is easy to understand. At rehearsal and concert alike, Rubinstein was like a man possessed, throwing himself about, screaming, sweating; his rehearsals were one long fight, but he carried perfection into the performance proper too; he would stop a symphony in the middle of a bar if he did not think the orchestra was following his conception of the music to a hairsbreadth. He cared for nothing and nobody; the audience would have to hear the work again from the beginning, just as the orchestra would have to play it over again. Of course the audience loved it; what was much more remarkable was that the hard-boiled musicians (most of them German who loathed Russians anyway) accepted it too; they rebelled, they declared themselves outraged, they swore they would not play for him, but they always did in the end and, what is more, when the concert was done they were the first to rise and applaud.

Then came the queer part of the man. After a performance— whether he had conducted or played as soloist—he would collapse on to a sofa and lie there like one dead. But he was not dead, he was calm and collected. Looking at him or listening to him, one could not believe that this apparently cold man was the gesticulating creature of a few minutes earlier. In his exhausted way he was businesslike, every faculty keen and alive.

When he taught in the Conservatoire the concerts were repeated on a minor scale. Enormous emphasis, temperament flying, students dismissed from class on the slightest pretext—this was daily fare, and Pyotr Ilyich watched and listened, fascinated. He saw him as a genius who had given his life to music, and that was enough for him.

He was soon acting as the Director's right-hand man in the students' orchestra and chorus formed by Rubinstein, and one student, A. L. Spasskaya, watched the "assiduous assistant" and wished, like many other girls there, that some of the absorbed interest given to the scowling Rubinstein might come her way. When Rubinstein was too busy to conduct they had their wish: Pyotr Ilyich conducted the orchestra and was made wholly responsible for the choir. When Rubinstein was there, or another student was entrusted with the baton, the young Tchaikovsky more often than not still held the unsteady orchestra together and from an unusual position: "his function was kettle drummer and his firm rhythm gave much needed support to the orchestra when it strayed from the true beat."

The girl students seemed to have sighed after him in vain—he had become altogether too singleminded for such frivolities as flirtations—and the boy student he adopted as his particular friend gave the key to the prevailing mood of the Conservatoire years.

Disciple would be the better word, for the seventeen-year-old Herman Augustovich Laroche, though something of a prodigy as linguist and composer, attached himself to Pyotr Ilyich from the moment of meeting. This clever boy of German descent was an unmitigated prig like so many prodigies and was to become a music critic of smug and often wildly inaccurate judgments. But he did see at once the possibilities of the Tchaikovsky student and his later reminiscences of the composer, though often suspect and with altogether too much of himself about them, do make clear that the impressionable and self-depreciatory Pyotr Ilyich came to depend a great deal on his earnest encouragement—to the point of becoming a rather comprehensive prig himself.

As a person, Pyotr Ilyich does not cut a very attractive figure in these years. What with the adulatory-monitor Laroche, his own excessive repentance for wasted years (he was in his early twenties), and his passionate regard for the self-righteous, self-worshipping Rubinstein, a young man of Pyotr Ilyich's pliant nature is apt to swing violently to extremes. As he did. Devotion to music is all very well but when the true self is sacrificed to it the result cannot be self-expression. If there was one thing he was decidedly never meant to be it was strait-laced. So, though working extremely hard and mastering his trade thoroughly, he remained a shadow of his true creative self; this was buried under the weight of idolization, remorse, and the effort to live up to the impossible —and undesirable—figure set up by Laroche.

His comportment in Zaremba's counterpoint class could stand as model for the dedicated student. "I can see him now," writes Spasskaya, "sitting by himself, his arms folded across his chest, seriously and attentively following the professor's every word, judiciously considering the example offered and often interrupting the already minutely expounded lecture with some question which led to its elucidation at still greater length." He seemed to take on the mantle of Zaremba in his presence and to feel the need to excel this virtually unexcellable man as music's exemplar —a recognizable trait in the young disciple. Hence the questions, hence too his frequent request that played examples might be sung. Zaremba was not the man to discourage such zeal: "so we all readily divided into the four required voices." One wonders whether Spasskaya's "readily" would have been echoed by the entire class.

The other rare company he kept in his new mood could not release the real man. Adamov was an edition of Laroche, altogether too earnest when Pyotr Ilyich was not opposing him with laughter and lightheartedness. Apukhtin was fading out of the picture and one sympathizes with him, though he was making an ass of himself in the low society of Petersburg. He was all in favor of his friend's outward picture of the romantic musician, furrowed brow, funereal clothes, and wild beard, but when Pyotr Ilyich abandoned drink and smoking and women and relaxations in general, he thought he was going altogether too far. He expected an artistic rake, he found a monk. They drifted apart.

One of the few gleams of humor in these grim and uncharacteristic years is seen in Pyotr Ilyich's begging letters. He was always short of ready money and devised a unique method of earning a meal or two or the price of a score he was mad to buy and study. He did not crudely write and ask for money; he put the request in music; strung out through his letters were a few bars of melody set to the refrain of "Don't deny, dear friend, this excessively reasonable plea" and so on. He evidently found the method effective for he kept going.

Unhappily for him, the antipathy between the Conservatoire and the Free Music School was growing ever more intense; so much so that it would have amounted to treachery of the deepest variety for the member of one to converse with a member of the other. Balakirev remained as unapproachable and unthinkable as if he and his group were in Timbucktoo instead of a few streets away.

The one man he did meet outside the Conservatoire group was of doubtful value to him. Alexander Nikolayevich Serov, twenty years his senior, had been yet another student of the Law School fascinated by music. He went much further than Stasov, for long his friend, because he intended to be an opera composer. Having heard Wagner, he abandoned Stasov and Balakirev's nationalistic aims; he and his old friend began to write articles in the press attacking each other's theories. Serov was as virulent about the old-fashioned Rubinstein as about the Nationalists, and occupied a platform of his own consisting entirely of Wagner worship. At least he put his theories into practice, and in 1862, the year Pyotr Ilyich joined the Conservatoire, his first lyrical drama, as he called it, *Judith,* was produced in Petersburg. It was more Meyerbeer than Wagner but it had a smack of the grand manner and caught on. Tchaikovsky said later, in one of his pithy comments on contemporaries, "Serov knew how to appeal to the masses. His work is weak in melodic inspiration and recitative, lacks organic sequence, and offers only crude harmonic effects with instrumentation which is no more than decorative, but he does manage to achieve dramatic effects."

To the student Pyotr Ilyich he was naturally a figure to be reckoned with. In fact Serov merely succeeded in confusing the young man still further vis-à-vis nationalist and conservative points of view and offended him greatly by his arrogance, but he performed one service. He emphasized what Pyotr Ilyich felt, Rubinstein notwithstanding, was essential to him as a composer of modern times—that was, to make use of a large orchestra and all the instruments available.

The next year, 1864, Tchaikovsky made his first attempt to break loose from Rubinstein's narrow orchestral gospel. He was a great admirer of the playwright Ostrovsky and specially of his fine play *The Storm* and decided to write an overture for it. In his score he defied all Conservatoire precepts by including parts for harp, tuba, and English horn as well as writing for tremolo and divided violins, all of which were regarded by Rubinstein as inventions of the devil. The result was certain harmonic novelties long afterwards to be recognized as characteristic of Tchaikovsky, and more than a hint of themes whose origin was not an inch west of Moscow.

The Director duly castigated the score and not for another year did any sign of the known Tchaikovsky appear. In 1865 Ilya Petrovich, then aged seventy, married for the third time. Pyotr Ilyich knew his stepmother well. She was a widow, Yelizaveta Mikhailovna Alexandrova, a homely and understanding woman liked by all the children. Had he been a victim of the Oedipus complex as so many have alleged, Pyotr Ilyich could never have accepted another woman in the place of his mother. As it was, he welcomed the marriage, discussed his music with his step-mother, and breathed a sigh of relief at the thought that the twins, now in their middle teens, would have motherly attention and a comfortable home to live in.

This event freed him from one anxiety, and when his father went off to present his new wife to the Davidov family in the sum-mer of that year, he did what he had long wanted to do; he seized the excuse to join the travellers and spend a long holiday with his sister at Kamenka.

4

The significance of this visit in the history of the composer has been strangely overlooked, for it provided the beginning of one of the most notable aspects of the mature Tchaikovsky and of Russian music as known today. His talks with Serov and the furor of Wagner's visit to Petersburg in 1862 to conduct excerpts from his operas put an idea in his head which appealed strongly, the use of a massive orchestra. His hearings of Berlioz, Liszt, and Meyerbeer in concerts and operas at Petersburg appealed to an-other but allied side of him, the use of instruments new to the Russians and the novel use of classical instruments. At once he grasped dimly the enormous possibilities of rich orchestral effects by including these new instruments and the new use of old in-struments in a large orchestra. Kamenka, following on his passion for Glinka, provided a third outstanding strand in his work.

The Ukraine is famous for its beauty, the province of Kiev in the Ukraine contains the finest Ukrainian scenery and architecture, and Kamenka in Kiev province provided one of the best examples of both. It had everything that the Russian novelists have made world-famous, the large balconied house with its suites for guests, its spacious reception rooms and ballroom, its lake, river, forest and extensive rich farmland bordering the flowered garden and orchard.

By 1865 Kamenka had become famous in another way, for it was there that Pushkin spent one of his many rustications forced on him by Nicholas I and there that he wrote *The Prisoner of the Caucasus*. The choice of Kamenka was perhaps a little curious since Lyov's father, Vasily Davidov, had been a notable Decembrist, one of the brave men exiled to Siberia for his resistance to the accession of Nicholas. By the time Pyotr Ilyich made this first stay at Kamenka, Vasily was dead; his wife, Alexandra Ivanovna, who had shared his exile, had moved to Petersburg with her daughters; the estate had passed to Nicolai Vasilyevich, the elder brother of Lyov, and the political atmosphere had become the reverse of the father's. All was conservative.

It may be doubted whether Pyotr Ilyich cared very much one way or the other; he was no politician. He spent hour after hour with Sasha. He went the rounds of the sugar-beet factory with Lyov, a born estate manager. He played with his sister's two little girls on the lawn and in the nursery. He practiced the piano in his suite every morning, and in the evenings entertained Alexandra and her guests on the magnificent grand in the drawing room. He fished, shot, gardened. He ate enormous meals—fresh country food—and walked them off. He walked for miles. The vast estate was not big enough for him; every afternoon he would take his stick and be off to the villages beyond it. The house was named Verbovka, but the family always referred to it by the name of the village, Kamenka.

It would be hard to say what he loved most in these summer months: to be reunited with Sasha, to luxuriate in the domestic life he craved for or to experience another kind of reunion with the true Russia of field, steppe and village and forest and lake that he had not known since the days of Alapayesk. He was to tell Alexandra, "I don't know what I should do without you, I can't be happy apart from you," and he did not exaggerate; he leaned on her love, sought her advice, could scarcely bring himself to go out of her sight. Her family life was exactly the life he imagined for himself, with a devoted mate, lively children and a home in which grandeur always gave way to homeliness; her calmness, her good sense, her faith in him soothed and encouraged him, it was so civilized and based on the only things that mattered in life.

But the solitary walks, when he stepped out briskly, strong and tireless, were a joy too. He could savor the country as one never could in company and he could begin to equate it with his music, the one thing suggesting the other. Like so many composers he worked on the move and at Kamenka in this summer of 1865 he was given his first hint of the rich source he was to find in the Russian countryside. Here Kamenka proved a rare boon, for it was in the center of the province in which the finest of all Russian folk songs were to be found. During his walks Pyotr Ilyich heard the peasants singing and began to note down their songs.

Back in Petersburg late that summer he finished a set of dances based on the Kamenka songs. This little work, "Character Dances," was played at one of the open air concerts outside the city that autumn and was well received. The work is not heard now but is historic not merely because it was the first performance of an orchestral work by him but because it pointed the way he was to go; it was wholly Russian and it was Tchaikovsky too, and several of the fascinating themes were to reappear in his mature compositions.

Almost immediately afterwards, a matter of weeks, came an unexpected offer which was to change the course of his life. After a number of successful years managing the Moscow branch of the Russian Musical Society, Rubinstein's younger brother, Nikolai, had just opened the Moscow Conservatoire. He invited Serov to be his Professor of Harmony. Serov accepted. Before the new year term opened, Serov's second opera *Rognyeda* had its premiere in

Petersburg. To his surprise it was an immediate success. His reputation soared. He was established. He withdrew his acceptance of the post.

Nikolai Rubinstein, left in the lurch at short notice, asked his brother if he had anyone else in mind. Anton recommended Pyotr Ilyich warmly as a hard worker and as a young man very well versed in the theory of composition. Perhaps he also said that this student could be had cheaply; at any rate Pyotr Ilyich was offered the post at a figure well below the salary Serov would have received, no more than fifty rubles a month.

Very much his father's son, Pyotr Ilyich did not give a second thought to the salary. Somewhat sadly, for he loved Petersburg and had only unhappy memories of Moscow, he accepted. In the early days of January, 1866, he left for Moscow. He was in his twenty-sixth year.

CHAPTER 7

Professor and Symphonist
1866-1869

THE RUBINSTEIN BROTHERS were small men, devoted to music and fine pianists but when this is said the resemblance ends. Nikolai was the finer musician though overshadowed by his brother's reputation even to the present day. One reason for this is that he detested to look or act the musician as his brother and Liszt had established him in the public eye. When he met Pyotr Ilyich at the railway station in Moscow and saw a taller version of his brother, long-haired, unkempt, and haggard, he gave an inward whistle, took the young man to his apartment in the Conservatoire in which he was to have a room, insisted on a shave, a beard-clip and haircut and borrowed a morning coat for him; he was not prepared to staff his Conservatoire with Anton Rubinsteins.

There was another substantial difference beside a sense of humor in the one brother and its absence in the other. Anton was a puritan, an austere, rigid-minded man, reserving all exuberance for the concert platform. Nikolai's dandified appearance suggested the fashionable roué. His carefully crinkled hair, moustache, and beard—a mere slip of a thing—his immaculate clothes, debonair manner, and witty speech all spoke of the gregarious man at home in higher society and its rather less high adjuncts. He was, superficially, the *bon viveur* in person, and within a day or two the astonished and somewhat apprehensive Pyotr Ilyich had been wined and dined expensively at the famous Var, whirled into the English Club where he consumed large quantities of liquor, and through a haze watched Nikolai Rubinstein gamble away what would have been his harmony professor's year's salary. He had been introduced to exclusive Moscow families where he learned from his Director how to flirt without committing oneself, and driven out of town to the gypsies where Rubinstein enjoyed himself without finesse of any kind.

All of this, the gambling excepted, was not new to Pyotr Ilyich, it seemed a sort of revival of the useless life he thought had gone forever. What was new was the style with which Nikolai Rubinstein carried out his fast living, a style which made the government clerks of Petersburg seem callow and crude. Confusing the new arrival almost beyond endurance was the thought of one of Russia's famous musicians, a man whose devotion to musical education was a Moscow legend, making a public exhibition of himself.

Pyotr Ilyich, it must be admitted, showed himself provincial and dense too in his reaction to his new Director. Then and for a long time afterward he looked up to Anton Rubinstein as the serious man, dedicated to his art and altogether admirable, and down to his brother as the frivolous one. This in spite of the fact, which also took his breath away, that after two or three hours sleep (Rubinstein never came home until the small hours) his Director would appear trim and businesslike, that he arrived on the dot of the hour in his classroom, that his students worshipped him and—most telling of all—that his comments to his newly engaged professor about his method of teaching, his music, his outlook, and his compositions were soberness itself and demonstrated a sound grasp of his subject and of men.

For all his equivocal reception of Nikolai Rubinstein, Pyotr Ilyich enjoyed himself well enough in Moscow after the first shock had passed. Nikolai was an admirable teacher, of staff as well as students, and once his new professor managed to subdue his nervousness in front of a class he began to make a quiet name for himself in the Conservatoire.

He found admirable foils to Rubinstein in the professor of singing, Konstantin Karlovich Albrecht, and the pianoforte professor, Nikolai Dmitryevich Kashkin, and his wife, a quiet couple who kept open house for him in their apartment where he had evening after evening of music and cards. If he wanted pretty girls and a luxurious home he had them in the Tarnovsky house where he and Rubinstein (only five years his senior) tried to outdo one another as gallants. If he wanted good talk and celebrities he could find them at another Rubinstein haunt, the mansion of the Superintendent of the Moscow Opera, Vladimir Petrovich Begichev, a strong supporter of the Conservatoire and one of Moscow's leaders in music. There Pyotr Ilyich met his future publisher, Pyotr Ivanovich Jurgenson, whose enthusiasm had made the founding of the Conservatoire possible, his literary hero Ostrovsky, and the ailing Dargomijsky, struggling to finish *The Stone Guest*.

If he wanted to meet these people all over again in less formidable surroundings he had only to drop into the Pukirev house on Tversky Avenue. There he could find on one evening or another members of the circle founded by Nikolai Rubinstein, Ostrovsky, and the old theater and music patron Prince Odoyevsky. Anybody who was anybody in the arts in Moscow, with a few lesser fry, gathered there—Maly actors, Bolshoi singers, dancers and choreographers, playwrights, poets, novelists, and musicians from every corner of the city. The talk was good, the drinks plentiful, and the music fascinating to a man who thought almost wholly in terms of his next composition. After the rigors of Petersburg where he had no entree into the only excitingly forward-looking music group, that of Balakirev, and was too little known to be invited to important literary or theatrical soirees, the camaraderie at Pukirev's seemed like heaven to the young professor.

The difficulty was to fit it all in. He was soon living in four worlds, the hectic world of Rubinstein, the gay world of fashionable Moscow, the cultured quiet of the Kashkins, and the studious world of the Conservatoire classrooms. The world of his own music began to blossom too. He found a sharp critic in Rubinstein —he was to agree with him in almost every particular after the first automatic resentment—but a loyal supporter too; when the Director thought he had written something worth playing he spared no effort to get it played.

The trouble was that Rubinstein was limited too. Pyotr Ilyich was not fortunate in his early leaders and supporters; Anton Rubinstein's crushing conservatism, the idiotic exaggerations of Laroche (who soon joined him in Moscow), and the conventional judgments of Nikolai Rubinstein all in their various ways put him off his true track. The first composition Nikolai Rubinstein approved and arranged to be played—Overture in F Major—was little more original than the beginnings of an opera, the Andantes, the Adagios, the Agitatos, the Allegros, the Oratorios, the Variations and the "Ode to Joy," Pyotr Ilyich had composed under the rule of Anton. The main result of the new influence was to encourage him to turn out too much music. What with the wrath of Anton at the slightest deviation from his norm and the bantering of Nikolai, who soon began to see in his new professor an irresistible object for practical and verbal jokes, Pyotr Ilyich was well on the way to becoming a writing machine. His fine technical background actually proved a disadvantage—he found composition only too easy.

The dichotomy in his nature grew more marked under the Moscow regime. He learned to drink heavily—he was never wholly to unlearn it—he went regularly to the English Club with his Director, to the society salons, he flirted, he was flattered, he went to the gypsies with the same taskmaster. Then, home again, he repented with the gusto he gave to everything and set himself, nerves jangling, to hour after hour of composition—often spending the rest of the night at his bedroom table—then to walk down to the classrooms in the morning, heady, nervous and dispirited.

From time to time he expressed himself half humorous, half despairingly on the subject of Moscow life, as when he told Anatoly "Our first concert takes place on Saturday and very glad I am of it for generally speaking they take their pleasures in Moscow more sensually than spiritually—they eat and drink enormously. The concerts will provide a musical pabulum I am greatly in need of. Without it I am like the bear in his den, I have to live on my own resources—that's to say my own compositions, and they won't always come out of my head. No matter how much I try to live quietly one can't get on in Moscow without guzzling and hard drinking. For example, for the past five days I've got back in the early hours with my belly filled to bursting point. But don't imagine I'm doing nothing, I keep at it every day from morning to late dinner."

This war of apparent opposites—for he could not resist the big meals, the drink, the gambling—left him after a few months hopelessly in debt. Nor could he resist generous gestures that drew him closer to the looming money-lenders of Moscow back streets. It was a firm principle with him that everyone connected with the family must be cared for, and in the letter to Anatoly already quoted he says "A week ago I sent 40 rubles in silver to Avdotya Yakovlevna [the twins' old nurse-governess] and 25 to Ditlova [an aged relative of his mother]." That was his month's salary given away in one day!

He was not only hopelessly in debt, he was in what often seemed to be a hopeless mental muddle: which world did he want, Anton's or Nikolai's? That he did not want either did not occur to him, so vividly did he incline towards the necessity of a guiding star. He must be counted unlucky that both Rubinsteins insisted on the very need which Balakirev, in his group at Petersburg, was then demolishing, the need to follow rigorously the classical sonata form.

For, inevitably, he was soon at work on his first symphony, and at once came up against that in him which could not accept the Rubinsteins' immutable law, the teaching he had accepted without comment from Zaremba. To have a pleasant nature is to find oneself at a disadvantage, as he began to discover; he was grateful to all three men, admired Zaremba's rectitude, worshipped Anton without reservation, and was in a fair way to think very highly of Nikolai. To differ from them was painful and caused him suffering which only the warmhearted know; he felt a traitor, an ingrate and, being naturally modest, felt sure that his instincts must be a form of original sin to be resisted and put down.

Later, he was to write, "In certain compositions such as the symphony the form is fixed and I keep to it. But only in its broad outlines and in the order of movements. When it comes to the details I think it permissible to take every liberty, believing that these are dictated by the natural development of the musical idea." But in the spring of 1866 he had not found himself, he had not met Balakirev, he was a grateful disciple, tried to bend his natural feelings into conformity with what he had been taught, and was in despair when he found his pen running away with him.

By April his feelings broke out in a cry of frustration. "My nerves are completely wrecked:

1. My symphony is not getting on.

2. Rubinstein and Tarnovsky, having discovered the weak joints in my armor, spend their time infuriating me.

3. I know I shall die before I have finished my symphony. I look forward to a summer at Kamenka like the promised land. From yesterday I have given up vodka, wine, and even strong tea. I hate everyone and want to live in a desert. I have already got my ticket for the coach on May 10."

May tenth came and went and the promised land eluded him. The coach could not make the journey owing to bad roads. He had not enough money to pay for a private carriage for three (he had planned to go with the twins) and compromised; he paid for Anatoly to go to Kamenka and made with Modest the shorter journey to Peterhof, near the Oranienbaum of his childhood. Here they stayed for the summer with the Davidovs' mother, Alexandra Ivanovna Davidova, and her four daughters.

Pyotr Ilyich was in high spirits when he set off. His symphony had not advanced but Anton Rubinstein had played his Overture in F Major at one of the Petersburg Conservatoire's concerts. It had been vigorously applauded and Apukhtin wrote to say how much he thought of it. This gesture by his old hero and the generous letter from his old friend lifted all depression and he opened the holiday in great form. The Davidovs were favorite companions—they had come to live in Petersburg some years earlier—and a special attachment had grown up between Pyotr Ilyich and the second daughter, Vera Vasilyevna. There is no sign that he thought of marriage—he was more interested in the prettiest of the Tarnovsky girls—but Vera was musical and intelligent as well as good-looking; they were often at the piano playing duets; they had long talks and walks together; and he felt a soothing sense of minds akin.

All went well until he began to orchestrate the symphony he had brought with him. The old difficulties sprang up and the longer he worked the more formidable they appeared. The first carefree days with the Davidovs had glossed over not only the threat of the symphony but the conditions which made him unfit to finish it. For all his cheerfulness he had arrived a wreck after months of teaching—twenty-six hours of it every week—after the strain of living up to Nikolai Rubinstein who, sensing a boon companion in him, rarely gave him a day's peace, after night after night of work on the symphony whenever he could elude his Director.

All his symptoms of the spring came back, redoubled. A great deal has been made of these symptoms which, we have been told, prove him once more to be the hopeless neurotic. If so, then most of us are neurotics, for his symptoms are well known to everyone who has overworked and is worried besides—insomnia, weird and alarming internal pains, violent headaches, palpitations.

The difference between Pyotr Ilyich and most men is not that he had certain symptoms and the others do not; it is that he frankly confessed them as he confessed everything. His reactions were more violent than most because he felt more deeply than most. Again he thought he was dying and—this was what mattered —that his symphony would die with him. Added to this, he had the further problem familiar to many creative people, of what to do with material which would only go his way and not the way of the men he admired? The result was neurasthenia.

A doctor was called in. He advised him to stop composition and forbade all night work. Pyotr Ilyich tried to obey, but, as he was to say, "I live on music. Apart from this I am good for nothing. I must hurry because I am afraid of dying before being able to pass on to others what I have in me to give."

Eventually he was persuaded to send the unfinished symphony to Anton Rubinstein and Zaremba. They were shocked by the liberties he was taking. They indicated at length what he must do to the score to make it acceptable—that is, to follow classical precepts exactly.

Crushed, he went back to Moscow and to months of revision as well as to months of rather desperate gaiety following the example of Nikolai Rubinstein. Almost all his companions were heavy drinkers and he found in wine and vodka a satisfactory solace until the next morning arrived. He had a better head for alcohol than Rubinstein but was entirely without his astonishing power of recuperation.

A letter to Anatoly on the first day of December, 1866, gives a good picture of his life, a medley of music and carousal after music. He describes a normal weekend—concert, drinking bout, masked ball, and painful Monday awakening.

The weekend began in examplary style with a recital by Rubinstein and the Austrian, Ferdinand Laub, who had joined the Conservatoire as chief professor of the violin and first violin of the Musical Society. They played "superb things by Schumann." But "after the music there was a magnificent supper—that's why I'm writing this letter under difficulties."

Actually, he was simplifying. By the time the concert was held he was already fairly drunk; with him in the audience was a fellow student of the Petersburg Conservatoire, the pianist Gustav Gustavovich Kross (then professor of pianoforte at Petersburg and later to be famed as the first professor of the young Sergei Rachmaninov), and "I spent four days with him. We were inseparable and went on the spree pretty fiercely."

Rubinstein, freed from the responsibility of the recital, then joined the two young men who were distinctly the worse for wear. Whenever Rubinstein entered the fray things livened up at a brisk pace. "Our orgy ended with a fancy dress ball on Sunday at the Bolshoi. I must say that I had a distinctly good time there. The whole evening a woman and I danced and flirted together. I don't think I knew her but she was exceedingly attractive and in a way I seemed to find something familiar about the face behind the mask. Then we joined Rubinstein and the 'mask' he had picked up and we all (I less than the others) drank a frightful lot—so much that I had to take Rubinstein home dead drunk. This is the first time I've seen him absolutely incapable. The next day my head was dreadfully painful and I was hardly able to sit in class."

Rubinstein notwithstanding, however, he stuck to the equally painful job of revising his symphony on the lines suggested by his old masters. Early in the new year of 1867 he finished the revision and submitted it to Petersburg. Anton Rubinstein and Zaremba damned it decisively.

This second blow did him a service, though he suffered severely; it loosened the musical ties still binding him to Petersburg. Only a few months earlier, when the Moscow Conservatoire was transferred to a fine new building, he had spoken at the celebration banquet, his chosen toast being Anton Rubinstein and the Petersburg Conservatoire. Now, Anton's attitude to the symphony which had been remodelled precisely according to his wishes was too unreasonable for even the fervent Pyotr Ilyich to defend. The vodka, the wine, and the strong tea were taken up again.

As Anton fell into the background, Nikolai advanced. In his tipsy moods he was still a sore trial, but his kindness and faith cheered Pyotr Ilyich through a bleak winter and spring. Nikolai had doubled Tchaikovsky's salary when he came back from the summer holiday. Rubinstein's suggestion that his professor should speak at the banquet was a compliment, as was his would-be scandalized face when Pyotr Ilyich sat down at the piano at the after-banquet concert and played from memory the overture to *Russlan and Ludmilla* so that, as he said, Glinka's music should be heard first in the new headquarters of music in Moscow. More importantly, Nikolai, understanding the depression caused by his brother's treatment of the symphony, offered more than once to play it. His offers were only accepted in part by the stricken composer who was in the state familiar to many, not knowing what to believe in, his own instincts or the advice of those supposed to know better than he did. The first performance of the entire symphony was still some way off.

In the midst of this indecision he was diverted by the first of his many ignes fatui. Taking his worship of Glinka too literally, he felt that he must write an opera, that Russian music must advance in that form. He approached Ostrovsky. Ostrovsky suggested making an opera libretto from his play *Voivode*. Pyotr Ilyich was much too flattered by the agreement to question the subject; he would have set to music anything written by such a man. In early spring he was at work, with enthusiasm yet not with success. In the symphony he had allowed himself to be guided by traditionalists. He now encouraged himself to take on a subject he was temperamentally unfitted to portray satisfactorily.

Because of this and the mutilated symphony, he was back once more in the toils of neurasthenia by the time summer came round. He had intended to go to Kamenka, so infuriatingly missed the summer before, but when the moment arrived he again changed his mind—this time for the characteristic reason that he would not present himself to Alexandra in a condition which could pain and worry her and (such was his unconquerable modesty) make her think less of him.

Instead, he took one of the twins, Anatoly this time, for a holiday in Finland. Most typically—to his dying day he was hopeless (or splendidly careless, according to the way you look at it) with money—he soon found himself without funds, having miscalculated the cost of the trip. After a hazardous but amusing voyage across the Baltic, they found themselves in the arms of the Davidov mother and daughters who most opportunely were spending the summer in Estonia, at the little seaport of Hapsal.

In such company cheerfulness soon returned and it became extremely difficult for Tchaikovsky to persuade himself that he was a born misanthrope. He had had the sense to leave the symphony behind or had forgotten to bring it—with him one can never be sure—and the work he did on the *Voivode* was one of the best things in that ill-fated opera; he reorchestrated the Kamenka "Character Dances." This apart, the only writing he did during another holiday of walks and talks and piano duets was the composition of three little piano pieces dedicated to Vera Vasilyevna. All three are charmingly melancholy, the last was to become famous as "Song Without Words" in F Major.

One could also say infamous, for this little piece has been castigated by great critics with such epithets as cheap and saccharine. But these critics miss the point; the notable thing about this light work, thrown off quickly, was that it provided the first demonstration of another facet of Tchaikovsky the great composer. One thing all great composers have in common is the ability to write good tunes. Tchaikovsky, as all now know, was to prove the master of all in this essential department of genius, and here, in this much-berated piano piece, was the first evidence of a fabulous gift.

By winter the opera was on its way and the symphony was returning by fits and starts to its pre-Anton Rubinstein content except for improvements which occurred in the act of scratching out the great man's instructions. In December Nikolai Rubinstein played the *Voivode* dances at a symphony concert—the first of three successful performances within a few months. A few weeks later Berlioz, recently the honored guest of Balakirev and Dargomijsky at Petersburg, came to give a series of concerts of his own works.

All Pyotr Ilyich's generosity and wish to praise came to the fore. Berlioz was one of the gods of The Mighty Handful, whom Pyotr Ilyich had been taught to regard as vulgar deriders of his own heroes, but no matter, he was courageous, original, and shockingly ill-rewarded and the young harmony professor said so. Not only in his letters and in conversation but—a tremendous ordeal for such a shy man—in a speech in French at a banquet given in the old composer's honor by the music lovers of the city.

Both Stasov and Balakirev had followed Berlioz down from Petersburg and after the Master's departure for Paris each met Pyotr Ilyich. These meetings were momentous. It was not possible to be five minutes in the presence of these men without realizing that they were far from the crude and bad-mannered nationalists Pyotr Ilyich had been led to believe. He was not the man to cling to a false conception for an instant in the face of such evidence. Stasov charmed and awed him, Balakirev exerted his usual mesmerism without apparent difficulty. Personalities were excluded, the future of Russian music was the one subject discussed. On this subject both Petersburghers were irresistible.

Thinking over the meetings after Balakirev and Stasov had gone home, Pyotr Ilyich began to adjust his mind. One aspect of the man which has never been understood widely is his common sense. Pyotr Ilyich was nervous, for instance—so much so that when he found himself on the conductor's podium not long after this he went stiff with fright and felt "that his head was going to tumble from his shoulders at any moment unless he held it absolutely rigid." He was seemingly without self-confidence in everything; he was extravagant and knew nothing about the value of money; he drank too much; he had no idea of time, orderliness, discipline, as these things are understood by the crowd. Nevertheless he had a strong vein of common sense in everything that mattered. He understood that art was a part of life—its finest part— and must not be divorced from it. He was the very opposite of that philistine Nikolai Ilyich, his elder brother. Nikolai, like all philistines, took with immense seriousness everything in life that was of no importance and treated with frivolity everything that was truly important.

One example of Pyotr Ilyich's attitude is enough. He had a very good appetite and never missed a meal but he ate largely not just because he enjoyed his food but because his common sense told him that he could not work at his music satisfactorily on an empty stomach. Now this common sense applied itself to Balakirev and the nationalist school. Having met Balakirev, all inhibitions dropped away but he did not succumb to his fascination as the members of the "Five" had done; he saw that Balakirev was genuine, perhaps great, that much of what he said was true and vital to the future of Russian music, but there he stopped. His fund of common sense was greater than that of the ebullient Balakirev. He saw the dangers of shutting oneself in a group and shouting abuse at the backward—the cramping, narrowing effect on one's music. He believed one could be truly nationalist without wasting time and energy on propaganda and labelling musicians as those one met and those one did not. He believed that if he wrote Russian music as he felt it, the music would do its own work.

So he sent his *Voivode* dances to Balakirev to play in Petersburg but reserved judgment about the offer to join the nationalist school. He began to think that one could be nationalist without flying any kind of flag. Balakirev finally released him from the Anton Rubinstein school but failed to lure him into another. He set him free to be himself.

At that moment Balakirev's influence was shown in a practical way in the work on the symphony. Tchaikovsky was never to throw off wholly the feeling that his deviations from the classical mold were faults in himself. This effect of Mozart-worship was expressed years later when he said, "I have always suffered from my inability to assimilate musical forms and handle them correctly. I have struggled hard against this defect and can claim, with legitimate pride, that I have made progress. But it is only too clear, nevertheless, that I shall never compose anything with a perfect form to the end of my days. In everything I write there are masses of faults which the most casual glance can discover easily."

If he felt like that in his maturity, his feelings in 1868 can be imagined. He was still trying to erase the sensation of guilt every time he differed from Anton Rubinstein, and his replacement of original material criticized by Rubinstein still seemed little less than crimes of ingratitude and presumption. Balakirev arrived in his life at precisely the moment best calculated to encourage his natural gifts. As soon as the nationalist leader had gone back to Petersburg, Pyotr Ilyich flew at his score, wiped out the last remnants of Zaremba and Rubinstein, and asked Nikolai Rubinstein to play it.

He did so in the middle of February with unquestionable success. How modest the composer was may be gathered from the fact that, sure of failure, he had not even troubled to dress for the occasion. The delighted audience, insisting on a personal appearance, were surprised to find, when Pyotr Ilyich had at last been routed out from his corner, that the young man who edged onto the platform looked rather like someone who had spent the night in his clothes.

From that day to this, the First Symphony has been neglected in the most extraordinary fashion. Most music lovers have never heard it, critics seldom mention it. What has been said about it since Tchaikovsky's death is better not repeated, it is so biased, so inadequate. Naturally the symphonies written in his maturity are finer works, but in this first symphony the Tchaikovsky of the future is plainly and often charmingly revealed. It deserves regular performance in its own right.

The work has a title "Winter Daydreams" as have all four movements, and the few critics who have dealt with it have not failed to exercise their wit: "Lots of daydreams, little winter" is a typical example; it is not very funny and is wholly untrue.

The first movement title—"Traveller's Dreams"—can be read in more than one sense, for the work it heads is a voyage of discovery into the mysteries of symphonic writing. Tchaikovsky uses his love of the Russian countryside—particularly the expanse of snowy steppe—symbolically and with the happiest of results. This first movement opens as if the composer had created the Tchaikovsky idiom many years earlier; flute and bassoon announce a cheerful melody which leads into the principal theme struck out by full orchestra. The way he manipulates this theme at once places him as a composer to be reckoned with; it runs the gamut of the emotions representing the changing moods of the traveller as he journeys on and it is tossed from section to section of the orchestra with a technical skill neatly screened.

The link between first and second theme is just as representative of the established Tchaikovsky, a series of chromatic scales taken from a primitive Russian instrument of the psaltery type, the gusli, chiefly famed for its rich arpeggios. It was to become a fetish in the composer to search for instruments which would add unusual color to the orchestral tone and the gusli was to reappear in all his symphonies.

The movement ends with another Tchaikovskian device, a thrilling orchestral crescendo dying away to the suggestion of a tolling bell—not a bell itself, be it noted. This too provided a foretaste of the future. Every lover of music knows how often Russian composers imitate or use bells in their orchestral works and for a very natural reason; church and town bells pealing far across forest and steppe are among the Russian's most familiar memories and at once bring his countryside to life.

This atmosphere is one of two outstanding points about the opening movement of the G Minor symphony which will quickly strike the listener—the extraordinarily skillful recreation which reminds one of Pushkin's great poem *Byesy*, building up without one false touch the picture of a traveller passing through a snowy countryside. It is a musical impression of the effect achieved in words by the poet. The other point is that the symphonist is ready-made and offers the certain sign of supremacy in this form. Besides giving fascinating proof of resourcefulness in orchestration he speaks throughout with one unmistakable voice and this voice is his alone.

Not until the transformation music in "Casse Noisette" was Tchaikovsky to rival this highly successful atmospheric score. It remains unique to this day in that, unlike most impressionistic music, it does not demand a certain mood in the listener, it creates it because Tchaikovsky's music is vigorous and manly as well as poetical.

The Andante—"Sad Country of Mists"—opens with one of Tchaikovsky's mellow themes and is ended with a stroke of ingenuity, the bassoon used against a background of strings. The theme is given, as one would imagine with this composer, to the woodwinds, the instruments he perhaps loved best and certainly used with the most ravishing effect. In this First Symphony the theme is melancholy and wistful, a theme which could have come only from Russia.

It is notable that Pyotr Ilyich had already adopted a proceeding which the mature Tchaikovsky was to carry out automatically; unlike a Rimsky-Korsakov who takes folk themes and orchestrates them more or less as they stand, he transforms them. When one listens to this Andante one has the sense of a Russian theme which has been spiritualized to meet a certain mood required by the composer.

The Scherzo opens gaily with the piccolo—the traveller is approaching the village in which he will stay the night—and moves into a waltz, yet another precursor of the world-famous Tchaikovsky. This waltz is not one of his best but his use of the orchestra is not far from masterly, providing the kind of delicate embroidery at which Tchaikovsky was to excel, the French elegance which was to pervade much of his work.

The last movement returns to the first theme of the opening movement, then—the traveller is watching a village fete—breaks into a fine rousing dance measure. This cheerful refrain, given to all sections of the orchestra with a full-blooded zest that reminds one of Glinka—of whom the composer was undoubtedly thinking—demonstrates not only that Pyotr Ilyich could be as lively as his hero but that he had already passed beyond him in the use of orchestral color.

Perhaps the most impressive point about this movement is the contrapuntal treatment of the dance tune. The counterpoint is most felicitous, striking without subtlety, and the coda, though equally obvious, is always varied and always effective. Indeed, one of the most revealing things about this symphony is the composer's command of the orchestra. He also senses what was to be such a joy in the work of the mature man, that constant change of mood and tempo is essential to hold the listener and, a further refinement by which the great composer can always be distinguished from the lesser, that a returned theme must be varied slightly—not simply by giving it to another section of the orchestra, but by actual changes in the writing. There are beautiful themes which could only have come from a Tchaikovsky and there are even hints of the elegant sophistication for which he was to become famous.

This First Symphony is a young man's work in many respects. It is often emotional but never soul-searching, often clever but never profound, but in originality, in charm, in genuine feeling it stands squarely on its own feet as a work able to give pleasure without reference to anything the composer might have written in later years. The idea of playing such a work as a curiosity because it happens to be by Tchaikovsky is as ridiculous as the attitude sometimes adopted by musicologists when they write as though no early Tchaikovsky symphony can be taken seriously. The reason given is that they are so little subjective and do not deal with a theme of importance to mankind.

The absurdity of this argument—which is mere snobbism—does not need to be stressed. A man can write a symphony precisely as he pleases; all one dare demand is that the form expresses the content truthfully, the rest is up to the composer. And in this First Symphony as in his next two, Tchaikovsky chooses to show himself pre-eminently the disciple of Balakirev the nationalist and as the man who was to give the world its greatest ballet scores. This Symphony in G Minor is not only the first truly Russian symphony and, as such, as important as *A Life for the Tsar,* it is far ahead of its time. When one remembers that Brahms was not to write his First Symphony for another ten years, one sees precisely how advanced Tchaikovsky was in this first attempt and how successful.

One further point of moment: this, his first large-scale orchestral work, offers the doubled drama that is found at its height only in Tchaikovsky and certain works of Stravinsky. As all concert-goers know, a Tchaikovsky symphony, concerto, or tone poem has the power to stir deeply for two reasons, that it provides both aural and visual excitement. This magic of the great composer who is also an inspired orchestrator can be seen as well as heard in the Tchaikovsky First Symphony.

CHAPTER 8

Suitor and Opera Composer

1869

TCHAIKOVSKY WAS MUCH MORE than a sympathetic man, he was that rare creature, a noble-minded man. He was incapable of spite or meanness, and in fifty-three years not one nasty action and very few unfair words were recorded against him. From the very beginning of his life he affected people favorably, from his softening influence on the sharp Fanny to the conquest of the little brutes in the Petersburg preparatory school. A list of his friends shows how every type of man felt drawn towards him, from the rake Apukhtin to the sedate Adamov, from the napoleonic Anton Rubinstein (who criticized his music but always spoke with unusual respect and even fondness about him) to the difficult Nikolai Rubinstein who began by laughing at him and ended by preferring him to any other man in Moscow.

The victory over Nikolai Rubinstein was a notable triumph of unassuming goodness. Pyotr Ilyich learned much from his Director—for instance, he became a man of the world in the best sense, transforming Nikolai's worldliness into a truly civilized approach to life and people—but he gave more than he received. By the time the "Winter Daydreams" symphony had been performed, Nikolai had quite changed his views. He did not change his manner of life but he began to understand in 1869 that the harmony professor who had amused him so much in 1866 might well become one of the hopes of Russian music and a particular advertisement for the Moscow Conservatoire, and was prepared, in theory at least, to give him every chance to compose and, in practice, to play what he did compose.

In his own way he too had been forced to respect the young man who had seemed at first little more than an admirable butt and an amiable drinking companion. And when one remembers that in spite of his apparently flighty manner Nikolai had held musical opinions as conservative as Anton a mere three years earlier, the feat achieved by the outwardly mild and gentle Pyotr Ilyich will be seen in its true proportions; to widen the views of a man in Nikolai's position was to provide Russian music with a powerful striking base. So Russian musicologists were to see the amusing spectacle of the moderate radical beginning in his quiet and common-sense way a revolution just as important and rather more successful than the violent upheaval preached by the rebels —for the Balakirev group had not the power of an established Conservatoire behind it.

In the Moscow Conservatoire Tchaikovsky had become in these three years the most popular professor; his classes were jammed, his lectures were listened to in respectful silence, and after he had finished he always found it difficult to escape to his room because of the crowd of eager young men and women besieging him with questions and invitations.

Some of his popularity with the young women was no doubt attributable to his looks and manner. At twenty-nine he had become a very handsome man, tall, upright, strong, his wonderful blue eyes contrasting with thick brown hair brushed back to show the full white expanse of forehead. The beard was taking the form it was to have for the rest of his life. He had beautiful hands—a legacy from his mother—and a melodious voice. And his manner was altogether charming, the manner of the well-bred man who expects—and gets—from others the polish and kindness he invariably offers them. The men students were just as taken with him; his approach was without favor, he simply and obviously loved music and wished to impart his love and knowledge in the clearest and most civilized way—the splendid Taneyev, for instance, afterwards admitted proudly that he owed everything to him. Tchaikovsky did not, in fact, like teaching; but in these early years he managed to conceal these feelings.

It was now the turn of the Balakirev group to fall under the spell of his charm and goodness. Balakirev and Stasov had carried back favorable reports of him but as he had refused to indulge in personalities he was still regarded with suspicion in the group as an Anton Rubinstein man. His charm was obvious; what lay behind it not so obvious.

Then came a charity concert in Moscow at which he conducted his *Voivode* dances (this was one of the occasions when he felt that his head would leave his shoulders at any moment) and he and his music were received rapturously by the fashionable audience.

Not so another item on the same program. This was one of the earliest orchestral works by the young Rimsky-Korsakov, "Fantasia on Serbian Themes." It was received coolly and the next day reviewed harshly in a Moscow newspaper.

Tchaikovsky had never met Rimsky-Korsakov and knew nothing about him except what Balakirev had told him; if he had had any feeling about him it could have been caution about a fervent nationalist group member. No such thought entered his head; he knew what most interested him, the young man's music, and that was enough. He thought the Fantasia was good, promising music. Putting himself in the composer's place, as he always did, he imagined the shock of this first Moscow review. He was not prepared to allow some anonymous reviewer, who could not have written a note of decent music to save his life, to discourage an obviously gifted musician at the opening of his career.

Burning with indignation, he at once sat down and wrote his first piece of music criticism, a long and favorable notice of the Fantasia, and sent it off to a well-known Moscow journal. When it was printed he found himself hailed as a critic of power and discernment in his own city. More to the point, the notice dispelled the last remnant of suspicion in the Balakirev circle; what he had done was courageous and disinterested, they all saw that. From that moment the name of Tchaikovsky occupied a unique position in the nationalist camp; he stood for a nationalist composer who preferred to go his own way, a man to be respected.

This attitude warmed into open admiration soon afterwards when Tchaikovsky spent that Easter of 1868 with his father in Petersburg and was introduced to the rest of the nationalist disciples. His easy and tactful manner pleased everyone, even the difficult Cui who had damned his "Ode to Joy" three years earlier. Some, notably Rimsky-Korsakov, and his future wife, the pianist Nadyezda Purgold admired the polish of the man and his work immensely.

For his part, Tchaikovsky liked their wholehearted love of music and of Russia and concentrated on this rather than on the more controversial points such as a lack of finesse in their work and a lack of charity in their general outlook. When he went back to Moscow he went in effect as their spokesman and sympathizer.

2

He came back greatly cheered by the new friends he had made and their obvious belief in his talent. He threw himself into *Voivode* and by the time the Conservatoire classes ended in early summer had finished it and sent it to the Bolshoi.

That June he had a welcome break and a much needed addition to his income when he accompanied Begichev and one of his stepsons to Berlin in the role of music teacher. The boy became ill and the whole party—Begichev never travelled without a large retinue—hurried to a chest specialist in Paris.

The boy, Vladimir Shilovsky, was one of his students at the Conservatoire and a brilliant one too—at fourteen he had had his compositions publicly performed. Shilovsky (the Volodya one meets so often in Tchaikovsky's early letters) also possessed immense charm, for Pyotr Ilyich and for the whole family. A few months later he is found at one of his many spas, Baden-Baden, where, as Pyotr Ilyich reports, "He spent the whole time with Aunt Katya [Alexandra Andreyevna's sister] and became extremely intimate with her."

Pyotr Ilyich had matured from the traveller of twenty-one who thought the Petersburg theaters mounted opera and stage plays so much better than the French. Possibly he had been jolted out of the last of his chauvinism by meeting so much of it in the Balakirev circle. At any rate in 1868 he looked at the Paris theaters with an unbiased eye and told Alexandra frankly that the Russians had no conception of the care taken in production by the French.

He had become an assiduous correspondent, pouring out letters by the dozen. His friends heard regularly from him, his family oftener still, and Alexandra almost every other day. "My future happiness is impossible without you," he had told her only a few weeks earlier; and in June, in a Paris which thrilled and delighted him, he nevertheless found time to think with longing of Kamenka, to picture it, and to insist that his feelings were there. "That smelly but beloved jasmin is now enjoying itself flowering by the side of the house that holds my nearest and dearest."

When he wrote this, he had already met the woman who was to arouse the deepest feeling in him of anyone outside his family. A few weeks earlier a touring Italian opera company had arrived in Moscow after a triumphant visit to Warsaw. The triumph rested in their star artist, Désirée Artot, who had performed the exceptional feat of singing the roles in *Il Trovatore* of Leonora and Azzucena on alternate nights. Tchaikovsky did not go to the Moscow performances—he was then in the final stages of *Voivode* —but was introduced to Artot at a supper given after her benefit night.

As his letters say nothing of her at this time, the meeting evidently made no impression on him. This is not surprising for Artot was a plain woman who, like so many artists, only "came alive" on the stage. He did, however, attend the opening night of the company's autumn season when he had come back to Moscow and the Conservatoire after a round of family visits. She played Desdemona in Rossini's *Otello*, and Tchaikovsky, like the rest of the audience, fell in love with her.

It is significant that at that moment, in the midst of considering various plans for a second opera, he was writing a tone poem which he was to call "Fatum." He explained the program. "Fate is a power of destiny which forbids us to be happy, watches jealously to see that our felicity and serenity is never unalloyed, holds itself over our head like the sword of Damocles and instils a slow poison into the soul. It makes sure that our existence is a succession of painful realities, of ephemeral dreams and mirages of happiness. One has to submit to it and resign oneself to sadness without end."

Nothing could have seemed more improbable a few weeks after he had begun work on this Byronic theme than that it could have any bearing on his present life, for he was obsessed by Artot and could think of nothing and no one else. Characteristically he could not bring himself to seek her out, thinking her far above the attentions of such an insignificant man as himself—and this even when, having met her again at a musical evening, she expressed hurt surprise that he had not tried to renew the acquaintance of the spring. The man to bring them together was, of all people, Anton Rubinstein. Visiting Moscow, he insisted that his old student accompany him to another reception for Artot. This time Tchaikovsky, for all his diffidence, could not hide his feelings and Artot was more than interested. She knew that he was rated as one of the most promising of young Russian composers and she could see for herself that he stood out of the ruck of men at the reception (and as he did at every gathering) with his distinguished face, fine carriage, and kind smile. They talked. She was Belgian and had been trained by Turgenev's Pauline Viardot.

They began to meet every day. Soon he was writing to everyone except, significantly, Alexandra, in high emotion. "Ah! If only you knew Artot!" he told Modest. "What a singer! What an actress! Nobody on the stage has ever produced such an effect on me. How I regret that you can't see and hear her! You would be in ecstasy with her gestures and the infinite grace of her poses."

He added, "I have become very friendly with her and she treats me in the most affectionate manner you can imagine. Rarely have I met a woman so kind, good, and intelligent."

They were soon the talk of Moscow. Prince Odoyevsky, who flourished on theater gossip, noted, "Tchaikovsky seems to be courting Désirée Artot prodigiously." The autumn production of *Voivode* was postponed; "Fatum" advanced lethargically; everyone was waiting for the announcement of an engagement.

On the first day of the new year, 1869, Tchaikovsky broke the news to his father. "If nothing prevents it, we shall get married in the summer."

But he had not written to Ilya Petrovich simply to announce the engagement but to ask his advice. "The worst of it is that there are obstacles to the marriage, several of them." He detailed the obstacles, which arose on both sides. On Artot's side there was the inevitable mother who went everywhere with her. "She thinks me too young (Artot was five years older) and is afraid that I should insist on her daughter living in Russia always."

On his side, the objections came from his friends led by Nikolai Rubinstein. "They are doing all they can to prevent the marriage. They say that if I marry a famous singer I shall become a 'wife's husband,' live on her earnings, follow her round Europe and have no time to write music."

On her side, "she insists that for all her great love for me she can't bring herself to give up her work which earns so much money for her and without which she would feel lost."

He sums up. "On the one hand, I am heart and soul in love with her and feel that I can't live without her, on the other hand, calm common sense insists that I consider carefully whether my friends' objections have any weight."

The mere fact that he thought it necessary to ask his father's advice—favorable though the advice was—showed how undecided he was. He and she were faced with the old and insoluble problem that neither wished to give up his art, that each feared that it would be submerged by the art of the other. They agreed that he should come to her home near Paris that summer and settle the matter one way or the other, but there was little chance that a woman of Artot's temperament would accept the arrangement for long; to her, a man who would agree to wait for six months to know his fate had declared in advance what his fate must be.

She did not hesitate for long. The company left for a return visit to Warsaw late that month. A week or so afterwards Nikolai Rubinstein came into the Bolshoi where Tchaikovsky was superintending final rehearsals of *Voivode* and broke the news: Artot had married the company's leading baritone, Padilla y Ramos. Rubinstein, who could be cruel, cried cheerfully, "Well, so I was right after all. You are needed by Russia. You were never meant to be a foreigner's valet."

Tchaikovsky said nothing. As white as a sheet, he walked out of the theater. Common sense told him that Rubinstein was right, his heart told him that he was wrong. He mastered the shock. Only once did he lose his self-control; he broke out against her, saying that after their intimacy a marriage to another man was farcical. For the rest, he controlled himself and behaved as though he had not been snubbed, as though the people of Moscow were not whispering about him behind his back. In the future he and Artot were to become good friends and he never missed hearing her sing, but the first time he heard her again (it was the winter of that same year and she sang Marguerite in Faust) he stared at her without taking the opera glasses from his eyes. Throughout the entire time she was on stage, tears ran down his cheeks, and he made no effort to check them because he did not know that they were there.

He felt, perhaps, what most people will think; that she had been right but that he had lost his best and maybe only tolerable chance of living a normal life. Suddenly and against all probability, his introduction to "Fatum" had been proved only too correct;

he was the sport of destiny and destiny would not leave him in peace until he died. And though Artot was probably right and he knew it, he can scarcely be blamed for feeling that fate had marked him out, and that his symphonic poem had been fate's work too. He was doing no more than express in his Russian fashion the despair felt by most great creative artists when they suspect that domesticity and all its joys are not for them.

3

Many biographies of Tchaikovsky, following contemporary reports, say that he reappeared at rehearsals calm and unmoved the day after Nikolai Rubinstein's dramatic news and the days following. They assume, rather naively, that his feeling for Artot had somehow died in the night, that it was shallow and worthless.

This point needs comment because it is generally taken for granted that Tchaikovsky wore his heart on his sleeve, that impassioned (and morbid) self-revelation was the rule of his life. In truth, nothing could be further from the fact. In his music and in his letters to and conversations with intimates, Pyotr Ilyich was absolutely frank and, as has been seen, when he felt wretched or guilty he said so with the utmost extravagance, in real Russian style. But with acquaintances and in his day-to-day life in Moscow he behaved as the aristocrats behaved with whom he had mixed for so much of his life, taking care not to worry others with his private sorrows.

Pride took a hand too; he knew that Moscow was buzzing with stories of the way in which its favorite young composer had been jilted by the French opera star, and would not for the world have given scandalmongers the satisfaction of seeing how hurt and mortified he was. So he appeared as the contemporary reports made out, calm, apparently unconcerned, possibly a little more silent than usual, but anxious to get on with the rehearsal. It was a notable victory for the last virtue with which Tchaikovsky is ever credited, self-restraint.

Work was, of course, the one answer, and he worked, leaving himself no time to think. He worked on the final stages of *Voivode* and "Fatum," and he worked at a new opera. At first it seemed as though his reaction to shock was to be rewarded. The premiere of *Voivode* on February 11 was a considerable success—fifteen curtain calls for Tchaikovsky—and Prince Odoyevsky, who never missed a first night, was so taken with what he called a "masterly work" that he decided to make the composer a gift. It was a curious gift, as Tchaikovsky reported home with a chuckle, nothing less than the replacement of the Bolshoi cymbals which the Prince did not think were fit for a man who had such talent for introducing them at the right moment. "So the dear old fellow scoured Moscow for a good pair of 'piatti' and sent them to me with a delightful letter."

Two weeks later came the first performance of "Fatum" under Nikolai Rubinstein, and this too was sufficiently well received to give Tchaikovsky the illusion that at last he had written a symphonic work which would remain in the concert repertory.

Both ventures disappointed. Both were damned, politely and not so politely by the critics. The opera did not last beyond its fifth performance and the disgusted composer destroyed the score. "Fatum" quietly died and this score too was destroyed by Tchaikovsky.

One of the most virulent critics was, of all people, Laroche, who had scarcely a good word to say of either the opera or symphonic work. Tchaikovsky was greatly offended—not so much by the tone of the reviews as by the secrecy with which his supposed friend had concealed his views when they met. He did not speak to Laroche for two years and never afterwards completely trusted him.

It must be said that Laroche for once had the rights of it, though his admiring attitude to Tchaikovsky while the works— which he knew well—were being written cannot be excused. Any hope of *Voivode* making a good opera was destroyed early, when Ostrovsky withdrew from the collaboration after the first act.

Pyotr Ilyich took over the writing of the libretto and the work was doomed from that moment. Tchaikovsky was singularly unlucky in his librettists and it is a question who was the worse, he or his brother Modest. It is almost always a mistake for opera composers to take any hand in their libretti, and Tchaikovsky was unfitted for the work in every way. He was no poet apart from his music and his taste in literature was generally unreliable. He could write a good, self-revealing through uninspired letter— he was to write thousands—and he wrote sensible music criticisms, but a creative writer he was not.

Sagging under the weight of its untheatrical and banal libretto, the score presented a melange of Italian and German operatic conventions leavened (or burdened) by writing which could only have come from one source, Anton Rubinstein. The strange eclipse of the First Symphony after apparent success—it was not to be played again until he was a well-known composer—had destroyed Tchaikovsky's self-confidence, and he turned back to what he had been taught at the Petersburg Conservatoire.

His destruction of the score was much less peevishness than self-knowledge. He kept what he still thought promising, and this was, specially, the dances and a song, "Romance of the Nightingale," which has been well described as an early effort in musical impressionism. Up to then soloist or chorus in opera had sung words which advanced the action, words accompanied by a tune which exploited the range of the voice but had little to do with the words sung. In *Voivode* Tchaikovsky tentatively changed the balance; he chose to make the music advance the story by conveying the emotion hitherto left to the words. He was to develop this Wagnerian innovation in his later operas.

One further point about the opera; the ever-searching Tchaikovsky had with much joy—and secrecy—embodied in the score a part for another instrument never yet heard in an orchestra. This was the celesta which he was to use to such effect in "Casse Noisette."

"Fatum," which was resurrected from orchestral parts and published after Tchaikovsky's death, is an unequal work but whether it deserves the total oblivion it has been consigned to is questionable. Like the First Symphony it has a very beautiful and wholly characteristic Andante, and the other movements, though less successful, possess much interest. The trouble is that the movements are not properly integrated and that the form is unsatisfactory. For, veering away from his conservatism in *Voivode,* Tchaikovsky, uncertain which way to pursue, wrote the work in free form.

The best comment comes as so often from Balakirev. Tchaikovsky sent the score to him soon after the Moscow premiere, asking him to play it and to accept the dedication if he thought the work worthy of it—the usual disarming approach which made Pyotr Ilyich so beloved.

Balakirev played it and accepted the dedication, but this did not prevent him from forthright criticism. "I don't really like the work," he wrote bluntly, "because I don't think you have thought enough about it. It shows signs of being composed in a tearing hurry—the joins are only too apparent—and the form just won't do. Laroche says this is because you haven't studied the classics enough. I beg to differ. I think the reason is that you don't know enough modern music."

Tchaikovsky accepted this plain speech. He did not in fact dedicate the work to Balakirev because he never had it printed, but luckily for himself and the world he swallowed his chagrin and allowed the older man to guide him to his first authentically Tchaikovskian composition.

Before this happened he had finished his second opera. He took a little time to find a suitable subject. Ostrovsky suggested Alexander the Great but Pyotr Ilyich wisely rejected the compliment. Eventually he settled on his favorite story, of Undine. Here, for the first time, he followed his instincts. The subject, as the future was to show, suited him precisely.

At this point fate intervened, comically in one sense, disastrously in another. La Motte Fouque's story had been splendidly translated into Russian by Vasily Andreyevich Zhukovsky, the

great translator of the Odyssey, but Tchaikovsky was led by his
goddess to a bookshop where he discovered a libretto after Undine
perpetrated by Vernoy de Saint-Georges, a charlatan who emu-
lated Scribe only too faithfully. And as if this was not enough,
he handed over the translation to Vladimir Alexandrovich Sologub. Sologub was a Count who moved in the Moscow social circles
frequented by the composer. Possibly he had personal charm, certainly his literary ability was slight; he was a poet without promise, a dilettante. The translation was abominable, losing all the
magic of the poetry.

With this heavy burden on his back, Tchaikovsky wrote freely
and often well, inspired by the subject. He was particularly
cheered on by the promise of Gedeonov, Director of the Imperial
Theaters, to stage it. As none of the work was then in a state to
be seen, the compliment was considerable. A date was even fixed;
in November of that year. He wrote so rapidly that by August the
score was in the Director's office.

And that, virtually, was the end of *Undine.* It took Tchaikovsky five years to get the score, or a firm comment, from the authorities. When it came, the comment was freezing: "Your opera
has been judged unworthy of inclusion in the repertoire of the
Imperial Theaters."

That score too was burned by the infuriated composer. But he
kept some numbers and remembered others with the happiest of
results; he had not been wrong, the subject suited him, and his
music—or that of it which has been preserved—indicated for the
first time where one great facet of his genius lay, in the portrayal
of the fairy world as no other man has done. The music of *Undine*
was to reappear in Ostrovsky's *Snyegurochka,* in the Second Symphony and, most important, in *Swan Lake.*

When he went off to Kamenka for the summer of 1869, Tchaikovsky had no conception of the fate awaiting his newly completed opera. He found most of the family there—the newly married Ippolit, well-established in the navy from which he was to
retire as an admiral; Anatoly graduated from the Law School and

posted to Kiev; Modest, who had no clear idea what he would do when he left the Law School; Alexandra, as great a joy as ever, the calm and affectionate Lyov Vasilyevich; and nieces, four of them, who would have commandeered him from morning to night if he had let them. He revelled in Kamenka as always, and when at last he had to return to the Conservatoire for the autumn term he did so with immense reluctance; he was no teacher, he told Alexandra, and longed for his compositions to bring in money enough to free him from lecturing.

In general he looked on Moscow with a gloomy eye, comparing it very much to its disadvantage with the peace and beauty of the Ukraine estate and the warm love of Alexandra and her family. Yet in Moscow, waiting for him, was Balakirev. This was the reverse side of the fate he thought of as always dogging him, for Balakirev was to open his true destiny to him.

Part Three

FULFILLMENT

CHAPTER 9

Balakirev and *Romeo and Juliet*
1869-1872

BALAKIREV WAS IN GREAT FORM; he had just composed his Overture to King Lear, was working on *Tamara* and trying to persuade
Borodin, who was in Moscow with him, to follow up his promising
First Symphony by getting to work on *Prince Igor* which Stasov—
who usually presented the disciples with subjects—had more or
less commanded.

No one ever hurried Borodin. He was not so much lazy as sus-
pended between two worlds—he was making valuable researches
in organic chemistry at the Petersburg Academy of Medicine—
and not even Balakirev could lure him from his interest in practical science. Tchaikovsky offered more hopeful material, and
Balakirev was soon suggesting that he too write on a Shakespeare
theme. He said quite firmly what the theme must be; for a Tchaikovsky *Romeo and Juliet* was obvious and inescapable.

It so happened that Tchaikovsky at last had a room into which
he could invite a friend with some hope of an uninterrupted talk.
He and Rubinstein had moved quarters. Ironically their old quarters had become less and less tolerable the more the Conservatoire
flourished. They were next door to the practice rooms, the walls
were thin, and Tchaikovsky, trying to entertain or to write music,
was distracted by students trying to make up for lost time with
piano, harp, every kind of woodwind and, worst, the violin or

113

their own voices. Rubinstein survived the racket without blench-
ing; he liked noise, made plenty himself and did not plan to be
at home in the evenings in any case. It was a very different matter
with Tchaikovsky; when he could avoid his director's blandish-
ments he made the motions of working but rarely managed to
write a tolerable bar until late at night when the students had
forsaken their instruments for bed.

The noise and the frustration not only interfered with composition but also with his eating. He grew into the habit of dining
with Albrecht and his wife every evening and staying on until
he thought his room would be reasonably quiet. But this was
frustrating too; he enjoyed Mme. Albrecht's meals but grudged
every moment away from the music which was at once the only
thing he really wished to do and the only hope of eventual escape
from the routine of teaching. He had never thought of himself
as a teacher and his popularity in class (which was to prove temporary) did not move him in the least. "My tortures have begun
again," he writes after the first day of the new term.

Now all was changed, at home if not in the Conservatoire, as
he cheerfully told Anatoly: "We dined at home for the first time
yesterday and Agafon's wife prepared an excellent dinner. I shall
not go to the Albrechts again for dinner but shall always dine at
home. You will eat with us when you come here." To which he
added a very typical, "Do excuse me, old chap, that I can't send
you more than twenty silver rubles for the moment; at the first
possible opportunity I'll send more."

His spirits soared as quickly as they fell and Balakirev found
him in excellent form in his new room. They discussed *Romeo
and Juliet* there, in restaurants, cafés, and during long walks along
the boulevards, the swarthy, broadfaced Balakirev doing most of
the talking. The meetings were not always free from silent resentment, silent because it was Tchaikovsky who felt it. Balakirev remained blissfully ignorant that his companion sometimes
seethed when treated like one of the disciples in Petersburg and
would have been astounded to know that his musical views were

being described in letters to the family as narrow and his tone as authoritarian.

But these unveiled tussles did not mar the general harmony nor his companion's view that he was a splendid man—for Tchaikovsky was fair to a fault and sensible too; he knew that the encounters with such a mind and such selfless enthusiasm could do him nothing but good. Whether he understood how much good is doubtful, but by the time Balakirev went back to Petersburg the farewells were very affectionate and the idea of *Romeo and Juliet* had stuck.

By November Tchaikovsky had sketched it out and had told Balakirev so. He was at once deluged with instructions, almost all pertinent. The most sound was Balakirev's advice on how to encourage the right ideas. Nothing showed better how perceptive Balakirev was; he had come to the conclusion that, apart from his friend's deplorable introduction to the classics by way of Zaremba, Tchaikovsky's worst enemy was himself, his habit of striking out music too rapidly and without due preparatory thought. So: "Put on your goloshes, take your stick in your hand and go for a long walk round the boulevards. Begin at the Nikitsky, let your mind soak in the theme and I don't mind wagering that by the time you reach the Sretensky you will have discovered something good in the way of an episode or motif."

Tchaikovsky did as he was bid and wrote such warmhearted letters to Petersburg that a much cheered Balakirev "ran out to the Nevsky Prospekt—not walking but dancing!—and composed *Tamara* on my way."

Reflection away from piano and composing table did all that Balakirev had hoped. Reflection took the place of immediate emotional reaction. Within a few weeks Tchaikovsky sent a sketch of the main themes to Petersburg and received with commendable patience the master's criticisms, sugared with a genuine "this is the first work you have written that I can unhesitatingly describe as thoroughly good in essence. It is full of wonderful things."

The collaboration continued in fits and starts for the next

eighteen months, long after, to Balakirev's dismay, the work had
been published in Berlin on the intervention of Nikolai Rubinstein. For Balakirev was not the only man to perceive that Tchaikovsky had at last found his subject and with it his true style;
though he was to blot his copybook more than once in the future,
Rubinstein never seriously doubted after reading this score that
in his harmony professor he had found one of the great hopes of
Russian music; with exceptions, one of them wholly inexplicable,
he was to back Tchaikovsky fully from then on.

The fruitful year of 1869 ended with the publication of a
group of six Tchaikovsky songs. The best of these was a setting
from Goethe's *Nur wer die Sehnsucht Kennt.* "None But the
Lonely Heart" is perhaps Tchaikovsky's most famous song. This
is not surprising since it provides a perfect vehicle for the poem
but is unfortunate because it has obscured the greatness of other
songs by the same hand just as Tchaikovsky the song writer has
been obscured by his more obvious gifts. This is a pity because,
as with the *Voivode* fragment already discussed, he added something all his own to vocal music as he was to add to almost every
genre of the art.

He was to write many songs and to fail in many. Few men of
high emotional range are free from occasional descents into sentimentality and Tchaikovsky's warm heart when linked to his
uncertain literary taste often led him astray. Some of the lyrics
he set to music are rubbish and the music, faithfully expressing
them, is rubbish too.

But he was to succeed in many too, whenever the words struck
real fire from him. For instance, "During the Ball," "Forgotten
So Soon," "Pimpinella," "Greek Song," "Corals," "Mignon's
Dream" and "Don Juan's Serenade" are all in their widely differ-
ing styles marked with the stamp of the master—the peculiarly
Tchaikovskian gift of conveying precisely, economically, and unforgettably the particular emotion roused by the lyric. Even in
Schumann, his direct exemplar, the piano is often little more
than an accompaniment to the words; with Tchaikovsky it is al-

ways a musical impression of the words; that is to say, if one does
not hear the words (which is not as unusual as it ought to be)
one still receives the full sense of them because of the composer's
complete identification of himself with them.

Some critics, anxious to point to the "morbid Tchaikovsky"
legend, have commented on the fact that most of his songs are sad.
This is true. But it is also true of all great song writers and naturally, since only when they portray struggle and sorrow and loss
can they feel and stir the most powerful emotions.

2

The year 1869 had been a year of fruitfulness, the year 1870 was
barren. The tone of 1870 was set by the failure of *Romeo and
Juliet* when Nikolai Rubinstein first played it in March—a failure
summed up in Tchaikovsky's comment on the would-be triumphant after-concert dinner at Gurin's, one of the smartest of the
Moscow restaurants: "Nobody said a single word to me about the
Overture the entire evening—it wasn't mentioned."

Such insensitiveness in the leading lights in Moscow music is
difficult to imagine today; music lovers will find it hard to credit
that an audience, let alone composers, musicians, and critics, did
not instantly rise to this work which contains in essence everything
that has made Tchaikovsky known and loved wherever his music
is played. There were, for example, none of the obvious flountings
of harmonic convention which were to make Prokofiev regarded
forty years later as a young monster of modernism. On the contrary the score of *Romeo and Juliet* is melodious without difficulty, filled with themes which the man in the street could reasonably be expected to whistle, it is romantic, it was brief. No one
has yet explained satisfactorily why Tchaikovsky was to have to
wait more than ten years before this masterpiece of romantic
writing became one of the most popular works in the concert
repertory.

Romeo and Juliet is now too well known and is played too

often (and too sloppily—a frequent fault with renderings of Tchaikovsky) to need analysis here, but one or two facts must be mentioned. The first is that the composer held strictly to his title;
the work is a Fantasy Overture and not a symphonic poem. Tchaikovsky makes no attempt to tell the Romeo and Juliet story in
order or in detail; what interests him and what he does is to portray a series of impressions of action and character just as he
would have done if this had actually been the overture to an
opera. *Romeo and Juliet* is, in short, an extension of his principle
in song writing, to illustrate states of soul.

Behind this, guiding all, is his obsession with the victims of
fate. Romeo and Juliet are the first of several to be dealt with by
him, and his sense of a fate menacing human lives gives the story
intense dramatic power. He conveys this, in notable manner, for
he chose to follow the pure sonata form. As has been seen, he
was to complain all his life of deviations from classical form.
Musicians know that he is a master of form in all his great works
and in many of his lesser—the kind of instinctive marriage of
form and personal expression—but in *Romeo and Juliet* even he
could not castigate himself, it was a tour de force.

Romeo and Juliet presents for the first time virtually the
whole range of the great composer. He revealed himself a born
dramatist, moving from scene to scene and mood to mood with
vivid contrasts of pace and feeling and always with the utmost
economy. The speed never slackens, the listener is carried from
one superb melody to another, from one climax to another. Such
rich orchestral writing had not been heard in a concert hall in
Russia; the composer was clearly in complete command of his
forces from first note to last, never thickening the texture and
making highly inventive use of the orchestra. The score is dominated by a controlled rapport between composer and subject; he
understood the fate which would part the lovers but he felt the
love too and recreates it with a touching blend of passion and
compassion; never before had the fire and poetry of young love
been communicated with such truth and charm.

He did not destroy the score of this unsuccessful work; his critical sense overbore the inevitable reaction and mood of hopelessness after failure; he knew that *Romeo and Juliet* would come into its own. But such a reflection is poor comfort to a man getting on to thirty who wants a home of his own and freedom from teaching so that he can write uninterruptedly. He remained desperately poor—his stipend inadequate, his optimism and generosity abnormal, his grasp of arithmetic negligible—and a week or two later he was writing urgently to Albrecht, "For God's sake send me four rubles or I shall starve!"

Four rubles! One dollar! And this was not the only frantic note to Albrecht and Albrecht was not the only friend to receive them. One recipient was a new and unusual friend, one of the most remarkable men of his time. Nikolai Sergeyevich Zverev was wellborn, a dandy and rake who had run through a fortune in Petersburg and returned to Moscow where, in his university days, he learned the piano under the famous Dubuque. Rubinstein had persuaded Dubuque to join the Conservatoire staff when it opened; Dubuque introduced Zverev to him on his return in 1870; and Zverev in turn became a teacher of pianoforte there.

But Zverev, who had no intention of reducing his standard of living, also stormed the aristocratic households of Moscow in search of private pupils and in short time had made himself the most talked of teacher in the city. More significantly, he took the three most promising boys he could find as boarder-pupils, refusing fees if their parents were not wealthy and bringing them up as if they were his own children. He could play the tyrant, falling into fearful rages if his pupils did not work as hard as he and come up to his own high standards, but the result of such concentrated coaching (the boys were not allowed to stay with their parents even in supposed vacation periods) was quickly apparent. Zverev, who had his fair share of vanity, made his boys play to the company after his vast Sunday dinners at which he royally entertained his Conservatoire friends and distinguished visiting musicians, and everyone, even the highly critical Anton Rubinstein, was astounded by their feats on the piano. All musical circles in the city were soon full of this unique experiment—an experiment which was to produce, amidst a galaxy of high talent, the young Sergei Rachmaninov fresh from his classes under Kross in Petersburg.

Tchaikovsky was a regular guest at these Sunday dinners. His friendship with Zverev began in a peculiar way. Zverev came to him and asked if he would give him lessons in musical theory. Zverev was then thirty-eight, eight years older than Tchaikovsky, and this impressive demonstration of his determination to put music before dignity (he was a man of fanatical pride) struck Tchaikovsky favorably. As a man Zverev appealed to him too; he responded at once to the good breeding which was not always conspicuous in the Conservatoire staff and to the forcefulness which was so lacking in himself. Nikolai Rubinstein quickly found a boon companion in Zverev, specially at the gypsies and the English Club, but Tchaikovsky came a good second. He and Zverev began to go about a lot together, theater and concert going (always in the best seats—Zverev would tolerate no other), dining, wining, and music making. They made a fine couple, the tall, stern-faced, black-browed Zverev, impeccably dressed and the essence of dignity, contrasting piquantly with Tchaikovsky's gentler good looks and appealing manner.

A large number of appeals for money date from this year of musical standstill, appeals made even more necessary by Tchaikovsky's efforts to live up to his new friend. Sometimes these appeals were lively—"You are a pig, you prefer Laroche to me. That will cost you five silver rubles. By messenger, please!"—and "Please send me ten rubles at once. If you don't, the next issue of *Sovremennaya Letopis* will carry a complete account of the man you really are!"—but more often they were sombre, always indicating bare pockets. He knew what poverty was and every time a work of his was damned he saw an extension of this poverty stretching ahead indefinitely. After *Romeo and Juliet* he retreated into melancholy, seeing no hope of a miracle.

He wrote the beginnings of a new opera *Mandragora* (a fragment of which became well known as the "Insect Chorus") when Kashkin stepped in firmly with such devastating criticism of the libretto—by a professor of botany—that he threw it out. He began yet another opera *The Oprichnik*, this time with an excellent libretto, but the repulse of *Romeo and Juliet* haunted him. The depression would not lift and he once again hated the streets of Moscow and longed for Kamenka. But it was to Paris and Germany that he went. Begichev told him that his stepson was dangerously ill in Paris and asked him to go there. Tchaikovsky left at once, glad to be away from a Russia which refused to recognize his genius, anxious to be with a young lad who was attracting him more and more.

This was the first of many disgusted flights from his homeland, all of which ended with a rush back, as homesick as he had been homehating a few weeks earlier. The Begichev boy recovered sufficiently to be moved to a German spa and there Tchaikovsky languished for a few weeks trying unsuccessfully to persuade himself that the waters were doing him good. His day was unvaried and unexciting, as he told A. Y. Bakireva, the twins' old governess. "We get up at six, drink the waters, then stroll about till eight. Then we drink coffee and at one o'clock we dine. Afterwards we walk or drive until evening, drink tea at eight and go to bed at nine."

The rest of the letter is much more interesting because it illustrates two unvarying facets of the writer, his moral courage and his true democracy at a time when governesses were household pariahs, too plebeian to associate with the family, too educated to mix with the servants. Of all this he was blissfully unaware; he took people as he found them, judging not by class but by heart.

The incident leading to the letter was obviously a derogatory reference by Avdotya Yakovlevna—not the most patient of women —to one of the many voluble nonworkers in the Tchaikovsky household, a dependent relative. "I parted from you so unpleasantly," Pyotr Ilyich now says, "that I must write these few lines to tell you that I love you as always.

"I very much regret that your morbid irritability led to a quarrel. I advise you to go to Papasha and apologize. He is a 75-year-old man and, what's much more important, one of the best people in the world. Consequently there will be no kind of humiliation for you in the act. Besides, you really did behave indelicately in abusing his kinswoman. What would you say if someone spoke so cuttingly about your sister?"

He was to continue to supply the old woman till her death with money he could not afford, to augment Ilya Petrovich's pension. For the moment, in Soden, he felt increasingly bored and unhappy. A few weeks earlier he had written to his sister: "I feel a passionate wish to hear children's voices. I want to be able to take part in all the little things that make up a home. In short, I long for a family life." The attractions of the German spa in no way compensated for the lack of a home and family of his own; the frivolity of the life there—aged rakes trying to prolong a useless existence—and the falsity of the friendships and flirtations struck up out of sheer ennui made this warmhearted man detest every minute of it.

The most lively part of this depressing German visit with an invalid who rarely showed signs of real recovery was a trip to Wiesbaden where Nikolai Rubinstein was busily losing his last ruble at the roulette tables. Tchaikovsky reported that his Director was "convinced that he will break the bank." Of course the bank broke him, and for the rest of the year he and Tchaikovsky (who was throwing his money away just as effectively in other directions) were impoverished.

In retrospect this moment can be seen as the beginning of a stage in Tchaikovsky's life which, in cruel contrast to the upward surge of his reputation as Russia's most promising composer during the same period, was to transform him into a haunted near-alcoholic, turn his hair prematurely grey and cover his face with a mass of nervous wrinkles. For it was then that the monstrous suspicion first crossed his mind—the trend of his letters is only too clear—that fate had ordained that he, most home-, woman- and child-loving of men, was to be denied them all.

It was highly significant that he wrote despairingly to Alexandra when supposedly enjoying the company of the brilliant young man he was so fond of. Shilovsky offered him everything a homosexual could ask—love, wealth, intelligence, wit, charm, a feeling for art. It was not enough; that was Tchaikovsky's shattering discovery at Soden. It was not enough, yet he found himself increasingly drawn in that direction for lack of another Artot, another Alexandra. Love of some kind, strong physical love, he had to have, and the so lightly assumed schoolboy habit of Petersburg days began to tighten its grip. And he knew it; he saw what was happening and was powerless to stop it.

And this was not all. Homosexuality was not only inadequate for him, as had just been demonstrated under the most favorable circumstances, it was dangerous. It was an offense punishable by imprisonment. Tchaikovsky's prolific imagination raced ahead; he saw himself publicly disgraced, an outcast from society, driven out of the Conservatoire, he saw his family ruined—his brothers' careers fatally cut short, his sister's heart broken, nothing was too lurid for him when in the grip of remorse.

No sane man would allow himself to dwell on such thoughts. For a long time the suspicion that he was emotionally doomed remained an occasional nightmare recurring with increasing frequency. But after the return to Moscow in the winter of 1870 many circumstances conspired to prey on his mind—the effect of weeks in a stuffy German spa with an invalid, the prospect of interminable Conservatoire lectures and interminable rejections of his music by the public, the prospect of a life lived alone or in fearful intimacies, all this added to, at that moment, bitter thoughts of the futile Franco-Prussian war in which his mother's country was being humiliated.

His answer to all this was to drink heavily, and this in turn led to deeper despair when he recovered from a drinking bout. He

saw possible disgrace there too, his life broken, his family humiliated if he should be dismissed from the Conservatoire for
perpetual insobriety. He was no Rubinstein, to lecture brightly
and clearly the next morning; already his popularity in class was
draining away because he was gruff, short with students, wrestling
with violent headaches and growing hatred of the academic treadmill. He saw himself a moneyless hack piano teacher in some
provincial town, his chance of composing great music forever
gone. And this threw him back on to more drink, more forgetfulness, more dreadful awakenings.

Rubinstein was not the best of company for a man in a state
he could not begin to comprehend; his remedy for low spirits was
high living and forgetfulness until the next morning when, in
any case, classes took one's mind off everything but music. He
merely succeeded in further damaging Pyotr Ilyich's nervous system while systematically making sure that his salary could not
possibly meet his expenses. Deep in debt himself, he could not
think seriously of his colleague's (to him) trifling embarrassments.

Tchaikovsky's ambivalent attitude to Nikolai began to turn
definitely towards a separation; he admired him as much as ever,
more than ever he appreciated his good nature and generosity.
He wanted to work under him if he was destined to work under
somebody, but to live with him he wanted no longer. Nerves on
edge, he longed for an apartment or room of his own.

Typically, it was Rubinstein who helped him to it. He suggested at the beginning of 1871 that Tchaikovsky promote a concert of his works. This would make his music better known and,
if he was lucky, bring in a sizable sum at the box office. The idea
of an all-Tchaikovsky concert had not occurred to the composer—
giving some idea of his extraordinary modesty even at this late
stage in his career—but he jumped at it.

At first he thought naturally in terms of a symphonic concert
with Nikolai Rubinstein conducting but had overlooked the considerable cost of arranging such a program; he wrote for large
orchestra and his music needed a large hall at a large rent.

Foiled, he turned to the idea of a chamber concert. The difficulty here was that he had not sufficient items to make up even a short program—merely his six songs and a number of little piano pieces. He decided to write a string quartet to give body to the program. By March it was done and at the end of the month the concert was held. Nikolai Rubinstein played two pieces in the middle of the program, a well-known soprano sang some songs and the audience was highly titilated by the unexpected arrival of Turgenev in the hall.

Modest claims that the presence of Turgenev went some way to make the evening, but the real success of the concert was its first item which Turgenev apparently did not hear—the First Quartet in D Major. This work at once established Tchaikovsky as masterly in yet another department of music. Like some later compositions of his—one thinks of the Trio and Serenade for Strings—this quartet has become famous for a single movement which is often, too often, played apart from the rest of the work. This Andante Cantabile consists of two themes, both regarded as essentially Tchaikovskian. The first theme he had taken from a peasant song he heard sung under his window at Kamenka two summers earlier, the second, almost equally luscious, was his own invention; his handling of each demonstrated his supreme musicality in this sphere.

As he sat in the hall and listened, Tchaikovsky wept throughout this movement as Tolstoy was to do whenever he heard it and as many lesser listeners have done and may continue to do; it was the kind of sweet music he was to write more effectively than any other man, just as he was to excel in vigorous romantic music too. This excessively Victorian movement has obscured the quartet as a whole and this is much to be regretted, for the work is first-rate from beginning to end. The glittering first movement shows Tchaikovsky at his most elegant, as adept at syncopation (as he was so dazzlingly to demonstrate in his Second Piano Concerto) and a master in counterpoint when he unites and develops the first and second themes. The scherzo is wholly classical in construction and includes a fascinating trio led by the cello, and the vigorous finale, in rondo form, brings the quartet to a rousing finish.

On the whole the concert paid handsomely, with good reviews, an enthusiastic audience, and a gratifying monetary return. Soon afterwards, partly as a result of it, Tchaikovsky was offered, was indeed almost badgered into, a job of reviewing. He did not care for the work although he did it conscientiously and well, but it made the financial future decidedly less gloomy.

True to his nature, Tchaikovsky took all this as an omen of a relenting fate and was galvanized into great activity. He turned to *The Oprichnik* again, spent the summer at Kamenka in excellent spirits (writing a ballet *Swan Lake* for his nieces to dance and, going to the other extreme, *A Guide to the Practical Study of Harmony* which Rimsky-Korsakov was soon to regard as his Bible) and when he returned to Moscow in the autumn moved at last to rooms of his own.

The opera forged ahead, with the inevitable periods of dissatisfaction, but was still unfinished when he went off for a round of southern visits, to Nice, Genoa, Venice, and Vienna, with Shilovsky still fighting his tuberculosis.

There were many wearisome moments, as in the German spa, yet Tchaikovsky's melancholy was not due wholly to dancing attendance on an invalid; he liked Vladimir Shilovsky and did it willingly. What subdued him, as it was always to do, was the realization that none of the undoubted charms of Italy, Austria, and southern France could compete for one moment with the solid virtues of his Russia. Like almost all creative men he had a strong compulsion towards movement; after a few months in Moscow his sources of inspiration seemed to dry up and he was eager to try anything new, the warm sunshine of the Riviera, the sophistication of Vienna, the brightness of Paris, to revive his failing muse, but unlike many great creators he could not escape his destiny. "I am Russian, Russian, Russian!" he was to cry; and this was so true that he was never to be at ease for more than a week or two outside his own country.

Back again in February of the new year, 1872, he worked hard at *The Oprichnik*. By May he had finished and the score was sent off to Petersburg to be considered by the Imperial Theaters Committee. He left for Kamenka as soon as the Conservatoire term ended, and found a new arrival there, a baby nephew, Vladimir.

The change from Europe to Moscow and from Moscow to Kamenka had put him in fine fettle; it had been a joy to get back to a Russian city but the joy paled before his rapture when he reached the countryside. Never had his family seen him so light-hearted. Again he ate great meals and went for great walks, played the piano, romped with his nieces, hung over his nephew's cradle, and talked animatedly to Alexandra and her husband. He stopped heavy drinking, partly because the strain of city life, of Rubinstein, and reviewing and lecturing had disappeared, but more because he was ashamed to worry Alexandra. He could never make up his mind whether she knew of his weakness; in the hope that she did not he said nothing.

This slight cloud apart (for he loathed anything even faintly suggestive of deceit), he loved everything about the long holiday, his family, the people of Kamenka, the Ukraine countryside, and as always this feeling immediately began to express itself in music; he wrote the beginnings of his Second Symphony.

CHAPTER 10

Second Symphony
1872-1874

THIS SUMMER SAW A TURN in Tchaikovsky's fortunes. By the time he had finished his round with a visit to the Begichev country house he had sketched out the entire symphony. He came back to Moscow to find his salary increased once more, and this, his reviewing fees, and the occasional sales of work which Jurgenson had begun to publish pushed his total income up to the three-thousand-ruble mark. It was not a fortune—about $840 a year— and he managed to make it seem even less than it was: "I'm such an ass with money that I'm always in debt." But he did one wise thing, to move to rooms he liked in place of rooms dictated by the lowest possible rent.

The move had one main purpose, to help him to compose more quickly—the apartment was quiet and roomy—and by the middle of November he was apologizing for a break in his letters because "I can't think of anything but the symphony."

By the end of the year it was completed and he took it with him to Petersburg where he had been summoned by the Imperial Theaters Committee for a hearing, on the piano, of his new opera. After the usual bout of nervousness—he could never accustom himself to perform or conduct in public—he managed to get through *The Oprichnik* sufficiently well to sway the committee in his favor, so the new year of 1873 opened auspiciously with a decision to stage the opera at the Maryinsky the following year.

He stayed as usual with his father and stepmother, and it can be assumed with some confidence that they all discussed his wish to get married, since he was constantly writing letters to his father about it. He was in a dilemma. He wanted to find a woman as like his stepmother as possible—an intelligent woman who would make the kind of home for him that Alexandra had made for Lyov—but he had never met a woman of this sort who attracted him. He also disliked the idea of asking any woman to take the risk of marrying a man whose income was small and much of it uncertain—a man who had not yet managed to make his mark as a composer even in his own country. He was still regarded in Moscow as a promising young composer, in Petersburg he was scarcely known at all. Yet he was nearly thirty-three. So: "If a man is single his debts are not of much moment, but if I had to keep a wife and children it would be a very different matter."

This kind of argument delivered him into his father's hands. For many years, ever since in a fit of conscience he had suggested a musical career for his son, Ilya Petrovich had set his mind against it. He had never hidden his view that Pyotr Ilyich was foolish to throw over the civil service for professional music instead of preserving music as a pleasant hobby, and the six years in Moscow seemed to have proved his point—his son was as unknown and as hard up as ever.

He listened skeptically when Pyotr Ilyich told him in these early days of 1873 that he had at last written a work which must surely make his name: "I think it the best thing I've done." He had been told this after every composition and his son's words were thrown away. Tchaikovsky no doubt believed them—it is a necessary characteristic of creative men to think their most recent work better than any other—but he must have had uneasy memories, not only of past rejections by the public but also of his own volte-faces.

He was soon to be vociferously supported, for the week he arrived in Petersburg he saw much of Balakirev and his disciples and was persuaded to play some of his symphony at a party held in his honor at the Rimsky-Korsakov apartment. It is not certain how much he played but he certainly played the last movement and as certainly swept his audience off its feet.

The meeting was not without humor. Tchaikovsky, as a Moscow man, was received with a certain reserve—the rivalry between the musicians of the two cities remained tense. Admittedly he was not against the nationalist school of Balakirev like so many of his Moscow colleagues, but as certainly he was not a member of it. He was, in their eyes, sitting on the fence. Yet as they listened to the finale of the new symphony they heard with stupefaction music more essentially and thoroughly Russian than any Petersburg nationalist had ever written. To their credit the response was immediate and heartwarming: "They almost tore me to pieces," he reported to the family, "and Madame Korsakov implored me to arrange the Finale for four hands." As it was, Nadezhda Niko-layevna arranged it herself as she had arranged the *Romeo and Juliet.*

He could not doubt that all present thought they were listening to one of the most important works composed by a contemporary Russian. Even the critical Stasov, who did not usually support works he had not suggested, had nothing but praise for the symphony, and Tchaikovsky was so overcome by the favor that he ventured to beg a subject from him for another work after the style of *Romeo and Juliet,* on a Shakespearian theme if possible.

The gratified Stasov followed him back to Moscow with a long letter suggesting three subjects—The Tempest, Taras Bulba, and Ivanhoe—and when Tchaikovsky chose the first, gave detailed instructions which the composer accepted without demur.

This meekness owed something to the events of the previous evening, February 7, when his symphony was played by Rubinstein for the first time with such success that a second performance was demanded "by general request." News of the new symphony— the first truly Russian symphony ever written, many claimed— travelled fast to the right quarters in Petersburg, and one month later Edward Napravnik conducted it there. Again it had a great welcome. And to round off weeks of triumph the repeat Moscow performance in April saw a spontaneous demonstration of esteem by the packed house. Tchaikovsky was called on to the platform at the end of each movement—the audience refused to stop applauding until he appeared—and at the end of the finale was given a silver goblet and a laurel wreath.

The public instinct was right as it so often is, and began a reaction to the old, snobbish prejudice against Russian music; Tchaikovsky had not only made his name known in his own country, he had cleared the way for others to write Russian music and to receive a hearing.

The Symphony in C Minor was called the "Little Russian" and the title is apt because three of its four movements owe much of their power and charm to Kamenka folk songs. Although this Second Symphony is played more often today than in the past it is still strangely neglected. It has been Tchaikovsky's fate to be known by a handful of works which crowd the rest out of the concert hall; the omission of the Second Symphony from the regular repertory is a considerable loss to all who love his music; it is not only a splendid work but exhibits the composer in a sunny mood which is a delight to share.

A word must be said about this mood in which Tchaikovsky wrote his music. He is often accused of morbidity, of a preoccupation with the dark side of life. It is true that he looked at life straight and that, not being unthinking or unfeeling, he saw it in general as a sombre pilgrimage. That aspect colors a great deal of his music, and as it is the aspect shared by all great and thoughtful men he can scarcely be blamed for expressing it. What he does, being a truthful man as well as an artist, is to show, above the groundplan of sobriety, the facets of life which make it tolerable—the love of one for another, the beauty in nature, the humor in human contacts, the style and charm of man's work and, above all, the sense of form which the unconquerable human soul imposes on the chaos by which he is surrounded. If a Tchaikovsky work is heard correctly it can give more to the listener than the work of an "optimist"—a word which usually means no more than a man who refuses to think—because it is a heartening as well as moving experience.

The Second Symphony is an almost wholly extrovert work, the result of a summer in the peaceful and unspoiled Russian countryside spent by a man who had recently been abroad. It is his joyful response to reunion with so much that he loved, the life of the home, leisurely bustle of the village, and the calm and grandeur of the country scene.

Tchaikovsky speaks of its satisfactory form—for once he is almost satisfied—and certainly the entire symphony is closely knit in the classical manner though built almost entirely on Russian themes. The pleasantly melancholy introduction, in no way sad, rather the mood of a man walking the country at evening, soon gives way to an Ukrainian version of one of the oldest songs in Russia, "On the Volga." This allegro vivo, which occupies the greater part of the first movement, is brilliantly handled—with constant variety, pace, and vigor. For the second movement, andante marziale, Tchaikovsky takes up one of the most fetching remnants of the destroyed *Undine,* the wedding march, and presents it with a masterly use of the woodwinds, always his most successful instruments, and with which he obtains original effects of poetical nostalgia. The scherzo goes back to folk song themes tossed about with audacious use of rhythm—a lighthearted movement into which the composer manages, true to his passion for novelty, to introduce the sounds of the balalaika.

The finale is the cream of the work and compares favorably with anything written by Tchaikovsky. The second and third movements owe something to Delibes and a great deal more to *A Midsummer Night's Dream;* the last movement owes nothing to anyone or anything but Russia. It is based on two themes, one his own, the other heard at Kamenka—but it is in his treatment of the latter that he shows his genius. It is a well-known song called "The Crane," a fascinating song, which the composer repeats no fewer than eight times. Although he enlarges he does not alter the theme, he obtains his variety by constant changes of orchestral color. It is sheer joy to hear, vigorous, charming, nostalgic; one can never have enough of it, a fact which speaks for itself. With deceptive ease Tchaikovsky gives the appearance of spontaneity throughout his repetitions; in fact they are devised with extreme skill. The counterpoint is masterly, the use of syncopation a joy. The Balakirev circle had understood at once when they heard this movement that they were listening to a great composer and the concert audiences of Petersburg and Moscow understood it too.

2

There were two immediate effects of the success of the Second Symphony. The first, as would be expected, was a rapid rise in Tchaikovsky's spirits and to the reader of today who cannot hear the composer keeping Moscow social gatherings in fits of laughter, this comes across in his letters. The bulk of the fantastically large number of letters Tchaikovsky wrote can be divided into four distinct categories. There are the personal and family letters in which, in exchange for news of the family doings, he replies with full details of his own life, triumphs, and failures, moral and concrete, and accounts of steps he is taking to help the latest of the many lame dogs attached in some way or other (often very tenuous) to the vast Tchaikovsky family group—he was the family conscience incarnate. There are letters devoted almost entirely to music and musicians. There are his begging letters, dozens of them in his early Moscow years, by means of which he comprehensively relieves Jurgenson and his Conservatoire friends, Albrecht, Rubinstein, and Kashkin foremost, of anything from four to fifteen or twenty rubles at a time—some of the letters gay and impudent, some written in desperation. There are also his bright and humorous letters which range at this time from a note to Jurgenson—"Nikolai Mikhailovich [Kashkin] tells me you are dropping in to see me tonight. Splendid! Three wine glasses filled with vodka, and a piece of pie, will be waiting for you"—to pure nonsense.

In general his humor, in line with the taste of his time, seems infantile to the present-day reader and embarrassing rather than amusing. But there are exceptions. As the twins had discovered with joy in their childhood, he had a penchant for word twisting. His nonsense letters and poems are often most refreshing and show a man too often forgotten by the reader brought up to think of the name Tchaikovsky as synonymous with gloom and struggle. The following letter, written just after the success of the Second Symphony, is a good example of the genre. In it Tchaikovsky demonstrates the fun to be had by a man who has half learned English and revenges himself on the intractable language by mocking its syntactical absurdities. It is easy to imagine Alexandra and Modest (then staying at Kamenka) revelling in this letter addressed to them jointly, and it is still very much worth reading.

"My good sister and my dear brother! I have know what motsch plesir that you learn the Englisch langage bot you cannot told that I cannot understand. I kan understand wery biutifoll oll what you will and enough bether. My brother! you are one fulischmen, bot you, my dear sister, are one biutiffoll women. I have not times to scrive this letter englisch bot God sawe the Quenn and collection of Britisch autors is one trifles. I can you told that the spanierds wear their hats cocked and I cocked my pistol directly. The King has conferred the order of the Garter on him bot i will cringe to nobody. We always deal with him and We dined on soup and fisch.

"Tell me: How did he come by so musch money and Why do you call out? Call un your brother and your sister, call down the servant. I will call for you at six. He assisted me with all his endeavours, i have atoned for my fault and i will ask him to dine. Do not argue withe me. You argue against reason and i abide by what I say: France abounds with fruit and several trees are bliwn down.

"My brother, what are you gaping at? My sister, you lies in with your first child.

"I are your affectioned brother Pither!"

So much for Tchaikovsky's reaction to success. The first practical effect of the welcome given to the new symphony was an invitation from the Imperial Theaters at Moscow to supply incidental music for Ostrovsky's new play *Snyegurochka*. The commission pleased Tchaikovsky in every way; he appreciated the compliment of being asked to collaborate with Russia's greatest dramatist, he needed the three hundred and fifty rubles fee and the subject suited him precisely. He flew at it and in three weeks had it ready for production in April.

Ostrovsky's lovely play was not to make its name until Rimsky-Korsakov used it for *The Snow Maiden*, one of the most charming operas ever written, but Tchaikovsky's music caught on and was often played as a kind of suite and published as Opus 12. The popularity of the music is not surprising—what is surprising is its disappearance from modern programs.

Tchaikovsky had to provide nineteen numbers—dances, solos, and choruses—and for three of them he used fragments of *Undine*. The first was the Prelude which became the Overture to the new work, transplanted en bloc. It was not one of his happiest thoughts, but the second and third borrowings were entirely successful. Undine's song "Little Storm, My Sister," became the first of Lel's three songs and the best, though all are charming. In this first song Tchaikovsky broke new ground by using a piano with the orchestra, a then hair-raising stroke of modernism.

An allegro for mixed choir became the young girl's chorus, a ravishing little theme, and just as attractive is Tchaikovsky's original theme for the flower scene. The carnival music is pure Russian, gay, tender, bright, and the clowns' dance is Russian too but at the opposite extreme and demonstrates the composer's virtuosity. Some critics were hard on this dance music—"Noisy and vulgar" was a typical comment—but they missed the unconventional use of instruments, the trumpets in particular, which was to reappear in *Petrushka* and in much of Shostakovich. Tchaikovsky was often to point the way to the future and this little number contains one of his happiest original thoughts.

Having money in his pocket meant a departure from Moscow as soon as term ended, and again he went off to the west, picking up the Jurgensons in Dresden and touring Switzerland, north Italy and Paris with them. He enjoyed their company (Jurgenson was a forthright, homely self-made man) and he dutifully and often sincerely admired the sights, the antiquities, the climate, but in the end, and not a far end, his continental ardor collapsed once more. In Switzerland he confided to a diary he had begun to keep, and which is chiefly notable for a record of excellent food and wine taken en route: "My soul yearns for Russia and when I see in my mind's eye its plains, fields and forests I feel a pang at the heart. Oh my dear country, you are a hundred times lovelier and dearer to me than these majestic mountain ranges famed for their beauty!"

In such a mood—and it became more frequent the longer he stayed away—nothing would quiet him but Russia. By August he was back in Moscow and only paused to collect what money he could rake together, having as usual spent everything, before he was off into the country. Kamenka was too far and too expensive to reach, so he again took up Begichev's permanent invitation to his country estate at Usovo in Tambov Province, only some two hundred miles southeast of the capital.

He had another reason for choosing Usovo: he wanted absolute quiet to work and would get it; the house was larger than Kamenka, there were no children to tempt him from music, and the Begichevs, like so many rich people, were forever dashing from one place to another in search of some new way of passing the time.

After a few days the family went off, leaving him in the midst of a countryside he loved almost as well as the Ukraine. He at once began work on *The Tempest* which, in the spirit of Balakirev's advice, he had been meditating more than six months.

The work leaped ahead: "At last I was alone, absolutely alone, in a marvellous steppe country," he was to recall years later. "I couldn't possibly tell you what great happiness I felt in this solitude. I found myself in a state of exhaltation, of uninterrupted ecstasy, of beatitude. During the day I wandered in the woods, in the evening I walked across the steppe, at night I stood by the window listening to the profound silence of the great spaces, a silence broken rarely by a confused noise from far away. Without the least effort and as though borne up by some supernatural power I wrote, almost in spite of myself, the entire first draft of *The Tempest.*"

In December Rubinstein conducted the first performance of the new work. It was hailed as the Second Symphony had been hailed and a repeat performance demanded, and from that time became one of Tchaikovsky's most popular works.

There are many mysteries in music, and *The Tempest* is one of them. It is difficult to understand why an audience which rejected *Romeo and Juliet* should welcome *The Tempest* with open arms. It is as difficult to explain why modern audiences have completely reversed the taste of Tchaikovsky's day so that we hear *Romeo and Juliet* often and *The Tempest* virtually not at all. For the first mystery there seems only one explanation, that *The Tempest* had a printed program which the composer followed religiously. This seems almost absurd, yet concert audiences like to get their teeth into program music, to be able to say that they are following every action of the drama set out before them. For the second mystery there seems to be no adequate explanation. Music critics know that certain works of every great composer are preferred to others not less good but they have not been able to explain the unaccountable except by the capriciousness of public taste.

The Tempest is in one respect a more remarkable work than *Romeo and Juliet* because Tchaikovsky obeyed Stasov's detailed instructions to the letter yet managed to write music which sounds perfectly integrated, unforced, spontaneous. Possibly his unusually long wait before writing the work released him from the sense of writing to order. Possibly again, those magical ten days at Usovo wove the spell that he in turn weaves in his score. It is melodious, balanced and orchestrated with an appearance of consummate ease and richness. If a fault must be found it is perhaps in the storm music. Tchaikovsky plainly did not wish to write this in the first instance but Stasov was adamant, indeed shocked at the thought of *The Tempest* without a storm. The result is a battery of sound that deafens rather than awes. Tchaikovsky was frequently to be attacked by contemporary critics for his penchant for noise. Usually the critics are at fault; here, when they said nothing, one feels that they would have had a case.

3

With a second successful orchestral work behind him, Tchaikovsky turned back to chamber music and in a few weeks in the new year of 1874—"in one breath," as he was to say—wrote his Second String Quartet. It had a wretched beginning; at a private first performance Anton Rubinstein, visiting Moscow, took his brother's place as honored guest and returned the compliment by comprehensively damning the quartet which, he declared, he could not understand.

Those who hear this work today will be unable to understand Anton Rubinstein, but Tchaikovsky, still the uncertain student Pyotr Ilyich whenever he came in contact with Anton, feverishly tried to rewrite some of it despite the protests of those who had played it. He might have spared himself the trouble; he could do no more than tinker with some of the parts, leaving the whole very much as it was, and when it had its first public performance in March it was praised by all.

Looking back on this quartet, Tchaikovsky claimed that it was one of the finest things he had written: "I have never composed anything so easily, so spontaneously." Opinions about it since his death have varied widely; some think it an advance on his first quartet, others find it labored, rather dull, and too long—it is half

as long again as the earlier work. This latter opinion is probably
due to the somewhat uninspired Finale; the first three movements
have all Tchaikovsky's genius for melody and dexterous use of
material and instruments. Nothing can be hidden in a quartet,
and he rises to the challenge.

Two points about the quartet are worth notice. In the Adagio
we can see plainly what disturbed Rubinstein, some extremely
advanced dissonances. The entire third movement, an Andante,
is as moving and beautifully written as the almost notorious
Andante Cantabile of the first quartet but has remained virtually
unknown. It is what is now thought of as typical Tchaikovsky
music, sweet and tender and a shade melancholy, but the robust
scherzo is just as typical and demonstrated the composer's innate
feeling for rhythm which he handled to the point of audacity. The
dissonances are now too ordinary to rouse a moment's surprise—
one has to remember when the work was written—but the rhythms
remain a joy as rhythm by a master always is.

The staging of *The Oprichnik* had been delayed so long that
Tchaikovsky embarked on yet another opera, this time taken from
Gogol's *Christmas Eve,* but soon after the quartet was played he
at last had word from Petersburg that *The Oprichnik* was sched-
uled for a premiere in Easter week and that he was wanted for
rehearsals.

Partly because of the long delay since he had finished the
opera, partly because of his enthusiasm for the new opera and
partly because Napravnik, the chief opera conductor at the Maryinsky, was a tetchy pedant, Tchaikovsky's faith in his work evap-
orated rapidly. No composer likes his work to be cut and Napravnik insisted on many cuts. Tchaikovsky had not been a week in
Petersburg before he began to look gloomily on the prospects of
the opera. From despair at the sight and sound of butchery he
deteriorated rapidly to dislike of his own music; stupefied with
boredom, he regularly walked out of the theater after the end of
the second act.

To add to his embarrassment, everyone he knew (and he had

dozens of friends) was determined to make an occasion of the premiere. The family had taken a box and colleagues and students at the Moscow Conservatoire clamored for tickets. He tried to discourage them all. He told his best student and most devoted disciple, Sergei Ivanovich Taneyev, for example, "If you're really thinking of coming up here simply to hear my opera, Seryozha, do think again, I entreat you. It doesn't contain anything out of the way and is not worth rushing up to Petersburg for."

His appeals were useless, and the Maryinsky was thick with his supporters from Moscow and Petersburg when the opera was finally staged on April 24. Ilya Petrovich, bearing his seventy-nine years well, was sitting stiffly in his bemedalled uniform in a box beside his "dumpling," as Pyotr Ilyich fondly called Yelizaveta Mikhailovna, the twins (both small young men) were in attendance and a highly nervous and despondent Tchaikovsky was walking uneasily up and down in the background.

There was not in fact any obvious cause for despondency except for the usual dingy production, but then all Russian operas were shabbily mounted, the Imperial Theaters Committee only dug its hands in its pockets for Italian opera productions. This relic of snobbery was to rouse ferocious and eventually successful complaints from Chaliapin nearly thirty years later. For the rest the opera was well sung, enthusiastically received and Tchaikovsky had to take a bow as early as the end of the second act. And at an after-performance supper given in his honor by the combined Conservatoire staffs the Director of the Petersburg Conservatoire announced that he had been awarded a prize worth 300 rubles for the outstanding Russian composer of the year.

It was an amiable weakness with Tchaikovsky that he was off with the old and on with the new, like so many creative men. His darling of the moment was the new opera *Vakula the Smith* and to him *The Oprichnik* was *vieux jeu*. The praise and the prize left him comparatively unmoved. He departed from Petersburg soon afterwards with relief—he had promised to review a La Scala production of *A Life For The Tsar*—and without waiting for the critics to give tongue.

The opera was praised by his well-wishers (prominently a forgiven Laroche) and damned by others, headed as usual by the vitriolic Cui. The keynote of the latter's notice was the absence of inspiration, and in spite of the fact that the opera was performed more often than most and always with acclamation, Tchaikovsky agreed with him: "For all its beastliness and obvious animosity, Cui's criticism is basically correct . . . the opera lacks style, action and inspiration."

If one is to judge by the number of representations a work is given, the composer was to be proved right. *The Oprichnik* is not heard today except for an occasional Soviet production and is unknown to most musicians in the West. Yet there is much to be said for it. It had, unlike most Tchaikovsky operas, a workable libretto after the play by the well-known novelist Ivan Ivanovich Lazhechnikov, and the plot was congenial to a man absorbed by the ironies of fate: Andrei Morozov, one of Ivan The Terrible's picked band of Oprichniks (a kind of personal bodyguard notorious for their suppression of all human feelings), meets the young Natalya and falls in love; Ivan revenges himself on the girl, Andrei revolts and is executed.

Here we have another version of Romeo and Juliet and even more obviously the forerunners of Tatyana and Onegin. Natalya is created with that heartwarming blend, so typical of the composer, of passion and compassion. She stands as model for the modest, artless Russian heroine drawn from life by all the great Russian novelists and poets, and Tchaikovsky's version is full-blooded and convincing. Her two ariosos express this type of Russian girl with tenderness and understanding. Balancing the heroine and hero (another full-bodied portrait) is the Countess Morozova, Andrei's mother, a symbol for Mother Russia, old, wise, farseeing, fatalistic. She is given a remarkable monologue in the lydian mode.

Three fine portraits, then, but the outstanding virtue of the opera is not its principals but the atmosphere surrounding them. The use of the chorus in particular gives the work an unmistakably Russian color. Tchaikovsky's operas often lack the vigor, the form, and even the melodiousness of his orchestral works, and the composer's symphonic dramatic sense often deserts him in opera. But in one respect he can scarcely be faulted; he faithfully set *The Oprichnik* in old Russia and kept it there. He was following Glinka but he improved upon him too. Moussorgsky went further than Tchaikovsky in his abandonment of key signatures and his insistence on a kind of realistic declamation with a vocal line based on the actual inflections of the words—all after Dargomijsky—but in creation of national atmosphere and in truthful recreation of a past age he was forestalled and sometimes excelled by Tchaikovsky, as this forgotten work demonstrates.

CHAPTER 11

Piano Concerto
1874-1877

AT THIRTY-FOUR Tchaikovsky had begun to make his name in Russia; his Second Symphony, *The Tempest,* his quartets, his songs, and to a certain extent *The Oprichnik,* had established him in general favor. He was by no means considered a "great" composer but as a very sympathetic one who happened to be a Russian without making an embarrassing parade of it. He could be reasonably sure of a public hearing for anything he wrote and quite sure that Jurgenson would print it.

So far, so good; but Russia, musically speaking, still lagged far behind the West. *The Oprichnik,* for example, was given single performances in Kiev and Odessa as well as one or two at Moscow and there its possibilities ended. The number of people from whom concert audiences could be drawn was, compared with any Western country or the United States, pitifully small and the hold of Western music was still very strong; Italian opera continued to be socially "the thing," and programs of concerts remained 90 per cent foreign.

Russian composers were therefore driven to look to the West for fame and fortune, and in this respect Tchaikovsky had not moved one inch since he began to write music; he was to all intents and purposes unknown beyond his own frontiers and not much played inside them, "popular" though he was supposed to be. He was not destined to conquer the foreigner by one dramatic flourish but he was on the point of securing a foothold, and a few weeks before the premiere of *The Oprichnik* he met the man who was to make the step possible.

This man was Hans von Bülow. He arrived in Moscow in March, 1874, to give a series of recitals. Many of the people who crammed the Bolshoi to hear his first recital no doubt did so to stare at the man whose wife, Cosima, daughter of Liszt, had left him for Wagner five years earlier—a European *cause célèbre* made specially piquant by the fact that von Bülow had studied under both men, one for the piano, the other for conductorship, and revered them both.

To the musical members of the audience he was known as one of the most renowned opera conductors in the world and one of the finest pianists. To Tchaikovsky his playing and his manner at the keyboard were a revelation, for he was the first of what may be called the restrained virtuosos. Instead of pounding the piano, he played it, as Tchaikovsky said, "with mastery, taste, and a remarkable gift for conveying objectively the spirit and mood of a composition." In appearance as in manner he was a scholar; the long hair of Liszt and Rubinstein had been discarded and replaced by a Louis Napoleon beard; everything about him bespoke intellect governing feeling.

Unlike many visiting virtuosos from the West, von Bülow interested himself in local talent; he met Tchaikovsky (they had in common an education in law) and awed the younger man who was fascinated by his wit and slightly alarmed by his caustic comments. Someone—it was certainly not Pyotr Ilyich and almost certainly Nikolai Rubinstein—showed him a group of pianoforte pieces Tchaikovsky had written a few months earlier. Von Bülow took them away with him on his tour of Russia and by the time he had got to Kharkov was writing home, "This man Tchaikovsky is very talented; I am working on his Variations with a view to playing them."

He did play them and, not content with this, singled out Tchaikovsky in an article he wrote about his tour when he got home. He had, of course, picked the one piece of any value from the six published under the one opus number. One could say, of considerable value, because although Variations on an Original Theme are rarely played today they are excellent in themselves and indicate plainly that in Tchaikovsky the musical world had found one of its great variation writers, perhaps the greatest. He was not to be an outstanding writer for pianoforte solo but his genius for variations shines out even in this uncongenial medium.

2

For the moment the brief rapport with von Bülow seemed to have faded away. Tchaikovsky did not forget, however. For a few months after his return from Italy (a fruitless visit since *A Life For The Tsar* was constantly postponed and he never heard it), he was entirely taken up with one of his most unhappy ideas, the opera after Gogol called *Vakula The Smith*. This formed the subject of a prize contest in honor of Serov (who had died in 1871 before he could begin work on it) and which offered one thousand rubles for the best entry and five hundred for the second best.

Tchaikovsky wanted the money—he dreamed always of escape from the Conservatoire—and even more wanted to write the opera he believed he had in him, but he was no business man and failed entirely to get the prize conditions into his head. The first condition and the most important was that the score should be delivered by August, 1875. He misread the date, tore at the opera in a frenzy, and triumphantly finished it in August, 1874. Having discovered his mistake, he could not endure the thought of his work lying idle a whole year and impulsively wrote to his friend G. P. Kondratyev, the Chief Regisseur of the Maryinsky, asking him to sound Napravnik as to whether the opera could not be mounted right away regardless of the prize.

This brought on his head general wrath from the prize judges and he received a sharp and rather suspicious letter from Napravnik, pointing out that he had no rights in the libretto and that such a request was dishonorable. His reply was absolutely typical of the man and banished any remnant of ill-feeling in Petersburg; it was not so much an explanation—"performance of the opera means much more to me than prize money"—as a reproof couched in the terms which made him so difficult to quarrel with: "Why couldn't you simply have asked Kondratyev to tell me what an ass I'd made of myself instead of imagining unworthy motives that never even entered my head?"

For the next year or more he was to wait with burning impatience for the fate of his opera to be decided and his letters are full of it. Fortunately for everyone he could not do anything about it and was obliged to turn to something else, and so, almost by accident, his first world-famous work came into existence.

The first open news of what he was doing was given in a letter to Anatoly: "I am at the moment completely absorbed by a pianoforte concerto which I am most anxious shall be played by Rubinstein. It is not going well—very slow progress—but I am sticking to it and manage to hammer passages for the instrument out of my brain."

The millions who have heard this first Piano Concerto must wonder not only why it came so hard to Tchaikovsky—"I bite my nails to the quick, smoke endless cigarettes, and walk up and down the room for hours before an idea comes to me"—but why he did not think of writing a concerto long before. There was no lack of examples; in addition to Beethoven's five, his god Mozart had written more than twenty—half of them entrancing concertos; Schumann's one and Liszt's two were both well known to him; and it seems likely that he must have heard the work of the man who was to become his greatest rival for European popularity, Brahms.

His feeling that he must carry on the work of Glinka literally was chiefly responsible for holding Tchaikovsky back from his right paths. He was not a man to be confined to any one branch of composition and he proved that he could write great works in every genre, but much of the time given to opera must be considered lost. Yet it does not seem that to the end of his life he ever fully realized that one could continue the work of Glinka without writing opera, and that he had in fact continued the master's work in almost all directions so successfully that Russian music had become known and loved all over the world.

What finally set him on the track of the piano concerto was the remembrance of the very effective use of the piano with orchestra in the accompaniment to the first of Lel's songs. And— irony could scarcely go further—he only recalled this to the point of doing anything about it because he found himself at a loss when *Vakula The Smith* was completed a year before time; like nature he abhored a vacuum.

In spite of his difficulties with the concerto at the outset he soon found himself very much at home in it, and in the end wrote the whole work before the end of the year. He had Rubinstein in mind all the time and wrote the piano part with a view to his special gifts as pianist. Naturally he dedicated the concerto to him. As naturally, he kept Rubinstein informed and on Christmas Eve of 1874, just before he, Rubinstein, and N. A. Hubert (one of his fellow students at the Petersburg Conservatoire who had followed him to Moscow as a professor) went off to spend the evening with Albrecht, they arranged that he should play it through to them in one of the classrooms.

The result of this first run through the concerto has become one of the best known stories in the history of music. Tchaikovsky was to describe the scene three years later. "I played the first movement. Not one word was said—absolute silence. Do you know the awkward and humiliating feeling one has when offering someone a meal cooked by oneself which he eats without a word? . . . But somehow I restrained myself and played to the end of the concerto. I finished and waited. Still not a word. I got up from the piano. 'Well?' I said. Then a torrent burst from Rubinstein, gentle at first, and gathering volume till it exploded in fury. My concerto was worthless and unplayable, the passages so broken, disconnected, and badly written that they were beyond mending. The work was bad, trivial, vulgar. In some parts I had stolen from others. Only one or two pages had any value, the rest must be destroyed or rewritten."

At this point Rubinstein sat down at the piano and demonstrated the unplayability of the score, turning round to Tchaikovsky and Hubert from time to time with: *"That,* for instance," "What does *this* mean?" "How could anyone possibly play such a passage?" and so on until Tchaikovsky went out of the room.

"I couldn't have said a word, I was so angry, so shaken. Rubinstein soon followed me and, seeing how upset I was, motioned me into another room. There he said the same things all over again, pointing out the revisions necessary. He added that he would certainly play the concerto if I made the alterations he wanted. I replied, "I shan't alter a note. I shall publish it as it stands."

It was at this point that Tchaikovsky remembered von Bülow. He reacted to the double blow—of Rubinstein's inexplicable attitude and the loss of a first performance with Rubinstein as soloist—with a defiant gesture. He scratched out the dedication to his friend and sent the score to von Bülow with an offer of a dedication if he thought the work worthy of sponsorship.

This act was more timely than Tchaikovsky could have dreamed. All he knew was that von Bülow had played his Variations nine months earlier and had said some kind things about his work. What he did not know was that von Bülow had been going into his work more carefully and with most gratifying result. He too had gone to see *A Life For The Tsar* at La Scala and, having greater patience than Tchaikovsky, had stayed in Milan until it was actually staged. Back in Germany, he wrote an article in the *Allgemeine Musikalische Zeitung* about the music he had heard in Italy. He dealt with *A Life for the Tsar,* then added, "At the moment we only know of one other Russian who strives and aspires like Glinka and whose works, though they have not yet reached full maturity, promise with certainty that the maturity is not far away. I speak of the young professor of composition at the Moscow Conservatoire—Tchaikovsky. One of his splendid string quartets has already been played with success in many German towns and many other of his works deserve equal recognition—his compositions for pianoforte, for example, his two symphonies and his extremely interesting overture to *Romeo and Juliet* which is both original and extraordinarily melodious."

Von Bülow ended: "Because of his many-sidedness this composer is in no danger of being neglected outside his own country as Glinka was."

Von Bülow saw what Tchaikovsky did not: that he could become the natural successor to Glinka without following Glinka precisely, that indeed he would succeed where Glinka had failed precisely because of his excursions into other fields than opera. When the score of the Piano Concerto reached him, the German was at once captivated. It was, he declared, the most perfect thing by Tchaikovsky he had seen. "The ideas are lofty, strong, and original. The details, though profuse, do not obscure the work as a whole and are most interesting. The form is perfect, mature, and redolent of style, that best of styles in which intention and craftsmanship are everywhere concealed."

He ended by accepting the dedication and by offering to take the concerto with him on an American tour he was to make that autumn. In Boston in October, 1875, he played the work as promised.

The Americans have always been noted for their appreciation of the modern. At that time, in 1875, they had no musical tradition of their own and were regarded by most Europeans as, artistically speaking, mere savages—the long and bitter caricature in *Martin Chuzzlewit* faithfully represented the feeling of the Old World towards the New. Yet the Americans already were offering virtuosi the most lucrative tours and their audiences were showing an enthusiasm which outrivalled the blasé Europeans. It was only justice that their freshness of approach should be rewarded by the honor—as it afterwards appeared—of providing the first

world performance of what was to become one of the most popular works of classical music.

The critics had certain reservations, specially with the first
movement which, one thought, "lacked a central idea around
which to assemble the host of musical fantasies which make up
the breezy and ethereal whole" and singled out, to the amusement
of the composer, "syncopation in the trills, spasmodic interrup-
tions of the subject and thundering octave passages in the finale."
The audiences had no reservations whatever. Von Bülow's reception was so emotional in Boston that he cabled the good news to
Tchaikovsky. When he played the work in New York under
Leopold Damrosch the next month his reception was even more
fervent and he wrote to a friend: "It was a distinct success and is
to be repeated next Saturday. In fact Tchaikovsky has become
popular in the New World."

How popular this work had made him at one blow—for scarcely
anyone in America had heard a note of his music before—he understood when von Bülow sent him press cuttings: "Just imagine
the capacity these Americans have for musical appreciation—after
every performance von Bülow had to repeat *the entire finale*," he
told Rimsky-Korsakov, with whom he had begun a correspondence. He added gloomily, "Such a thing could never happen
here."

His prophecy was proved only too correct when the concerto
was played, first in Petersburg on December 1, 1875, then in Moscow two days later with Sergei Taneyev as soloist—only his second
appearance on a public concert platform. The work was received
enthusiastically by the public but in almost every case was politely damned by the critics. In general they echoed Rubinstein,
though more temperately, and Laroche stood for almost all when
he summed up: "It is unrewarding for pianists and has no future." That this remark was a criticism of the inadequate technique of the pianists of his day and a compliment to an original
composer, Laroche did not see—not until the work had become
one of the glories of Russia.

The concerto is a refreshing proof of the fact that in the long run the public knows a good thing and will have it whatever its mentors tell them. The one unfortunate aspect of the concerto's popularity is that it too often rules out performance of works not less worthy, though less obviously so—one thinks in this connection of Tchaikovsky's splendid Second Concerto.

There is of course a sound reason for this, the reason why the Mozart A Major Concerto is played far more often than any other of the many great concertos by that master. That is, its thematic felicities. One essential attribute of the great composer is the ability to write good tunes and Tchaikovsky excelled in this respect; in the B Flat Minor Concerto, just as in Mozart's A Major Concerto, there is not one indifferent or ordinary theme.

For the rest, von Bülow's analysis can scarcely be bettered. The obvious merits of the work have often been pointed out but it is filled with minor felicities too, such as the little second movement cadenza, a piece of writing for pianoforte at least fifty years ahead of its time, and the witty comments by the woodwinds. In general its enduring popularity stems from its summing up of the entire romantic movement which in this unromantic age men and women regard nostalgically. It is written throughout with great panache and is a masterly demonstration of the art that conceals art; it covers a great range of emotion and expression, it is fiery, tender, impassioned, lyrical and, above all, it is essentially noble.

3

In the six months or so which elapsed between the finishing of this concerto and its first performance Tchaikovsky worked almost without a break. He did so partly to take his mind off *Vakula The Smith* which obsessed him to the point of telling Anatoly, "If it doesn't change my luck I think I shall go mad. I'm not interested in the prize, I despise it even though the money would not be a bad thing to have, what I want is to get my opera performed."

As the winner of the prize, and so the performance, would not be known for the best part of a year, something had to be done to keep down his rising anxiety. Work was the answer and he had not long finished the concerto than the answer appeared—or seemed to appear—in a most gratifying commission from the Imperial Opera to write a ballet on the theme of Swan Lake. "I accepted the invitation," he told Rimsky-Korsakov, "because I could do with the money but also because I have wanted for a long time to try my hand at this kind of music."

The reader, who knows what Tchaikovsky did not, will think this a most inadequate statement, particularly when one recalls the little sketch of this very ballet written for his nieces some years earlier, but the flatness of the composer's epistolary style—so often directly opposed to his music—is misleading. What Tchaikovsky wanted was to write the music in the appropriate place so that he could get the right atmosphere.

He had, besides, already determined to write another symphony, and it was this that he got down to the moment he left for Usovo at the end of the Conservatoire term, having finally despatched the score of *Vakula* to Petersburg. Between the completion of the concerto and the beginning of his holiday he had written some notable things—the "Serenade Melancolique" for violin and orchestra, a sort of preparation, pleasant but rather thin, for the violin concerto he was soon to compose, and a group of songs, melancholy too but including the powerful "Corals."

By the time he left Usovo late in June the symphony was sketched out, and he began to orchestrate it right away at his next port of call. This was one of his favorite country places, the estate of a wealthy amateur of music, N. D. Kondratyev, at Nizi in Kharkov Province.

He finished the orchestration at his sister's house by the end of July. Nizi was roughly halfway between Usovo and Kamenka, so that Tchaikovsky progressed farther from Moscow as the summer deepened. It was convenient to travel that way but it also expressed his wishes, for he always preferred to end his summer break with Alexandra.

He did not travel alone. He had with him his "beloved Dinochka," the nine-year-old daughter of Kondratyev who was so devoted to him that he had not the heart to leave her at Nizi. Besides, she loved Kamenka almost as much as he. She found Alexandra "bewitching and with all the charm and fascination of Pyotr Ilyich" and she managed to support his absence or the loss of his sole company (they used to take long walks together at Nizi) by cultivating Alexandra: "who looked amazingly like him." Besides, to come to Kamenka after the quiet of her father's house was a never failing joy; the household was always lively and "time passed like lightning in this merry circle."

This time Alexandra was not at Kamenka (which was owned by the elder Davidov) but at nearby Verbovka to which she had moved to better accommodate her now large family. Here, after Tchaikovsky had finished orchestrating the symphony, he wrote the Prologue and first act of *Swan Lake* in two weeks.

The speed of composition tells its own story. At Verbovka were not only Alexandra and her children and husband but Ilya Petrovich and his wife and Anatoly, and Tchaikovsky was doubly happy, in the heart of the Ukraine and of his family. He was to write a revealing letter to Alexandra a year later which can be quoted now since it explains his feelings in the summer of 1875 and so explains the sense of effortless felicity in the *Swan Lake* score.

The letter was caused by a sad one from his sister. In her way she was as sensitive as Pyotr Ilyich, and a harsh word from her husband or an unloving one from her children was enough to drive her to the depths of self-abasement. "My darling," he replied, "you probably weren't very well when you wrote. The note of heartfelt melancholy in your letter is only too well known to me. With me too there are hours, days, weeks—yes, even months— when everything looks black and I am tormented by the thought that I am forsaken and that none loves me. And why should they?

What use am I to anyone? If I vanished from this earth today it would be no great loss to Russian music and no great loss to any-one personally. . . . But for *you* to give way to depression, *you* who are indispensable, who make the happiness of us all—this I find incredible. How can you for a moment doubt that everyone who knows you loves and admires you? How could anyone *not* love you? No, there is none in the world more dearly loved. For me to speak of my love for you would be absurd. I love you far above everyone else in the world—you, your family, my brothers and our old father. And I love you all, not because you are my relatives but because you are the best people in the world."

This has the air of an infatuated man even in a country where partiality for one's family was the rule rather than the exception, yet his view of the Tchaikovskys was widely held. Ilya Petrovich was loved wherever he went, Ippolit was a highly popular officer on his ship, Nikolai was respected for his uprightness and good sense, Anatoly was winning golden opinions in his office, and Modest had enormous charm as his career was to prove. Alexandra had one of the loveliest characters and natures imaginable; every-body who met her responded instantly to her goodness. Pyotr Ilyich the reader will know for himself. Many witnesses can be produced, including the entire Conservatoire staff, but perhaps one of the best is the young Nadezhda Kondratyeva. She was to know and love her hero to the day of his death and when grown up was always included in the after-theatre supper parties and dinners he gave whenever he was in Petersburg. Here she met "all the most interesting theater and musical people in the city." For a young woman fascinated by the arts these artistes must have had a magnetism that the Tchaikovskys, whom she had known most of her life, could not possibly offer. Yet in her account of Tchaikovsky's social life in Petersburg she goes out of her way to add that members of his family were always included in these parties when in town and that she found one and all "notable for their unusual likeableness."

To Tchaikovsky this had been gospel from the moment he

learned to feel and observe at Votkinsk, and in this mood, surrounded by the people he loved in the country he loved, he wrote the first half of *Swan Lake*.

Back in Moscow that autumn he soon heard that his opera had won the prize and would be produced at some unspecified date. This news virtually coincided with von Bülow's triumphant cable from Boston, but so little are men unable to judge their own work that most of Tchaikovsky's joy was given to the promised presentation of the opera rather than the actual promise of world fame in the American reception of his concerto.

A few weeks later his Third Symphony had its first performance by Nikolai Rubinstein. Tchaikovsky was in Petersburg at the time but heard the symphony when he returned and wrote rather coolly about it to Rimsky-Korsakov. "I can't see any specially happy ideas in the work but its form is an advance in the right direction. I like the first movement and the Scherzi best."

The public was mildly enthusiastic, though not to the point of demanding repeat performances, and the critics differed. The work was not destined to hold concert audiences and today it is rarely played. This virtual extinction is too severe—the first movement ought to be heard often—but the symphony in D Major is an undeniable disappointment after the high promise of its predecessor.

It is curious that Tchaikovsky should feel happy about the form because that is just what worries so many listeners. The two scherzi are a stumbling block to the purist but, this apart, most people would probably agree that this work should have been called the First Suite instead of the Third Symphony—though it must be added that this definition could be regarded as a slur on the suites he was to write. One of the most valid criticisms of the symphony is that it does not hang together, that there is no true progression or development of thought—in short, that it is not symphonic. If Tchaikovsky had an idea or feeling which insisted on expression, it does not emerge. His letters, often so explanatory of the music he is writing, do not help here.

The symphony was to be the only one he was to write in a major key and seems to prove that he was happier in the minor which offers so many more opportunities for dramatic effect. Yet no one could quarrel with the Introduzione e Allegro. Throughout it is Tchaikovsky almost at his best, introducing three disarming themes—all highly characteristic—and handling their very complicated and interesting development with equally disarming ease. It is a bright, cheerful, melodious movement, a pleasure to hear from first bar to last.

From this impressive opening, unhappily, the work degenerates. The Alla tedesca is the first of the scherzi, placed unusually before the Andante; it is reminiscent of the waltzes made famous in Vienna but is altogether too slight to form the basis of a symphonic movement, though not without charm. A pale shadow of the Tchaikovsky of the future emerges in the Andante elegiaco, a nostalgic theme merging into dim suggestions of a ghostly waltz. A shadow indeed, for there are obvious echoes of Delibes and the theme is banal.

The fourth movement, a true Scherzo, is Tchaikovsky in reverse, the lover of speed and bustle, but is again built on overslight material and the best of it is not his own but taken unashamedly from Kreisleriana. The composer does not recover his grip in the Finale. He uses a Polonaise—hence the symphony's title The Polish which was not his—but the theme is one of his poorest and its development is unsurprising and uninspired. The movement could be described, a little unkindly, as a ragbag of tricks, ending with the inevitable contrapuntal treatment of the main theme.

One conclusion will be reached by many listeners, that this symphony is a mournful example of what happens when a composer is technically advanced and emotionally retarded. By this time there was not much Tchaikovsky did not know about the handling of an orchestra but there was a lot he did not know about life. Within a year or two he was to grow up painfully and all his magnificent equipment as a symphonist was to flower into the Fourth Symphony.

One further point about the Third Symphony. It has been described, like so much of Tchaikovsky's work, as primarily ballet music. It is true that echoes of the great ballets to come are often heard. But the description is commonly used as a reproach. Later on, Tchaikovsky was to deal with his critics and demolish them. Here it need only be pointed out that ballet music, as Tchaikovsky conceived and wrote it, became for the first time symphonic. That was his great gift to ballet, to compose music for it in the grand manner—in the symphonic manner. So that when ballet music can be read into the Third Symphony it is no discredit either to ballet or symphony; in the hands of Tchaikovsky the two were to become one.

The symphony and the piano concerto were heard in Moscow by a distinguished visitor, Camille Saint-Saëns, who was to play and conduct his own works in the two capitals. He met Tchaikovsky at a reception—the change in the Russian's status at home was shown by the fact that he was one of the first to be introduced to all visitors of moment—and the men took a fancy to each other. The forty-year-old Saint-Saëns, five years older than Tchaikovsky, was the antithesis of the Russian, small, vivacious, amusing in a brittle way, and the tall, strong, unassuming Pyotr Ilyich admired him as usual for all that he himself did not possess and as a famous representative of his mother's nation. He thought at first that Saint-Saëns was beginning a new era in music, combining the elegance and wit of the French with the solidity of the Germans, a superficial judgment owing a great deal to the visitor's charm (he was like another Nikolai Rubinstein) and his formidable technical equipment.

The meetings between them were not notable for anything creative in music; Saint-Saëns understood the originality of *Romeo and Juliet* well enough to propose an entire Tchaikovsky concert in Paris as an excuse to play the work—"*Cela l'a posé, cette overture*"—but the compliment carried its own criticism of the rest of the composer's output. The notable fact about their brief friendship is the view it provides of a side of Tchaikovsky almost buried beneath the weight of evidence of the serious and painfully sensitive man. This other side was very much alive, however; it was the Tchaikovsky who had drawn appreciative audiences to the *dacha* in Petersburg to see him take off the Maryinsky ballerinas with lighthearted deviltry, the Tchaikovsky who played the fool with Nikolai Rubinstein, who larked with his nieces and nephew so youthfully that they would not let him go, the romping, hugely popular Tchaikovsky of the Kamenka village dances. So the story, though so well known, must be repeated: he and Saint-Saëns together wrote a little ballet *Pygmalion and Galatea* and danced it themselves on the Conservatoire stage with Rubinstein accompanying—Tchaikovsky as Pygmalion, Saint-Saëns as Galatea.

To meet a Frenchman was quite enough to turn Tchaikovsky's mind westward, and he celebrated the winning of the opera competition by a short trip to Paris that winter. He used the break to see Modest who had caused him little but trouble ever since he left the Law School and indeed at the school too. Tchaikovsky took his self-imposed responsibilities towards the twins with an earnestness that would surely have caused Alexandra Andreyevna to raise languid eyebrows. He had not been particularly well repaid but the affection both undoubtedly felt for him seemed reward enough. He agonized often and uselessly. Probably the money he was always sending them—money he certainly could not afford—did more harm than good.

Of the two Anatoly was the steadier. His trouble was a perpetual restlessness; wherever his job took him he always discovered that he wanted to be somewhere else. This meant a letter to Petya asking for help. Like most young men brought up in a capital city he abhorred the thought of a provincial town, and his brother was forever trying to get him out of them.

Shortly before the visit to Paris just such an occasion had happened. Anatoly, posted to Kiev three months earlier, demanded that he be removed to one of the capitals. Tchaikovsky at once got to work for him. He shot up to Petersburg for a couple of days—the excuse was Shilovsky, ill and begging a visit. "I wanted to be incognito but on Nevsky I met Ditlova and though I took to my heels she spotted me and soon everyone knew I was there. However I didn't go to see anyone except Balakirev, Apukhtin, and Adamov."

The last visit was as much for Anatoly as for himself—both men being in the law—and he persuaded his old friend to write to Anatoly's chief in Moscow, Motovilov. As soon as he got back to Moscow he followed up the Adamov letter with a personal call—several, in fact, as Motovilov was hard to catch.

When at last tracked down, Motovilov proved more sensible than any of the Tchaikovskys; there was some plain speech which Pyotr Ilyich toned down as best he could: "He promised not to forget you but added that it wouldn't do you any harm to stay at Kiev for at least a year. . . . I left him with misgivings but don't lose hope, I'll write to Adamov today."

In this same letter he told Anatoly not for the first time, "I have had a very silly letter from Modest" and had no sooner sealed his own letter than he was writing one to Modest. "I'm told you have done something very dishonorable and nasty. I don't yet know what it is but I know your character well, you are so spineless that you will do absolutely anything to be able to go on the spree and have a good time." And he added a familiar cry of "Ah, Modka! I'm seriously worried about you. Have you forgotten already how I spoke to you about your utter lack of purpose, the way you never think of doing something with your life. For heaven's sake do consider your future instead of always trying to enjoy yourself."

Modest was a playboy and rather unscrupulous. He had got into bad company at school and never got out of it, much to Tchaikovsky's distress, until suddenly, moved by some quirk (which could have been unpayable debts), he found a job as tutor to a deaf and dumb boy, Nikolai (Kolya) Konradi and took him to Lyons for treatment for deafness.

Tchaikovsky went to Paris chiefly to call at Lyons and see whether Modest was pulling his weight as tutor but his trip was memorable for the birth of a lifelong passion for Bizet—he went into raptures over *Carmen* at the Opera Comique—and for the beginnings of another quartet.

Back in Moscow, he worked hard; by March the quartet was finished. It was played five times within the next few weeks. As this indicates, it was immediately appreciated but Tchaikovsky was not pleased with it and talked gloomily of having written himself out. He was mistaken as time has proved; this Quartet in E Flat Minor is the best of his string quartets.

In one sense the work is a little unbalanced. It was dedicated to the memory of Ferdinand Laub, the violinist for whom Tchaikovsky had written the "Serenade Melancolique," and as a compliment to the dead man the composer threw the onus of every movement on to the first violin. Like so many of his works, the quartet has become famous for one movement, the Andante Funebre, but this partiality of the public does real disservice to the rest of the quartet as well as giving quite the wrong impression of its mood. Though written as an elegy the general tone of the work is serene and even joyful—not the joy of the thoughtless but the joy of a man who is coming to terms with himself about the problems of life and death.

The first movement opens and closes as an Andante sostenuto, a kind of mourning theme, but so free from morbidity as to be undisturbedly beautiful, and is broken by a lyrical Allegro moderato portraying by strong syncopated rhythms man's refusal to accept death as the end. The Scherzo-Allegretto is marked vivo e scherzando and is one of the most brilliant little movements Tchaikovsky ever wrote for strings, fiery, fanciful, and bubbling over with so many ideas so briefly treated that the listener is as much tantalized as fascinated. This is the Tchaikovsky who danced the ballet with Saint-Saëns, gay, defiant, determined to enjoy life while he had it.

It may be mentioned here that Tchaikovsky was the most meticulous of composers; he gave no excuse for wrong tempi on the part of performers or conductors, going so far as to include metronome markings on his scores. The third and best known movement of this third quartet is a case in point; it is marked Andante funebre e doloroso, ma con moto. All the weight is given to the first violin which sings the funeral march, a plaintive melody of infinite charm, sad but never hopeless, never sentimental. The Finale, an allegro, lifts one at once into the village dance measure so much loved by the composer, brisk, vigorous, full of gaiety and with sparkling tunes. It is not namby-pamby stuff and has offended some critics just as the clown's dance in Snyegrochka offended them, as vulgar. It is vulgar in the true meaning of that word; in the phrase of a more discerning critic it has a real "whiff of village streets."

The quartet is a model in the writing of an elegiac work; it is not stuffed with dripping sentiment but is manly, thoughtful, positive, keeping a memory alive, not burying it. It is also a lesson in how to stress the importance and value of the first violin without overloading the part to the point of formlessness. It has always been regarded as his best work for string quartet and as proof that he was never content to rest in his tracks.

The quartet completed, he turned back to Swan Lake and finished it most suitably deep in the country that Easter. He did not pause, he was in a rage of work, and at once began a symphonic poem on Francesca da Rimini. He had toyed with the idea of making an opera on this Dante theme but disliked the libretto when he read it and abruptly abandoned the opera in favor of a symphonic work.

He did not rest until summer when he went abroad again, first to see Modest and his pupil at Lyons and to take the waters at Vichy—without effect, he thought—then to move to Bayreuth for the festival. There he met Wagner and Liszt (whom he found amiable but something of an actor) and groaned his way through The Ring in company with Rubinstein, Laroche, and Cui. He was there in the capacity of critic for his Moscow journal as well as a Russian composer who, he was gratified to discover, was not entirely unknown in the West. His report to the journal was a model of fairmindedness, his private opinion was refreshingly blunt. "After the last chords of the Götterdämmerung had ended and we were allowed to go I felt as though I had come out of prison. *The Nibelungen* may be a great work of art—it is possible —but it is certainly a crashing bore; it goes on far too long."

The music evidently proved together too much for Laroche. He had become a heavy drinker but at Bayreuth, "he is drunk from morning to night." Tchaikovsky's effort to occupy his mind was unsuccessful: "I threw him together with Cui only to see them quarrel after a couple of hours."

He went back very happily to Russia feeling that he was breathing a purer air in every sense of the word in the heart of it, Kamenka. And there he unleashed a minor bombshell.

4

The atmosphere of domestic happiness was too much for him that summer and he announced to Modest an underlined "I have decided to get married."

This sounded tolerably definite but would not cause much of a flutter in the family dovecot, as he knew, he had been talking for years about marriage so he added, "This decision is irrevocable"—as much to nerve himself to the act as to stop family discussions.

Alexandra, Lyov, Modest, and Anatoly all protested because they foresaw disaster if Pyotr Ilyich married without love, simply to get a home life. Many men could and did marry "sensibly" and made a success of it, but the sensitive, romantic Tchaikovsky who had adored a highly romantic soprano was not of this type much though he insisted on his strong common sense.

The subject was debated, heatedly at times, through the summer holiday and beyond it; when he returned to Moscow he was followed by an agitated letter from Alexandra, to which he answered, "Don't worry about my marriage, my angel. It is a long way ahead, certainly not before next year." He then added, ruining all his attempt at consolation, "Next month I shall begin to look about me."

He was to explain this decision in a letter to Modest which has become notorious; the purpose was to stop Moscow gossip. He claimed that he wanted to save his family and friends from the disgrace of having him publicly branded as a homosexual.

There is no doubt that this was his main preoccupation; letter after letter expresses his conviction that all the people he loved might be "ruined"—he uses this word often—by the connection with him. His imagination was lively; he visualized his brothers forced to resign their posts, Alexandra and Lyov socially snubbed, and their children's future blemished, and the last years of his father and stepmother blighted. But he was thinking of his music too. If, as seemed only too possible to him, he was hounded out of the Conservatoire how would he get his compositions played? The official view of homosexuality was strict and at moments he lived in dread of sudden arrest and shameful imprisonment. He owed his years of immunity to the good and powerful friends he had made. But could even they protect him if the growing rumors threatened the good name of the Conservatoire?

The decision to marry was not sudden; it had been forming in his mind for years, as far back as the understanding with Artot six years earlier. They had been years of steadily increasing bouts of wretchedness as he realized that what he had once taken so lightly had become an unmanageable force that might bring him and everyone he loved down in shame.

A conclusion of this kind is slow to mature—everything in a man's mind tempts him to ignore or underrate it. Tchaikovsky had good reason to play down his fears. If one judges by the evidence of his early letters he was like many teen-agers and young men; his inclinations were bisexual. The first open references to his homosexuality occur, as expected, in the years immediately following his graduation from the Law School. The references are all carefree, those of a young man sowing his wild oats. At the same time he is flirting often and persistently with the young women of his circle and writing of them with the kind of besotted devotion common to "bloods" of the day.

Obviously it has never entered his head that the first inclination might destroy the second. If he thought much about the matter—and there is no sign that he did—he plainly assumed, in the style of numberless boys and young men, that this delightful indulgence would prove superfluous and indeed tame in the course of nature—that is, when he had the money to marry, met the right girl, and began to raise a family, his homosexual impulse would fade away. Certainly he never dreamed for a moment that he might not enoy the domestic life he loved with a passion rare even in the purely heterosexual male.

In this he differentiates himself sharply from the true homosexual to whom the thought of sleeping with a woman and begetting children would be a form of nightmare. What he anticipated so lightheartedly in those Petersburg days was not unreasonable; nine out of ten young men who carry schooldays' homosexuality into their late teens and early twenties find the habit dies imperceptibly and painlessly when they fall in love with a girl and marry her.

There is no reason to suppose that Tchaikovsky's sexual life would not have followed this normal pattern. That it did not was due to a stroke of irony, an irony so cruel that it was to preoccupy him for the rest of his life with the workings of fate in human lives. This irony was nothing less than his decision to follow the great love of his youth and take up music professionally.

The decision was a late one—he was twenty-two when he joined the Petersburg Conservatoire—and in practical terms meant that the safe and marriageable income he would soon have reached in the civil service was reduced to a pittance barely enough to keep him alive.

The crucial years began when he went to Moscow as professor. He was then twenty-six, very badly paid (marriage was out of the question), and very lonely. In this he differs from the average young man who reacts positively to fresh surroundings and flourishes on his own. Tchaikovsky was ambitious too but with him ambition always came a poor second to affection. He was deeply feeling to a degree few could rival. When he moved to Moscow he lost his best and surest hold on a normal sexual life, his family.

A man of twenty-six in those days was sexually mature, was expected to settle down, and usually wanted to settle down. Tchaikovsky was no exception to the rule; his wish to settle down was even greater than the norm. But he had not the money, he had not any reasonable prospect of earning enough money for many years. His sexual desires were strong. Failing marriage, the delightful pastime of Petersburg became a necessity in Moscow. The one or two Petersburg friends with whom he had enjoyed himself were no longer available. The inevitable happened. Love of some kind he had to have. He began to pay for it.

From that moment he was lost. No man will admit that he is lost. For years Tchaikovsky kept up the pretence of normality; he talked about marriage, wrote about it, dreamed of it, longed for it, tried to convince himself that only money and the right woman were lacking and that in time he would have both. He was helped in the illusion by the undeniable fact that for several years his salary in Moscow remained utterly inadequate to support two people let alone a family, and that he loved women and children and the idea of a home with ever greater fervor.

But a Tchaikovsky—extraordinarily sensitive, self-analytical, physically fastidious—could not live a secret life which he felt to be reprehensible, weak, and disgusting without extreme reactions. In these first Moscow years his letters begin to reveal his sufferings.

Yet he was not fully committed to homosexuality until the unsuccessful understanding with Artot when he was twenty-nine. After that he seems not to have abandoned hope so much as relaxed guard. It is from this time that the first of his begging notes date. All his Moscow friends received them. Not all this money— for he seems never to have been refused—went on those expensive luxuries, the twins in Petersburg, old nurses and governesses, and the hundred and one small charities he was busy about. Nor was it all absorbed by the alcohol he was drinking increasingly to try to stun his uneasiness and misery. He no longer made a secret of his vice, as it had become, nor did he try to justify it; he confessed freely and often to all these good friends, almost all married and with families; he protested again and again that he wanted nothing better than to be like them.

The protests were genuine. For the tragedy of Tchaikovsky was not that he was homosexual but that he was a reluctant one. As his ravaged face, his prematurely white hair, agonized letters and deeply introvertive music show, the further he got into the toils of homosexuality the more he longed for the normal life that had once seemed so inevitable, for a wife, children, home. Not for him the arguments that what he did was highly civilized and sanctified by the Greeks, that he wanted nothing better. Whatever physical satisfaction he may have had was fleeting and left a dreadful sting. His attitude after the first years in Moscow was one of almost unrelieved self-disgust as both letters and diaries bear witness. The most he could find to say in extenuation was that he could not be held responsible for a bodily urge implanted in him by the Fate of which he thought so much and so bitterly.

The truth was that he had all the instincts of the bisexual but, owing perhaps to his long enforced celibacy, had lost a vital part of one, the ability or the will (it is difficult to separate them) to consummate marriage. Of course he suspected this some time before the 1875 announcement that he had decided "irrevocably" to marry but, feeling as he did, he dared not face its full implications. On the contrary he insisted that he needed only the "habit" of marriage to restore his sexual life to normal.

What he was forced to face as the years went on and his occasional homosexual excursions fastened into a virtually unbreakable desire were the repercussions on his family and friends. How he first came to hear of the growing Moscow rumors is not known. A professor in a college of music is fair game and he had a thou-

sand ways of learning, from anonymous notes to sotto voce remarks in class, that he was becoming the talk of the town.

This stirred him as nothing else could do. His letters began to
reflect the new terror. He no longer borrowed money with a joke
but a cry of fear. His loyal Moscow friends began to receive notes
such as, "Send me 15 silver rubles for God's sake and save me and
my family from certain ruin!"

They paid up uncomplainingly and, it seems, uncritically—they
were all very fond of him. Tchaikovsky paid in another fashion.
Living from hand to mouth, with exposure and disgrace hanging
over one day by day, night by night, would break a far less sensitive man. He made effort after effort to fight his homosexual instinct. He always failed; it had grown too strong. Then he loathed
himself because of this thing in him he could not conquer, an
unclean thing which, unless something were done and done
quickly, would kill his dreams of becoming one of Russia's great
composers and wreck the happiness and peace of mind of everyone
he loved.

And it was at this point, in the summer of 1875, that he announced his irrevocable decision to marry or—for the first time
in his life he admitted that marriage might be beyond him—"at
least form some public bond with a woman which would silence
contemptible creatures whose judgments mean nothing to me but
who have the power to hurt those I love."

5

His compositions went on regardless—which, incidentally, puts
his state of mind that summer and autumn in truer perspective—
and he worked hard at *Francesca da Rimini*. In the summer,
moved by the war between tiny Serbia and the Turkish Empire,
he had written "Marche Slave." It is a jingoistic piece of music,
unashamedly emotional, but is extremely well done and still has
the power to move even against one's will. *Francesca* is emotional
too but the love he gave it was quite another thing from his out-

burst of slavophilism. He finished it late in October and tried to get it put on right away in Petersburg but failed; it had to wait until the next year and by that time other matters had reduced its importance.

This work has become as popular as *Romeo and Juliet*. The subject is, superficially, similar and is treated just as brilliantly, with an array of unforgettable themes and a barrage of magnificent orchestral sound. In truth, Tchaikovsky here attacked a very different subject. Francesca is no Juliet, she is the languorous lover, the eternal temptress, the femme fatale, and remarkably— for his instincts were all towards the Juliet type of woman—he creates her without one false note.

When the music of *Francesca de Rimini* is not martially vigorous it is sultry, sensual, exotic, and at the risk of undue harping on argument it must be said that Tchaikovsky was to offer few better proofs than this symphonic poem that he was not a natural homosexual; otherwise, such a theme and such treatment of it would have been quite beyond him. But the final thought after a hearing of *Francesca,* as of so many of his major works, must be of his marvellous orchestration. The word is used advisedly, for he has a supple genius for wielding the orchestra rivalled only perhaps by Rimsky-Korsakov and one more fellow countryman then not born, Igor Stravinsky.

Another link with Stravinsky was forged a matter of days after *Francesca* was finished, for on December 6 the long-awaited premiere of *Vakula The Smith* was held at the Maryinsky and one of the major roles was taken by Stravinsky's father, Fyodor. Neither he nor anyone else in the cast could save this opera. Tchaikovsky had a sense of humor but it was not the kind needed for a comic opera. Throughout the Overture and the first scene he managed to keep up the fun and earned considerable applause. After that it was a tale of mounting disappointment for the audience and it ended with as many jeers as applause at the curtain calls. To complete his chagrin the composer overheard a comment during one of the intervals which summed up audience reaction: "I came here to amuse myself, not to be bored to tears."

Tchaikovsky's ability to divert every failure to himself—a refreshingly rare trait in creative men—was hard pressed when he had to admit failure once again; unlike his previous operas, in which he had lost faith before they were even staged, he attended the first performance of *Vakula* filled with optimism—a rare sensation buoyed up by a most unusual event, praise from Cui at the dress rehearsal.

Later, in his review of the first performance, Cui, who was perceptive when he was not being merely catty, put his finger on the fault of all Tchaikovsky operas up to date; the music was symphonic, not operatic, he wrote, and though often beautiful and always noble, did not match the action on stage. Tchaikovsky afterwards agreed with the criticism in toto. He did not take the hint, however; before leaving Petersburg he asked Stasov for a libretto for yet another opera, on Othello, and at first refused to accept Stasov's reaction, that the subject would not suit him. Later he dropped it, but not opera; he was merely biding his time.

For the moment he demonstrated both courage and his real gift in humor, for in spite of the failure of *Vakula* and of performances of *Romeo and Juliet* in Paris and Vienna, he immediately began work on Variations on a Rococo Theme. Nor was that the end of the surprise—one that he often has in store for the categorist of human behavior; the work does not bear a single trace of pique or sorrow.

This is the more surprising because the Rococo Variations were written for his friend W. K. F. Fitzenhagen, the noted cellist, who played in the Conservatoire quartet, and dedicated to him. It might be thought that of all composers Tchaikovsky would respond emotionally to the obvious manifestations of the cello and that anything he wrote for it would be luscious and sentimental to a degree. That is what we have been taught to think of Tchaikovsky. Instead, he showed the instrument in a new light, as graceful, witty, elegant, and himself as a man with a real sense of humor.

It has often been said that the Variations show Tchaikovsky in his most Mozartian light. It could be added, in his French style too and, of course, as a master of the variation form. This work can be heavily treated but if one hears, for example, Rostropovich play it under Rozhdestvensky, the full beauty of the composer's wit is brought out and from first bar to last it is a joy—economical, pithy, inventive. It is what is known as a light work, that is to say the composer is not plunging into the profound, merely enjoying himself. If all enjoyed themselves as Tchaikovsky did in the Rococo Variations, the world would be a more bearable place to live in.

The year of 1876 ended in comedy. Tolstoy visited Moscow and called on Tchaikovsky. To the composer, as to millions in Russia, Tolstoy was a god, the maker of the greatest novels ever written, and a psychologist to be dreaded. The honor of the visit was therefore clouded: "The great prober of the human heart must obviously possess the power of reading the inmost secrets of mine; I felt sure that neither the smallest weakness nor sin could escape his eye and that it would be useless to try to show him nothing but the best in me."

In such a mood Pyotr Ilyich braced himself for trouble, which, with his imagination, could end only by a contemptuous Tolstoy turning on his heel after expressing disgust at having come into contact with such a vile creature. He was right in thinking that his visitor had the power to make men tell the truth—everyone who met Tolstoy was agreed that under the scrutiny of those extraordinary eyes dissimulation was useless—but to his immense surprise Tchaikovsky passed muster. Typically, he did not once think that Tolstoy had found him worthy and interesting. No, for him, "evidently the great analyst of human nature did not consider me a fit subject for dissection but simply decided to chat about music."

Tolstoy, having satisfied himself at a glance, put the conversation, as always, on the other man's level. In his relief Tchaikovsky rebounded into criticism: "He seemed to enjoy depreciating Beethoven and even directly questioning his genius. This is an unworthy trait in a great man."

Tolstoy was not at all disturbed by his companion's agitation at this slight on the god of music. He attended a concert arranged in his honor by Rubinstein at which the Andante Cantabile from Tchaikovsky's First Quartet was played, freely wept during it to the unspeakable emotion of the composer sitting next to him, and, when he left, promised to make a collection of the folk songs of his region which he was sure "will become wonderful gems in your hands." And when, a few days later, he duly sent the songs, he added unregenerately, "for God's sake treat them in the Mozart-Handel style and not in the manner of the Beethoven-Schumann-Berlioz school which strives only after the sensational."

The comedy reached its height when, mastering his anger, Tchaikovsky dutifully looked through the songs. They were absolutely useless and his letter to Tolstoy informing him of this fact is a masterpiece of tact. "I must tell you frankly that the songs have been taken down by an unskillful hand and that almost all their original beauty has disappeared. The chief mistake is that they have been forced artificially into a regular rhythm. Only the Russian choral dances have a regularly accentuated measure; the legends (Bylini) have nothing in common with the dances. In addition, most of these songs have been written down in the cheerful key of D Major. This is quite out of keeping with the tonality of genuine Russian folk songs which are always in some indefinite key like the old church modes. . . . I could not make them into a folksong album because such songs must be taken down exactly as the people sing them. This is highly skilled work which calls for the most delicate musical perception as well as a thorough knowledge of musical history. With the exception of Balakirev—and possibly Prokunin—I know no one who really understands this work."

Having stated the fact, he added, "But your songs can be used as symphonic material—and very fine material too—which I shall certainly take advantage of."

6

Early in 1877 Tchaikovsky began to write his Fourth Symphony.
It was intended to deal in a more extensive form than ever before
with his preoccupation with the workings of fate. It can be no
surprise that Tchaikovsky's belief that he was born under an unlucky star had strengthened; and in truth many a less emotionally
introspective man than Pyotr Ilyich might justifiably have considered that fate had been sporting with him with particular
malice during the past three years.

At the beginning of 1874 he was poised ready for fame and
fortune, well established in his own country and on the point of
invading the West. Since that time he had written many works
he considered an advance on anything he had done before, but
apart from a success in the United States which had not been
followed up and one or two minor triumphs in Russia he seemed
to have slipped back everywhere. In England he remained little
known and even less thought of (the pianoforte concerto had
made no mark there), in Paris he had been frigidly received and
very badly played, and even in Germany where he had a staunch
champion in the powerful von Bülow neither critics nor public,
absorbed by Brahms, would take him seriously. In his own country he was in danger of being relegated to the position of the
second-rater who wrote pleasant but rather ineffective music, a
man who could not make the grade. Even critics formerly hostile
had begun to treat him leniently and this he well knew to be the
last stage of infirmity; when a man like Cui began to talk of his
nobility, he could almost write himself off.

This he was not for one moment prepared to do. He often said
and wrote the most absurd things—he was past his prime, written
out, not far from senile—and believed them at that moment, but
the letter posted, the speech made, he was once more the ambitious man conscious of his superiority to most living composers
and determined to give his music to the world. Yet there he was

in early 1877, nearly thirty-seven years old, the finest living composer in his own country and one of the finest in the world, but who would acknowledge it? He thought of Brahms, idolized in Germany and with a strong foothold in every civilized country, and felt as bitter as he was able.

There was, in short, every reason for a symphony which would try to express his feelings about the inexplicable, incalculable hand of chance, one of the strongest powers in man's life. Tchaikovsky was not one to accept such a phenomenon without trying to resolve it in musical terms. The Fourth Symphony was intended to do that.

It probably originated in the deplorable production of *Swan Lake*. The ballet was staged at the Bolshoi on March 4—five days before the first performance of *Francesca da Rimini*. The success of the latter was a mockery to Tchaikovsky after the stupendous, the almost unbelievable bungling of *Swan Lake*—a record in mismanagement even for one of the Imperial Theaters. Everything went wrong that could go wrong; the ballet was appallingly badly costumed, the sets were a disgrace, the choreography farcical, the dancing poor, and the rendering of the music—which most of the orchestra had not troubled to learn and the rest could not play—was incredibly inept. To round matters off, the score had been hacked about on the grounds that some of it was too difficult for both dancers and musicians. What Tchaikovsky must have suffered as he looked and listened defies imagination.

Naturally, the ballet was an abject flop. After a few performances it was taken off. *Swan Lake* was not seen again for the best part of twenty years, when the Petipa version swept the world. Tchaikovsky was then in his grave.

It would be absurd in this day and age to comment in detail on Tchaikovsky's score. The one point of interest not always known is that the most famous part of it—the First Act pas de deux—came straight from *Undine*, probably the happiest piece of borrowing that any composer has ever thought of; it fitted

Swan Lake like a glove, and the solo violin theme has become immortal.

It is almost impossible now to imagine the kind of ballet music Tchaikovsky had listened to ever since he first came to Petersburg as a boy, the kind of music still being played in the Russian capitals when he wrote *Swan Lake*—and for that matter the kind of ballet music played everywhere and accepted as normal fare in the 1870's. Occasionally the balletgoer of today will hear a Minkus pas de deux, and that gives some idea of the triviality, the inanity of music considered good enough for ballet. Yet it is only if one can imagine oneself back into that now distant past that it is possible to understand exactly what Tchaikovsky did with *Swan Lake*. For the first time in history he gave ballet music symphonic proportions, he gave it dignity, elegance, and true feeling.

Today the *Swan Lake* music sounds simple and inevitable; it was anything but that in 1877, it was daring to the last degree. As it happened, it was not to be the first of Tchaikovsky's scores publicly to revolutionize ballet (for it demanded and so created great choreography and great dancing); this honor was to fall to *The Sleeping Beauty* thirteen years later.

Thirteen years! That is the measure of the loss that millions of balletgoers have sustained. For thirteen years after the shambles of the *Swan Lake* production Tchaikovsky wrote no ballet music. Although *Swan Lake* was not to make its mark first, it is regarded by millions today as the very essence of ballet—the art at its purest and greatest.

In the spring of 1877 nothing of this was even faintly imaginable to the distressed composer. As usual he tried to take much of the blame for the fiasco on his own shoulders, but his feeling that fate was against him deepened and darkened, and those who examine his life dispassionately must feel that he was severely tested. Something of this was due, of course, to his disposition and to his public standing; every creative man takes his life in his hands every time he offers something to the world. But when all is said, Tchaikovsky seems peculiarly vulnerable to the buffets of fortune, and never was this to be more true than at the time he had now reached, for it was then, early in 1877, that he made the acquaintance of Antonina Ivanovna Milyukova and Nadezhda Filaretovna von Meck.

CHAPTER 12

Nadezhda Filaretovna
1877

ANTONINA MILYUKOVA WAS the first of these women to come into his life. She had been a student in his class but had made little impression on him at the time. This was not surprising for he did not think much of his women students: "Although it is a dreary business to have been forced to explain to my young men's classes for eleven consecutive years what a triad consists of, at least I have had the consolation of feeling that I am ramming essential knowledge into them because they intend to take up music as a profession. But the young women's classes! Heavens above! Out of sixty or seventy only five at the most will ever make musicians. The rest come to the Conservatoire to fill in time or from motives which have nothing to do with music. They are not less intelligent or less hard working than the men, rather the opposite . . . but they all come to grief the moment they are unable to apply a rule mechanically or use it by rote. I often lose patience with them—and my head—and go quite frantic with rage."

As this remark indicates, Tchaikovsky's dislike of lecturing had long since passed the stage of silent resentment and his widespread popularity in class had gone. One of the Conservatoire pupils A. M. Amfiteatrova-Levitskaya, who was later to create the role of Olga in *Eugene Onegin*, described Tchaikovsky the professor with refreshing frankness: "He was handsome but very stern and the expression on his face was of almost constant displeasure. When he came into the classroom he looked sombrely at us under eyebrows drawn into a frown and answered the students' greeting with a barely noticeable nod of the head."

The opinion of the classes was divided: "Some thought he was not only a composer of genius but an ideal teacher. According to these students Pyotr Ilyich always went through their work with great interest and care, correcting mistakes patiently and giving them the most valuable advice. Others were convinced that he neglected them."

That he could be sharp and severe was demonstrated by a student in his harmony class who told Amfiteatrova-Levitskaya indignantly what happened when he came to her desk one day to look at a specimen score she had written out. She had forgotten to add the tails to the thirty-second notes and he at once fell into a fury and slashed the page across with a red pencil. "You'd better try to master the art of making tails before you try to master harmony," he said coldly, and moved on to the next student.

This story, and his grim manner in class, impressed Amfiteatrova-Levitskaya so unfavorably that she eventually complained to Kashkin. All she got for her pains was a shout of incredulous laughter and, "Pyotr Ilyich irritable! Why he's the kindest, gentlest, most sympathetic man breathing. He's far too kind, that's his trouble, he pities every poor, unfortunate, and oppressed man and woman to the point of absurdity. As for ragged, deserted children, he can't even speak of them without tears!"

She was not convinced; to her Tchaikovsky remained a harsh taskmaster who only interested himself in promising students, and by 1877 this was no doubt true. He had never been able to convince himself that he was a good teacher let alone a born one. He felt trapped for life at the Conservatoire and resented every moment spent away from composition unless he was dealing with a student he felt might make his mark in music if carefully trained. His horror of stupidity and laziness had reached a pitch of ferocity that burst on his classes week after week. Hence "I go quite frantic with rage" and the dismay of students who meant well but had little hope of becoming serious musicians.

But there was a third type of student who was anything but dismayed by these classroom scenes. Tchaikovsky did not understand that his explosions made him even more attractive to those who had joined "from motives which have nothing to do with music." It is doubtful whether, of all the hundreds in this category who had passed through his hands, a girl was ever as indifferent to music as Antonina Milyukova. She had one thought in her head—men—and at that particular moment, one man, the lecturer whose furiously glaring blue eyes gave her such a pleasant thrill. She had joined his class at the Conservatoire four years earlier, when she was twenty-four. She had not joined the class to learn harmony; like most of the other young women, she had joined to stare at the handsome professor and to try to engage his attention.

Of this Tchaikovsky had no notion; the numbers in his class were too great for him to distinguish every girl and young man; he only became intimate with the most gifted and Antonina was not among these. When he met her for a few moments at the end of term parties he remained innocent; she was pretty, with fine eyes and a mass of fair hair, a good figure, and a manner which a more experienced man than Pyotr Ilyich would have found difficult to penetrate; she said little and looked much; she was apparently a demure, rather shy, and earnest girl deeply interested in music in general and his in particular.

He was mildly attracted. He was accustomed to student crushes, and when this student completed her course towards the end of 1876 and left his classes he forgot her completely.

2

In the five months before Tchaikovsky was to be reminded of her he had won the friendship of the second woman who was to influence his life powerfully. Just about the time when Antonina

The Tchaikovsky family, photographed in 1848. From left to right, Pyotr Ilyich, Alexandra Andreyevna, Alexandra Ilyinishna (seated in front), Zinaida, Nikolai, Ippolit, and Ilya Petrovich.

Tchaikovsky in 1859, the year he was appointed to a post in the First Division of the Ministry of Justice.

Lyov Davidov and Tchaikovsky's sister, Alexandra Ilyinishna, on their wedding day in 1860.

Tchaikovsky in 1861, at the time he began preparing himself for a career in music.

Tchaikovsky while he was in the Conservatoire, 1863-4.

Anton Rubinstein, about 1880, Director of the Conservatoire.

Nikolai Rubenstein, Anton's younger brother, in 1872.

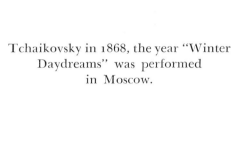

Tchaikovsky in 1868, the year "Winter
Daydreams" was performed
in Moscow.

Tchaikovsky's friend and publisher
P. I. Jurgenson in 1870.

Vladimir Stasov, a leader of the nationalist school of Russian musicians, who charmed and awed Tchaikovsky.

Tchaikovsky photographed in 1875.

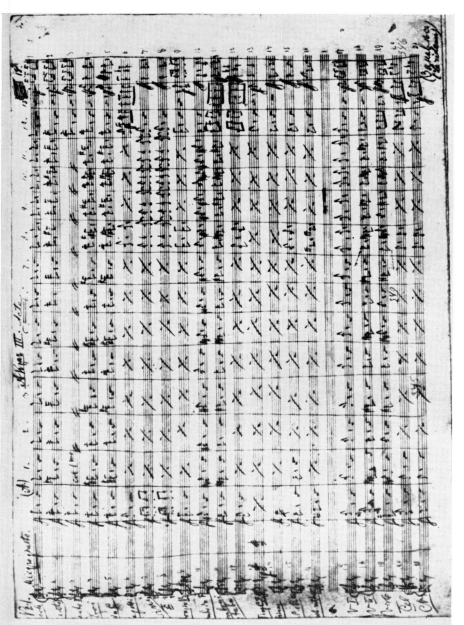

Page from the score of the third act of the ballet *Swan Lake*.

Pyotr Ilyich (right) and his brother Modest (left) with Kondratyev and Antoly, photographed in 1872.

Tchaikovsky greeted by local notables on the way to Tiflis, 1886.

Nadezhda Filaretovna von Meck photographed in 1877, the year this wealthy widow became Tchaikovsky's patroness and, by correspondence, his confidante.

Brailov, Madame Von Meck's mansion on her enormous estate in the Ukraine.

Désirée Artôt, the French singer whose career prevented Tchaikovsky from marrying her.

Tchaikovsky and Antonina Milyukova, the student he married on July 18, 1877, who made his life miserable.

Tchaikovsky, Kolya, and
Modest photographed in
1878.

Tchaikovsky in 1888
with A. A. Brandukov.

Tchaikovsky with his brother-in-law
V. L. Davidov in 1892.

Herman Augustovich Laroche, left,
Tchaikovsky's friend from student
days at the Conservatoire, with Alexander Konstantinovich Glazunov the
prodigious composer.

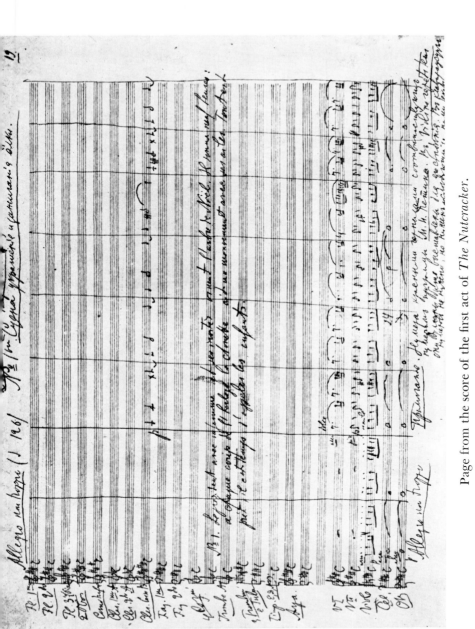

Page from the score of the first act of *The Nutcracker*.

Tchaikovsky's last house at Klin, now the Tchaikovsky Museum.

The music room at Klin.

Milyukova left the Conservatoire he was offered and accepted a commission to arrange some orchestral music for violin and pianoforte. The commission came through one of his favorite students. Yosif Yosifovich Kotek, who had just finished his Conservatoire course. This young man had obtained a post as violin tutor in the household of Nadezhda Filaretovna von Meck, and had raved to her about his god Pyotr Ilyich, what a noble soul he was and what wonderful music he composed.

Tchaikovsky knew a good deal about Nadezhda Filaretovna. Indeed all Moscow was gossiping about her, for earlier that year her husband—a railway king—had died and left her a great fortune. He had also left her eleven children, ten of whom were alive, and there was one still unborn. The talk in Moscow salons was all about what she would do with herself and who would share the money with her—for she was only in her mid-forties, nine years older than Tchaikovsky.

He knew more than the town gossips. Whenever he met Kotek the young man talked about her autocratic manner, her violent change of moods, her equally violent headaches when the whole household trembled, her journeyings in search of health, her vast retinue of servants, her enormous estate at Brailov in the Ukraine and above all of her passion for music.

Nikolai Rubinstein filled in some of the gaps left by Kotek. He had come to know her fairly well in the past year or so—as Director of the Conservatoire he was the only man unconnected with the household who was allowed to visit her—and made fun of her and her queer ways. If he was to be believed—never a foregone conclusion with him—she was half-demented but very well worth cultivating. She had already helped the shaky Conservatoire funds and would almost certainly do more. She never missed a Moscow concert. Rubinstein predicted that she would not marry again but would give her life to music; she was a fair pianist, she surrounded herself with a staff of musicians and would be forever demanding arrangements for two pianos and violin and piano for which she would pay handsomely.

Rubinstein, it may be assumed with fair confidence, urged Tchaikovsky to accept the commission which she offered him for the violin and pianoforte arrangement. Nadezhda Filaretovna was the kind of patron no Director of a penurious Conservatoire dare offend. He would be anxious to help his friend too; he knew that Pyotr Ilyich, constitutionally unable to say no to a borrower, had at last fallen into the moneylender's hands, he knew that he could turn out the required arrangement with the greatest of ease; everything seemed to add up to the beginnings of a lucrative period for all.

Tchaikovsky agreed, supplied the arrangement quickly just before the end of the year, and received by return a payment which must have made him open his eyes together with a short but gratifying note. From this note it was clear that the great patroness of music preferred his music to that of all others; she said so no fewer than three times in a few lines, ending "I simply ask you to believe as a fact that your music makes my life easier and more endurable."

Tchaikovsky's reply to this considerable compliment from such a quarter was restrained, a mere formal letter of thanks. There was a short interval of two or three weeks before he heard from her again. In that time the industrious Kotek who oscillated between his mistress of the von Meck mansion and his idol of the Conservatoire had provided more information about this unusual woman. She had vowed, he said, to live for the rest of her life as a recluse. She did not think this period would be very long; she had tubercular symptoms and regarded her dreadful headaches and attacks of nerves as the beginning of the end. She was an atheist. She had two photographs of Tchaikovsky prominently displayed in her music room; she talked at length of him and questioned Kotek and Rubinstein closely about him.

This news must have made Tchaikovsky thoughtful. As everyone must have their god an atheist will search for a human god. To worship a human being is to long to possess him; everything he heard about this woman suggested that she was a tyrant; not one person in her house could really be said to call his soul his own.

He was soon tested. In February of the new year, 1877, he was offered and accepted another commission to make an arrangement for piano and violin. He again made it quickly and before the end of the month had received an even more generous payment with a covering letter at once reassuring and challenging. "I should dearly like to tell you fully what I think and feel about you but I don't want to waste your precious time, so let me just say that my feeling for you is spiritual and one of my dearest possessions."

There was only one answer to this and Tchaikovsky made it. He was a human being and had his fair share of vanity. He could not forget that this woman who had voluntarily offered her admiration was fabulously wealthy and could at one stroke relieve him of all money worries. But apart from the money and the flattery he was touched. Kotek and Rubinstein had both made plain that this Nadezhda Filaretovna was unhappy. She was lonely in spite of her large family and huge household. She loved music. She appealed to all the kindness in him. In reply the next day he urged her to write to him as she wished, fully: "Perhaps I know you better than you think."

He believed what he said. He considered himself a lonely man in Moscow for all the company he kept and was not entirely mistaken. By and large he detested Moscow social life—or, to be exact, he detested himself every time he came back from a soiree chiefly given over to gossip and insincerities. He was not a prodigious letter writer for nothing; he preferred a letter friendship to a drinking bout which was what most friendships in Moscow led to. He was sorry for the rich woman in her mansion in Rozhdestvensky Boulevard and admired the stand she was taking, the stand he had so often talked about, to give up the world for music. He thought she could be right, that he and she had in common the greatest love on earth.

His note opened the floodgates. In the middle of March he

received the first of what was to become a unique collection of long and intimate letters. This first one began with a request for a photograph. "I want to discover in your face the thoughts and feelings which inspired you to write music that transports me into a world of high emotion, of hope, of an unquenchable craving."

She explained that her ideal man was a musician but that she expected to be able to look up to the man as much as to the musician—she could not divorce the one from the other. She had been searching for this man and thought she had found him after she heard for the first time a Tchaikovsky work, *The Tempest*. "I couldn't possibly describe the impression it made on me; for days afterwards I was practically out of my mind with excitement."

Being the business woman she was, she immediately set about to discover "what kind of man had created the music that had given me such unparalleled joy. I seized every opportunity to learn more about you, I listened to everything that was said about you, in general and in passing, from those who knew you and from those who only knew about you. . . . I am interested in everything about you, where you are and what you are doing all day and every day. And already I feel from what I have heard, favorable and otherwise, an enormous conviction that we are one in thought and feeling."

Raptures of this kind were not strange to Tchaikovsky; he had been receiving them, in writing and speech, from men and women students alike, for the greater part of the ten years he had been teaching at the Conservatoire. But Nadezhda Filaretovna was forty-five, one of the richest women in Russia, famed for her strong business sense, her rigid morals, her unapproachability. And as if she realized that even the composer of emotional music might balk at such an outpouring she hurriedly added that she had lost all her wish to meet him: "I prefer to think about you, to hear you in your music and to feel it with you."

As Kotek had said, she was a confirmed hypochondriac. One of her many delusions was that she was dying—she was in fact to outlive Tchaikovsky—and as further evidence that she was not pursuing him, she implored him: "Don't grudge a woman who is nearing the end of her life, who is almost at the point of death, the chance to feel so divinely alive for a fleeting moment."

She offered another commission in her own way. "In your *Oprichnik* there is a theme that drives me distracted. What music! I could give my life for it, I long to die hearing it! Could you please, Pyotr Ilyich, write me a *Marche Funebre* on this theme? I enclose the score with the passages marked. Do please, I beg, arange it for four hands."

He wrote the March and at the end of the month was overwhelmed with thanks: "It is so superb that, as I had hoped, it elevates and transports me into a state of such frenzied happiness that I forget everything bitter and offensive in the world. I couldn't describe the disorder reigning in my head and heart every time I hear it. My nerves are shaken by a thrill, I long to sob, to die, I have visions of another life, not the one all men believe in and wait for but quite another life, inaccessible, indescribable. Life, death, pain, joy all disappear as I wing my way above the earth, my temples beating, my heart palpitating madly, my eyes misted so that I see nothing and hear only that magnificent, enchanting music. I forget the exterior world, I feel only the beauty it has to offer, I dread to waken from the spell. My God! what a great man he is who can give such moments to a fellow spirit!"

There was a great deal more—all her letters were lengthy and all set the key in which she had determined the correspondence should be written. The very next letter, in the middle of May (each had been away from Moscow in the interval), was a love letter pure and simple, though cast in a spiritual mold: she confessed to terrible loneliness without a letter from him, she begged him to "save my sinless musical soul for earthly musical joy" by permitting her to write whenever she felt inclined to "the pure prophet of my beloved art." She also sent another commission, this time not an arrangement of music already written but a new composition on a theme she outlined.

At this point Tchaikovsky put his foot down. He showed the

strong common sense which was to be so wretchedly absent within the next few weeks. What he thought about Nadezhda Filaretovna must be a matter for conjecture. That he considered her entry into his life as the hand of fate is certain. That he rode her extravagances with ease is probable; he was a Russian and emotional himself. That he was flattered is inevitable.

But he was no fool. By this time he knew his correspondent fairly well. He believed that she felt what she said she felt about his music but must have been uneasy about her wish to worship him. He knew that he could not live up to her portrait of him and had told her so. He was unquestionably uneasy about the form their relationship would take in spite of her protests that she was content to know him by his music and his letters.

But what worried him most of all was the fear of being dominated. He knew her to be a born autocrat. Her love of music was only one side of a complex character; from the moment she left her domineering mother to marry von Meck at the age of seventeen she had ridden roughshod over everyone. The famous railway which had made the von Meck fortune was her railway in every real sense, for it was she who had forced her husband out of the civil service. When she met him he was a government engineer much less well placed than Ilya Petrovich and without even the moderate future of the Tchaikovsky father. As soon as Nadezhda Filaretovna took over the reins, von Meck struck out on his own and, after years of struggle and sacrifice (mostly on her side, since she continued to bear children regularly in spite of their poverty) her energy and faith were rewarded, the railway was built and her husband became one of Russia's biggest industrialists.

All this Tchaikovsky knew. He knew too that an autocrat in one sphere is an autocrat in all. Nadezhda Filaretovna might genuinely love music and passionately admire him—he did not doubt it—but she remained a woman who must rule. Her household proved it; it was a household of slaves and her lavish payments merely turned their work into gilded slavery.

It was this that made him dig in his heels. His fear was less for himself than for his music. In that house in Moscow she had secured tame piano teachers and now a violin tutor; she was soon to own a complete quartet which would include the young Debussy. These young men were at her beck and call; they had to play for her or with her whenever she felt the mood. Now, in her latest letter, she showed her hand; she wanted a tame composer too, a man who would write music on themes chosen by her, a man who would be in every real sense her property.

Tchaikovsky dealt with this subtly and boldly. If their relationship was to survive she had to understand his terms. He proceeded to test her feeling for him and for music. This is what he said: "Every time I get a letter from you I find money in it. Everyone assumes that an artist is never humiliated by being paid for his work, but in order to write the kind of creative work you are now asking for, the artist must be in a certain frame of mind (inspired, as we say) and he can't produce this mood to order. I am not prepared to deny the artist in me for the sake of money. I refuse to give you bad coin for good by using my technical skill."

Having affirmed his principles, he came to the test. "But I need those coins very badly all the same! I won't bore you by explaining how a man who ought to be able to live on his income has managed to get into such a state of debt that his life is often poisoned and his ability to work is crippled by worry; all I need say is that I have managed to get myself into serious financial trouble and can't get myself out without help. I have decided to ask you for that help."

He explained why: "You are the only person living I am not ashamed to beg money from, because you are kind, generous, and wealthy. I want to free myself from the clutches of the money-lenders by placing all the repayments of my debts in the one hand. If you would have the kindness to *lend* me the money to do this I should be intensely grateful. The total is not small—3000 rubles."

He outlined the methods by which he intended to repay the loan: by making piano arrangements for her, by sending her a percentage of his monthly salary, and of his royalties from operas.

He ended with an appeal which was both skillful and genuine, that she should allow him to dedicate his Fourth Symphony to her. This was the work he wanted to get on with instead of commissions from her and he said so pleasantly but plainly. The compliment was not only flattering but truthful; he wanted to make the dedication; in a symphony intended to illustrate the workings of fate in human lives, what could be more apposite than that it should bear the name of the woman whom fate had sent him at such a moment?

She accepted her defeat in a good spirit. To such a woman, accustomed to rule, only this determined stand was necessary to raise her feeling for Tchaikovsky to the highest level, for she was now forced to feel respect as well as admiration. He had made plain in the best possible way that if their intimacy was to grow as both wished she must help him to write the music she professed to love and not hinder it by telling him what she wished him to write. He would not be her tool but he would allow her to be associated with the work he truly wanted to do.

From this moment, in the middle of May, 1877, the lines of one of the most civilized friendships ever known were clearly drawn. He had found a champion of immense influence and a woman who felt as he did in the thing dearest to him—his music—and she had found her ideal in a world she hated and despised.

When she replied to him with a surrender and with the three thousand rubles (which she of course said she did not wish to be returned—the sum was nothing to her) Tchaikovsky must have felt that at long last the fates were smiling on him. He was out of debt, he had won a friend in a million and a powerful ally, he could write as he wished free from worry.

All this was true but he had not reckoned on the fate he talked and thought about so much. If it gave with the one hand it took with the other. As he learned within a few days of receiving her letter. For it was then that he received a letter of a very different kind. It was from Antonina Milyukova.

CHAPTER 13

Antonina Milyukova
1877

BEFORE DEALING WITH THIS LETTER it is necessary to look at the work which, in spite of Nadezhda Filaretovna and her commissions, Tchaikovsky was continuing in spurts. The Fourth Symphony was only one item; he had begun another opera and this work was soon to provide him with more horrifying proof of the macabre caprices of fate.

As usual he considered several subjects before, at a musical party, the then favorite Moscow soprano Lavrovskaya asked him why he did not write on Eugene Onegin. He rejected the idea; then, while dining that same evening, began to think more favorably of it. He at once went out to buy Pushkin's poems and, astonishingly, had trouble in getting hold of a copy. He finally came across the book, took it home, read the verse novel and was so excited by its possibilities that he did not get a wink of sleep that night. He never thought of sleep, he was hard at work, and by the morning had made a rough sketch of the opera. He went straight off to Shilovsky to beg him to write a libretto.

He told Modest excitedly that he was almost out of his mind with joy at having found such a subject. "What bliss to be free from boring Pharaohs, incredible Ethiopian princesses, poisoned goblets and all the rest of the lifeless rubbish. What riches of poetry Onegin possesses! It has faults, I know, it doesn't offer much scope for stage effects or treatment, but the splendor of the poetry, the humanity and simplicity of the subject, expressed in Pushkin's inspired verses, make up for all its shortcomings."

The humanity and the simplicity—here were the keynotes of a subject which went straight to Tchaikovsky's heart. The pure and innocent Tatyana fascinated by the roue Onegin and writing him one of the most moving love letters ever created—the story continued, but with a genius unknown to him before, a trend of Pyotr Ilyich's mind ever since he had begun to write music. In Tatyana he saw and felt yet another Russian heroine whom he equated as always with Alexandra. He loved her with a passion. And he hated Onegin—equated with himself—so fervently that he felt ill when he thought of his hero's rejection of Tatyana, his failure to see in her avowal his one chance to break free from a useless life and win lasting happiness.

To think of Alexandra as another Tatyana is not difficult, to think of Tchaikovsky as an Onegin seems impossible. But he managed it. To himself, he had all the makings of just such a villain, and by the middle of May he had reached a frenzy of fury at the thought of Onegin's heartlessness. He had forgotten long since that he was dealing with a story; for him the fantasy did not lie in Pushkin's poem but in the people around him, the professors, the students, the men and women in the streets and restaurants; reality was in the drama, the true, everyday drama he was setting to music. "I am in love with Tatyana," he told Modest.

At this point came a letter from Antonina Milyukova.

The letter was devastatingly simple. It said that she had loved him ever since she had first come to the Conservatoire four years earlier. She begged him to come to see her.

Tchaikovsky was no stranger to love letters or proposals; they were regular fare for the most handsome professor in the Conservatoire and one of Russia's outstanding composers. No doubt these letters caused him some worry, for he was considerate to the point of folly, but he had resisted the temptation to reply; he believed that the kindest thing was to remain silent and let the infatuation die even if his image suffered in the process. But though she could not know it, Antonina's letter was perfectly timed. To a man who was obsessed by fate the coincidence was extraordinary. Tchaikovsky was reading the love letter of a modern Tatyana to the modern Onegin. His immediate reaction was that he was being given the chance to prove that he, in Onegin's place, would act differently.

He replied to the letter. He said that he did not feel love for Antonina (in truth he could scarcely remember her) and could offer her only friendship. He listed some of his failings in an effort to show that her love was given to a romantic girl's vision, not a flesh and blood man. No doubt he thought that he was acting cautiously; in fact the moment he put pen to paper he had sealed his fate; Antonina was not the kind of woman to let him go if given the slightest encouragement.

She replied promptly and at length. "I don't expect I shall stay in Moscow but wherever I go I shan't forget you or stop loving you and I have no hope of finding in any other man what I love in you." She then added a sentence which would have told a more sophisticated man all he wanted to know about her. "Only last week I had to hear the declaration of a man who has been in love with me ever since I was at school and has been faithful to me for five years."

To Tchaikovsky this meant only one thing, as she intended him to think, that she was desirable but pure, that she would marry only a man she loved. Again the perfect identification with his image of Tatyana, as were the final sentences of her letter: "I am dying with wretchedness and frustration because although I long so desperately to sit by you and talk to you I'm afraid that at first I shouldn't be able to speak one word. Why bother to list your failings to me—nothing could stop me loving you. My love isn't a passing whim, it's for life."

Modest and faithful. Apprehensive too, making him feel that her fate was in his hands. For Antonina, fearing that his first letter was intended as the last, had slipped in a pathetic, "Is it possible that you could stop writing to me before I've even seen you? You wouldn't be so cruel."

This was decisive. No, he would not be so cruel. Onegin would, he would not. He went to see her.

At the interview he repeated what he had said in his letter, that he was not the hero she imagined but a faulty man, that he had nothing but friendship to offer. Again unknowingly she said the right thing; her reply, banal enough and inevitable, chimed in with the thoughts he had long been having on the subject of marriage. She said she could expect no more than friendship at the moment; love would come if they married.

Now this was precisely the argument he had been using to placate his protesting family over the past two years, ever since he told them that he intended to get married, and unlike Antonina, he believed it. That was why, when actually faced with a decision, he ignored all the material advantages of his connection with Madame von Meck, which must have been beyond his most optimistic imaginings, and acted in a way calculated to put an end to it. There he could see only gratitude and flattered vanity, not a substantial base for a man-woman relationship to rest on.

Nadezhda Filaretovna was not merely a dominating woman, she was nine years his senior and not attractive—the photograph she had sent him shows a forbidding face notable only for fine eyes. He could not bring himself even to try to see her.

What he did was to go to a woman nine years younger than himself, an attractive woman with considerable sexual charm, a woman who, if her words and manner were to be believed, would rely completely on him, a woman who was not well-born or well-off, quite the contrary. In short, he behaved just as most normal, red-blooded men would behave; he chose youth, looks, femininity. As for his music, one woman matched the other, for Antonina assured him that she loved his music as she loved him.

One flash of prudence—or what he liked to tell himself was prudence—remained. He asked a friend to find out what kind of reputation the girl had in Moscow. The reply seems to have been unfavorable—no details have come down, nor would one expect them—but could have said little more than that her reputation was suspect because she lived alone and not as was customary with her family. It certainly did not reveal the real truth, that she was a nymphomaniac, completely unbalanced, and obsessed by delusions of being desired by all men. Had this been the reply to his enquiry even the gallant and unworldly Pyotr Ilyich would have thought better of his impulse.

As it was, he was given little time to ponder what he had been told. Two days later he had another letter from her. She had discovered that he had been out of town the previous day (when he went to consult his friend) and, as a result, "I didn't leave my room all day, pacing from corner to corner like a mad thing. I could think of nothing but the moment I should see you again. And when I do I don't know how I shall prevent myself from throwing myself into your arms and kissing you. But you have given me no right to do that and you would think me shameless."

This demanded an explanation. "Don't, please, think badly of me because I confess what I feel for you. My reputation is good, I can tell you, and I have nothing to hide. When I kiss you it will be the first time I have ever kissed a man."

She once again dismissed his attempt to show her what he was really like—"You are only wasting your time"—and ended with a formidable threat. "I can't live without you and shall probably kill myself very soon. But please let me see you once more and kiss you so that I can carry the memory of that kiss into the next world."

There it was; the challenge had to be taken up or he had to surrender. Readers knowing the sequel and the true character of Antonina will feel that a letter of this kind should have been ignored, that no decent woman would write it. But Tchaikovsky saw himself as Onegin and Antonina as Tatyana; he had long wanted to get married and probably wished it more than ever then to protect himself from the somewhat alarming warmth of the widow Nadezhda Filaretovna, and Antonina was sexually very attractive.

Add to these reasons the most powerful of all, that he was a man of extraordinary innocence and nobility, never thinking ill of men or women unless proof stared him in the face, and his next action becomes almost inevitable.

He was to explain himself a few weeks later, just before his marriage, to Nadezhda Filaretovna. It was a difficult letter to write; he knew he would hurt her, he feared he would disappoint her, he thought it probable that he had thrown away the support which promised to free him from money worries and allow him to write music unhampered. The letter took him weeks to write yet in the end it was an honest letter without special pleading and gives a truthful account of the affair except that, naturally, he did not enlarge on Antonina's youth and charm.

These are the salient points of his letter: "Some time ago I had a letter from a girl I had once known. The letter told me that she had done me the honor of loving me for a long time past. The letter was so sincere and so affectionate that I felt bound to break my rule in such cases and answer it. I was careful however to hold out no hope that the feeling could be mutual. But I had answered and the result was that in the end I agreed to go to see her. Why? After thinking it over I believe that I was destined to go by Fate. At the meeting I repeated what I had said in my letter, that I could only return her love with friendship and gratitude, but after I had gone away I began to question my actions. If I did not love her and did not want to encourage her feelings, why had I gone to see her?"

That was the first stage. The second stage was her suicide threat, which he typically thrust on his own shoulders. "In her next letter she made plain that if I did not continue the acquaintance after writing to her and going to see her I should make her utterly wretched and drive her to make away with herself. I was at once faced with a dreadful decision. I had to marry her to save her, or preserve my freedom at the cost of her destruction—I don't ex- aggerate, she seems to love me to the point of desperation. How could I choose anything but the former? . . . So I went to see her, reiterated that my character was difficult—irritable, temperamental, unsociable—and my means slender, repeated that I did not love her but said that I would be a faithful and devoted friend. I asked her if knowing all these facts, she would be my wife. She accepted me."

He described Antonina. "She is twenty-eight and not unattractive. Her reputation is without flaw. She earns her own living so that she can live an independent and free life, but she and her mother love each other. She is poor and has been educated according to her station in life, in the Yelizaveta Institute. She seems to have a very kind nature and to be willing to identify herself with her husband without reservations."

His final thought was "My conscience is clear. Heaven knows I have nothing but good will for my future wife. If we are not destined to be happy it will not be through any fault of mine. Though I am marrying without love I could take no other course with honor."

When he wrote this letter in the middle of July only three days were left before the marriage. Soon after the engagement he had gone to the country for a month to think things over calmly. So little did he understand the woman he was to marry that he actually persuaded himself into a sufficiently placid state of mind to work hard on the opera which had caused all the trouble. By the end of the month, before he came back to Moscow, he had written two thirds of it.

In every direction a fatal blindness—or obstinacy—fastened on him at this critical moment of his life. Of all men he was the most family-loving; his frequent letters to father, brothers, and sister were full to the point of absurdity; he revealed his mind in the minutest detail. Yet he did not tell any of them about his engagement until on the point of marriage and evidently did not once ask himself why. When he did at last write his letters were deceptively calm—he had mesmerized himself into a fatalistic trance. Ilya Petrovich was deceived and replied with many congratulations, but not Anatoly; he took the first train to Moscow.

By this time Nadezhda Filaretovna, also told very late in the day, had responded gallantly; she wrote a courageous letter, concealing her feelings until the very last. "Never forget the one whose whole soul is devoted to you."

Tchaikovsky approached his marriage with this load off his mind; the friendship with Nadezhda would continue. Anatoly was not so obliging; he insisted on seeing Antonina, was horrified and said so. He tried to stop the marriage. Tchaikovsky would not listen. On July 18 he and Antonina were married.

2

Only when he was in the train to Petersburg that evening on his way to present his bride to Ilya Petrovich did Tchaikovsky begin to come to his senses. He did not understand Antonina any better, but after having to entertain her until the train reached Klin and she fell asleep in her chair he began to realize that she was, as he put it, "very limited."

Even this he tried to see as a benefit, that it would prevent her from interfering with his work. This negative consolation did not last long. A glimpse of the truth came to him when at last she slept beside him. It is a glimpse that has come to many newly married men. He had undertaken to live with this stranger for the rest of his life. This frightening thought was followed by "the conviction that all that is best in me—my music—has been destroyed."

In these sleepless hours he hated her. During the next few days —they spent a week in Petersburg—his feelings veered wildly. At one point he was declaring that he thought he would love her when he got used to her: "All she asks is to caress me and look after me." At another moment these apparently simple wishes had become unendurable: "Physically she has become thoroughly repulsive to me."

Three days after the marriage he temporarily forgot his plight when he heard that Laroche was on the verge of delirium tremens. He had kept clear of him; Laroche was one of the many Petersburghers—the Aleksandrinsy Theatre actor Delazari (professionally known as Konstantinov) was another—who always thought Tchaikovsky good for a few rubles. But as ever he had second thoughts. "How hard and unfeeling I was when I told you I wouldn't go to Laroche for fear of parting with 25 rubles," he told Anatoly repentantly. "What selfishness! So I went to him after all and thank goodness I did go. In the first place I found him on the verge of complete ruin and clutching at me like a straw. I want to be that straw for him. I must do everything I can to rescue the poor sinking fellow."

He was rewarded. "He came to dinner and spent the whole evening with us; he was very nice to my wife and above all he broke up our irksome tête-à-tête. However the irksomeness is all on my side; *she* seems perfectly happy and contented. In the evening we all went to the Kamennoostrovsky Theatre then drank tea and beer (a lot of it) chez moi. His presence was a great help."

His feelings towards Antonina Ivanovna can be gauged by his immediate reaction when he met old friends unexpectedly. "In the morning, walking arm in arm with my wife on the Nevsky, I ran into Niks Litke and spoke to him but for some reason couldn't bring myself to tell him that the lady was my wife. On the way to the theater in the evening I met Konstantinov. I said nothing to him either and managed to escape for once in a while with no more than a loan of 5 rubles. Money flows like water. I feel that the happiest day of my life will be the first of August."

The first of August was the day he was due at Kamenka but much was to happen before then. Four days later, his last day in Petersburg, he told Anatoly: "Tolichka, yesterday was the most frightful since July 18. In the morning it seemed to me that my life was completely smashed and a dreadful attack of despair possessed me. At three o'clock *a great number* of people gathered at our place: N. Rubinstein, his sister Sofya, Malozemova, K. Y. Davidov, Ivanov, Bessel, Laroche. We all dined together. In the evening we first of all saw N. G. [Rubinstein] off to Moscow, then Malozemova and Sofya to Peterhof."

The dinner evidently put heart into Tchaikovsky, for he goes on to tell his brother "Today the awful crisis has passed. I am recovering. But the crisis was *awful, awful, awful;* if it weren't for my love for you and all the other people I'm intimate with, the thought of whom supported me through *excruciating mental tortures,* it could have ended badly, in illness or even insanity."

His last thought was of the worry he must have caused Anatoly and he assured him, "I give you my word that there's nothing for you to worry about. I'm recovering completely." This was unhappily no more than a pious hope which scarcely outlasted the arrival back in Moscow. There they took lodgings before going on to Antonina's mother for a week's stay. They had planned to rent an apartment to come back to but Tchaikovsky found himself virtually without money—his wife was even more spendthrift than himself and in his guilt at not feeling more for her he had splashed more money about than usual since the marriage. Besides, he had relied on her assurance that she owned a forest which was on the point of being sold. The forest was not sold. It may not even have existed for, as he was soon to discover, Antonina was incapable of telling the truth.

Penned in one lodging house room with her, all his optimism vanished. He thought he would go mad. He could still only see that his bride was a silly woman. He could not write a line of music—she was forever leaning over him, heavily scented, in an effort to get all his attention for herself—and began to drink deeply so that he could restrain himself from telling or showing her what he was feeling. He did restrain himself but could think of nothing but an apartment where he would have his own room in which to work. At moments he was still hopeful that time and habit would give him strength to live with her contentedly.

He wrote to Nadezhda Filaretovna and begged a loan to rent an apartment. His letter was more than honest. He could have blamed his wife and assured himself of sympathy; instead: "My wife is not to blame; she did not ask for marriage."

Self-reproach could scarcely go further. By the time he had her reply he had spent the week with Antonina at his mother-in-law's.

He came back from this visit desperate to get away; he felt that he must have some respite if he were to continue the marriage. He had not had one moment to himself since they married, and the week out of Moscow was absolute agony. For the first time he realized that Antonina had lied to him. "I disliked the mother and the entire family. They have narrow ideas, they express themselves coarsely and all of them are at daggers drawn." He began to see why Antonina had lived by herself in Moscow, but why had she lied about it? "It may be unfair but my wife grows more abhorrent to me every hour."

His wretchedness was increased by news of the sudden death of Adamov; their friendship had never faltered since the days of school, and Pyotr Ilyich felt as though the abrupt end to the long tie was a sign that his own life had changed course and was bound irrevocably for the philistine surroundings symbolized by the Milyukov family.

Nadezhda's letter was waiting for him. She lent him the money willingly. No doubt she could foresee the future if he could not. She sent the money and her advice, that he should go off for a holiday by himself and think things out.

As she had reckoned, the money freed him. He knew enough of Antonina by this time to feel sure that she would be happy enough looking about for an apartment and furnishing it when she found one that pleased her. As it turned out, she saw him go off in the second week of August without any regret, promising to have a home ready for him when he came back. They had then spent three weeks together without a break, two of them in the homes of relatives.

He intended to take the waters at Essentuki in the Caucasus but not surprisingly changed his mind at Kiev and went to Verbovka where Alexandra, Lyov, Modest, and Anatoly were waiting for him. The change was part bliss, part an increase of despair. He was once again with civilized people who did not snarl and bicker, people who loved art, people who lived creatively, people who loved him, whose life was built on truth. The contrast between what he had left and what he had around him was almost too painful to be borne. When the children showed their joy at seeing him by frisking about, he remembered that Antonina had told him—after the marriage—that she did not like children and did not want them. The tastefulness of the house threw up in horrid relief the dreadful nothingness of the Milyukov home where commonness of behavior was matched by vulgarity of surroundings.

In the end the influence of Kamenka and its surroundings soothed him back to composition. He continued, not the opera, but the symphony. Perhaps he tried to think of Nadezhda Filaretovna as he wrote, but the idea behind the work was now appallingly justified. When he began it he had thought of fate's perverse handling of his reputation as a composer; her latest caprice put this long injustice completely in the shade.

Yet finally the musician expelled the man as always, and was soon absorbed in a novelty which still gives a thrill of pleasure nearly one hundred years later. "The Scherzo will display a new orchestral effect that I think will be most effective. The strings at first play pizzicato by themselves, in the Trio the woodwinds are given a solo passage followed by the brasses, and towards the end of the movement all three groups converse with one another in brief phrases."

By the time in mid-September Antonina wrote that she had found and furnished an apartment, the orchestration of the symphony had gone far and he had even orchestrated the first act of the opera, about which he now had the deepest doubts: "The story is simple, the stage effects are practically nil and the music is without brilliance or grandeur. All the same I feel that when a few chosen people hear my music they may respond to the emotion I felt when I wrote it."

The Conservatoire term was due to begin, the apartment was ready, he could delay no more. He dragged himself back to Moscow after a final note to Anatoly who had gone back to work ahead of him, an Anatoly who had not embittered the Kamenka stay with "I told you so." "A man only realizes just how strongly he loves a person when that person is far away. Tolya, I love you enormously! But oh, how little I love Antonina Ivanovna Tchaikovsky! With what colossal indifference does that lady fill me! How little am I enlivened by the thought of seeing her again!"

He added, "It is not that she alarms me, she is simply a bore."

3

This was bravado or a forgetfulness. Up to this time he had discovered in Antonina a common young woman, apparently stupid and with little regard for the truth. He came back to find a new Antonina or, correctly, a woman who was beginning to show her true colors. When she met him at the station on September 23 she felt a security she had not felt earlier; she had her own apartment, she was married, her husband was famous. She began to blossom out.

In public she maintained the façade that had so much impressed Tchaikovsky. At a dinner for the couple given by Jurgenson she said little, seeming to wait for her husband's prompting. She had all the cunning of the near insane and her act of the dependent female took in every man present.

Tchaikovsky's attitude in his classes successfully misled everyone too; he made a special effort to be brisk and carefree. In the tiny apartment matters were different. It was not big enough for him to escape his wife; she was in the room hour after hour. He tried to work, it was impossible. Another lie disclosed itself. "After assuring me that she had loved me for four years and was a devoted musician, I found that she didn't know a single note of any of my works . . . and had not once gone to the concerts of the Musical Society where she knew that I, whom she had loved for four years, could always be found."

This music lover, then, was not interested in music. What did she want? To talk, the horrified Tchaikovsky discovered. And what talk! "Everything she said always led to the same topic, the numberless men who had loved her (she harped on this theme incessantly), all of them very important, mostly generals, relations of well-known financial wizards, famous actors or members of the royal family."

That was the main stream of her conversation—"she is extremely talkative"—but the subsidiary theme though less mad was even less bearable. "All the wickednesses, the baseness and abominable behavior of her family were described incessantly and with a fury quite beyond all sense. Most of her venom was directed at her mother."

So much for the day—a stream of insane and vitriolic commonplaces interrupted by nauseating lovemaking. "I know now that she never loved me," he said a few weeks later. But the nights passed beyond description. "She lavished her caresses on me to the point of satiety."

All his abomination of the workings of fate returned a hundredfold. Fate's instrument became more and more abhorrent to him each day. The prettiness which had attracted him vanished. He saw beneath it. Antonina's lips, he now realized, were unpleasantly thin, her smile calculating and abnormal, and her affectations—she put on a cultured accent, she used her arms and hands in a bad imitation of the best society—almost drove him out of his mind. "As soon as I met her again I saw that I could never love her, that the affection born of habit on which I had counted was unattainable. I felt absolute despair and longed for death."

After a week his feelings had become dangerous. "My whole being was filled with such hatred of the poor woman that I longed to throttle her." One particular night—he was to remember it fearfully for the rest of his life—"I was within a hairsbreadth of succumbing to that blind, unreasoning, diseased loathing that ends in murder. I was only saved by a miracle."

To protect her—for he persisted in thinking that all the fault was on his side—he began to go out every evening. He could not go where he was known, to the theatres, well-known restaurants or cafés, because he might be seen and asked why he had not brought his wife. He roamed the streets like one lost—his mind was beginning to cloud—and at last, one night early in October, he could bear the strain no longer. He walked down to the river, waded into it and stood in the bitterly cold water up to his armpits.

Even in this extremity he thought of others. His death must not be accounted suicide, that would unbearably hurt all who loved him and make his wife the subject of hostile gossip. He chose the way of death which could be put down to an accident.

He never knew afterwards how long he stood there, praying for death. At last he stumbled out of the water and went home, sure that he had caught a fatal chill. He told the astonished Antonina that he had had a fishing accident, went to bed, and prepared for death.

The next morning he was as well as ever; his strong constitution had thrown off even this extraordinary exposure to cold and wet.

There was only one thing left to do if he was not to murder Antonina. He invented a sudden call to Petersburg. On the evening of October 6 he caught the train.

When Anatoly met him at the station he did not recognize Pyotr Ilyich. He got him to a hotel. There Tchaikovsky had a kind of fit. He lay unconscious for two days. The doctor, after giving him up, said that he must get away as soon as he was able to move, go right out of Russia.

The moment Tchaikovsky came out of his coma and had explained everything, Anatoly took the train to Moscow, had a long talk with Rubinstein and together with Rubinstein went to see Antonina.

The meeting was short. They told her that Tchaikovsky could not live with her, that he would keep her with a home and generous allowance wherever she wanted to be. For the moment they suggested that she took a fully paid holiday in Odessa, out of range of Moscow gossip.

She scarcely seemed to take in what they were saying, and her final words indicated that she had been far too much preoccupied to listen. She thrust tea on them and did nothing but stare enraptured at Rubinstein who, to those who liked that kind of looks, appeared smarter and more distinctive with the years. After he had hurriedly swallowed his tea and left, she said to Anatoly in a kind of ecstasy "Who would ever have thought that Nikolai Rubinstein would have drunk tea in my house!" If Anatoly had had any doubt of his brother's action it disappeared in that moment. He left her plenty of money to enjoy herself in Odessa, then went back to Pyotr Ilyich.

A few days later he and Tchaikovsky left for Switzerland.

4

Tchaikovsky's retreat abroad has been quoted by many as yet another proof of his lack of manliness; faced with a woman at close range, they say, he went to pieces.

It is a pity that those who so glibly take away the character of a great man cannot be obliged to spend one night with a woman like Antonina Milyukova—just one night, not the thirty-five spent by Tchaikovsky. What the extraordinarily sensitive Tchaikovsky suffered defies the imagination; for weeks afterwards he was like a man half insane, whose reason was barely preserved by heavy drinking.

His misfortune in becoming the object of Antonina's attentions justifies his preoccupation with fate only too well. There were tens of thousands of reasonably decent women in Moscow but he had to receive a letter from one of the very few who could have done such harm to him at precisely the moment when circumstances made him least fitted to deal with her advances. Had he been a worldly man, or anything but the trustful creature he was, he might have seen what kind of woman he was dealing with. He might; but it must be said that he was not alone; no one who saw Antonina at that time dreamed what she was really like. The sexually half-mad are cunning as well as stupid. She misled every-one.

One person who could not credit the necessity for her brother's breakdown was Alexandra Davidova. She had been against a love-less marriage but once the marriage was made she felt that her brother ought to have tried harder to make a success of it. Pure and normal herself, Alexandra walked blindly into trouble; she went down to Odessa and fetched Antonina home.

Her eyes were soon opened. Antonina adopted a new role, of the deserted wife, and spent much of her time whining about her hard lot. She wept copiously, day after day and most of the day. Sympathy only made her weep the more. She told Alexandra and Lyov that she had been duped by Pyotr Ilyich, that he had caught her by a trick.

As she accused him she fell to biting her nails. It was an old habit of hers, one of the many habits which had sickened the fastidious Tchaikovsky when he saw it for the first time in that apartment in Moscow. Antonina did not merely bite the tips of her nails, she bit them to the quick, she bit round the edges until they bled. Drops of blood began to disfigure the Davidov furnish-ings. Nothing Alexandra could say would stop the disgusting habit; Antonina merely wept more violently and bit harder.

The complaints of the deserted wife did not end at the Ver-bovka household; she wrote long and largely incoherent letters to Anatoly and to Tchaikovsky. Neither could understand what she wanted except to cause trouble; she showed no great wish to live with Tchaikovsky again.

To try to cheer her, Alexandra invited guests. She succeeded beyond her wildest hopes; Antonina immediately developed a passion for one of the better looking of the men, flirted madly with him and would afterwards talk of nothing but the manner in which he was pursuing her. It was, she assured Alexandra, her fate to attract men like flies.

At first Alexandra had begun to try to convince Pyotr Ilyich that his wife only needed to be educated in a happy and good-mannered family circle—the Kamenka circle—to "make an excellent companion for life." She dwelt on the girl's many good qualities and begged her brother to be patient.

As autumn moved into winter her letters changed; she was discovering that she had taken on the impossible. She ended, inevitably, by wondering how Pyotr Ilyich could ever have seen anything in the girl and, only too humanly, blamed him in her heart for this too. By this time she had begun to drop broad hints to Antonina Ivanovna that her stay had lasted long enough. Antonina feigned ignorance; she was doing very nicely where she was. She stayed on. By the end of November the household was in chaos and Alexandra wrote urgently to Anatoly demanding that he come and remove her visitor.

Tchaikovsky read this and a "poisonous" letter from Antonina enclosed with it and for the first and last time wrote to his sister a letter which was not wholly loving. "I'm glad she has at last dropped the role of meek sheep which moved you so much. I have replied to her letter and enclose it. *I beg you* to give it to her and read it with her. Then, my angel, please explain to her that I acknowledge my guilt fully. But let her know, too, that I remember everything down to the smallest detail that took place before our wedding and that she ought to remember even better than I how our intimacy began. Obviously she has forgotten everything that really happened and, indulged by you, has persuaded herself that I angled for the marriage and touched her heart by writing amorous letters—in short, that I alone am to blame.

"But this is not true. She must share the blame. I can't conceal from you that Antonina Ivanovna's stay with you has wounded me painfully. I'm glad that you have been kind to her but I am far from glad that my history is known now to every inhabitant of Kamenka. How can I ever stay with you again when even Baby will look accusingly at me? How can I look Alexandra Ivanovna in the face and all the rest of the inhabitants of your big house? Much time will have to pass before I can come to your so dear and so necessary home without unbearable moral and mental torments."

Having said this mildest of reproofs, he immediately tried to qualify it. "For God's sake don't think I am reproaching you! I know that you've done everything out of love for me. I admit I would have been happier if you had confined your meeting with Antonina Ivanovna to Odessa. To be absolutely honest, I had even hoped that my miserable history, in detail at any rate, would never be known at Kamenka, but your angelic heart carried you too far. I'm even glad that you have caressed Antonina Ivanovna though it is painful to me to think that these caresses have been lavished in vain and always to my detriment. But the thing that shames me most horribly is that every hour of every day you have in front of you a perpetual reminder of my wretched situation."

This letter did not fall on deaf ears. Alexandra was only too ready to forgive. She was not yet to escape the consequences of her quixotic impulse in carrying her sister-in-law back from Odessa; it was not until the end of December that Anatoly—surely the most obliging brother ever known—removed Antonina from Kamenka on his way back from Vienna. He settled her in her Moscow apartment, evading as best he could her persistent attempts to make love to him and set him against Pyotr Ilyich, and paid over the first installment of his brother's extremely generous allowance.

He left her apparently contented. But a woman who is slowly going mad cannot be contented. The letters to Tchaikovsky continued—a stream of insane complaints mingled with accounts of her triumphs with other men. By the early years of the next decade she had had affair after affair and had borne at least two children to different lovers. Even more embarrassing to Tchaikovsky, she began to borrow money from his friends; she would call at the houses of well-known Petersburg and Moscow men, insist on an interview, pour out a long and largely incomprehensible story of her woes at the hands of her husband and demand help as an abandoned wife.

By the end of the decade she was no longer responsible for her actions but the authorities hesitated to act, possibly because they were naturally sluggish, possibly because Tchaikovsky was then world-famous. Eventually she was put into a Petersburg mental home where she spent the last twenty years of her life.

But this was not until 1896, three years after Tchaikovsky's death. All the time he was alive she was left free to plague him, as she did. In vain he paid her the allowance regularly, in vain he tried to reason with her. His response to that declaration of love in 1877—a more innocent and well-meaning act could hardly be imagined—was to poison the last sixteen years of his life.

His reaction to this embarrassment, worry, and public humiliation was characteristic. He loathed the very thought of Antonina and loathed himself even more for every encouragement he had given her. He was therefore all the more careful to treat her with particular generosity. He offered her a divorce though this meant publicly branding himself as an adulterer. She refused, doubtless because she feared that the courts would award her alimony very much less than the allowance he voluntarily made. Later, when she stood self-confessed as a loose woman, he would not take divorce proceedings against her. At first he accepted the chance to free himself joyfully. Then he had second thoughts. He reacted violently from the lies which would have to be told in court. More important, he could not rid himself of the feeling that he had started her on the downward path. Then every argument his friends put forward, showing plainly that the girl was irredeemable, had no effect on him. He not only continued to pay her allowance to the day of his death but several times sent her extra funds after she had written a particularly outrageous letter to him.

One of the most revealing incidents in this long purgatory was to occur in 1886. Antonina Ivanovna that year excelled herself by demanding not only money and compassion but also that Tchaikovsky relieve her of her illegitimate children so that she should be freer to enjoy herself.

Like all the rest of these shattering eruptions into the world he was trying to rebuild, this letter made him ill—"Have been like a madman all day," was a typical diary entry after an Antonina letter—but when he recovered he wrote a kind reply and enclosed more money than usual in the hope, which must have been rather faint, that the children would benefit from some of it.

Above all, he wrote in his diary, that repository of absolute truth: "I feel very sorry for her in spite of all she's done and all she is. She must be one of the world's biggest misfits but all the same everything has gone wrong for her, poor thing."

How much this extraordinary generosity was due to pity, how much to guilt, how much to pure humanity must be left to every reader to decide for himself. This much is certain, few men would have acted as he did.

CHAPTER 14

Fourth Symphony and *Eugene Onegin*
1877-1878

ONE INEVITABLE RESULT of Tchaikovsky's tragic marriage was to turn him decisively towards Nadezhda Filaretovna. He was relieved of one considerable anxiety—she could no longer marry him—and there remained his immense gratitude to her. The result was to be a series of letters, and a number of great works arising out of these letters, which are without parallel in musical history. The works are now part of our staple musical fare. The letters have become famous yet are little read. And this is not because the full range of letters is available only in Russian. The letters are not to be read for pleasure alone—on her side the key is too often pitched uncomfortably high, on his side there is frequently a note of falsity, of a man trying to live up to an emotional standard he could not match. But unusual they certainly are.

He needed her faith as much as any man when he was taken away by Anatoly late in October, 1877. He needed her good sense even more. He was a nervous wreck; his dreams were nightmares, his waking hours were tormented by dreadful feelings of guilt that he had wrecked not only his own, but another life as well.

They went to Switzerland, then to Italy. For all his intense Russianness and his longing to get home when he was abroad, Tchaikovsky felt a natural kinship with the Italians and responded to their open-hearted expression of feeling, but this winter Italy could do little for him. He yearned for Alexandra and Kamenka, "the one place that is always home to me, that has always been my refuge in trouble and doubt, and that will always remain for me the most loved spot on this earth." But Kamenka was barred to him; Antonina was still there, hanging on persistently, deaf to every hint.

From Petersburg came a welcome surprise. Apukhtin, now one of Russia's most famous living poets, had the happy knack of producing a letter just when it was needed. He sent one now. He tended to be bellicose and detested injustice. Tchaikovsky always called to see him when he visited Petersburg and though their correspondence had dwindled he loved him dearly—the more so that his other schoolfriend Adamov had gone. Apukhtin demonstrated his feelings by writing forcefully and in lordly disgust of the gossipers. He instructed Pyotr Ilyich in school style to ignore the "scum" who had nothing better to do than make a nine day's wonder of the Tchaikovsky marriage: "Your country is going to be proud of you. . . . Turn your back on these nobodies and ascend the creative heights where you can't see or think of them. From there fling the rabble another Romeo or Tempest and let the weight of your fame squash them!"

Back in Moscow, Rubinstein acted promptly and generously; he granted Tchaikovsky unlimited leave of absence and persuaded the board of the Musical Society to vote a special sum of money as a token of appreciation for his eleven years of work in the Conservatoire.

Anatoly was with him, a tower of strength as they moved restlessly from Switzerland to Italy and back to Austria, but Anatoly, for all his affection and common sense, had one grave defect as healer of the mentally sick man—he was not musical. Tchaikovsky's recovery was assured by the letters from Nadezhda Filaretovna; they finally pulled him together and made possible the masterpieces still to come.

We do not know whether she had wished to marry him—as she

was to offer him ten thousand rubles to pay for a divorce, there may be a presumption that she had. Short of accomplishing this, she won a great victory for herself and every lover of music. The manager, the artist, and the woman in her all had cause for gratification in the next few months, for in that time she gained Tchaikovsky's confidence and affection. In every sense but the purely physical one she could think of the composer as her property, providing always that she did not try to force work on him that he had no wish to do, providing also that she was content to limit her personal demands on him.

Readers often find her letters absurdly overemotional—she wrote in the sentimental climate of that day and was at times definitely unbalanced and naive as when she tried to make Tchaikovsky explain exactly how and why he wrote as he did. She was curious, she was possessive and occasionally forgot that she was dealing with a genius and a human being with his own soul. Tchaikovsky was to rescue the relationship from the impossible strain she wanted to put on it, but she was in general extraordinarily good for him, and never more so than in those winter months of 1877-78. She restrained herself from reproach and, for a time, almost from questions. The practical and kind part of her nature came to the fore, and combined to rescue him from the pit.

She showed her instinctive wisdom there and then by two actions. She wrote to beg him to accept an annual allowance of six thousand rubles and enclosed the first installment before he could hesitate. That freed him at one stroke from money worries and allowed him to visualize another longed-for freedom, from lectures at the Conservatoire. She also urged him in letter after letter to get down to composition as the only way back to sanity and health. She refused to hear of inability to write, and her faith and strength of character came through the letters. This faith and his feeling, once he accepted the allowance, that he must justify it, actually set him to work again.

It is true that Tchaikovsky would have come back to music on his own; nothing short of complete mental breakdown would keep him from composition. No one can now say what would have happened to him without the faith and the financial help of the woman he had so recently discarded in favor of Antonina, but it would be less than generous to deny her the credit; he certainly was to regard her for the rest of his days as the main source of his recovery.

2

He spent almost exactly six months out of Russia—from October, 1877, to April, 1878—and the proof of the new spirit that was born slowly and agonizingly in him remains today in the major works he wrote during this time; he finished the Fourth Symphony and *Eugene Onegin* and he composed a large part of his violin concerto. Early in January, 1878, he sent off the completed symphony to Moscow. One month almost to the day, *Eugene Onegin* followed it.

This sounds like the Tchaikovsky of old, pouring out music day after day, even though much of the opera and symphony had been sketched out before he left Russia. In truth he could scarcely bring himself to write a note until the new year opened; he was fighting the horrors.

When Anatoly had to go back to Russia early in December, Tchaikovsky was for a time left to himself. Other rescuers were to make the long journey to support him, Modest and Kotek among them—an indication of the love he inspired—but not until he had fought his fight and won it.

His recovery was hindered by a new crisis that once more thrust music into the background. Nikolai Rubinstein was an impatient man who had not a nerve in his body. He thought that Tchaikovsky was coddling himself and needed shaking out of hypochondria. He suggested that Pyotr Ilyich go to Paris as Chief Delegate of Russian Music to the World's Fair just opening there.

The suggestion threw Tchaikovsky into despair, and when Anatoly supported Rubinstein, Pyotr Ilyich retired to another line of defense. He refers to it in his reply to Anatoly's attempt to persuade him to go to Paris. "If you could see my wretched face and could see me pacing up and down like a madman you would say, stay where you are. I have not told you that since you left I have drunk several glasses of brandy at night. I drink a lot during the day too. I can't do without it. I only feel calm when I have a lot of brandy inside me. I have grown so accustomed to this solitary drinking that the very look of the bottle—which is always by my side—gives me a thrill of joy. I can't write letters until I have had a drink—that shows how ill I still am. If I went to Paris I should be at it from morning to night to cope with the excitement of life there."

Anatoly dropped the subject. Not Rubinstein. Furious at the loss of such an advertisement for Russian music and the Moscow Conservatoire, he angrily accused Tchaikovsky of "putting it on."

Tchaikovsky's reply shows why he was so widely beloved. "Have it your own way—I am *putting it on*. But if I am, that is exactly what my illness consists of." And he added an irresistible, "How often must I tell you that though I loathe being a professor chained to the Conservatoire for life, I can't imagine wanting to be anywhere but in Moscow and with you." To which he added in his next letter, "I would gladly give up all the beauties and sunshine of this place to be in my beloved Moscow again." And to this again, he made a kind of postscript, to Nadezhda this time. He was moving slowly through northern Italy—Venice, Milan, Florence, Genoa, San Remo—and he felt for Italy what he felt for no other foreign country, as his music testifies. All the same, "I have never met anyone so passionately in love with Mother Russia—specially Great Russia—as I. . . . I love the Russian people, language, spirit, customs, yes, even the Russian face, with fervor."

There was another reason why he would not go to Paris. It is a reason which demonstrates what is too easy to forget with Tchaikovsky and all modest men, that true modesty does not preclude true pride. How, Tchaikovsky asked, could he be expected to explain Russian music to people like the French? "You know I'm a useless kind of man apart from my music."

He believed this but there was more to come. "Pride expresses itself in many ways. I show it by refusing to meet people who either don't know my real worth or don't appreciate it. How frightful, for instance, to be forced to stand meekly in front of Saint-Saëns and allow myself to be graciously condescended to when I know in my heart that I stand *as high above him as the alps*. In Paris my self-respect, which is considerable for all my outward modesty, would be bruised every second of the day by having to mix with celebrities who would all look down on me. To brag to them about my works, to try to persuade them that I am a person of consequence—this kind of thing is quite beyond me."

Rubinstein gave way with a growl—obviously he would have to go himself—and, the question settled as he wanted it, Tchaikovsky felt a good deal better for the sharp fight and began to orchestrate the symphony and opera and discuss them with Nadezhda and his friends at the Conservatoire who had already seen much of the work in sketch. The first reaction came from Taneyev. Tchaikovsky had enormous faith in this old pupil—Taneyev was fast becoming one of the most erudite musicians Russia had ever known—and felt mingled despair and irritation when told that *Eugene Onegin* would not be effective on the stage.

Like every born creative man, the composer, who had said the same thing himself a few months earlier, flew to the defense of his child. "If it really wouldn't be effective then it had better not be staged. I composed the opera because I was moved to express in music everything that seems to me to cry out for expression in *Eugene Onegin*. I spit on 'effectiveness.' What are effects anyway? If *Aida* is effective I can tell you I wouldn't compose an opera on such a subject if you gave me a fortune. I want to create human beings, not puppets."

He was to say this in another way a week or so later to Nadezhda Filaretovna. She was pouring out letters to him as well as money and every letter contained questions as well as encouragement. She wanted to know how the clock ticked—that was the gist of it—and Tchaikovsky, trying conscientiously to satisfy his patroness, had to attempt more than once to describe the indescribable, the creative process in himself. His reply to a less impossible but more intimate question—Had he ever experienced anything more than platonic love?—has a direct bearing on his defense of *Eugene Onegin*.

His answer to the personal side of the question, which ought never to have been put, was vague. "Yes and No. If you had asked, Have I ever found complete satisfaction or happiness in love? I should have answered No and again—No."

He then firmly placed the subject where it should always have been. "My music is my best answer. If you had asked, Have I ever known the full power and indescribable torment of love? I should have to reply Yes, Yes, Yes! Time after time I have tried to express through my music the intolerable anguish and supreme bliss of love. I must leave it to others to say whether I have succeeded, but this does not affect the validity of my attempt. I don't agree at all with your view that music is incapable of expressing the universal nature of love. On the contrary, I believe that music *alone* can do it."

In this spirit he continued his defense of *Eugene Onegin* to Taneyev. "What do I want? you may ask. . . . Above all I want an intimate but dramatic story based on a conflict of circumstance or character which is within the bounds of my imagination and which I feel deeply."

He showed his good sense by admitting that it would never do at the Maryinsky or any big opera house; he would like to see it put on by the students in the Conservatoire theatre. "I won't even describe my modest work as an opera but as something like 'lyrical scenes.'" He ended defiantly, "If my enthusiasm for *Eugene Onegin* merely underlines or exposes my limitations, my stupidity is not understanding the basic requirements of an opera, I apologize. But this I will say, that my music comes *literally from my inmost being.*"

His postscript was an uneasy wonder what Taneyev would think of the symphony: "I know you are absolutely sincere and I think a great deal of your judgment. But I also fear it."

He had some reason for alarm. When Taneyev at last told him, early in March, what he thought of the symphony, the letter made hard reading; he disliked it and said so, as was his way, plainly. Curiously enough, Taneyev had completely changed his view of *Eugene Onegin* after playing the full score over time after time. As a sop to this letter mutilating the symphony he said, "But your opera is without parallel in the world." And, in reference to one of Tchaikovsky's despairing moments, "And you talk of giving up composing!"

Tchaikovsky brushed aside this volte-face which he would normally have received in high delight. Taneyev's chief complaint about the symphony was that so much of it sounded like ballet music. He was particularly savage about the Scherzo of which Tchaikovsky was so proud: "I can't stand it." But for that matter, wrote Taneyev, almost every movement reminded him of Moscow's prima ballerina, Sobyesychanskaya—the middle of the Andante, the Trio, and the March in the Finale.

Tchaikovsky sat down and tried to control his fury sufficiently to reply coherently. He succeeded, and his answer stands to this day as a complete disposal of the same stupid objection which some critics still raise. "I can't imagine what your idea of 'ballet music' is nor why you should object to it. Does every melody in a lively dance rhythm seem like 'ballet music' to you? If so I don't understand how you can endure most of Beethoven's symphonies for melodies of this kind are found on every page. Or do you mean you think the Trio of my Scherzo is like Minkus, Gerber, or Pugni? I can't really believe it is as bad as that.

"In any case, why should 'ballet music' be considered a derogatory term? The music of a ballet is not always bad, it can be good—Delibes' *Sylvia*, for instance—and when it is good what does it matter whether Sobyesychanskaya is dancing to it or not? I can only think you don't like some parts of my symphony *because they remind you of the ballet* and not because they are intrinsically bad.

"You may be right, but I really can't see why dance tunes

should not be used from time to time in a symphony even when it is with the declared intention of introducing a touch of down-to-earth humor. Let me appeal once more to Beethoven who often used such effects."

He ended his defense of this aspect of his symphony with an outburst every musician will understand and love him for. "But how on earth did you manage to find 'ballet music' in my Allegro? I have racked my brains but can't think of a single bar that could possibly come under that heading."

So much for ballet music. Evidently it had not occurred to the serious young Taneyev (though it ought to have done so after he had heard *Swan Lake*, which Tchaikovsky was too modest to give as an example) that the very man he was writing to had already lifted ballet music to the plane of the symphony—the exact opposite of his charge that he had degraded the symphony to the level of dance music.

There remained the other major objection by Taneyev, that the symphony obviously had been written to a program and that this degraded a noble form. This leads once more to Nadezhda Filaretovna and her letters. She of course expected to be kept *au fait* with "our" symphony, as it had become. Particularly, she wanted to know exactly what it meant, what Tchaikovsky had in mind when writing it. He obliged, as he always did. His description of the meaning of the symphony is well known—it is printed in every concert program when the Fourth Symphony is played—and will not be repeated here. Even to her he prefaced his attempt to provide a literary program with, "How is it possible to express what one feels when writing an orchestral work since one has sensations for which words have never been invented? Didn't Heine say, music begins where words leave off?"

He did his best for her, however. He was a very personal composer and though he could not properly explain what was in his mind because it was also in his heart, he was almost always moved to composition by a reaction to some manifestation of life. The Fourth Symphony can be said, briefly and inadequately, to express man's struggle with fate throughout his life. The word fate is Tchaikovsky's own; everybody will insert the word which most closely represents his own view of life and its hazards.

Tchaikovsky, then, though he balked at the thought of putting a program on paper as Balakirev and Stasov did, was not going to deny the existence of a program; that would be to deny his whole raison d'etre as artist. So he replied to Taneyev: "I never want to write a symphonic work consisting of meaningless harmonies and modulations and a rhythmical scheme expressing nothing. Of course my symphony is program music but I couldn't put the program into words; it would merely sound ridiculous and give you an excuse to laugh. But isn't a program precisely what one would expect from a symphony, the most lyrical of musical forms? Should it not express everything that words cannot— things that rise in the heart and cry out for expression?

"In my innocence I thought the idea behind my symphony was so plain that everyone would grasp it, or at any rate its chief outlines, without the need of a written program. Please don't think I want to pose as a man of profound emotions and lofty ideas. I don't express any new thought and haven't even tried to. The idea behind my work is basically a reflection of Beethoven's Fifth —not the musical content, naturally, but the central plan."

He allowed himself a friendly dig at the pedant. "Must I tell you that the Fifth not only has a program but such an obvious one that everybody agrees about it? The same thing ought to apply to my symphony. If you haven't grasped the program there, all it proves is that I am no Beethoven—and I shan't dispute that!"

Then came a characteristic display of Tchaikovsky's honesty. He began by protesting in high emotion that there was not "a single bar" in the symphony that he had not felt deeply. He had no sooner written the words than he hurriedly qualified them: "Yes, there is perhaps one exception, some forced passages and a few labored and artificial things in the middle section of the first movement."

Men warmed to him for this kind of attitude, and his end to

the letter begun in such anger was absolutely typical and helps to explain why Taneyev worshipped him. "I can see you laughing as you read all this, you skeptic and mocking-bird. In spite of your great love of music it seems you still can't believe that a man can express his inmost feelings in his compositions. You just wait!"

The little battle put him into tremendous form, and for the first time for a year he got down to his work with all the old speed and enthusiasm. He began a violin concerto and wrote it *con amore,* as it was to appear when heard, and shot off a warning letter to Jurgenson. "I hit on the idea by chance, was quite carried away and the sketch is all but done." He added in the kind of mock fear he knew his publisher loved: "One way and another a considerable number of works are hanging over your head and I shall need to hire a railway truck to get them all to you. I can imagine your 'The devil take you!' when you get them all."

Jurgenson's fondness for him will be understood by one or two notes from Tchaikovsky at this time. First, he refused the large sum the publisher offered him for *Eugene Onegin* with, "I shan't take anything unless the opera is done in an opera house and even then nothing like the sum you offer." As for some translations he had made of a group of German songs at Jurgenson's request, "I can't take a ruble for them, they're so frightfully bad!" When the "truck load" finally reached Moscow there came with it a list with all the items priced—a piano sonata he had written in Italy, some songs, a children's album, and so on. The total came to nine hundred and ten rubles. "In round figures, say nine hundred rubles," said Tchaikovsky's note, "but as I've written such a lot all at once you can have them for eight hundred." That Tchaikovsky would never grow rich is clear from these business dealings; that he would never be without good friends is equally clear.

Late in February, 1878, the Fourth Symphony was given its first performance by Nicolai Rubinstein in Moscow. Nadezhda Filaretovna, who was there, sent Tchaikovsky a telegram which gave him the impression that the work had succeeded, and he was rather irritated by a telegram from Rubinstein and his colleagues containing a bare mention of the performance. Mercifully, he did not know the truth for some time. He moved back to Switzerland in April, full of the violin concerto. Kotek, who had had much to do with the inception of the concerto, was still with him; he had left Nadezhda Filaretovna and was supposed long since to be in Berlin studying under Joachim, but simply could not bring himself to leave Pyotr Ilyich until the work was done to everyone's satisfaction.

By the first days of April, Tchaikovsky had written and Kotek had played over the first two movements to the rapture of the composer and Modest, who was also with him, but not until Kotek approved the last movement would Tchaikovsky budge. Then, enormously exhilarated, he left for Russia. By the twenty-third of the month he was at Verbovka, Kamenka, where he was greeted by a penitent Alexandra. They had differed for the first and last time.

Only after he had settled happily in this blessed spot did he hear the truth about the Fourth Symphony. It had been received with incomprehension and with little but the vaguest of comments. Not until the winter, when the symphony was first played in Petersburg, was its importance to be recognized.

3

In this day and age, when the Symphony in F Minor has become one of the most popular symphonies in the world, a detailed analysis would be absurd. A case could be made for it as Tchaikovsky's most masterly symphonic work, virtually faultless in construction and with a taut grasp of argument developed with an unobtrusive skill throughout, yet it has never had the appeal of its two famous successors. Some people find the opening movement with its insistent Fate theme a little on the grim and gaunt side. For Tchaikovsky the orchestral color and thematic material sound subdued, but this was deliberate. He succeeds in his aim, to present man's dilemma in the world, a very real one as he knew only too well. And who could deny that life is precisely as he illustrates it in this movement, a continuous ebb and flow of fortune? No living person can be sure that he will not be dead the next moment, or rebuffed, or humiliated, or become the victim of one of a thousand accidents unimaginable the moment earlier. This is the picture the composer paints. He sets the scene so that he can follow with his own comment.

But if the first movement is sparing in the charm and color associated specially with Tchaikovsky, the Scherzo amply makes up for it—its delicate originality delights to this day—and the splendor of the Finale remains breathtaking when conducted by a man who feels the composer's thought and emotion, observes his markings, and can breathe enthusiasm into an orchestra which has rehearsed adequately.

The Fourth Symphony has been hailed as the first great Russian symphony, comparable to anything written in Western Europe. This claim is unjust to the symphony's predecessors, but it is true that in this work Tchaikovsky shows himself for the first time as the complete master of his art. Throughout it is written with superb confidence and drive which communicates itself to every audience.

Some critics have complained that the symphony is an earthly work, that the spiritual is not found in it. They tread difficult ground—who is to decide or agree on a spiritual work as distinct from an earthbound one? In any case they are criticizing a man for not doing what he never intended to do, which is absurd, though critics are forever basing their criticism on nothing more potent than this. Tchaikovsky was preoccupied by the problem of Fate in the lives of men on earth. His Fourth Symphony is his intensely personal answer to it. The rest is up to the listener. One can enjoy it as pure music or one can get strength from his truthful presentation.

CHAPTER 15

First Suite
1878-1880

THAT SUMMER OF 1878 saw Tchaikovsky returning to something of the state of mind he was in before his marriage. He was never again to be free from regrets—it is a commentary on the fate he thought so much about that he no sooner attained the surety of comparative affluence than he was tormented by conscience—but at least he was reconciled with Alexandra, an essential condition of a tolerable life for him, and was tackling his work with real determination.

He had another cause for relief too. He had decided to resign his post at the Conservatoire and give the rest of his life to composition. His feelings will be understood by many less exalted people who have come to the end of a long drudgery and face the prospect of doing what they really believe in and think they were born for.

At Kamenka he tidied up his recent compositions, big and small, and completed the violin concerto which he had decided to dedicate to Leopold Auer, violin professor at the Petersburg Conservatoire, the man who had asked him to write the "Serenade Melancolique." He played over the opera to the family. All were in tears. He wrote in his notebook, "If only audiences of the future feel as the composer does about this music!" For once a wish of his was to be granted.

From Kamenka he moved half way up to Moscow, to a place he was to know well, the great Brailov estate of the von Mecks. Nadezhda Filaretovna was not there, of course; the entire vast house was left to him. His comments read rather amusingly today. He was evidently overwhelmed by the attentions of the staff left behind to look after him. One not unexpected result was a feeling of extreme exhaustion followed by heavy sleep after dinner, and his diagnosis was refreshingly frank; his dreams were often blissful but not much work followed: "Too often, alas, a pickled gherkin has played a vital role in the highest functions of the human intellect."

But though stifled by grandeur he revelled in the garden and countryside. He spent hours walking and working too; he wrote the Scherzo of what was to be one of his most charming light compositions, his First Suite. He planned it in five movements.

Back at Verbovka, he worked on the Suite at top speed until he was obliged to return for the last time to the Conservatoire in autumn. He saw Moscow again with mixed feelings; Antonina was there—he had had the usual incoherent letter from her as well as a gushing one from her mother—and he stood in daily dread of her appearing at the Conservatoire with some cooked-up story for the first person she could persuade to listen. However, the step had to be taken.

How difficult it was to be he had no conception until he met Nikolai Rubinstein. They arrived back in Moscow on the same day, September 22, Rubinstein full of the great success of the Russian concerts at the Paris World's Fair. Full of congratulations too, for of all the music he had conducted and played at the Trocadero, Tchaikovsky's had proved by far the most popular. The Tempest and the piano concerto were particular hits and the latter swept the audience off its feet to such a degree that Rubinstein had to repeat it at the final concert. Never, he now told Tchaikovsky, had he seen and heard such scenes of uninhibited rapture in a concert hall.

Tchaikovsky's gratification was quickly replaced by embarrassment which reached a pitch the following evening. "Rubinstein's reunion with his Conservatoire," he told Modest, "was an absolute festival. At six o'clock we gave him dinner at the Hermitage. There were a lot of speeches and the first Rubinstein made was in my honor. He said that my compositions had made an enormous impression in Paris and spoke about the happiness the Conservatoire felt in possessing such a celebrity. All congratulated me."

At this point Tchaikovsky broke off into a characteristic comment. He loved success, few men have loved it more, but was rarely blinded by it. Not all the congratulations showered on him at the dinner were genuine and he quickly spotted the false. One of the company was the Professor of Dramatic Art, I. V. Samarin, a florid man who had begun life as an actor and still played at the Maly Theatre from time to time. Tchaikovsky often made up a foursome with him at the Kashkin's evenings of cards. He liked him well enough except when he carried the stage into everyday life, which he did frequently. He could scarcely avoid histrionics, and indulged himself at the dinner. "Samarin wept publicly," continued Tchaikovsky, describing the scenes after Rubinstein had praised him. "He gave us all a display of tender emotion. In a word, he acted out a comedy that was extremely disagreeable to me."

But the embarrassment remained. Rubinstein described him at the dinner as one of the pillars of the Conservatoire. How the pillar managed to hand his resignation to his Director the next morning Tchaikovsky never knew. But Rubinstein rose to the occasion as he usually did. Before the talk was ended it was agreed that Taneyev should take the place of Tchaikovsky—a good exchange, the latter thought.

He went to Petersburg lighthearted but, after a round of dinners with Apukhtin, had the misfortune to attend a revival of *Vakula The Smith.* His reaction was in character. He felt very angry: "With *myself.* Heavens! What a mass of unforgivable mistakes which no man except me could ever have made!"

This sentiment had no effect whatever on his passion for opera, however. After he had spent a few more autumn days at Verbovka where he finished sketching out the Suite, he went off to Italy—Nadezhda Filaretovna had taken an apartment for him in Florence—and one of his first acts there was to decide to write an opera on Schiller's *Jungfrau von Orleans*. At Kamenka he had read Zhukovsky's translation, in itself a work of art, and the more he thought about the subject the more he liked it.

He forgot that he had just written the kind of opera that suited him perfectly, he forgot that he had said so, he forgot his contempt for grand opera and his condemnation of his work on *Vakula;* all he could remember was that his first childish poem at Votkinsk had been written on Joan of Arc and that his reading of Zhukovsky brought back all the old love and worship. Not once did he pause to wonder whether his particular genius was able to handle historical subjects in the grand manner or whether Joan of Arc could be treated successfully in this or any other way. He began at once to write the opera.

The truth was that for him Joan of Arc was yet another of the girls who fascinated him by their purity, their innocence and unshakable moral strength; she was a Tatyana on the grand scale. That was why he could not resist her. He did not consider what followed Joan's belief in a divine mission; her sense of power, her essential ruthlessness. He did not see further than Tatyana because he did not want to.

As usual when writing quickly on a subject close to his heart, he was in the highest spirits, dashed only from time to time when he heard of Antonina's extravagances in Moscow or received one of her insane letters. He was enormously cheered by news of the success of the Fourth Symphony in Petersburg in December, and when he moved to Switzerland at the end of the year so that he could concentrate more strenuously on the opera (Italy attracted him too much and was too lively for hard work) he was soon writing to Jurgenson in a way which showed plainly, if somewhat clumsily, how pleased he was.

To make this letter understandable, it should be said that he wrote his reviews (given up with the professorship) under one pseudonym and his translations of German lyrics for Jurgenson under another. "I don't have to introduce you to three extraordinary people," he writes. "The feeble scribbler N. N., the late music critic B. L. of the *Russkiye Vedomosti* and the composer and ex-professor Mr. T. An hour ago Mr. T. invited the other two gentlemen—who live with him—to the piano where he played the second act of his new opera, *The Maid of Orleans.*

"Mr. T., who is on the most intimate terms with Mr. N. N. and Mr. B. L., overcame his natural modesty without much trouble and played with great skill and even inspiration. I wish you had seen the enthusiasm of the two gentlemen! To see them strutting about the room, one might have thought they had written the opera. . . . They tried without success to convince Mr. T. that operas can't be tossed out like pancakes. His answer was to bemoan the limitations of a mind and body that couldn't write down in one night all the music tormenting him with the wish to be composed and which might so easily vanish unless captured right away."

This lightheartedness did not survive the later stages of the opera. When he was reading everything he could lay his hands on about Saint Joan he had found the end of her life unendurable even to think about and when he came to sketch out this part of the opera his sufferings were terrible, as was his hatred of the English. He was never to like the English, not even when, later, they were among the most enthusiastic followers of his music. In these first days of 1879, he loathed them for what they had done to Joan of Arc. For a time he could neither bear to go on with the opera nor bear to leave it alone.

In February he went off to Paris—*The Tempest* was to be played by the Colonne Orchestra and he was curious to hear it—after a most affecting leavetaking at the Villa Richelieu at Clarens, as he told Jurgenson: "The landlady wept, the landlord gave me a preternaturally long handshake, the maid (a very nice girl) wept too, so what could I do but join in?"

Paris was quite another matter. One did not weep in Paris nor did one agonize about Joan of Arc. In a very few days he had become the dandy. He bought a new overcoat and promenaded the streets in his silk hat twirling a cane with an elegantly gloved hand. He did not see many people—he refused to call on Turgenev (who had been rude about the libretto of *Eugene Onegin*) on the grounds that great men were better known by their works than their company—but "I feel at home, I feel happy." He added in a moment of attempted realism, "The performance of *The Tempest* next Sunday may have something to do with it." It may have had, but that was not all; Paris enlivened him and by March the whole opera was sketched out and he had turned to the Suite (parts of which he had left in Petersburg and which had only just reached him) for a final orchestration.

The Tempest was not well received, as it happened, but he put the whole blame for the failure on himself as usual. "I still write like a gifted young man. What miserable orchestration!" Once again the French escaped scot free, and though he told Nadezhda Filaretovna that he remained the misanthrope, this was true only in a limited sense, for in Paris he like everyone else preferred to walk the busy streets and drink in the crowded cafes and listen to the buzz of talk even if he took no part in it.

He was still there in April, working hard, listening hard, and generally loving life, when he heard that *Eugene Onegin* was to have its premiere at the Maly; the Conservatoire students were to sing the opera as he had wished. He hurried back to Moscow and was just in time to attend the dress rehearsal.

Perhaps the most moving feature of this performance was the unanimous tribute paid by the entire Conservatoire staff and students; they insisted on crowning the composer with a wreath. The performance itself was chiefly notable for the reactions of the supposedly unemotional Taneyev and the flighty Nikolai Rubinstein; Taneyev subsided in tears, Rubinstein could not raise a joke. "He's really fallen in love with it," cried Tchaikovsky, scarcely able to believe eyes or ears.

This apart, the opera fell rather flat. There was plenty of applause but, as the composer saw plainly, "for me rather than for my work." With the best will in the world the students were not up to it.

However, the evening was not yet over. Anton Rubinstein had been lured down to Moscow for the event and he rather than the composer became the guest of honor at the after-performance supper at the Hermitage. Tchaikovsky waited on tenterhooks for his comment during and after the supper. He waited in vain; Rubinstein did not say one word about the opera.

Tchaikovsky was angry. Over the years since he first joined the Petersburg Conservatoire in 1862 his devotion to Anton Rubinstein had been subjected to increasing strain: Anton had damned the First Symphony, damned the Second String Quartet and criticized in the most wounding terms almost every other Tchaikovsky work he had seen or heard. On top of this he had deterred (one could almost say forbidden, so great was his reputation) Tchaikovsky's old student friend V. V. Bessel from printing a score.

This last snub hit Tchaikovsky hard: "Isn't it strange," he wrote to von Bülow who made a point of sending good news from the West when he heard it, "that of the *two most famous artists* of our epoch you *who have not known me long* have supported my music so splendidly and Anton Rubinstein who was my master has not? That Olympian god has never shown anything but supreme contempt for my compositions and I can tell you under the seal of the confessional that I have always felt deeply hurt by this. Apropos of my quartet whose success you tell me about, may I reveal a small detail which will enable you to understand *how* great this contempt is? When I suggested to the publisher Bessel of Petersburg that he publish (without any payment to me) this same quartet that you tell me has found favor in America, he went to Rubinstein to ask his advice. Was the work good enough to be published? he asked. 'No,' said my old master decisively.

Thereupon Bessel sends me the most formal and humiliating refusal.

"And the great master is still treating my works in the same fashion—utter contempt. But let me add, Monsieur, that I tell you this only to show you how great my gratitude is towards you who are neither my master nor even a compatriot."

There was, then, every reason why Tchaikovsky should consign Anton Rubinstein to the devil in so far as his ability to judge his work was concerned, yet such was his habit of reverence from years past that he could never shake off the wish to win the master's approval. Once again he thought this triumphant moment had come; he believed *Eugene Onegin* was his best work to date and felt that Rubinstein must surely respond to the genuine feeling in the score.

Anton did nothing of the kind. Obviously he did not like the opera but he refused to say why, refused even to discuss it. Only when he had returned to Petersburg did he explain to his wife why he could not congratulate his old student: "It has none of the style of grand opera."

2

Anton Rubinstein's objection was to dog the fortunes of *Eugene Onegin* for two years in Russia and many more outside Russia. It must be said that those who hear the opera for the first time must dismiss from their minds every preconceived notion about opera if they are to appreciate it. It is now generally agreed to be Tchaikovsky's operatic masterpiece. One might go further and suggest that he invented a new kind of modern opera, the intimate drama, which must be played on a small stage in a small theater if it is to have its full effect.

People have often wondered how a symphonist who revels in the broad sweep and large effects goes to the other extreme when he writes opera that suits him. Clearly *Eugene Onegin* could have been written in quite another way. For instance, Prokofiev, who loved both the opera and its composer, often expressed his amazement that Tchaikovsky had omitted some of the more obviously dramatic parts of the story—parts which would have brought it nearer to grand opera.

But when Tchaikovsky brought people on to the stage his instinct was to keep them lifesize, as he and his audience would understand them from their own experience. He resisted every temptation to inflate them to the size of gods. The first definition of tragedy limited the participators to those of high estate. Tchaikovsky, who did not lack courage (after an attempt on the Tsar's life at this time he wrote, "As long as all of us—the people of Russia—are refused a say in the government of our country there is no hope of a happier future"), insisted on presenting from everyday life characters whom he knew and could understand. His Tatyana was the kind of Russian girl to be found in every town and village in the land. He had met Lenskis and Onegins by the score in Petersburg and Moscow. Even the duel in which the wrong man was killed had been fought out in cruel fact when Pushkin was virtually murdered by a nobody who lived into his eighties.

The music follows the characters. It too is unpretentious, quiet, avoiding bombast and heroics. It takes its cue from the heroine who is in the worldly sense nothing, in the spiritual sense everything. The composer does not strain himself to produce unforgettable themes as he could well have done; he chooses to rely on music precisely suited to character and situation, to a small event happening in remote Russia, to people who might be expected to live and die without raising a flutter outside their little provincial circle.

Lenski's aria and the letter song, justly famed though they are, do not constitute an opera; lesser known parts of the opera are as unique and as satisfactory. All the Overtures are little works of art, and the three main scenes between Tatyana and Onegin are beautifully constructed; they do not possess one notable theme, they possess something far better, music perfectly attuned to the moment and the people occupying the stage. This is the secret of the opera's success; it does not swerve from truth for one instant— has any opera ever ended on such a note?—and truth, as Tchaikovsky unforgettably demonstrates here, is beauty.

3

Tchaikovsky did not fret about the cool reception of his opera, chiefly for the old reason that he was too much taken up with its successor, *The Maid of Orleans,* the Suite, and a second piano concerto he was meditating. He was also preoccupied by Antonina. From Moscow he went up to Petersburg as usual to see his father and friends (he never let many months go by without this visit to the old man) but was poorly repaid by the sudden irruption of his wife. She hung about outside his rooms until she found him, but it was difficult to understand what she wanted except money; she talked incessantly about her love for him and of his for her and of those who wanted to keep them apart. She also threw in for good measure a long and rambling recital of the latest scalps she had added to her belt. Nothing he could say would calm her or stop the flow. She took the money he offered her, however.

In the end she drove him out of the city by taking a room in the house in which he was staying. He went back to Moscow. She followed him and again forced her way into his rooms. The Petersburg scene was repeated. He retreated to Kamenka and she bombarded him with letters.

The significant fact about this revival of persecution was the manner in which he dealt with it. A year earlier it would have driven him abroad, a guilty man struggling with a nervous breakdown. By the early summer of 1879 he had rationalized his guilt feelings and had begun to understand that he was dealing with a woman who could not be held responsible for her actions. But to deal with a half-mad woman face to face is a terrifying experience. He was terrified but he kept his head because he was compassionate too. He could not acquit himself from responsibility and did not try, but he refused to allow her (sometimes he thought the only guiltless party) to affect his work.

This attitude he demonstrated effectively at Kamenka. He finished *The Maid of Orleans* and quickly polished off the orchestration of the Suite. He added a sixth movement, a Divertimento, which he placed second and very good it was, but the movement which caused something of a sensation in the Davidov house was an Andante. "Everyone here is mad about it," he told Jurgenson. "When I played it with my brother as a piano duet one girl fainted!"

From Kamenka he went on to Brailov. Not to the main mansion, as Nadezhda Filaretovna was there; she had left open a smaller house at Simaki on the Brailov estate. He went with some misgivings: "I've grown so used to thinking of Nadezhda Filaretovna as some sort of remote and invisible godmother that the thought of her so close to me in the flesh is a little disturbing."

His concern was well-founded. She would not at all have cared for being cast in the role of godmother as she began to show. In Florence she had lived within a short way from him and he had passed her one day in the street. Now, at Simaki, she wanted to send her youngest daughter over to him. He stopped that politely but firmly. Then, in August, she drove through the Simaki grounds and came face to face with him in a wood through which he was walking. Both were confused and he was not pleased. He understood, if she did not, that a flesh and blood friendship would never do; it could not stay that way, on her side at any rate, and it would destroy the spiritual basis on which the relationship had to rest if it were to last.

He could not explain this in so many words, but he was soon to make clear enough what he felt—he was driven to it by more obvious signs that she was thinking in terms of a closer tie.

She had already broached a marriage between one of her sons and one of Alexandra's daughters so that the Tchaikovsky and von Meck blood could mingle literally as well as spiritually. He did not dissent—he could scarcely do that—but replied coolly to her request for an opinion as to which Davidov daughter would be most fitted as her daughter-in-law. This cold-blooded marriage-making was not to his taste—his own marriage had exposed it forever—and he would not give an opinion. For him, the young people must meet and make up their own minds, as, later on, they did.

All this was as nothing to her outburst a few weeks later. It was caused, she said, by the piano transcription of the Fourth Symphony which she had received shortly before she wrote. She had been playing it ever since.

Her letter had little to do with the symphony. After the first sentence she broke out: "I don't expect you could ever understand how jealous I am of you in spite of the fact that we have never even spoken to each other. Let me confess that I am jealous in an unforgivable way, as a woman is jealous of the man she loves. Can you imagine how I felt when you married? I had a dreadful struggle, my heart was all but broken. The thought that you were with that woman was scarcely bearable torture. And that is not all. I must tell you how wicked I was—I was overjoyed when I realized that you were wretched to be with her. . . . I hated her for not making you happy but if she had made you happy I should have hated her a hundred times more. I felt that she had stolen from me what ought to belong to me only, what I have a right to possess for the best of all reasons, that I love you more than anyone else and cherish you more than anything else in the world."

At this point she seems to have realized what she was saying and what Tchaikovsky might think of it. She did not tear up the letter as she could so easily have done; she added a would-be re-assuring statement that in spite of her feelings she had no wish to alter the present relationship—a statement she went far to render valueless by another addition which bore a horrifying resemblance to a somewhat similar remark by Antonina more than two years earlier. She said that before her life came to its end

she would like to feel sure that nothing was changed, that nobody. . . . She did not finish this sentence, having no need to do
so. She then threw in an Antonina-like remark: "But I have no
right to say that."

Tchaikovsky's feelings on receiving this letter are not difficult
to imagine. He could no longer believe in Nadezhda Filaretovna's
imminent decease. He knew from Rubinstein, from Kotek, and
from another Conservatoire violinist who had taken Kotek's place
—V. A. Pakhulsky—that she suffered much physically. He also
knew from his own experience that if one tears one's nerves to
pieces one will feel physically unwell. But to die was another
matter; the way his patroness dashed about Europe in search of
cures did not suggest death.

He had to proceed on the assumption—quite correct as it
turned out—that she would live as long as he. He was not a stupid
man; he could imagine something of what she must have felt
when he wrote to tell her about his engagement to Antonina. But
her reply then had been calm, two years had passed and he, familiar with the flowery epistolary style of the day, had been encouraged to think that she really wished their friendship to be on a platonic level. Recently, as has been seen, her attitude had worried
him; now she had come out into the open.

About one thing he was definite; he would neither live with
her nor, should such a thing ever be possible, would he marry her.
He did not even wish to meet her; he felt with reason that any
kind of intimacy other than the kind they enjoyed would be fatal
to the relationship.

Yet he did not wish the relationship to end; the mere thought
dismayed him beyond words. He needed her money for himself
and his music chiefly, though for others too, but he needed her
faith and moral support just as much. He was still unrecognized
abroad as an outstanding composer and still had far to go in his
own country. Her faith and her money kept him writing and
hopeful of eventual triumph; without them he could no longer
feel sure of going on. Besides, he was immensely grateful for what

she had done for him in the past two years; she had almost literally made a new man of him.

It was up to him to save the relationship. He did so with great
skill. She had given him the opportunity to put down everything
she had written to the effect of playing his symphony. He took
the opportunity. "I can't bear to think," he wrote after reaffirm-
ing his belief in the dedication of the symphony as truly meant
and earned, "what might have happened if you had not been
sent to me by Fate. I owe you everything—life, freedom that had
seemed out of my grasp, and indeed so much good fortune that I
could never have dreamed of it coming my way."

Then came the crucial sentence; it was no more than a repeti-
tion of what he had told her many times, particularly when she
had questioned the power of music to convey the feeling of love.
"I read your letter with such gratitude and love that I can only
express what I feel by means of music."

He had said in his own way what he was and was not prepared
to do or feel. She submitted, more fearful than he of losing what
she had. From that moment there was a change in the balance of
power; the relationship, its limits and its scope were henceforth
left in his hands to decide. He was never again to receive such a
letter from her.

4

To this tactful and wise Tchaikovsky must be added a demonstration of the businesslike one, forceful and quick. It is a Tchaikovsky little known, thanks chiefly to the diffidence which so
often falsifies his letters. Here for once the man of affairs comes
into the open, released, as might be expected, by a threat to the
well-being of someone he loved.

He heard suddenly that Anatoly was likely to lose his job. He
took the next train to Petersburg where his brother worked, demanded full particulars and, having got them, made a round of
calls on Anatoly's superiors. What Pyotr Ilyich said and how he

said it we shall never know but we do know the immediate result; Anatoly was reinstated.

The taste of triumph did not last long; he had no sooner reached Moscow on his way back to Kamenka than Nikolai Rubinstein and Jurgenson called. He was having his morning tea but they routed him out and insisted that he come along with them to what was euphemistically called breakfast. By the evening he had drunk more than was good for him. "Oh, Moscow!" he wrote to Anatoly the next morning. "One has scarcely set foot in it before one begins drinking. At five o'clock I had to go along to the Jurgensons' where it all began over again. This Moscow tippling is more abhorrent to me than I can tell you."

As he was writing to a brother who deplored drinking in any shape or form, and specially his own fondness for it, his excess of regret may be suspect. Nevertheless he was sick of what went with the drink in Conservatoire company—gossip and not much but gossip. After a few more weeks at Kamenka, where he began his Second Piano Concerto, he developed "an intense Italian craze." That is to say, he longed for blue Italian skies and hot sun and longed too for the wine on which men did not become fuddled but merely more amusing.

By November he was in Paris en route for Rome. "I'm so happy!" he cried as always when he first left Russia.

The stay in Paris was prolonged. Nadezhda Filaretovna was there busily bribing Colonne to play the Fourth Symphony. She was determined to make Pyotr Ilyich world-famous and was prepared to buy fame for him if he could get it no other way.

He deprecated the whole business. His pride was wounded. But he had just checked his patroness in one direction and had temporarily to allow her latitude in another; he washed his hands of the whole affair and kept away from Colonne. But he was determined that this should be her first and last excursion into the world of concert and theater management. There were times when the business woman in her offended him deeply. This was one of them. When she next brought up the subject, as he knew she would, he insisted that no more payments should be made. Either his music was good enough to force people to play it or it was not. He stood firm and she was obliged to give up.

Neither Colonne nor the symphony would have kept him in Paris, but the new piano concerto was going splendidly and he would not risk moving and disturbing the flow of ideas. The moment the sketch was completed, in the middle of December, he went to Rome.

Soon afterwards, the First Suite had its first performance in Moscow. The success—as it was—was soured for the composer by hearing from Jurgenson that Nikolai Rubinstein said the music was impossible to play (though he had done so) because the writing for some of the parts was too difficult.

Tchaikovsky flew into a rage. "If he is right I had better give up writing music."

When Taneyev tried to pour oil on the waters he merely let himself in for another storm from Rome. Defending Rubinstein, he particularized: some of the woodwind writing, he explained, especially for the oboe, was unplayable; Tchaikovsky had not allowed enough time for the instrumentalist to take breath.

Tchaikovsky denied the imputation comprehensively and hit back. "I can see plainly that Rubinstein was in a bad mood and took it out on my Suite. For ten years I taught instrumentation at the Conservatoire—not very well, admittedly, but without exactly disgracing myself—and now, two years later, I have to endure remarks which should be confined to backward students! Let's get this thing straight; either I have never known how to write for an orchestra or Rubinstein's criticism is on a par with his remarks about my piano concerto. In 1875 he said it was impossible to play but by 1878 he had found it perfectly possible!"

This was a cruel cut—Rubinstein had become one of the concerto's most ardent advocates and was playing it brilliantly. But Tchaikovsky, who did not bear malice, soon found a likelier explanation than ill-humor in Rubinstein when he heard that the leading oboist had complained. All the same, what was Rubinstein doing, listening to the growlings of a lazy man? Tchaikovsky knew him, a German who was more preoccupied with flirtations than with his instrument. "So the high notes I have written will spoil the beautiful shape of my German friend's lips, will they!" he wrote in high sarcasm. "So his kisses won't be quite so emphatic or luscious! All right. But this tragedy won't stop me from writing high notes that every oboist can play!"

The fuss blew over and the supposedly impossible writing—of which every advanced composer has been accused in his time—has long since been proved eminently playable. The Suite was to be immediately popular everywhere it was played and one of the many mysteries of music is its complete disappearance from the concert repertory. It is never heard now and no recording is available at the time of writing.

The Suite is not and was not supposed to be great music. It is very pleasing music written with superlative skill and many a concert program would be the happier and the more popular if it opened or closed with this work. One notable feature is the use of the woodwinds. Tchaikovsky never failed in this department of an orchestra and in this First Suite, written in one of his sunniest moods, the writing for woodwinds is wholly delightful. Four of the six movements open with woodwinds—The Introduction and Fugue (a fine pastiche) opens with the bassoon, the Divertimento with the clarinet, the Intermezzo with flute and bassoon and the final Gavotte with bassoon, clarinet, oboe, and flute each echoing the same phrase in turn against a string background.

But the triumph of the work is unquestionably the little "Marche Miniature." There are only 124 bars in this tiny movement but all are magical. They also point ahead. Just as the first movement of the First Symphony points to the Transformation music of "Casse Noisette," so this Suite—and specially the "Marche Miniature"—points to the first act of the same ballet.

Within a few months this Suite was to be played and praised by a much greater musician than Nikolai Rubinstein—none other than the young Debussy. Nadezhda Filaretovna engaged the eight-

een-year-old boy during the summer vacation of the Paris Conservatoire. He was to play four-hand arrangements with her.
When he did, she was critical; he wasn't, she thought, much of a
pianist—"There is no comparison between French and Russian
pianists, ours are so much better in technique and as musicians"—
but she recognized his astonishing gift as sight-reader.

He was soon exercising this gift on the Suite, which they played
together, and, said the gratified Nadezhda Filaretovna, in doing
so disclosed another virtue: "He likes your music. Massenet
teaches him theory, so naturally Massenet is a hero of his, but
after we had played your Suite he was so pleased with the fugue
that he volunteered, 'I've never come across anything so beautiful
in all modern fugues; even M. Massenet could not have written
it.' "

The composer's mind was soon and unhappily taken off this
fine little work; from Petersburg and Kamenka came bad news
early in the new year of 1880; Ilya Petrovich was ill at the one
place, Alexandra at the other. Tchaikovsky prepared to go back
to Petersburg but before he could move he had a telegram an-
nouncing his father's death.

Those who pursue the well-worn spectre of the Oedipus complex have lost no time in pointing out that the death of Ilya
Petrovich did not cause Tchaikovsky the grief he had felt when
he lost his mother. This is a typical example of wishful thinking.
No one knows what Pyotr Ilyich felt—grief is not measurable—
and those who say they do are talking nonsense. Moreover, Alexandra Andreyevna was forty-one when she died, her husband
eighty-five! Forty-one was young even in those days, eighty-five a
great age. What Tchaikovsky said when he had the news was,
"What an angelic old soul he was! It is a bitter grief to me that
I shan't see him again." He meant exactly what he said.

Part Four

FAME

CHAPTER 16

Serenade for Strings and
Violin Concerto
1880-1881

ILYA PETROVICH DID NOT LIVE to see his son a famous man. He had heard him applauded in the Maryinsky and the Petersburg concert halls. He had also read the newspapers afterwards and had watched Pyotr Ilyich growing more and more despondent and looking older every time he saw him; already—he was not quite forty—there was gray on the head which was coming to look so much like his own, hair brushed back stiffly from the forehead. It seems most probable that Ilya Petrovich died with his original opinion unchanged, that his son would have lived more happily as a very talented amateur. Had he read the letter from Apukhtin two years earlier he would surely have felt himself justified, for after twelve years as a professional musician and with all the lustre and help of a Conservatoire post and powerful friends, his son could only draw from the poet, "Your country is going to be proud of you." He might well wonder whether this was not merely poetic license.

Yet had he lived another few months he would have seen his son's and Apukhtin's faith justified, for the year 1880 was to be notable for the beginnings of world fame—fame to a degree that no other Russian before or since has enjoyed.

The opening of the year gave little sign of what was so soon to come. Nadezhda Filaretovna could splash her money about but the recipient was only obliged to fulfil the letter of the law as Colonne demonstrated. He played the Fourth Symphony; how he played it was another matter. It was a comparative failure. There were mitigating circumstances. The French were to prove one of the stubbornest audiences to move—regular and enthusiastically received performances of Tchaikovsky in Paris have only recently taken place—but by 1880 they were at least aware of him as a possible force in modern music. The triumph of his First Piano Concerto during the World's Fair did much to advance his fame; his name was known though his music was not often played, and comments on the Fourth Symphony, if cool, were respectful. Besides, he was succeeding in Paris with other works; both the Third Quartet and the "Serenade Melancolique" were praised rapturously, the latter far beyond its merits.

Elsewhere this year his music went from triumph to triumph. The First Suite was given a wonderful reception in Petersburg, then in New York under Leopold Damrosch. The Concerto in B Flat Minor was at last welcomed by the Germans—it was played three times within a few weeks—as well as making its mark in Budapest, and in New York it scored a renewed ovation with Franz Rummel at the piano.

This was not fame but a hint of it was in the air and when he returned to Russia in March he found in the capitals that subtle but unmistakable change of climate when a man begins to advance from purely national to international notice. In Petersburg he was in such demand at dinners and soirees given by musical and social celebrities that he panted to be away into the country; he never had a moment to himself and, feeling that this widespread notice might well have been given some years earlier when, for one thing, his father would have been alive and would have revelled in it much more than he, his comments were unflattering to those who suddenly discovered that it was the thing to patronize the local boy who had made good.

Even a performance of his Second Quartet, with Leopold Auer playing first violin, after which Tchaikovsky was presented with a wreath amidst scenes of enormous enthusiasm—even this could not rouse him. It had all come rather late. He stayed on for one purpose only, to try to see that *The Maid of Orleans* was given a fair hearing by the Imperial Theaters committee. His disgust with the creatures who had sensed correctly (as they almost always do) the prevailing wind of change was natural enough, but his assumption that their praise was nauseatingly worthless was going too far; that the Petersburg musicians and aristocrats could be right for the wrong reason seems never to have occurred to him, so obsessed was he by this latest opera.

At last he escaped to Moscow, dead tired and rather cynical, only to find that one of his most persistent new admirers, the Grand Duke Konstantin Nikolayevich, had followed him and wanted to repeat the banquet he had given in his honor in Petersburg. Tchaikovsky hurriedly made his excuses and fled to Kamenka.

There he found Alexandra still unwell and Lyov waiting to take her to Carlsbad for treatment. Leaving Pyotr Ilyich in charge of the children, they went off soon after he arrived. He was not in the best shape for dealing with the children's demands on his time—they were all growing up fast and were very lively—but he kept them in some sort of order and himself in good physical trim and managed to get down to some work too. Before he broke the Kamenka stay with a few weeks at Brailov and Simaki as usual, he had finished orchestrating the piano concerto and a *Capriccio Italien* he had written very quickly in Rome.

At Brailov he did more work, getting *The Maid of Orleans* ready for the printer, and went for more great walks. At Simaki too he was forever out of doors when the weather allowed and one day his passion for Russia expressed itself. He was walking through a field of millet when suddenly the beauty of the Russian countryside came over him with such a rush of feeling that he fell on his knees and thanked God for the joy he felt. "Everywhere beauty and space!" he wrote in his notebook that night. "What moments life holds! Thanks to them one can forget all the rest."

Back at Kamenka he had more news of the latest addition to

the von Meck musical staff, the young cellist Danilchenko fresh from the Moscow Conservatoire, and of the boy Debussy whom Nadezhda Filaretovna insisted on calling Bussy. She sent a photograph of him—Tchaikovsky thought he looked very much like Anton Rubinstein when young—and asked whether he might take back to Paris (his vacation was almost up) a copy of *The Maid of Orleans* score. Tchaikovsky agreed readily and sent the score but by the time she received it Nadezhda Filaretovna had changed her mind; she had remembered the French magpies.

Debussy went off without the score. "I was afraid," she explained to Pyotr Ilyich, "that those thieving French composers, Massenet, Delibes, and the rest of them, would steal whole handfuls of your opera and play them to Parisian audiences as their own." She hastened to forestall an incredulous objection—she thought she knew the French better than her correspondent and tended to look on the uncharitable side—with, "They have already stolen from you, Pyotr Ilyich, believe me. For instance only the other day when we were playing the fourhand arrangement of your First Symphony I noticed passages I had heard in Paris, *not* under your name."

Tchaikovsky was hard at work again—Kamenka had an extraordinarily good effect on him—on two very different compositions, the "1812" Overture and Serenade for Strings. He wrote "1812" with his tongue in his cheek—Nikolai Rubinstein had been plaguing him to write something suitable for the Moscow Exposition of Industrial Art in 1882—and it is not mentioned in high critical quarters. It is difficult not to laugh at the bombast—"It will be very noisy" he warned Nadezhda Filaretovna—yet it is also difficult to deny that it is effective. Tchaikovsky was a consummate workman—a professional musician who knew his job—and this piece precisely filled the need; it roused patriotic fervor, it was dramatic, and it did not go on too long.

The Serenade for Strings was a very different matter. When he had finished it early in November he told Jurgenson, "I am violently in love with this work and can't wait for it to be played."

He had to wait a while but scarcely had time to notice it, for the moment he left Kamenka he was caught up in a veritable barrage of first performances of works written earlier. A man's own country rarely hails him as great until the outside world shows signs of doing so, and this was what was happening in Russia in the beginning of the 1880's. The musical members of high society in Petersburg had already given him a foretaste of the kind of public life he must expect; now came a rush of Moscow performances as if there could not be enough Tchaikovsky music.

Apart from chamber concerts—his songs and quartets were becoming firm favorites—the first orchestral work to be heard that winter was the "Capriccio Italien"; it was played several times in both capitals and public and critics alike (Cui excepted as usual) received it rapturously. Too rapturously perhaps; it is popular music and was not intended to be anything else. To complain, as Cui did, that its brilliance was all on the surface was to mistake the composer's aim. Tchaikovsky had no wish to write a profound work but to give his own personal impression of Italy in music, and the impression was deliberately of Carnival in Rome, using the tunes he had heard sung in the streets. A superficial impression, possibly, of an event which, based on religious feeling, was absolutely true of the Italian people at that time. The work has held its popularity for almost one hundred years and is likely to hold it, for, given the restricted aim, it is brilliantly worked out, tuneful, varied, and economical.

At the Bolshoi was a revival of *Oprichnik*—applauded more because the composer had suddenly caught public favor than for its real merits—and at the other extreme came a Musical Society performance of a Liturgy he had written some months previously, a work which produced vast applause and violent opposition by the church.

A few weeks later, after Tchaikovsky had spent a thankful Christmas and the New Year of 1881 with the Kamenka family and an Alexandra somewhat recovered, *Eugene Onegin* was given its first Bolshoi performance with a professional cast. This time it gradually won its way with the public who not for the first time proved themselves more malleable than the critics. To accept this chamber opera—specially in the vast Bolshoi—when one has been accustomed to a diet of grand opera is not easy. It took some time for the audiences to adapt themselves to the change but they made the effort. While the critics were still harping on the old objections of lack of large-scale dramatic effects, quietness of the music matching undistinguished happenings on stage, the people were obstinately coming back for more. They would not let the opera die and from that moment its fate was certain; unlike previous operas by the same composer, *Eugene Onegin* was to go from success to success as the years passed.

Three weeks later his Second Symphony had its first performance in its revised form—he had rewritten much of the first movement and tightened up the rest—and received great acclaim. One has the impression that anything he wrote then would have been acclaimed; Moscow had become Tchaikovsky-conscious at last, realizing that this undemonstrative composer possessed all the dynamism of the Russian spirit and would change world opinion of a supposed backward country.

The quiet and popular ex-professor did not hear the ovations; he was in Petersburg showing quite another Tchaikovsky to the producers of *The Maid of Orleans*.

2

Tchaikovsky's use of his new status in Russia was typical of the man. We have seen what he thought of the adulation; when it did not bore it sickened him, with himself and the flatterers. Now he saw the practical side and seized it.

As his scores demonstrate, he was a punctilious writer of music. He left nothing to chance; he knew just what he wanted and explained it in the clearest possible manner. In performances of chamber works and occasionally in the symphonic works he had had his way; that is to say, he often managed to impress on the members of quartets and on Nikolai Rubinstein as conductor that his markings were meant to be followed and that if they were not his music was not being played, only a travesty of it. But in opera he had had to stand aside and watch and hear his work mutilated. He had no power to influence the bureaucratic conductors, producers, and the dozens of hangers on of the state opera houses, including a nonmusical government representative who would cut and change the score and libretto at will. Chaliapin was to rage against these backstage Napoleons many years later. What Tchaikovsky suffered impotently during earlier rehearsals in the Imperial Theaters beggars the imagination.

Now, in February, 1881, he went up to Petersburg determined to use his sudden rise to fame to some purpose, which he did, to the general amazement of all the theater people. They knew him well, as they thought, by this time, and rated him a mild and easygoing man. They now discovered during rehearsals a meticulous tyrant insistent that his work should be produced and played and sung as he had imagined it during composition and who was prepared to keep singers, producer, conductor, and orchestra in the theatre all night if he did not get his way.

Napravnik's chief assistant, O. O. Palyechek, was to put everybody's astonishment into words: "He attended all the rehearsals and had something to say about everything that went on. He literally cavilled at every phrase that was played or sung. . . . Assisted by Napravnik and me, he worked out every move on stage with the singers, every note they sang, every gesture they made. He insisted that we study the character of the music as he had written it before allowing it to be played and sung. . . . And I must admit that his directions were so very much to the point that it would be true to say that he alone was the real producer of the opera."

To this Palyechek adds a plaintive note: "Although I know that everyone thinks of him as simply a mild, good man, at such times he was extremely severe."

In this instance it is sad to have to report that all his trouble was wasted. He attended the first performance at the Maryinsky before leaving for his usual winter in Italy and, not for the first time, was deceived by the applause in the theater as he had long since deceived himself about the opera: "I believe it will make my name as an opera composer" he had told Modest.

The near future was to show that the applause was almost wholly a tribute to him and his work in general rather than for the opera on stage. He had not reached Rome before newspapers warned him that the critics to a man were likely to condemn the opera.

As it turned out, they tore it to shreds, and for once one can say, justly. Tchaikovsky's taste, which was not impeccable, had failed him badly. He presented Joan of Arc as a Russian girl whose spirituality did not prevent a hopeless love for an imaginary Lionel of Burgundy and gave them a love duet as one of the central pieces of the opera. His historical sense was not equal to the challenge; he surrounded Saint Joan with a chorus which was in essence nothing more than a crowd of Russian peasants.

But then, as has often been said, Joan of Arc is not a fit subject for an opera stage; like Faure's Requiem in a concert hall, it is out of place. Having chosen to present her in an opera Tchaikovsky was no doubt obliged to follow the conventions but could not hope to succeed. He made bad worse by reacting violently to criticisms that he was incapable of writing grand opera—this in spite of his many asseverations that he had no wish to attempt it. It is true that he chose for his grand opera a real person and not a puppet but his treatment of the work is painfully reminiscent of Meyerbeer.

At times he wrote good music, as the critics acknowledged, but the action on stage made nonsense of it. Only twice did he manage to create a Joan of Arc in which one could believe, when she makes her farewell to her birthplace—a very moving aria—and again in the second act when, in an inspired solo, she invokes the blessing of God and his angels. These apart—and they are still sung—the opera is best forgotten.

3

Tchaikovsky was prevented from too much brooding on this latest operatic disaster by two events, the one intermingling with the other. So soon does fame spread even in a country which scarcely knew his work that his new reputation had preceded him. He had no sooner arrived in Rome than he discovered that the days of anonymity were over; the society hostesses set their sights on this latest lion. He found himself in a Roman version of the Petersburg of his last two visits and rapidly tired of it.

He was, besides, worried about Nikolai Rubinstein and the chatter at dinners and soirees seemed indecent as well as silly. For the last few months his old Director had been troubled by severe stomach pains. In spite of everything Tchaikovsky and every other friend could say he would not see a doctor nor would he give up his gargantuan meals washed down by wine and brandy.

A few days after Tchaikovsky left Russia, Rubinstein felt so ill that he was forced to see a doctor. The doctor sent him off immediately to Paris for treatment accompanied by his close friends, the Tretyakovs. They had got no farther than Vilna when news came that the Tsar had been assassinated. Tretyakov, Mayor of Moscow, had to return; his wife and Nikolai went on to Paris.

Tchaikovsky did not know of the hurried journey to Paris; he knew only that this old friend was seriously ill and would do nothing about it. He feared his obstinacy. Rome quickly became unendurable and Tchaikovsky went down to Naples hoping to forget his uneasiness in the work he could never get time for in the capital. He had scarcely put pen to paper before he heard that Alexander II had been assassinated, which made him long to be home; and, before he could do anything about it, that Rubinstein was in Paris and dangerously ill with tuberculosis of the stomach.

Pyotr Ilyich forgot all about Russia and the Tsar and got ready to go to Paris. He had not reached the train before a second telegram told him that Nikolai was dead. His death was absolutely in character; on his last morning he demanded a plate of oysters followed by an ice and would accept no refusals. He died a few hours later.

In the train Tchaikovsky spent long hours of wretchedness. He describes what he felt and at once sets himself apart from the ordinary man. The difference between the great man and the ordinary one lies not so much in what they think as that the one says what he thinks and the other does not. Tchaikovsky in the Rome-Paris express provides the perfect example. His thoughts during the journey were given less to sorrow at the loss of an old friend and companion than to sheer horror at the thought of seeing Rubinstein's dead body.

This is one of the commonest of fears and is shared by most people but not one in a thousand would ever have the moral courage to say so. Tchaikovsky frankly confesses it. "I was afraid I would break down under the shock." His journey was one long struggle "to try to brace myself to conquer such shameful cowardice."

All his fears were unnecessary; Rubinstein's body was already lying in the Russian church by the time he arrived. Anton was there, so too at the Paris funeral service were Turgenev, Lalo, Pauline Viardot, and Massenet.

Tchaikovsky would not go back to Moscow with the funeral party for the strange reason that he resented the fact that Anton appeared to show relief rather than grief at the death of his brother. It seems that Tchaikovsky's long hero worship of Anton Rubinstein, twenty years of it, had finally expired. Anton's attitude at The Hermitage had been deeply wounding, not for the first time, and his apparent attitude towards his dead brother—which Tchaikovsky must surely have misread—settled the matter.

A few days later Tchaikovsky followed them to Moscow. The choice of a new Director had to be made and he must have suspected that his name would be raised; he had already refused the Directorship at Kiev.

Surely enough, he was unanimously begged to take the post. He refused and recommended Taneyev. His refusal was courageous because he had recently heard that the von Meck fortune had suffered serious inroads and had begged Nadezhda Filaretovna to stop paying him an allowance; he was free from fear of poverty, he told her, and could always go back to a Conservatoire if the need arose.

She would not listen; Brailov might have to go (she did in fact sell the estate) but she had plenty left and in any case, heavily underlined: "I absolutely refuse to abandon my right to look after you."

He did not protest further. He could use the allowance. Although his income was going up steadily—the sale of songs and piano pieces in particular had grown substantially—his expenditures kept pace with it. Unlike most men who begin to flourish he became increasingly generous. The fact that he had been poor and might well be poor again had no effect whatever. He helped every genuine hard luck case brought to his notice—his begging post had become enormous—and many spurious ones. He had begun his charity at home with the lame duck Modest. He made him a handsome allowance that left him free to write, with the result that he had a play due to be staged in Petersburg shortly and was soon to be in demand, heaven knows why, as a librettist.

Although a few of his own completed works were hanging fire—the Violin Concerto was waiting for Leopold Auer, the Second Piano Concerto needed a suitable soloist and the "Serenade for Strings" was delayed for Eduard Napravnik—Tchaikovsky returned to Russia anxious to write. What he wanted to write was an opera—obviously he would never learn his limitations—and again he made a mistake at the outset by choosing what was for him an impossible subject. In Petersburg before going to Kamenka for the summer he was told by K. Y. Davidov the cellist, one of his professors at the Petersburg Conservatoire who had become Director, about a Pushkin libretto that had never been used—with some reason, it turned out. But when Tchaikovsky sent for the libretto, by V. P. Burenin on *Poltava*, he thought he could make a good thing of it with a few judicious alterations. He made the alterations—as has been seen, he rather fancied himself as librettist—and by the autumn, before leaving for another Italian winter, he had renamed it *Mazeppa* and had sketched out some of it. He was tremendously enthusiastic about it; if he never learned, he never grew up either, which is refreshing even when it leads to trouble.

In October the Serenade for Strings had its first performance in Petersburg. It was immediately hailed by public and critics as a splendid work. Anton Rubinstein, breaking a long silence, said that it was the best thing his old student had done; no doubt he meant the only tolerable thing. The Moscow premiere, some months later, confirmed the success of what has become one of Tchaikovsky's best liked works. The most popular movement, the Waltz, has suffered the fate of so many of Tchaikovsky's delightful themes and is so much overplayed as to make it difficult for a modern listener to evaluate it. The other three movements are more substantial and show the composer at his brilliant best; as a lesson in writing for strings they have rarely been surpassed. If any doubt existed that Tchaikovsky was a master of his craft it was finally dispelled when the Serenade was first played.

Less than two months later, when Tchaikovsky was settled in Rome for the winter, the Violin Concerto was played at last. For the second time he had to scratch out a dedication. Auer, he discovered, not content with declining the dedication after three years, had been trumpeting the legend of the unplayability of the violin part to all and sundry. Two possible substitutes, Sauret and Kotek, had withdrawn after listening to him. A third, Adolf Brodsky, could not face the difficulties for more than two years, then saw the possibilities if he could brush up his technique. With more gumption than the others he proceeded from words to deeds, learned the solo part, and was all on fire to play it. He persuaded Hans Richter to put it on in Vienna early in December of 1881.

The reaction of the Vienna audience is difficult to credit today when the technique of violin playing has advanced enormously;

the concert hall was pandemonium, a battle between the modernists and traditionalists. The critics parted company in much the same way, some hurling abuse at the "brutality" of the work and its insensitive handling of the solo instrument, others welcoming the composer's original use of the violin. In fact Tchaikovsky had the absorbing idea of using the kind of violin playing he had heard with Rubinstein at the gypsy encampments outside Moscow within the framework of one of the most classical orchestral scores he was ever to write.

Nowadays, when the technical feats of violinists have ceased to amaze, the form of the concerto is perhaps its greatest virtue. The violin writing is difficult even by present-day standards—the double stopping, the glissandi, the trills, the hair-raising leaps are formidable by any standard, and the Cossack Dance in the Finale tests every soloist—but as Tchaikovsky felt instinctively, the excitement and joy of this superb work must stand or fall by the mingling of classical and barbaric, of form and freedom. The themes are too familiar now to comment on; one and all are Tchaikovsky at his best and what more could one say?

As for the manner in which he introduced these themes, one is still overcome by admiration after innumerable hearings. Consider, for instance, the first movement of the concerto. It opens with what could be called a broadcloth introduction. Out of this rises the principal theme but so gradually and so inevitably that one is scarcely aware what is happening until the theme is all about one, radiant and glowing. It is Tchaikovsky magic.

It is instructive to note that the errant Auer, who was to become a renowned teacher of the violin, recanted and spent his later days urging the work on all his pupils. This is perhaps the best tribute ever paid to a rejected work. Tchaikovsky was not to write a second violin concerto. This is understandable; he was an artist; the merits of the one he did write could scarcely be repeated, could certainly not be excelled.

CHAPTER 17

Trio and Second Suite
1882-1884

TCHAIKOVSKY HAD BEEN THINKING a great deal about Nikolai Rubinstein. He was possibly suffering from a guilty conscience—he spent much of his life in this state—about his immediate reactions to his old friend's death. These were that he would have felt his death much more if it had taken place some years earlier. This was the truth; he and Rubinstein had gradually fallen apart since giving up their joint apartment. Rubinstein's private life had gone from bad to worse in these years and Tchaikovsky neither would nor could keep pace with him. Rubinstein's rejection of the piano concerto had left a wound—it was heartlessly done—and his later championship of it was almost cancelled out by his criticisms of the Fourth Symphony.

These were some of the forces which drove the men apart. Yet there were many other reasons for Tchaikovsky to feel grateful and affectionate; with few exceptions Rubinstein had championed his compositions for all his Moscow years and had played his work as conductor and pianist with understanding and generosity. He had been, for all his silly side, a thoroughly decent man.

Tchaikovsky's sentiments with the effect of time—we all miss the dead much more after the first shock—were finally and inevitably expressed in music. The surprise was the form the music took. He decided early in 1882 to write a piano trio in memory of Rubinstein. It is true that the inclusion of a piano was essential in a work in memory of a pianist. It is also true that Nadezhda Filaretovna had asked him some time before to write such a trio. He had replied that he did not care for this combination of timbres. Yet before the old year was out he was not only at work on a trio of this kind but it was to prove one of his most satisfactory compositions.

The work was broken into by a marriage in the family. Vera Lvovna, Alexandra's daughter, had already married a Rimsky-Korsakov and by doing so (though her husband was only a distant relative of the composer) had drawn Tchaikovsky closer to the man he most admired in the Balakirev circle. Now Anatoly was to marry, and Pyotr Ilyich greeted the news of the engagement with a recommendation that his brother should read *Anna Karenina* and especially the descriptions of Levin's love for Kitty; he had just reread them with ecstasy and sadness too. "How I long for a woman's caresses!" he cried.

The marriage, in Moscow that April, struck him as a tiresome bore. Some envy may have been inspired in him by the event. His recent fame had made him lonelier, for he could no longer distinguish good friend from false, and the domestic happiness of others made him sad. When he wrote "None But The Lonely Heart" he wrote it from the heart, that is why it has an undying appeal.

This loneliness was perhaps why Constantin Stanislavsky, a distant relative of Anatoly's wife, found the composer "nervous" in society. The men were to meet often—Stanislavsky's Moscow Art Theatre was a dream of the future but both were ardent admirers of the Maly Theater productions and actors, and Stanislavsky became a director of the Moscow Musical Society. The younger man, however, rarely saw the composer as a man of the world; unlike most witnesses he was impressed more by Tchaikovsky's unusual modesty.

Tchaikovsky went off sombrely to Kamenka that May to work on his Trio and his new opera. He was not in Moscow when

Anton Rubinstein opened the musical side of the Exhibition of Industrial Art with a concert in which the chief item was a first performance of the new Second Piano Concerto. Taneyev played the solo part.

The generous applause then seems to have set the style for the reception of this work ever since, that is, applause for the pianist for mastering a fantastically difficult part, and applause for the composer more because he is loved than for that particular example of his genius. Astonishment has frequently been registered that this Concerto in G Major has failed to establish itself in the concert repertory and one can only echo this astonishment. Criticisms of the form are beside the point; a composer has a perfect right to write a concerto in which the piano is as much accompanist as solo instrument, the only issue of moment is whether he has done it successfully and no one has seriously doubted this.

The concerto is almost as rich in typically Tchaikovskian themes as anything he wrote, it is both grand and continuously effective. The construction is better than the construction of the First Concerto and if the mood behind the work is more detached than usual with this composer, if the work is more of a showpiece than an expression of deep feeling, one can scarcely complain. Critic after critic has inveighed against the Tchaikovsky who "wears his heart on his sleeve"—a curious complaint, this—but most of them are equally annoyed when the composer steps outside his work. This does not make sense.

Music-loving men and women are happily untroubled by these extra-musical considerations and the concerto would become a firm favorite with them if only they were allowed to hear it frequently. That has never yet happened. A criticism could be made of the Andante; it is a little slight and a little sentimental, though the lush melody is difficult to resist. But the first movement is as magnificent a piece of writing as Tchaikovsky or any other man was to produce and reminds one of Mozart's great C Major.

The Finale, however, is the surprise of the work. It reveals a witty man and a master of original rhythms. Apart from his

"Clown's Dance" in *Snyegurochka* (which was more humor than wit) nothing remotely like this movement had been written before this concerto and nothing remotely like it was to be written for many years. It was almost half a century ahead of its time. Stravinsky was the first to take advantage of what it taught; Prokofiev improved on him (listen to the first movement of his Fifth Concerto); and the cycle was finished by Shostakovich. The Finale of the latter's Concerto for Piano and Trumpet is a logical and inevitable result of Tchaikovsky's lead.

2

Tchaikovsky's growing stature as the leading Russian composer of the day became more marked as 1882 wore on. The musical part of the Moscow Exhibition was completely dominated by his works and culminated in an all-Tchaikovsky night when the Violin Concerto had its first Russian performance. Abroad, the concerto roused immense enthusiasm in London—it was the first Tchaikovsky composition to take a firm hold there—Prague staged *The Maid of Orleans* (watched by Alexandra on her way back from another visit to Carlsbad) and this first performance of a Tchaikovsky opera outside his own country was sufficiently successful to bring about a revival a few months later. In New York his works were becoming well known and his music was selling fast. He was winning disciples abroad as well as at home where Arensky was begging to be allowed to use the libretto of *Voivode;* Brodsky and Hans Richter joined von Bülow as converts and in Prague the young Anton Dvorak, like the young Vincent D'Indy in Paris, was an enthusiastic admirer of *Eugene Onegin.*

But perhaps the surest sign of his supremacy as a contemporary composer came out of the blue from the still half-barbaric Votkinsk. It was a letter to her dear Petya from his first piano teacher, Maria Markovna Palchikova. She had married but was no more prosperous than when he had known her more than thirty years earlier. She begged for money.

He sent the money, more than she asked. He said that he owed a lot to her. At first sight this appears no more than sentimentality since he in fact taught her as much as she taught him. But that was not the point; his memory was good—indeed, he largely lived in the past of those happy days the more the present fame disappointed him—and he remembered not so much the girl who could never struggle through a piece unaided as the humble champion of hard pressed music when the all-conquering Fanny was bent on making a writer of him.

The result of all this notice was, unhappily, an extension of the kind of life Pyotr Ilyich could not endure and by August he was crying, "Life in Moscow and Petersburg is becoming impossible for me. I shall have to stay in the country or go abroad. Why this is, God only knows—the strain of it is driving me half mad. Perhaps in some better world I shall be told why I can never spend one hour in either capital without horrible suffering."

Like many other men he felt impelled to struggle after fame but when the first signs of it appeared the gratification was almost always outweighed by boredom and worse. He could no longer enter a room in Moscow without being besieged by people. He became tired and cynical. He knew that most of these people were merely running with the hounds and that they would be equally fulsome with the next sensation, not necessarily a musical one either. He suspected that they would be just as intrigued if a champion ice skater or trapeze artist suddenly made his appearance in the city.

He also despised himself. His natural kindness forbade the snub. Afterwards he berated himself for feebleness and for a more serious fault, of actually enjoying praise from those who he knew in his heart were completely false.

Finally and inevitably his gloomy view of the lionhunters made him suspect almost everyone, even the sincere—it was the old story of the rich unable to trust a single profession of friendship or love—and this made him think unkindly even of people such as the Rimsky-Korsakovs. He wrote bitterly that they were turning a fond face to him in Moscow and saying and writing nasty things in Petersburg. This was nonsense—he was confusing them with Cui—and he was eventually to recognize it; he was then specially irritated with Rimsky-Korsakov for writing *The Snow Maiden* but was to be among the first to appreciate the lovely opera when he heard it.

This came later. At the moment he yearned for the country whenever he was obliged to be in town (which was increasingly often) and when he got back to Kamenka gave a deep sigh of relief: "How marvellous to be oneself again instead of being forced to play a different part a thousand times a day. How insincere social life is—and how senseless!"

In October his Trio had its first performance in Moscow. The public response was warm, the critics were cool, but Taneyev delighted the composer by writing, "It is a glorious work. I have been studying it six hours a day for more than three weeks!"

The public won, as usual, and Taneyev has been justified; this long work—it is the size of a full symphony—has since become one of the most admired pieces of chamber music in the world. It is curious that Tchaikovsky should have been repelled by the thought of using pianoforte with violin and cello for he blends them as if he had been writing for this combination all his life; despite its enormous length the Trio holds the listener throughout.

The construction is unusual for an elegiac work; the composer devotes the whole of the massive central movement to an evocation of Rubinstein. It is a musical impression of the life of Nikolai and, one could say, of any artist, of his struggles, failures, successes, and the composer creates it by means of eleven variations on a simple but memorable theme. Here he illustrates the career of a man who was a musical educationalist (symbolized by a skillful fugue) an outstanding pianist (symbolized by a mazurka to be played with great verve) and finally a man who had to face death.

Tchaikovsky understood Rubinstein's love of life—he too did

not want to die—and since the death of his friend he had been examining himself closely. In his letters to Nadezhda Filaretovna, who stoutly denied the possibility of another life, he wavered; his intellect told him that it was impossible, that she was right; something else told him that she was wrong: "There *may* be another life," he was to tell Anatoly (he was discussing the subject widely). "My heart rebels against the idea of complete annihilation and my instinct is repelled by it. They both compel me to believe that another life does exist."

In the final variation of the "Rubinstein" theme he transfers the argument to music; it is a moving and convincing picture of man coming to grips with this final problem and accepting death. It was certainly true of Rubinstein; he died as gaily as he had lived.

The first movement of the Trio can be said to represent Tchaikovsky facing Fate and conquering it on behalf of a man who was taken out of life at forty-five and in the prime of his career and talents. He does so by two warring themes, the first sombre, the second almost gay, both fascinating examples of the writer of supremely lyrical melodies. The richness of the writing set a new standard in chamber music; listening, it is difficult to believe that there are only three instruments, the scale and sound suggests a chamber orchestra. The only other man of his time to give such an impression—Brahms—had not yet met Tchaikovsky.

The Finale also presents two themes in opposition but in a totally different manner; it is altogether lighter until the end of the movement when a splendid funeral march, solemn but never joyless, brings the work to a close.

3

By January of the new year, 1883, he was off on his winter travels again, *Mazeppa* still unfinished. This time he did not go to Italy direct but to Paris where once again he was enchanted and loathe to leave. He saw Bernhardt in *Fedora* and thought her an "arch genius" he saw De Musset, he listened night after night to *Figaro* at the Opera Comique and marvelled at its magic. He worked hard, too, at *Mazeppa* and at two commissioned compositions in connection with the forthcoming coronation of the new Tsar, Alexander III. One of these, the Cantata "Moscow," was much more than a routine job that Russia's most famous composer could not avoid, and it is difficult to understand why it is now never sung.

He enjoyed Paris as usual and felt the better for it. One day he went to a service in the Russian Church where Rubinstein's body had lain two years earlier. He had been overcome by one of his violent longings for his country and estimated correctly that, short of taking the train, he could only recapture the feeling of Russia there. "I felt rather moved when I held the wax taper and kneaded the little pellets of wax after each gospel, then I began to feel impatient—I wanted the service to end—and when it did I felt miserable because it was over!"

While he was in Paris Wagner died. Drinking punch at a café— the winter and spring were bitterly cold—Tchaikovsky read the newspapers and listened caustically to the flood of talk. All of a sudden Wagner had become the rage, every orchestra competing with its Wagner program. Men could talk of nothing but his greatness. Pyotr Ilyich could remember, if the French could not, when Wagner's operas were howled down and the critics excelled themselves in vituperation. Though he was no great admirer of the composer—he had recently seen and described *Tristan and Isolde* as "an endless void, without life or movement"—he could see in him the fate of all artists. He could with particular clarity see the French and art: "Curious people, the French. One has to die to catch their attention."

He might criticize his hosts but on his way back to Russia that summer—he had worked so hard that Italy was never reached— he stayed a night or two in Berlin and this put Paris in perspective; after all, Paris was a capital city not a provincial outpost, he said.

He did not leave Paris until he had finished the score of *Ma-zeppa* but he continued to tinker with it in the country all summer. He heard that the opera would be performed both in Moscow and Petersburg the next year—an exceptional honor, the one city vying with the other for the honor of first performance—but by this time he had begun to weary of the subject. He was more interested in a new Suite—the second—which he was writing at a great rate, and by the end of the year he had finished it and a rewriting or, to be exact, a trimming of his First Symphony.

The battle for first performance was won by the Bolshoi, and in the middle of February, 1884, a few weeks after a Davidov girl had married a von Meck boy as Nadezhda Filaretovna wished, *Mazeppa* had its Moscow premiere. Four days later it was produced at the Maryinsky. The opera was greeted warmly in Moscow, coldly in Petersburg, and this difference fairly indicates how much of the applause was due to the work and how much to the composer—Tchaikovsky was present at the Bolshoi but absent from the Maryinsky.

By this time he could fill a theater or concert hall if audiences knew they could bring him on to the platform after the work was played; the sight of him roused tremendous enthusiasm. Fame only reaches its climax when people can worship a creator in person. That was why Tchaikovsky's fame abroad was still confined to composers, musicians, musical coteries, and their social hangers-on. His reputation as Russia's leading composer had become, for many Russians, little more important than his reputation for kindness and good humor. Besides, he was a man worth seeing, the beautiful fast greying head poised on a perfectly proportioned body. He walked and moved, as he held himself, with natural grace—and his modesty endeared him to everyone just as the habitually sad expression on his face tugged at the heart.

Conductors were in despair when he refused to attend an opening night but could not move him if his mind was made up. He knew by this time what a hold he had on the public affection but refused to trade on it. He still loathed publicity and personal appearances, he still had to force himself on to a platform though years of experience had taught him how to conceal nervousness. But he did as little of it as possible. So after the Bolshoi first night he left for Paris.

Some time before, keeping Nadezhda Filaretovna *au fait* with his doings as usual, he had written "So far I haven't managed to work up the enthusiasm I felt for *Onegin*. The score advances gradually but I must confess that the characters haven't really caught my imagination." These were ominous words, and *Mazeppa* bore them out; to the very end he felt it to be more a task than a necessity and the music sounds like it; the only suggestion of inspiration comes in the mad song of Marie, the rest is so much conventional melodrama. Even the orchestral writing seems to have become stereotyped, as if the composer cannot believe in his characters or their situation.

All this was pointed out by the critics; respectful now because they were dealing with a great man. Disappointment was the keynote of their notices and it was understandable. Yet no one asked why Tchaikovsky continued to write operas.

He heard the truth in Paris. He was despondent but not overwhelmed—he must have been getting used to this kind of thing—and had in any case a swift consolation. The Second Suite had been unreservedly welcomed in Moscow and plans were already on foot for repeat performances.

It is to be feared that the composer found this consolation fairly thin; he was rarely to judge his own work correctly and his passion for the theater was too strong to be shifted. Yet the difference between the pasteboard drama of *Mazeppa* and the cheerful charm of the Second Suite might well have struck anyone, even the man who had written both. The opera was competently written—he could scarcely be other than competent by this time—but the Suite was much more, a charming example of his genius for handling an orchestra. The variety of the five movements, the economy, the fascinating rhythms, and the delightful themes make the work a rare pleasure from the first "Jeu de sons" to the final "Danse baroque."

Tchaikovsky probably thought less of the Suite as a whole than of his splendidly humorous use of four accordions in the third movement, the "Scherzo burlesque." It lives up to the description. This was the first time accordions had been included in a classical work and he had great fun with them; they are only used for a total of some sixty bars but most effectively. Also included in the orchestra was a tambourine and harp with very telling glissandi by a devotee of that instrument for the latter in the Fourth Movement "Reves d'enfant."

The Suite was described on the score by the composer as "Suite caracteristique." Like everything he wrote that had to do with music, the title was exact. This is characteristic of Tchaikovsky but a side of him all too little heard. He had enjoyed writing the work as he enjoyed writing the First Suite—the mood was as identical as the place he had written them in—and the enjoyment and the high spirits come through to the listener with a thrill of pleasure and surprise.

It is a great pity that so few people are allowed today to share the pleasure. The Second Suite is played little if at all more often than its predecessor and concert audiences are the losers for it. That it is beautifully constructed goes without saying, that it is all great and tuneful fun cannot be said too often. Regular performances of the first two Suites would make a serious dent in the stubbornly prevailing impression of Tchaikovsky as the melancholy Slav.

CHAPTER 18

A Home of His Own
1884-1885

TCHAIKOVSKY'S NEXT YEAR was an eventful one—one in which he was to change his mode of life drastically. But that was far from all: in the period ending in April, 1885, he was to be decorated by the Tsar; to write his popular Third Suite, his strange Concert Fantasy and the opening pages of yet another opera; to find a country home for himself; to re-establish relations with Balakirev and his group; and to begin the Manfred Symphony.

The decoration by the Tsar—The Order of St. Vladimir of the Fourth Class—for which he had to return from Paris in the spring of 1884 was a confirmation of his position as Russia's great contemporary composer. But it was more than that. Alexander III did not decorate him just because public demand insisted on it (the public being, of course, the aristocracy and influential musicians); he really liked his music and proved it in the most arduous way, by sitting through the entire performance of *Mazeppa*. This would have been a rare enough sign of condescension by a Tsar whatever the work (etiquette and inclination usually resulted in members of the royal family coming into their box when an opera was half way through or leaving it before it ended) but the incident was all the more remarkable because the composer was not in the theater—he was on his way to Paris.

Nor was this the end of the Tsar's obvious interest; he sat

through and congratulated the composer on *Eugene Onegin* which was having a long run in Petersburg. He returned more than once to it, an unprecedented honor. Most remarkable of all in the political climate of the day, he told Tchaikovsky that he would be permitted to write an opera on Pugachev, the Cossack rebel Pyotr Ilyich's great-grandfather had fought against. This was a quite staggering compliment. One might think that such an opera could only increase whatever patriotic fervor was still left in Russia but the court and government mind did not work that way; the mere suggestion that a man could rise against his Tsar was considered highly unwise, not to say treasonable.

Tchaikovsky did not in fact write the opera. He took up a subject which Modest, rashly it could be thought, claimed as his suggestion. This was to be *The Enchantress*.

But first came the Third Suite and the Concert Fantasy, both written at Kamenka in the summer of 1884 and both played for the first time early in 1885.

The Suite arrived first; it was performed in both capitals in January. In Petersburg it had the benefit of a world-famous conductor, none other than Hans von Bülow on a triumphant return visit to Russia as conductor and soloist. His admiration for Tchaikovsky's music knew few bounds and he made the very most of the Suite. Everyone, public and critics, hailed it as one of the best things Tchaikovsky had written. The Moscow premiere a few days later lacked the sparkle of the northern city's effort, possibly because von Bülow had changed roles and was playing the First Piano Concerto in the same program which rather stole the thunder. Nevertheless the Suite was praised.

This Suite has become too popular to discuss at length. Whether it is a substantial improvement on its two predecessors is questionable; there is some reason for thinking that chance alone has led to its elevation as Tchaikovsky's most successful composition in this genre. This is not to say that the Suite is anything but excellent throughout; it has splendid themes, variety of mood and treatment, and the advantage of ending with a long and substantial movement that everyone has found memorable. This Theme and Variations is often played apart from the rest of the Suite with much success (Tchaikovsky began the practice on his first concert tour) and it could be claimed with some reason that even he never excelled this example of the variation form. The Suite in general is rather less joyous than its predecessors though it gives a similar impression of spontaneity in the writing. Like them it is light classical music at its best—varied, melodious, and perhaps above all, finished—the rich scoring is beyond praise.

There have been several splendid orchestrators in the past century—Borodin and Rimsky-Korsakov, Stravinsky, and Shostakovich come naturally to mind—but Tchaikovsky's special and unrivalled gift was his ability to score superbly for every instrument, by itself, when blended with other instruments, and again when used with full orchestra. The Third Suite offers a near faultless example of this extraordinary talent.

The Concert Fantasy which Taneyev played for the first time in Moscow in March, 1885, is a curious work. It puzzled the listeners then and has puzzled them ever since. It began as a Third Concerto; then, the composer's inventiveness for once giving out, dwindled to this queer hotchpotch, formless and leaving one with the feeling that Tchaikovsky had decided to display his gift for dazzling pianoforte writing. The solo part is difficult to such a degree that few pianists can get through it without exhaustion. It could be called bravura stretched to the point of excess. Yet when every criticism has been made the work has undoubted charm and one must regret, when regular public performance of pianoforte concertos is limited to so few works, that the Concert Fantasy is not given an occasional airing. The themes are not Tchaikovsky at his best—that is to say they are, for him, a little ordinary and even sentimental—but they have wide appeal and the work as a whole has moments of real grandeur.

2

The difficulty he had in writing this work and his inability to extend it to concerto form were not without significance. A fluent and highly skilled writer like Tchaikovsky does not dry up for nothing. There were two special reasons for the fact that the world intruded on him with particular vehemence at this time. The lesser reason—though Tchaikovsky would not have described it so then—was the serious illness of Kotek. The young man had contracted tuberculosis and was about to go to Davos for treatment. As Tchaikovsky well knew—in those days the disease was regarded as virtually incurable—the move to Davos was almost equivalent to a death warrant.

Kotek could not be said to have behaved well to the composer— his withdrawal from the Violin Concerto was cowardly to say the least—but Tchaikovsky typically remembered only the good things; Kotek enthusiastically praising him to Nadezhda Filaretovna, Kotek practicing the concerto at Clarens hour by hour, day after day. Also typically, he was to hurry to Davos that winter of 1884 and to leave instructions that all expenses in connection with the illness were to be charged to him. Kotek in fact died in the first days of 1885 but in the previous summer Tchaikovsky worried about him and this was sufficient to cloud his usually fertile musical imagination.

Yet this was the lesser by far of the troubles of that summer and the work he did then, troubles which even show through the would-be high spirits of the Third Suite. After nineteen years of bliss at Kamenka the place was losing its charm for him and so its power to draw good work from him. In most of those years a great deal of his best work was initiated, written or completed at Kamenka or inspired by its domestic peace, its fascinating rural surroundings. By the summer of 1884 the magic had largely gone.

There were many explanations for this. First and strongest was the change in Alexandra. Her health fluctuated; the now regular trips abroad to take the waters did her good but could not cure her. She was ill and was not to recover. To Pyotr Ilyich she was a shadow of herself when there and when she was not, the thought of her illness distressed him beyond measure. In those melancholy days he learned the truth that when one loves, no scenery on earth can compete with feeling for a human being. The beauties of Kamenka might have not existed so little did he see in them.

If Alexandra was often absent during his summer months at Kamenka, others were only too much present. The children had grown up. They brought their friends home and the house was stuffed with boys and girls turning the place upside down. Tchaikovsky was one of those men who love small children much more than the hearty types they so often turn into, and however glad he may have been to see the young people enjoying themselves, the racket they made effectually prevented him from concentrating for any length of time on composition; either they insisted on having his company or they made such a din that he had to walk out to the village in despair.

Then there were the usual hangers-on. Every large Russian house had them, as readers of Russian literature well know. At Votkinsk there were cousin Lidia and Aunt Lisa, at Alapayevsk Cousin Anastasia, and at Verbovka in 1884 Tchaikovsky found Lyov's mother and her daughter Vera Vasilyevna. Time had changed them; they were far from the cheerful and loving people of Petersburg and Hapsal days. The mother, Alexandra Ivanovna Davidova, was going blind and depended on company, the daughter had married unhappily and was forever hinting to Pyotr Ilyich that she could have been happy if he had only married her; her half-melancholy, half-flirtatious references to the love they had for one another in past years and the suggestion that she still felt as before drove him almost to distraction. Mother and daughter were obviously there for life, in the Russian way; neither Alexandra nor Lyov would have dreamed of asking them to leave.

There was one ray of sunshine in this gloomy summer and one only. During a walk Tchaikovsky went deep into a wood a few miles from Kamenka. In the center of the wood he came across a forester's cottage. The man was pleased to see him—passers-by were rare—and asked him in. He met the wife and her child, a girl of four. He and the little girl took to each other at once and every day after that until he had to leave Tchaikovsky walked to the forester's cottage to see her, talk to her, and play with her. They became great friends. "I love her dearly," he wrote.

Had she lived he might not have had the heart to give up Verbovka as his summer retreat but to his fury she died that winter of diphtheria. He was furious as well as frantic with grief because, as he said, her life had been thrown away like the lives of thousands of children every year. "She need not have died if our people would take the most elementary precautions."

After that everything pointed to an end to Kamenka as a home— the only home he had ever known since he took the professorship at Moscow in 1866, nearly twenty years earlier. His apartments in Moscow were never more for him than perching places for they provided none of the essentials to home life for him, a woman or children or, failing them, country surroundings. They were essentials to good composition too; and as in the last resort his music always had the final say, he took the plunge; in February, 1885, he rented a furnished house at Maidanovo.

With this move he began an association with the Klin district which was to last for the rest of his life. Maidanovo was a village on the outskirts of Klin, and Klin, for Tchaikovsky, had two great advantages; it was surrounded by fertile and beautiful country and it was on the main rail and road between Moscow and Petersburg. From it he could reach Moscow fairly soon and was at the same time within reasonable striking distance of the northern capital. Before he departed for this new life, he had written, what was virtually a birthday note in his diary (actually made on May 6, 1884). How little Tchaikovsky saw himself as he was is illustrated here. "I shall very soon be forty-four," he writes. "What I have been through in those years and—without any false modesty—how little I have accomplished! I have not written a single perfect composition. I have written nothing worthy to stand as a model for others to follow. At this age I am still searching and still vacillating. I read nothing and I know nothing." He adds, "I don't want to be young again. Once is enough!"

3

Surrounded by trees, Maidanovo was beautifully situated in a large park bordering a river, and Tchaikovsky took his walks through the flower garden, then struck into the wood, or sauntered by the river bank according to his mood.

His first walk was usually made as soon as he had got out of bed and dressed, which he did every morning at seven-thirty to the minute. At half past eight he breakfasted—usually taking no more than several cups of strong tea with lemon—went for another walk, then settled back in a chair and, helped by many cigarettes, read any book he fancied, or studied—in the summer months of 1885 he was trying hard to learn English which he could read after a fashion but not speak. After an hour or so of this he took a third walk and came back to compose. He broke off to lunch at mid-day, a substantial meal washed down with much wine. More composition followed until five or six o'clock when he walked again and came back to the evening meal. After this he worked once more, helped by stronger drink than wine—brandy or vodka most commonly—until late at night. A final walk, and bed well after midnight.

This was his unvarying routine when alone. Often he had guests, picked ones. Modest, the Jurgensons, Kashkin (sometimes with his wife and daughter), Taneyev, Albrecht, Zverev, and Hubert—these were the regulars. Occasionally he would invite a famous soprano or tenor who was to sing in one of his operas, the producer, the conductor, or one of his Petersburg friends down in Moscow for a few days. But whoever was there the rule remained absolute, that if he felt in the mood he was to be left alone to work until evening.

He had a curious way of indicating his wishes. If he wanted to

work through the day he would not speak during breakfast. If he
felt unlike composition that day he would invite his guest to walk
with him after breakfast and would talk freely and entertainingly.
That was a sign that he would spend much of the day catching up
with his vast correspondence and dealing with the many begging
letters he received. If he did feel like composition no one saw him
except at meals until the period after the evening meal. He was
then at his guests' disposal.

As a host he was a great favorite, generous, undemanding, tactful, unfussy, and a fine and amusing talker. He preferred to play
the part of intelligent prompter or appreciative listener but he
could tell a good story. One of his best was the confounding of a
bore they all knew, the professor of mathematics at Moscow University, N. V. Bugayev. Bugayev is known today as the father of
the symbolist poet Andrei Bely; at the time of the Maidanovo
gatherings he was known and feared for his habit of buttonholing
some inoffensive musician with the remark, "Now take a point
in space"—an opening gambit which led to an interminable dis-
quisition on the relationship of space and time.

The mild I. V. Gazhimali, Professor of Violin at the Conservatoire, one day told Tchaikovsky that he was to meet Bugayev for
the first time at a soiree in Moscow that evening. Gazhimali was
particularly well-liked by the composer; he had led the quartet in
the Moscow section of the R.M.S. since 1875 and was a specially
understanding interpreter of Tchaikovsky works. Knowing that
he would fall an easy victim to Bugayev, Tchaikovsky took him
aside and primed him how to deal with "that dangerous chap."

That evening Bugayev duly fastened on his prey—he had the
uncanny gift possessed by all bores of spotting a likely listener—
and, eyes gleaming, opened fire with the usual, "Now, Ivan Voitsekhovich, let us take a point in space."

Gazhimali said mildly but firmly, "I regret, Nikolai Vasilyevich,
that I cannot admit the possibility of a point in space."

A little disconcerted, Bugayev put another proposition to him.

"I don't admit it," said Gazhimali.

There followed a stream of propositions, each simpler than its predecessor. To each Gazhimali replied, "No, I don't admit it."

Bugayev, badly flurried, at last snapped, "Well I suppose even you, Ivan Voitsekhovich, will admit the passing of time."

"No, I don't admit it," said Gazhimali.

Bugayev went off in a huff and from that moment Moscow musicians were spared for ever after.

Modest, Jurgenson, Kashkin, and his wife all commented later on these lively evenings and the good talk everyone enjoyed. They do not seem to have cared so much for the food; Tchaikovsky relied absolutely on the choice of his manservant Alexei. Nor did they admire the furnishings, also the work of Alexei, but Tchaikovsky seems never to have questioned his taste; all he had eyes for were his piano and desk and the pictures of other composers and the family spread liberally over the walls.

The liveliness of the Maidanovo evenings, like the speed of the evening work when Tchaikovsky was composing, owed a great deal to the drink taken. The Russians have always been heavy drinkers, partly because the severity of the climate demands it, and Tchaikovsky could drink most of his guests under the table if so inclined. He was not so inclined, he was no Rubinstein, but when the company was all male it was generally understood that some stiff drinking would be the order of the day at Maidanovo and the conversation flourished accordingly.

Tchaikovsky was one of the most open-eyed drinkers; he knew just what he was doing and could be worth hearing on the subject of teetotallers. Gone was the old sense of weakness and sin; he needed the drink and blessed the day he first came across it, and if he met a critic he would point to the work that drink had made possible. When he read cranks, he made gentle fun of them, as he did of one of Tolstoy's many extreme followers who had founded a Tolstoyan colony and, describing the life lived there, wrote an article in which he condemned the "poison" of alcohol. Tchaikovsky read the article and protested humorously in his diary that he could not live without such poison. Of course it could be abused, like everything else in life, but that was a far cry from the Tolstoyan "boasting that he has never known the pleasures of vodka." "Isn't it unjust and a little arrogant to judge other people by oneself and to forbid them everything one doesn't happen to like? How about me for example? Every evening I drink 'more than is good for me' as such a man would say. But I can't live any other way."

He did not want, or think that he ought, to live any other way, what was more, and continues his note: "Anyway, is this man right? When I drink I feel absolutely wonderful, specially at first when gently tipsy, and my brain functions a good deal better than it does when I abstain from the 'poison'!" And he dealt with the usual accusation, that drinking ruined a man's constitution, with "If my health has declined, I haven't noticed it, nor has anyone else. For the rest, Quid licet Jovi, non licet bovi."

His life proved the truth of his claim that, if anything, alcohol preserves a man; he never knew serious illness except the sort that comes from the highly sensitive nervous system he was born with, and up to a few days before his death he was strong and healthy.

4

These convivial Maidanovo evenings formed only one aspect of Tchaikovsky—the man-of-the-world aspect, the good talker and excellent host. Another side of him is shown by the childlike man who gravitated naturally towards children for his chief pleasure and had a genius for getting on good terms with them. One reason for his restlessness at Kamenka recently had been the growth of the children he had loved so much in their early years; to him the movement into teens and twenties was mostly sad; he remembered his own childhood days with a pang of regret as great as the shudder with which he thought of his youth and young manhood.

When the Kashkins came to Maidanovo their young daughter usually came with them. In the first year at Maidanovo she was thirteen but her love for Tchaikovsky had begun with her first memories of him, when she was six. That evening her mother and father had a number of people in to play cards and Sonya Niko-layevna was allowed to stay up and help to carry round refreshments.

One of the Kashkins' most frequent visitors was Ivan Vasilye-vich Samarin, the famous Maly Theater actor, Professor of dramatic art at the Conservatoire, and the producer of the first performance of *Eugene Onegin*. The ostentatious Samarin would draw attention to himself by suddenly breaking out of normal conversation into a stentorian monologue taken from his latest play. Sometimes this habit was effective, sometimes merely boring, but to a child it could be frightening too.

When the cardplayers were ready for refreshment on this particular evening, Sonya's nurse carried round a trayful of glasses of tea and Sonya carefully followed her with a bowl of sugar. When she came to the table where Samarin, Zverev, and Tchai-kovsky were sitting, the actor, seeing a chance to shine, abruptly addressed a "thunderous monologue" straight at the child.

"Understanding nothing," says Sonya, "I was struck dumb and quite lost my head. I couldn't move because Samarin kept one hand on the sugar bowl and when I tried to detach it from him he said loudly, 'Wait, wait. Stay where you are. I'm going to have more sugar. Besides, I like little messengers.'"

He did not help himself to more sugar but launched himself again into the monologue at the top of his voice. Sonya was terrified. And at this point Tchaikovsky, seeing what she felt, came to the rescue; he gave her the bowl of sugar and stopped the declamation in midstream with a few sharp words.

"To this day," recalled Sonya Nikolayevna, "I remember how grateful I felt. I can't remember what he looked like then; all I felt was a general impression of a friendly man, a man with whom you feel you can be simple and at ease although you also feel that he is not really simple but special—but what his specialness is you don't know."

This extremely pertinent account of a child's reaction was followed by another incident about a year later. "I ran out of the nursery and saw Tchaikovsky coming out of the anteroom. I was very glad to see him but for a moment or two I couldn't say anything because I had just noticed how grey his hair was."

Tchaikovsky understood immediately that she was embarrassed, walked up to her and, saying "May I kiss you?" bent down and kissed her on the top of her head. "I'm awfully fond of kissing children on their hair!" he explained in a boyish fashion which at once put Sonya at her ease.

He knew that she had begun to have pianoforte lessons from Zverev and asked how she was getting on and whether she would like to play for him. They went into the music room where she proudly went through her scales. "And do you play anything of mine?" he asked afterwards.

"Now by this time," said Sonya, "I knew that he was a composer and very celebrated—in fact in my eyes he had a kind of halo—but for all that I wanted to show off, so with great pride I played an old-fashioned "French Song" from his Children's Album. He said it was very good and my day was made."

From that time onwards she loved him dearly and waited impatiently for him to come to her parents' apartment to play cards or hear or talk music, theater, or books. She had divined as children do that he loved children and persuaded herself that he loved her best. Looking back when she had grown up, she understood what a rare thing his manner with children was: "He treated them particularly nicely and kindly. Like my father he seemed to know that grownups must not talk to children in a special way, talking down to them, but simply, as if they were grown up too. He always did this, that's why I and other children were so happy to be with him; he felt one of us and conveyed this to us so that we all understood without a word said."

By the time of the Maidanovo days, when the Kashkins came up for a weekend, Sonya was more observant. She noticed, for instance, that Tchaikovsky could never go out for a walk without being hailed by groups of the village children. "They had discovered the times he went out and, as he always gave them something, sweets or a small coin, they used to lay in wait for him.''

One day he and Kashkin went out for one of their usual country walks when Tchaikovsky felt in his pockets and, grimacing, said that he had forgotten to bring anything for the children. Not wanting to disappoint them, he told Kashkin to continue by the usual footpath; he would make a detour and meet him in the forest they were making for. But when the children saw Kashkin alone "they at once guessed Pyotr Ilyich's ruse, rushed off and rounded him up in great triumph. And in the end my father heard Tchaikovsky running towards him, crying, 'Nikolai Dmitryevich, lend me a coin or two, will you?' "

Tchaikovsky, it may be added, was not content to spoil the village children, much though he liked to see their faces light up when he came into sight. He thought further: why were they always free to catch him during his walks? He asked the local priest who told him that there was no school and no money for one. Tchaikovsky forthwith provided the money and guaranteed it in the future, and the school was opened early in 1886. And though Tchaikovsky was not to stay at Maidanovo all the rest of his life he never forgot the children or their school; each year his grant arrived without fail.

One last word about the daily life at Maidanovo. If Tchaikovsky had any doubts about the growth of his fame, they were unpleasantly dispelled by the crowds of tourists who found their way to the village seeking autographs, wishing to show him their work, to beg or simply stare. With them he dealt firmly. He got Alexei to paint and fix to the entrance gate a notice: "Pyotr Ilyich Tchaikovsky. Receives Mondays and Thursdays, 3 to 5. Otherwise not at home. Please do not ring or knock."

The first work he did in this first home of his own was to revise an old opera, *Vakula The Smith*. Unlike most of his operatic works, which he usually came to dislike, he had rarely wavered in his opinion of its merits. He did see plenty of scope for revision, however, and believing correctly that with his present-day reputation he could almost dictate presentation of a work, he got down to such rewriting including a change of title. It now became *Cherevichki,* the Russian name for the boots worn by the women in Kamenka.

After this revision, which he made with great speed, he turned with a certain reluctance to Manfred. This symphony had been in his mind for two years, ever since Balakirev had suggested it to him. When he went up to Petersburg about the staging of *Cherevichki* he seized the chance to have a word with Balakirev about the symphony. Much had happened to Balakirev and his group since the days when he had recommended *Romeo and Juliet* and praised *The Tempest* and First Symphony and we must go back some years to understand what Tchaikovsky found when he called on him.

CHAPTER 19

Balakirev and Manfred Symphony
1885-1886

THE PAST HISTORY of Balakirev had best begin in 1867, a few weeks before he came down to Moscow to hear Berlioz and met Pyotr Ilyich for the first time. He came from a spectacular triumph in Petersburg, an appointment as conductor of the Russian Musical Society concerts in place of his great rival Anton Rubinstein. When he returned to Petersburg after meeting with Tchaikovsky he soon took another forward step, when he was appointed Director of the Free School of Music in place of Lomkhin.

In the next eighteen months he did a great deal to popularize advanced Russian music and the more adventurous works of Western composers. He made plenty of enemies and one of particular power, the Grand Duchess Helena Pavlovna. This "scourge" as Moussorgsky called her, was furious when Balakirev supplanted her favorite Rubinstein at the R.M.S. and determined to get rid of him.

Balakirev set no store by charm or tact; indeed he often went to the other extreme, setting people by the ears for what appeared no better reason than contrariness; he always said exactly what he thought and usually very pungently. He would not fawn or even be moderately pleasant to wealthy or highborn patrons who did not care for music. He might have paid court to the Grand Duchess, who was interested in music of a kind, and won her over to his way of thinking—even she might have found it hard to resist his immense conviction—but he would not. He ignored her and all who sympathized with her.

In Petersburg in the 1860's one could not offend anyone close to the throne and hope to survive. By May, 1869, he had been forced to resign the conductorship.

These events were followed with high feeling in Moscow where, thanks largely to Tchaikovsky's advocacy, Balakirev's reputation actually stood higher than in his own city. The forced resignation infuriated Tchaikovsky and he worked on Nikolai Rubinstein to the point that the Director offered Balakirev a professorship at the Moscow Conservatoire.

Balakirev refused with a modesty that charmed and surprised everyone in the Conservatoire; he was not fitted for such a post, he said, because his technical background was faulty.

He could not be persuaded to change his mind so Tchaikovsky, whose temperament demanded action of some sort, risked his own future by printing an article in a Moscow journal praising Balakirev and openly criticizing the moves that had led to his resignation.

The article did not change the situation, it merely relieved Pyotr Ilyich's feelings, but it led to much for himself. Somehow he escaped official rebuke—which might have extended to his own dismissal—and he won the gratitude and respect of Balakirev, already well disposed. That summer Balakirev's father was ill at Klin, and after his death he stayed in Moscow until late autumn. It was then that he suggested *Romeo and Juliet*—a practical and historic repayment of debt.

For the next year or so the two men saw a fair amount of each other and corresponded largely about *Romeo and Juliet,* but towards the end of 1870 Balakirev began to fade out of Petersburg musical life and Tchaikovsky lost touch with him. The Free School Concerts, which Balakirev had taken up, did not pay their way and he was forced to take a menial job in the freight department of the Warsaw Railway in Petersburg. Even this drastic step did not save him from humiliation; three quarters of the way through the 1871-72 season the concerts collapsed—people refused to support them—and he lost his Directorship. This crushing blow was followed by the loss of the railway job, and for the next four or five years he withdrew from all public life. He went through a spiritual crisis from which he emerged as fiery a believer as he had formerly been a scathing skeptic. He kept himself alive by taking a few pupils. Nobody in his old group saw him; Tchaikovsky did not hear from him.

The death of the Grand Duchess in 1873 saw the beginnings of a more liberal-minded phase. Everybody in Petersburg who knew anything about music was well aware that Russian music could not afford the loss of a man like Balakirev but he was difficult to persuade. Eventually, in the middle seventies, Glinka's sister Ludmilla Shestakova, the one person who had not deserted him, managed to turn his mind to music again. She had never accepted his withdrawal and under her influence he began to compose again and to take up the long-planned editing of Glinka's scores.

When Alexander II was assassinated in March, 1881, the last obstacle to Balakirev's reinstatement disappeared. Once more the Muscovites tried to tempt him to their Conservatoire; after Tchaikovsky refused the Directorship it was offered to Balakirev. He stuck to his plea of insufficient technical knowledge but at once agreed to resume the direction of the Petersburg Free School and the conductorship of the concerts when offered later that year. He finished his *Tamara* about which he had written to Tchaikovsky many years earlier—it was first performed in March 1883—just one month after receiving the official benediction of an appointment as Director of the Imperial Court Chapel.

It was a few months before this appointment that Tchaikovsky heard from him again after a break of nearly ten years. He had not been without information all this time but the information did not come from an unbiased quarter. He kept up with the Rimsky-Korsakovs and Rimsky-Korsakov was already in the early stages of the resentment that was later to distort completely his view of Balakirev, that his teaching had deprived him of thorough technical training.

Unhappily Tchaikovsky did not at all understand the noble character of Borodin any more than he understood the extraordinary merits of Borodin's Second Symphony when it was played in Moscow in the same program as his "Capriccio Italien." Instead of Borodin's kindly and concerned comments on Balakirev, therefore, he had the rather waspish ones of the Rimsky-Korsakovs. He took them with a grain of salt—he disliked gossip—but he was forced to agree with Rimsky-Korsakov that Balakirev had done him harm as well as immense good and this, with his hatred of interference, may have prevented him from trying to come to the rescue of his old hero.

But if he had any reservations about Balakirev by the time he received his letter of November, 1882, they did not survive a reading. All the old magic came back because the vigorous letter was in character; it proposed a work which, in the writer's view, only Tchaikovsky could compose and a work which ought to be written for moral as well as musical reasons.

The suggestion was a symphony based on Byron's *Manfred.* Balakirev obviously had the *Symphonie Fantastique* in mind and had first asked Berlioz if he would write the new symphony. This was far back in 1867 when the master visited Russia at the suggestion of Stasov and Balakirev. Berlioz had refused; he was too old, he said. Now, fifteen years later, Balakirev reverted to the idea after a hearing of *Francesca da Rimini;* that convinced him, he told Tchaikovsky, that he was the only man who could take the place of Berlioz. He added a typical comment, "providing you take great pains, subject your work to stringent self-criticism, let your imagination run freely and above all, don't hurry."

He enclosed a detailed program for the symphony with a final word, "The subject is not only very profound but in line with present-day feelings since all modern man's troubles stem from the fact that he has no idea how to preserve his ideals—they rot away and leave nothing but bitterness in the soul. And that explains all the spiritual sufferings of our age."

Tchaikovsky took the adjuration "don't hurry" in quite a different sense from that intended by Balakirev; he was not anxious to go back to the kind of plan beloved by the Balakirev circle and particularly not in a symphony. He had not written a note of it when, late in 1884, he went up to Petersburg and had a long talk with Balakirev. He found the master as irresistible as ever despite his moods and when he left, he was committed to the work.

2

He found that youth had succumbed to the old fascination; in the few years since his return to normal musical life Balakirev had attracted a new generation of Russian modernists, all of whom worshipped him. Moussorgsky was dead and Rimsky-Korsakov disapproving but Cui was there still and so was Borodin. To Tchaikovsky, however, the newcomers were the real spirit of this Balakirev evening and one of them he knew very well.

This was an ex-pupil of his at the Conservatoire, Sergei Mikhailovich Lyapunov. He had joined Balakirev as assistant at the Court Chapel and was to be the sole faithful disciple after his master's death. With Lyapunov in Balakirev's rooms Tchaikovsky found a number of extremely bright and enthusiastic young men. He knew only one of them slightly; he was Anatoly Konstantinovich Lyadov, slightly senior to the others, a fine pianist and promising composer. Lyadov had just gone back to the Petersburg Conservatoire, where he had studied under Rimsky-Korsakov, as professor in harmony and composition. Together with Lyapunov and Balakirev he had been given a grant by the Imperial Geographical Society to collect and score folk songs in several districts. One of these districts, Tchaikovsky now heard with great interest, was the province in which he had been born.

The other unusually gifted young man present that evening, like the rest of the crowd except the few elders, was unknown to

Tchaikovsky, yet was to become one of his most devoted admirers. This was Alexander Konstantinovich Glazunov. Tchaikovsky had heard about the feats of this prodigy who had written his first symphony, first quartet, and pianoforte suite at the age of sixteen, all so highly thought of that the extraordinary sight had been seen in Petersburg of a Balakirev and Rimsky-Korsakov disciple (inspired by the first and taught by the second) being played by Anton Rubinstein at a concert of the Musical Society. When Tchaikovsky met Glazunov at the Balakirev gathering the boy was nineteen, his symphony had just had its first foreign performance, and all musical people in the city were prophesying the most brilliant future for him.

One would never have guessed this from Glazunov's attitude when Tchaikovsky entered the room, nor would one have thought that any of the young men there were anything but overgrown schoolboys. Glazunov explains: "Although the Balakirev circle was no longer as isolated or exclusive as it had been before my time, Tchaikovsky did not belong to it and that at once raised a barrier in our minds. Balakirev used to hold him up to us as an example of fine writing but was critical of his deficiencies. We esteemed *Romeo and Juliet, The Tempest, Francesca,* and the Finale of the Second Symphony; the rest of his work we either did not know well or it did not fit in with our tenets."

For all this, the news that Tchaikovsky was to brave the temple of modernism had caused a considerable flutter. "We young members discussed the visit very seriously. How should we treat this outsider who was not a member of our group? We decided to be very reserved with him. The result was a certain stiffness in the atmosphere when Tchaikovsky arrived. It did not last long. We were all staggered by his dignity, his refinement and well-bred self-command that we thought of as exclusively European. We began to breathe freely and when he spoke, the atmosphere of reserve—you could call it disapproval—melted away because he obviously felt no constraint whatever. We younger ones said nothing, partly because we were overcome by admiration at the way he spoke about music, partly for fear of putting ourselves forward. *Manfred* was talked about, I remember, and at one point Lyapunov and I each played our works."

It may be that Balakirev sensed that Tchaikovsky was stealing the evening and his disciples' admiration; he was a proud and touchy man. At any rate he decided to introduce a controversial note—for, as Glazunov puts it, "in spite of his genuine cordiality and generous hospitality he loved to make caustic and derisive remarks calculated to offend one or more of his guests."

He decided to strike home: "He began to describe in sharp and uncomplimentary terms a Moscow musician and his wife, knowing them to be friends of his guest of honor."

For a moment all the disciples felt uncomfortable and Glazunov had the impression that the evening was on the verge of collapse, "but Tchaikovsky quickly and playfully took up the remark; he showed no sign of offense, but merely asked, did Balakirev know them, had he met them?

"To this Balakirev returned an evasive answer—everybody spoke about them, it was common property, etc., etc. Tchaikovsky made only one comment and made it in the friendliest manner: Here-say, he said mildly, was a dangerous stick to lean on."

The reproof and the way in which it was made, allowing of no quarrel or even argument, settled Balakirev: "His eyes shifted about nervously and he made no more attacks that evening."

All the young men were tremendously impressed and, soon after Tchaikovsky left, Glazunov, Lyadov, and Lyapunov went off to a tavern to talk their visitor over. Lyadov summed up the evening by saying that it had been a rare honor to meet such a great composer but what they all talked about until the early hours was the enormous charm of Tchaikovsky's personality, his tact, and his moral courage. Never before had they seen the hallowed Balakirev bearded in his own den and worsted without a single harsh word or lifted voice. From that moment Tchaikovsky and his music had doughty champions in the Balakirev circle.

3

What the young disciples did not know and could scarcely have guessed was that for all his sangfroid and dislike of gossip Tchaikovsky had come under the spell again in spite of everything Balakirev could do to ruin the effect of his own strong personality and genuine wish to glorify Russian music. Within a few months, by April, 1885, he had settled into Maidanovo and down to *Manfred*. After that he never seriously turned away from the symphony he had delayed so long. There were times when he felt that it would wear him out and at one point he complained rather curiously that he would become a Manfred if he went on with it much longer. When the work became too arduous and he felt downright ill—the symphony was drawing out to a fantastic length to include all Balakirev's instructions—he turned for a day or two to his new opera, *The Enchantress,* with enormous relief. He found it beautifully easy to write. This ease was significant too, though he was not aware of it. Occasionally he put in an hour or two on yet another future Opus, a sextet, but for most of spring and summer and the greater part of autumn he labored on *Manfred*.

Early in October it was done and six months later played for the first time in Moscow. It was received with a certain bewilderment that has lasted to this day. Cui, strangely enough, was its most enthusiastic supporter, a new role for him and a lonely one on this occasion. The great length of the work places a severe strain on everybody, orchestra and audience alike, and it is difficult to think that the program is sufficient to carry such a burden.

It is surprising that Balakirev, who first thought of Tchaikovsky as the obvious composer because he had just heard a performance of *Francesca,* did not follow this thought to its logical conclusion. Why he suggested a symphony after listening to a symphonic poem is a mystery; it would seem that he was influenced by purely literary considerations.

At first Tchaikovsky announced almost automatically that this was his finest composition to date. He had forgotten all his weariness of the previous summer with Manfred and his doings, a Manfred he was afraid he would turn into if he went on long enough. That this remark indicated clearly that he was tackling the wrong subject did not dawn for a long time although it was no doubt symptomatic that he refused to allow Jurgenson to pay him for the printed score; it would be lucky if it was played once in a decade, he said. Eventually—in 1889—he turned right around and damned everything but the first movement. He described the work as repulsive, the second and third movements as trivial, and the last as impossible. He said it must be made into a symphonic poem.

This is a fairly comprehensive discredit. He was too severe. The last movement with its pseudo church music does seem to be beyond the pale, but with this admittedly considerable exception there is much to admire. The Manfred theme is altogether fine— a large and noble theme treated in every conceivable manner throughout the symphony but used at its most impressive in the opening movement. One has glimpses of Byron's hero—there are moments of real feeling—and the almost complete oblivion that has fallen on the symphony cannot be justified; we are not so rich in symphonic wealth as all that. A success it can never be; Tchaikovsky was no Manfred; but the splendors are there and the public ought to be allowed the chance of relishing them from time to time.

CHAPTER 20

Composer—Conductor
1886-1887

Two WEEKS after the first performance of *Manfred* Tchaikovsky set off for his most romantic and, though he could not dream of it, one of his most triumphant vacations. He was bound for Tiflis, now Tbilsi, a place which to a Muscovite was synonymous with the ends of the earth.

Anatoly had been posted to Tiflis. That was the origin of the journey. Anatoly seems to have thought it hopeless to try to persuade his famous brother to risk the dangerous roads and appallingly dirty hotels between Russia proper and its outlying Trans-Caucasian province. The initiative came from a local musician, Mikhail Mikhailovich Ippolitov-Ivanov, the conductor of the Tiflis symphony orchestra and the genial inspiration behind the flourishing arts movement there.

As soon as Ippolitov-Ivanov heard that a Tchaikovsky had come to the town he got in touch with him, persuaded him to join the board of the local musical society and, later, begged him to use his influence to get the great composer there.

The two men put their heads together. What, short of Anatoly in trouble, could they put forward as a convincing reason for his brother to make the journey? As Anatoly was flourishing and had a loving wife and child with him this excuse would not convince even the unsuspecting Pyotr Ilyich. Anatoly finally produced the answer as Ippolitov-Ivanov recalled long afterwards: "He said that his brother loved the country with a passion and that he might be induced to come down to us if he suspected how beautiful our Caucasian countryside was."

Thereafter a barrage of propaganda went out to Maidanovo about the semioriental beauties of Tiflis and its surroundings, of the magnificence of the Caucasus mountains which one crossed en route, of the fine city, the hospitable people, the great strides they were making in music and the greater still if a certain famous man would only come and convert the waverers.

By the beginning of April, 1886, Tchaikovsky had succumbed— he was fast growing into an inveterate traveller though he preferred to travel in comfort—and before the end of the month he was there after a journey which had taken in a visit to Ippolit on his ship at Taganrog, nights of fearsome discomfort at bug-ridden inns and days corkscrewing alarmingly up and down fabulously romantic mountain passes.

Like almost everybody who gets to Tiflis he found the journey handsomely repaid and shared the usual surprise that the city was so beautiful and so up-to-date with its theater, opera house, and concert hall in which the latest plays and operas and symphonic works were performed, including his own. The countryside was all the conspirators had claimed and the climate superb.

The biggest and most joyful surprise, apart from seeing Anatoly and his family again, was the obvious determination of every musical person, not in Tiflis alone but in the entire vast province, to show appreciation of the visit of a great man. If Tchaikovsky doubted whether his fame extended farther than Moscow and Petersburg he was soon and unforgettably undeceived.

He had met Ippolitov-Ivanov once before, at the house of K. Y. Davidov, and now became very much attached to the enthusiastic young champion of Caucasian music who was also, as he demonstrated, a very good conductor. His feeling was reciprocated to the point of idolatry and the two men became almost inseparable. The gratified Tchaikovsky (he could never quite bring himself to take anything for granted) was escorted into the country, through the city and to every play, concert, and opera. He loved every moment of it. These wonderful people even had their own drink, and very potent it was.

The climax of his stay came on the first day of May when a gala performance of his work was given at the Opera House. Never in his life had he seen or heard such enthusiasm. Ippolitov-Ivanov had thought of everything, even of finding out by devious means what his favorite flower was. This flower did not grow in the Tiflis area, so Ippolitov-Ivanov sent to Kutasi, some three hundred miles away. He ordered an entire railway carriage to be filled with them.

When the composer entered the theater he was simply staggered by the look and scent of it. "Spring that year," said Ippolitov-Ivanov, "had been marvellous and the wealth of flowers was almost unbelievable—in particular, of Pyotr Ilyich's beloved lilies of the valley. So the theater was decorated with greenery and an assortment of flowers and the box set apart for our dear guest and his relations was filled with lilies of the valley—Tchaikovsky was seated in an absolute bower of them."

"Sharp at eight o'clock," Ippolitov-Ivanov continues, "Pyotr Ilyich, his brother Anatoly Ilyich and his wife and daughter entered the theater in which the whole of musical Tiflis had been waiting in impatient expectation for the best part of an hour. Everybody rose to their feet, and choir, chorus, soloists, and audience burst out with 'Glory to our dear and honored guest' which we took, with suitably altered words, from the first act of *Mazeppa,* 'Praise to our great genius!' "

Before the performance began, music teachers from Tiflis and every other large town within a radius of several hundred miles presented Tchaikovsky with a portrait of himself surrounded with a silver wreath, and a long line of city notables and leaders of local institutions followed with their own presentations, chiefly wreaths and costly silver gifts. After the performance the Musical Society arranged a vast banquet at which hundreds of people filled tables stretched the length of the great hall of the civic center building. Addresses and toasts lasted into the small hours.

The guest of honor did not get back to Anatoly's house until close to dawn. "Never have I known anything remotely like this before!" he wrote to Modest. "The cheering seemed unending."

He sailed a few days later from Batum for Italy but had to change his plans. Naples was cut off by cholera and the ship went on to Marseilles and Pyotr Ilyich to Paris and another experience he was not to forget.

In Paris he was made much of for the first time, meeting Delibes, Lalo, and Faure (whom he particularly liked) and being dined and feted by all the musical leaders of the day. But what thrilled him was not these signs of fame but an evening he spent at the house of Pauline Viardot. He had always felt a sentimental regard for her because she had taught Artot and he listened patiently to a long recital of her relationship with the dead Turgenev. He was rewarded beyond his wildest dreams when Viardot finally produced the autograph score of *Don Giovanni* and left him to pore over it by himself. He was still fingering it reverently two hours later. "I felt as though I had spoken to Mozart and had shaken him by the hand," he said afterwards, and those who know the magic of autograph scores by the great masters will understand exactly how he felt.

He was back at Maidanovo in time to enjoy the summer—he had become a keen if haphazard gardener—and to exclaim in his notebook, "I'm at my best when I'm alone with trees and flowers and books." To which, being an honest man with a sense of purpose that no garden could entirely lull, he added, "But God! How short life is and how much I still have to do!"

2

By the beginning of the next year, 1887, this thought had driven him to what, given his temperament, can be described as little less than an act of heroism, or rather a succession of them. He decided that if he was to make his work known as he wanted it to be known throughout Russia and the West he must conduct it himself. He had listened to many performances under other conductors. He had praised often but still more often had writhed with anger at the travesty of his music that was dragged out of orchestra or singers. There was only one answer and after struggles that can scarcely be overestimated he made up his mind to conquer what he called "the contemptible coward" in himself. He took lessons in conducting and, after surviving several rehearsals under his baton, took charge of the first performance of *Cherevichki* at the Bolshoi on the last day of January.

His conducting proved a greater success than the revived and recast opera (it had been greatly improved but his sense of humor had not changed for the better). In spite of a sudden shock before the second performance when he heard that his eldest niece Tatyana had died of heart failure at a masked ball, he carried on though feeling like death himself.

The experience did nothing to free him from the terrors of public appearances but he endured and agreed to conduct an all-Tchaikovsky concert at Petersburg in March. His uncertain confidence was nearly shattered when he noticed Balakirev (whose conducting he particularly admired) sitting in the stalls at the final rehearsal, but somehow he got through the evening and on the first night won praise from everyone, even the critics— Cui was to say of his next opera that the conducting was a great deal better than the work.

He did not allow this new and forced interest to get in the way of composition; by May he had at last finished the orchestration of *The Enchantress,* had sketched out the beginnings of a new suite and made notes for the sextet that had been in his mind for more than a year. All this before, unable to resist Tiflis, he set off to go by water, the inns of the previous year having effectively made him wary of the land route. He chose the romantic and much more comfortable route by Volga and Caspian, arrived in Tiflis fresh and threw himself into a month of music, theater, and excursions about a countryside so different from the woods and rivers and villas of Maidanovo that he might have been in another world.

If he was not quite so happy there the second time it had nothing to do with the town or the country or the amazingly hospitable people but to the workings of his conscience. His old friend and champion, N. D. Kondratyev who had placed Nizy at his disposal so often was seriously ill and had been sent as a final resort to take the waters at Aix-la-Chapelle.

Tchaikovsky dreaded sick beds and invalids who could scarcely be recognized for the men they used to be, but he went just the same, making the long and tiring journey from Tiflis. He was at Aix-la-Chapelle by the end of July. It was obvious to him at once that Kondratyev was dying and that his death would be slow. He stayed on for six weeks, until his old friend no longer knew him.

What he felt during these six weeks is within the imagination of us all. What he wrote about it shows, as with his openly confessed fear of seeing Rubinstein's body, that he stood head and shoulders above ordinary men. He said: "I sit in my hotel filled with thoughts that cause me extreme disquiet. Life is going by and nearing its end and I still don't understand it. What is more, far from trying to understand it I shirk all thoughts about another life and try to run away from them by thinking of something else. How can I be right? Is this the way to live? Look for instance at my behavior now. Everybody is admiring the way I *sacrifice* myself by staying here but there is no question of sacrifice—I am leading a life of ease, stuffing myself with food, and doing nothing but spend my money on luxuries although I know that other people need this money for necessities. What gross egotism! I don't act towards my neighbor as I ought."

The final effort to be absolutely honest came with a diary note about his reactions to the dying man. "I haven't felt *pity* once all day, only *horror* and a longing to be home."

He was home by September after going to see Kondratyev's wife. Six weeks later he was continuing the fight to overcome his

fears of conducting by taking on an even more formidable task—
the first performance of *The Enchantress* at the Maryinsky. In
spite of the usual rehearsal and first-night attacks of nerves he
looked calm enough when he stepped on to the rostrum and his
conducting was praised by all. It was overpraised; a spontaneous
wish to compensate a popular man. Once again a Tchaikovsky
opera had failed convincingly. The libretto of *The Enchantress*
is so stupid, even by operatic standards, that one is baffled to
know why Tchaikovsky ever gave it a second thought. However,
as we know, the most incredible stories can make great opera.
The Enchantress did not and the blame for this must rest fairly
and squarely on the composer. He had said again and again that
he must be able to put himself into the place of his operatic characters if he were to write living music for them. How, one wonders, did he ever imagine that he could put himself into the place
of a young widow who keeps an inn and fascinates in turn a
Prince and his son to such a degree that the Princess poisons her
and the Prince murders his son and goes mad with remorse?

No doubt artists exist who could have performed the feat but
not Tchaikovsky, and his attempt to write an opera on this and
similar types of libretto merely shows how little he knew himself.
In truth his imagination was a limited one and when he said that
he must imagine himself into his characters he really meant that
he must actually have met people who could stand as models.

When he failed completely to do this, as in *The Enchantress,*
the characters are wooden and unbelievable and, worse, his music
is flat. He was accused of failing to write music that created dramatic situations. The accusation was as true in *The Enchantress*
as it would have been untrue in his symphonies or the two operas
in which he felt completely at home.

He was not given long to brood about this new failure—treated,
it should be said, with considerable gentleness by critics and public. The public simply stopped coming to the theater, the critics
preferred to look ahead to the future of this great composer who
had merely taken a wrong turning. They even forebore to say

another wrong turning. Towards the end of November he had a concert to conduct and a second premiere, this time in Moscow. The concert was an all-Tchaikovsky one, the novelty the Fourth Suite.

The concert was a roaring success and his spirits leaped. He felt, he said, that he had never conducted so well and that the audience knew it. They would not let him go. Even his experience at Tiflis paled before the Moscow cheers: "I've never known such enthusiasm nor have I ever had such a triumph."

At this distance from the concert it is not possible to know what the cheers were chiefly aimed at beyond Tchaikovsky himself; obviously the applause was deafening for every item—*Francesca,* the Concert Fantasy, songs, "1812 Overture," excerpts from *The Enchantress* as well as the new Suite. "1812" was certainly a winner at the end of the program, but as one movement of the new Suite had to be played twice it must be assumed that this work caught the public imagination.

Nearly one hundred years later, when it is no longer possible to watch this extremely handsome and graceful man conduct his work the reaction to the Suite has become more critical. It was called "Mozartiana" and is now not often played. This neglect is not without reason. Tchaikovsky truly loved Mozart and his own work often possesses a Mozartian grace, elegance, and wit. But when, as in the Fourth Suite, he actually uses Mozart's themes or what he chooses to regard as Mozartian themes the limitations of hero-worship at once become apparent. It may seem harsh to say that any orchestral work of Tchaikovsky is dull but that is the impression left by this Suite; dull and even trivial in the sense that one has the feeling of the composer working himself up over very little. The previous three Suites made no claim to depth but they had charm and they were Tchaikovsky in light and happy mood. In the last work he was to write of this kind only the lightness is left.

No such considerations harried the composer at the end of 1887. He was to have second thoughts about this new work—he almost always did—but he was chiefly triumphant in quite another direction. He had won the fight to prove that he could conduct his own work—that was the real source of his pleasure. It was a moral victory and a practical one too. These efforts over the past twelve months to make a conductor of himself had a secondary purpose, to fit himself for a European concert tour. A few days before the end of the year he left for Germany, the first stage of his first tour.

CHAPTER 21

European Tour and Fifth Symphony
1887-1889

ONE CONCERT TOUR is very much like another. The orchestras are good, bad, or indifferent, the public and critical reaction likewise. Meetings with local musicians form an inevitable part of the routine as do the dinners in the visitor's honor with the appropriate speeches. It is all very exhausting and, after a time, very boring. Tchaikovsky's tours during the next five years were to follow the pattern—they varied only when he visited the United States, still considered far away and which Russians had yet to conquer.

The first tour, however, is important and even vital, specially for a man coming from a country which most people in the West continued to regard as barbaric. So when Tchaikovsky left for Berlin he was embarking on a course that only the virtuoso Rubinstein, more German than Russian, had taken before him. Glinka had travelled but his attempts to popularize his own work had been few and not widely spread. They had also failed. Tchaikovsky was trying to blaze a new trail as composer-conductor of modern Russian music.

Weeks of living in the limelight and no private life whatever involved everything he hated. Only his love of music provided the impulse to launch himself upon a tour of this magnitude. Of course he enjoyed applause at the moment of receiving it as everyone does but this played little part in his venture. What he set out to do was to show Europe some of his work as he knew it ought to be played. He thought that the world would be the better for his music and had come reluctantly to the conclusion that he alone could, or would, interpret this music so that Europeans were given a fair chance of deciding whether it was good or not.

This first tour lasted three months. He conducted concerts of his own works in Leipzig, Hamburg, Berlin, Prague, Paris, and London. He did not have one failure. In London he came into contact with the insular arrogance so many foreign artists have had to endure; no one met him after a terrible journey across a rough channel and far from being feted he was left entirely to himself and to the mercies of the Russian embassy. But if the musical organizers did not know their manners the English musical public atoned for the boorishness as they have so often had to do. They took to his music and made their feelings plain. Even the critics were kind though they pointed out with some justice that the composer might have treated them to some of his larger works—he conducted only the Serenade for Strings and the last movement of the Third Suite. He did not meet English composers because there were none.

In the London concert hall, as everywhere else on the tour, he had half won the fight before he ever lifted his baton. By this time, early in 1888, his hair and beard had turned completely white. It may be doubted whether a more romantic figure had ever ascended the conductor's podium, and the people who filled the hall were not only mesmerised by him but astounded that such grace and dignity could come out of a country which they thought of dimly as populated by bears and muzhiks swathed in furs and driving troikas along snowy roads—when they were not too drunk to drive, that is. That a Russian could wear evening dress with more elegance than an Englishman had not occurred to them. Hence the shock, and to do them credit, it was a pleasurable shock. When this distinguished man played music which went straight to English hearts the battle was completely won.

Never again was England to lose its passion for the music of Tchaikovsky. And it may be added, never again was Tchaikovsky to be suffered to land there without a greeting which probably sickened him by its obsequiousness as much as the neglect of 1888 had done by its coldness. But the people rose to him and his music. That he remembered.

Before London came Paris. There he was feted to the point of satiety, by his own embassy, by all the leading composers and leaders of musical society—not at all the same thing—and by emigre Russians of every description. He was called on by Fauré, Gounod, Massenet, and Viardot among others. He gave two concerts at the Châtelet and conducted the Colonne at a private festival. He never had a moment to himself. He was the toast and talk of the town.

He might have been excused for thinking that he had gained a considerable triumph. Yet it was not so. All was gallic froth. At the actual concerts he had great difficulty in inducing the orchestra to follow his beat and not gallop off on its own, the audiences cheered in the wrong places and the critics launched with much satisfaction one of those smart half-truths beloved of journalists. They had been reading Cui's recent book on music in Russia, appropriated great gulps of it, and came out with a judgment supposedly all their own, that Tchaikovsky was not one of the true heirs of Glinka such as Cui, Borodin, and Rimsky-Korsakov, but was a Germanized Russian. Then, having seen him off in the train to London with enormous enthusiasm they promptly forgot all about him and his music and turned to the next sensation.

Cui's judgment has long since been put into perspective—the Balakirev circle was influenced knowingly by Liszt and Schumann just as much if not more than the early Tchaikovsky—but in 1888 the Paris critics annoyed Tchaikovsky. That is, when he was not laughing, for he had not long left a Germany in which the critics were complaining that he was a trifle too French.

In the eyes of the Parisian journalists he was a Russian version of Brahms and it was as well for the composure of Pyotr Ilyich, tired and sickened by meaningless adulation, that he had already met Brahms. His attitude to Brahms for the past few years had been less than generous and not typical of his usual reactions to other men's music. In many letters to Nadezhda Filaretovna he attacked his contemporary savagely. The gist of his criticism of the man who was leading him in European popularity was that his work showed more intellect than feeling. No doubt he thought so but it was a superficial judgment nevertheless. It is difficult not to wonder whether his harsh words on Brahms were not due in some part to the fact that the German, who was not a theater man like Pyotr Ilyich, had had the sense not to try to write opera. Plain envy could have influenced his resentment too, for Brahms was not only accepted by his own country much more quickly than Tchaikovsky by his but had made Tchaikovsky's struggle to get his work played in Germany much more difficult. It may even have occurred to him that he and Brahms were not as un-alike as he could have wished.

Then, on the first day of 1888, the day after he had arrived in Leipzig on the opening stage of his tour, he found Brahms waiting to greet him in the house of the plucky soloist in his Violin Concerto, his young colleague at the Moscow Conservatoire who had moved to the Conservatoire at Leipzig. Brodsky introduced the men and Tchaikovsky's instinctive hostility began to wane. He found that Brahms was not at all the kind of man he had been picturing all these years. Instead of a dried-up and vanity-ridden intellectual he found "a handsome man, rather short and stout . . . and very friendly." When they sat down to a meal he discovered that Brahms liked a drink just as much as he did, that he was in fact a heavy drinker. This soothed him still further.

The course of their acquaintance was not without humor in the spectacle of Tchaikovsky fighting a losing battle with prejudice. After they had spent many hours together he noted, "He tries really hard to be kind to me but we never become intimate because we don't fundamentally care for each other."

The next day Brahms had become "very pleasant and not

nearly so vain as I expected." Later again, he studied Brahms' head and found it fascinating: "The soft contour with its pleasant curves, the longish grizzled hair, kind grey eyes and thick beard going white all reminded me of the pure Russian type so often found in our priests." This thought was hard to resist in a city where the fiercely Russian Pyotr Ilyich found himself surrounded by excessively Saxon faces. In the end Brahms, who must have worked hard with his visitor, won a tribute: "He has a simple manner without a trace of vanity, a nice sense of humor and altogether left me with a very pleasant impression."

The acceptance of Brahms (with certain reservations) was delayed by Tchaikovsky's fascination with Grieg who called at Brodsky's house to welcome Pyotr Ilyich just after they had all sat down. Tchaikovsky watched him walk into the room, "very short, middle-aged with a most fragile appearance, one shoulder higher than the other, fair hair brushed back, fair beard, and moustache slight and almost boyish."

Although Grieg was neither handsome nor immediately striking to look at, Tchaikovsky was at once won over by his manner: "Unusually charming, and his small blue eyes, rather like the eyes of a child, fascinated me with their charm and candor."

Their friendship progressed like lightning—"he has completely won my heart"—and Grieg's wife was soon included. Tchaikovsky found them both "extraordinarily sympathetic and appealing." They spent much of the time together at the dinners and concerts (Tchaikovsky not only had to conduct his own works but to listen to the work of other men) that seemed almost without end. Brodsky was a tower of strength, as was Alexander Siloti, a former Tchaikovsky student who had become professor in his turn as well as one of the most noted young Russian pianists of the day.

The musical fraternity of Leipzig generally wined and dined and praised their guest to the point of exhaustion and the reception of the First Suite, which he conducted, and a performance of the Trio and First Quartet, which he listened to sitting between Grieg and his wife, were greeted with respect and even enthusiasm. This from a town considering itself the fountain head of music and reluctant to admit the serious existence of any music other than German, was a tribute Tchaikovsky appreciated with a smile. His buoyant spirit was somewhat crushed by earnest Germans. That no doubt is why he took so quickly to Grieg and could have hugged Siloti and Brodsky for their Russianness.

The next German port of call was Hamburg, and there, for all the warm greeting he was given, he succeeded less than in any other city of his tour. He had plenty of applause but the piece de resistance of his concert, the Piano Concerto in B Flat Minor which he threw in for good measure, was not played to the critics' satisfaction.

Learning his lesson, Tchaikovsky persuaded Siloti to play the solo part at his Berlin concert. The concerto and indeed every Tchaikovsky work in the program, which included *Romeo and Juliet,* was received rapturously and he went off to Prague believing that he had established himself in Germany as a considerable composer. It could not be said that he was enamored of the Germans. He respected their devotion to music but their formality went against the grain with a man who liked to be open and free. Russians do not mix well with Germans, they never have and presumably never will, but the compliment even of being taken seriously was too rare for him to reject. He had undertaken the tour and had to accept patronage as well as triumphs.

Prague could not have been more different. "I never dreamed how much the Czechs love the Russians and hate the Germans," he told Nadezhda Filaretovna. From the moment of arriving he was caught up in a world of what, through dazed senses, seemed to him not far from adoration—not for him alone but as a representative of Slav culture in, musically speaking, a German world. Dvorak piloted him through a mass of delegations, receptions, dinners, and tours of the romantic city and its surrounding countryside. He heard concerts and operas and he conducted two all-Tchaikovsky concerts, Siloti again playing the solo in the First

Concerto, which were received with such rapture that the composer-conductor was almost overwhelmed.

He was not quite overwhelmed, however; the experience of the German part of the tour stood him in good stead; he not only kept his head to such effect on the podium that the orchestra played admirably, but managed to pick up enough Czech to reply to speeches of honor. He did not even complain of a surfeit of visitors, banquets, and speeches or a shortage of sleep. He was far too excited and gratified. He at last knew what happiness was, he said, and felt that all his very real terrors had been nobly repaid. He was finally cheered off to Paris in a flower-filled carriage of the train, a touch reminding him of those other friendly and generous people at Tiflis.

It was to Tiflis that he went for the third time at the end of the tour and nothing could have better illustrated his feeling for the Georgians and their beautiful capital than this; after covering thousands of miles in three months he chose to travel thousands more in anything but comfort to see Tiflis again and be with Anatoly, his wife and child, and Ippolitov-Ivanov.

But the real glory of the tour for him has not yet been mentioned. He came away from it knowing that he had made his mark as composer and conductor in most of the important musical centers of Western Europe and hoping that his music would be played there more often and listened to with greater attention. He was right; the Tchaikovsky furor had been set in motion and was never again to be arrested. Yet he thought much less of this at that moment than of an encounter in Berlin. Almost as soon as he had set foot in the city he met Artot. The meeting was quite by chance. She was fifty-three but still singing unforgettably, she had grown fat but he saw only the old charm. They spoke and the twenty years since they had met rolled away. "I was inexpressibly glad to see her and we were friends again at once."

He had to leave for Leipzig but they planned another meeting. When he came back a month later she gave a dinner for him.

She was with her husband and happy and Tchaikovsky rejoiced in it. He realized that she could appear elderly, stout, even absurd to those who did not know her. To him "she is as fascinating as ever." It was the rare perfect ending to an impossible romance and he knew it.

2

By May he was at home again. Not the same home. Maidanovo was becoming too popular and he moved a few miles to another, quieter village outside Klin. This was Frolovskoye. It was less developed than Maidanovo where the wealthy people of Klin had begun to build villas for themselves; Frolovskoye was still surrounded by the woods Tchaikovsky loved. The house Alexei had taken for him was only a one-story affair but Tchaikovsky had never worried much about luxury, what he wanted was a snatch of true Russian country to look at and walk in and this he had.

He had also in front of the little terrace outside the house a pond in the middle of which rose a hump of earth he proudly called an island. The garden had been neglected and he threw himself at it with all the abandon of a man who had had more than enough of travelling, conducting, applause, and overeating. "I have won a certain amount of fame," he told Jurgenson, "but I ask myself again and again, what is it all for? Is it worth while? My answer is, a quiet life without fame is infinitely preferable."

In that spirit he managed to turn himself for a few weeks into gardener, walker, and observer of the Russian scene he loved. He thought of little but the seeds he had planted—would they come up and when—and the moment when the garden would be gay with flowers. He may not have been a skillful gardener but was certainly an ardent one; he never could do anything by halves and he did not now. Having sown the seeds he used to lie awake wondering whether the night frosts, still heavy there, would kill off the seedlings and what he could do about it. In his intense way he was happy.

Of course it could not last. He excused himself by telling Nadezhda, "I am desperately anxious to prove to myself and others that I'm not yet written out." In fact he simply wanted to write music and by the end of May was hard at work on a symphony and a symphonic poem and was meditating on an opera.

He worked fast, not at all like a man who had written himself out; by the end of August he had finished the Fifth Symphony, by the end of October he had written *Hamlet* as well as celebrating his meetings in Berlin with a group of songs—"Six French Songs"—dedicated to Artot.

He conducted the first performance of the symphony in Petersburg towards the end of November and followed it a week later with a repeat performance and the premiere of *Hamlet*. He repeated the Symphony for a third time in Prague a few days afterwards as well as conducting *Eugene Onegin*. He then trailed dolefully back to Frolovskoye convinced that he was a failure.

This belief was not unconnected with two deaths, both of which hit him hard, the one of Hubert, the other of Alexandra's second daughter, Vera, the girl who had married a Rimsky-Korsakov. His niece had been young, happy, and apparently healthy; Hubert, one of his best friends at the Conservatoire, was younger than he and apparently set for a brilliant academic career—he had succeeded Rubinstein as Director until his illness. Once again he was faced with the incalculable strokes of fate. And this plunged him into deeper gloom for in his last two works he had tried once again to grapple with the problem of fate. Now he felt that he had done so most inadequately.

His depression had been given weight by the reception at the concerts—receptions which, for him, must be considered almost lukewarm. One critic went so far as to say that Shakespeare could not be expressed in music. Few people will agree today. Tchaikovsky had written *Hamlet,* or had agreed to write it which is not quite the same thing, as a kind of bargain with Lucien Guitry whom he had met in Petersburg some time before. The bargain was, if he would write incidental music to *Hamlet,* Guitry would play the role.

What actually happened could have been foreseen; when he got down to the work Tchaikovsky was inspired by the character of Hamlet as he had been by Romeo and Juliet. Hamlet too was a figure of fate, a man with every apparent advantage in the world yet destined to die young and, one must think, unnecessarily. The final score was not incidental music (he had to write this later) but a symphonic poem, a triumph of characterization and condensation.

In twenty minutes Tchaikovsky carries his hearers through the cogent events of the long drama, giving one vivid impression after another of the characters and their interaction. The score is intensely dramatic, fast moving and filled with telling themes and one must ask again why, like *The Tempest,* this brilliant evocation of a great poet's masterpiece is virtually never heard while *Romeo and Juliet* is overplayed. Had not the score been used for a ballet the probability is that the music might have remained unplayed in Western Europe for the past quarter century. The mental processes of concert planners are beyond computation; *Hamlet* possesses everything concert audiences demand, good tunes, romance, drama, and superlative use of the orchestra (woodwinds specially) so that the mere sight of it at work is highly exciting.

It is unnecessary to commend the Fifth Symphony; it has become too popular in so far as it has kept the three early symphonies out of the repertory and shares with the Fourth and Sixth the reputation of being one of the most played symphonies in the world. Yet in 1888 only one man seems to have grasped its merits to the full. He was Taneyev who was "enraptured." Tchaikovsky declared in those unhappy December weeks at Frolovskoye that it was a failure, insincere and, excelling himself in self-depreciation, "repellent."

More than any other of Tchaikovsky's symphonies the Fifth demands feeling and accurate interpretation. It does not often get it. If one is fortunate enough to hear it conducted by, say, Rosh-destvensky, then Tchaikovsky's intentions and his mastery become apparent and the most frequently criticized parts of the symphony—the waltz and the last movement with its possibility of barrel organ effect—come into focus as the composer imagined them, parts of an integral and majestic whole. The much belabored Finale, for instance, contains a masterstroke in the change from E Minor to E Major following the pensive clarinet statement of the motto theme.

This particular example is given because it illustrates Tchaikovsky's program so well. Like the preceding symphony, the Fifth deals wholly with man's reaction to fate or, as Tchaikovsky sometimes preferred to describe it, to the decrees of providence. Where it differs from the previous symphony is that the argument is lifted to a higher plane. Tchaikovsky has moved from earth to the spiritual and for the first time he poses the question, should one not resign oneself to fate and choose the way of faith? There are the inevitable rebellions which he had known only too well, but in the end he tends to accept the consolations of faith and even sees men as happy because of it.

The contrast between the two fates, or their presentation, in the two symphonies, is fascinating. In the Fourth, the Fate theme is earthy and militant as if the composer visualizes an implacable enemy in the form, say, of a Greek god. In the Fifth, the majestic Fate theme has been elevated far above earth and man is seen, not as fighting a force which thinks in his own terms, of revenge, hate, spite, but a wholly spiritual power who subjects him to checks and agonies for the betterment of his soul.

It is possible to hear this and every other important musical work with a pleasure and an emotion which has, consciously at least, nothing to do with the composer's program. The Fifth Symphony is splendid music, grand and dignified, and its form expresses the content more satisfactorily than in any other of Tchaikovsky's large works for orchestra. But the final thought must be, as with so many of this composer's works, a thought transcending the obvious pleasures of tunefulness, superb orchestration, and passionate self-questioning; it is from first note to last noble. Never querulous, never playing to the gallery, it exposes the soul of a man which all must feel the better for knowing.

Some musicologists have written as though "the poor, tortured soul of Pyotr Ilyich"—to quote one of them—had no concern with others, as though his own private battle was fought out in his music simply because he was a weakling prone to unhealthy fancies. Nothing could be further from the truth. What he tries to resolve in his three Fate symphonies is a universal problem. Every man and woman is a potential victim of fate and will remain so through life. Many shirk the problem as Tchaikovsky tried to shirk it in the Aix-la-Chapelle hotel after sitting by Kondratyev's death bed but sooner or later it catches up with one and all. Tchaikovsky would have been the last man to claim that he could provide an answer; what he has done is to present the problem of all in a framework which allows every listener, if he so wishes, to reflect. Most people will no doubt wish simply to enjoy the music; those further concerned may find, if nothing more, a sense of kinship with an honest but troubled mind.

He had little time to agonize about the reception of the symphony and *Hamlet;* he had waiting for him at Frolovskoye a subject after his heart and as far removed from self-communings about Fate as could be imagined. This was nothing less than a commission from the Imperial Theaters at Petersburg to write a ballet on a libretto after Perrault's fairy tale *The Sleeping Beauty.*

Unlike the unhappy *Swan Lake, The Sleeping Beauty* was to have the benefit of choreography by one of the greatest masters, Petipa. At once Tchaikovsky felt immense confidence; he was not only asked to write ballet music on a subject which he thought one of the most poetical in the world, he had a detailed description by Petipa of the action as it should be danced and mimed. It is not every composer who can work closely with a choreographer, reading his mind and feeling the steps with him, but

Petipa was an artist in a thousand and Tchaikovsky rose to his instructions with genius.

He was anything but free to concentrate his attention on this congenial subject unhindered, he was much too good and easy-going a host for that. In these winter weeks he had the usual crowd of visitors at Frolovskoye plus his devoted Siloti and two old friends, Laroche and the architect-musicologist A. A. Klimenko. He also had to fill an enforced engagement to conduct at Petersburg, and was often seduced from work by his garden, which he still tended in furious bursts, and always by his walks through the woods.

All the guests reported that they had never known their host in better form; they rallied him about his pessimistic views of the Fifth Symphony and his hero worship of Mozart, they argued furiously about Tolstoy—whether the disappearance of the novelist was a disaster or not—and about the merits of Doestoyevsky and Chekhov. Tchaikovsky had just been reading Chekhov with high excitement and was one of the first to see that he was reading the early work of one of the great literary giants in Russia.

In spite of all these pleasant distractions he was so much in love with the ballet that he had sketched out the first four scenes by the time he had to go to Petersburg again at the end of January, 1889. There he saw how a master choreographer worked; at rehearsals he and Petipa discovered that they thought as one man. The score scarcely needed any alteration. When it did, Petipa had only to act out his requirements and Tchaikovsky altered the music on the spot. There were no disagreements; it was a case of mutual admiration and empathy.

Had he been free he would surely have stayed in Petersburg and finished the ballet there and then. But he was not free. In spite of his genuine hatred of concert tours he had agreed to make another one and early in February he took the train for Berlin.

CHAPTER 22

The Sleeping Beauty
1889-1890

FOR THE FOUR YEARS left to him Tchaikovsky's life was to form
a pattern as regular as he could make it. With one exception he
went off for a foreign tour as conductor-composer in the early
months of each year, followed this with a visit to his family or
friends, settled in his own home for a summer of composing and
spent a large part of autumn and early winter trying to satisfy the
demands of his own country.

The pattern was broken into increasingly because not only
Moscow and Petersburg but all the provincial capitals began to
pester him to conduct his works or to help local composers to a
good debut by introducing their latest composition. If any kind
of celebration was afoot—and it sometimes seemed to him that
the Russians did little but celebrate or commemorate something
or other—he was always expected to be there to give the occasion
the finishing touch and counted himself lucky if he was not asked
to compose a piece as well.

It was an exhausting life and he was forever complaining of it
but he could not give it up. Few men have been able to resist the
lure of fame and he was not one of them. He worked himself into
a state of agitation before each concert, being constitutionally
unable to believe that he could get through it without disaster.
He always did but he remained a stern self-critic. In a sense he

was right; he was not a very good conductor. What saved him time after time was his feeling for his work and his practically patho-logical sense of duty to audience and orchestra.

The second European tour, in the early months of 1889, fol-lowed the lines of the first. The broadened itinerary was much the same—Cologne, Frankfurt, and Dresden took the place of Prague—as were his agitation and boredom and gratification; the gratification was greater, that was all. He took with him some of his more substantial works this time—the Fourth and Fifth Sym-phonies—and these had the effect of convincing many musicians that he was not only a good but an important composer. In gen-eral his concerts were very much more successful than in the previous year, particularly in Berlin, Cologne, and London, and the English musical public confirmed a Tchaikovsky passion that has lasted to this day.

By the time he left London for Marseilles in April he could feel that he had established himself as a European composer of moment and that all the countries he had visited would be eager to see him back. But what gave him more pleasure than all the tumultuous applause of the past three months put together was the recollection of the first week in Berlin before the tour really got under way. He spent that week with Artot and her husband. He and she were inseparable and went to all the theaters and con-certs and operas together. "I do love her," he wrote home; and surely this was one of the nicest loves on record, for he loved to see her happiness with her husband and got his own happiness simply from being with her, looking and listening.

After this the tour was bound to be something of an anticlimax to a man who always put the affections first and it was as well that he scarcely had a moment to himself and that, being very human, he thoroughly enjoyed the clapping, cheering, and footstamping even though he told himself that he had not earned them.

The curiously erratic relationship with Brahms was resumed at Hamburg where Brahms stayed on to hear Tchaikovsky rehearse the Fifth Symphony. He told him afterwards that he liked all but the Finale which he did not like in any sense whatever. He said this in the kindest possible way and Tchaikovsky, also in the kindest possible way, confessed that there was much in the work of his fellow composer that he also could not like—or perhaps understand. They parted on excellent terms but, on Tchaikovsky's side at least, rather hopelessly; he was never to understand why he could not relax with this obviously excellent man.

At Hamburg too he made one of his pithiest comments. After the concert he was entertained by all the musicians of the city. It was a thoroughly Germanic evening with much hearty laughter and a lot of beer. The comment of the guest of honor was brief and to the point: "German humor! Pleasant people, though."

From Marseilles he sailed off for Batum and Tiflis—his fourth visit in successive years—and there Ippolitov-Ivanov organized a forty-ninth birthday dinner for him as well as played many of his works at a gala concert.

Tchaikovsky left at the end of May with particular regret, not only to leave such a wonderful city and country and people but because he was bound for a most uncongenial task. Towards the end of the year Anton Rubinstein was celebrating the fiftieth anniversary of his first appearance as concert pianist and Tchaikovsky as the reigning Russian composer was expected to play a prominent part. He was in fact expected to conduct concerts of Rubinstein's works and this was what was causing him such pain. He still admired his old Director for what he had done for Russian musicians, he admired him for founding the Conservatoire and Musical Society, he even admired him with reservations as a pianist, but he regarded him as a composer with considerable distaste.

He had expressed this distaste in his diary with unusual bitterness three years earlier when he forced himself to play through Rubinstein's much-acclaimed opera *Nero*. "Idiotic fool!" he scribbled in a fury one day, leaping up from the piano. "And insolent too! By God, when I go through this score my soul writhes in anger. I only play this vile composition because it makes me feel that I can't be too bad. At least I am sincere. I think *my* writing is rotten do I! But I've only to look at this insipid rubbish and I cheer up. And it has actually been treated as a serious contribution to our music!"

His opinion had hardened in the three years since he wrote this yet he was to be obliged not merely to hear the master's compositions but to rehearse and conduct them and look as though he liked them. He could not possibly withdraw. Alexander III refused to acknowledge the existence of the anniversary because Rubinstein was a Jew. Balakirev refused because, as he said briefly, "the man has done nothing but harm to Russian music," but these public slights only had the effect of clamping the unhappy Tchaikovsky to his duty. He went off to Petersburg in a very bad temper and was in such a state after a preliminary interview with a "gracious" Rubinstein that only one remedy was left him. He joined the men who were writing the kind of Russian music he loved, Rimsky-Korsakov, Glazunov, and Lyadov, and sat in a restaurant with them drinking steadily. By the time they were ejected at two o'clock the next morning he was feeling much better and went off to Frolovskoye and *The Sleeping Beauty* almost resigned to the November celebrations.

By the early days of June he had written a complete sketch for the long ballet. Never in his life had he written with such a sense of felicity. The whole thing had taken only a total of forty days. The orchestration was another matter; not until the end of August had he finished it and then only after days of such intensive work that he wondered at times whether his brain would not burst.

He had a curious ally in the writing of this marvellous score, a little girl. Small children always fascinated him. His passion for the young Vladimir Davidov is shown by page after page of exclamatory entries in his diary, his love for the forester's daughter at Kamenka had completely absorbed him for the whole of one summer. Now he found another tiny child and at just the right moment.

This girl was the daughter of Lyegoshin, who was Kondratyev's manservant. During the first stages of Kondratyev's fatal illness Lyegoshin used to come over to Tchaikovsky's house with news of his master. Tchaikovsky admired him tremendously. "What a splendid personality he has!" he wrote in his diary, and with him this thought led inevitably to another. "Good God! And people are capable of looking down at such a man because he is a servant! Men are equal whatever their position in society and Lyegoshin is a wonderful proof of it. I don't know any man with a purer or nobler soul."

When Kondratyev died Lyegoshin was left without work and Tchaikovsky lived up to his words, he got him work near his house and made sure that he and his family did not want.

He was handsomely repaid when Lyegoshin's little daughter came into his world. She fascinated him; he saw her every day. She used to "help" him with the garden, and they were very happy together. Her prattle of princes and fairies and beautiful princesses and magic castles in the midst of deep forests kept his imagination clear and sweet for the writing of *The Sleeping Beauty*. Nor did the influence of the child end there, for the germ of another ballet was planted in his mind then; the entrancing portrait of Clara of *The Nutcracker* was to owe much to the composer's kindness to Lyegoshin.

The ballet was completed just on the stroke of the opening ceremonies in honor of Rubinstein, and Tchaikovsky took an apartment in Moscow for the rest of the year; he could not keep up with the demands on his time if he stayed at Frolovskoye. He was faced in these few winter weeks with charity concerts at which his presence was essential to their success, repeat concerts of all-Tchaikovsky programs, and also two unavoidable contributions to the Rubinstein celebrations, the writing of a cantata in praise of the great man and the conducting of all-Rubinstein concerts.

He did not enjoy these months but there were compensations— a few drinking evenings with his growing band of young admirers, the exquisite pleasure of working with a man like Petipa who knew exactly what he wanted and could actually make him wish to cut and alter a score, and a meeting with Chekhov.

Chekhov was not yet thirty and still churning out short stories in order to support his shiftless family. His fame was still to come, so he was overwhelmed by the news, which soon reached him, that the great Tchaikovsky was recommending this work to all his friends and prophesying a wonderful future for him. He decided to express his thanks in the only way possible, by dedicating his latest volumes of stories to him.

Tchaikovsky heard of the intention. He called on the writer to thank him for the honor, a typical touch from this great man to a virtually unknown one. Chekhov was nervous—a state of mind in such a level-headed man which gives a good indication of Tchaikovsky's status—but they soon got on very well together. Chekhov said how much he loved *Eugene Onegin,* and Tchaikovsky, always on the lookout for a new librettist, had no difficulty in persuading the writer to think seriously of it. They even decided tentatively on a subject, the *Bela* of Lermontov, and when the dedication appeared it was signed "from a future librettist."

The anniversary rites advanced remorselessly and at last Tchaikovsky was buried in them, a solid procession of concerts, banquets, and speeches ending with two all-Rubinstein programs on successive nights, the unhappy Pyotr Ilyich conducting both concerts. As a final blow came the last item on the last program, Rubinstein's fantastic *Tower of Babel* in which he set out to rival Berlioz with augmented orchestra and a choir numbering several hundreds. A martyrdom, Tchaikovsky told Nadezhda Filaretovna.

There was no possible retirement to the quiet of Frolovskoye, he was booked for concerts and ballet rehearsals to the end of the year and beyond it. He abandoned all thought of the now usual European tour and began to long for a country he had not seen for several years; he decided to winter in Italy.

He did not get away as soon as he had hoped; *The Sleeping Beauty* dress rehearsal was delayed and did not take place in the Maryinsky until the middle of January of the new year, 1890. The occasion was one of the most magnificent in the recent history of Petersburg, no expense spared, the Tsar in his box, the nobles in their stalls and boxes in glittering uniforms, the women thick with jewels, the talk all of the fortune the production had cost. The moment should have been historic, the culmination of the composer's career. In fact it almost misfired. The Tsar's comment when he summoned Tchaikovsky to his box was the infuriatingly inadequate "very nice." The audience applauded dutifully, following the Tsar's handclaps, but were plainly all at sea.

No one can wonder, for this Petersburg audience was hearing and watching a revolution in ballet. If *Swan Lake* is the essence of poetry in ballet, *The Sleeping Beauty* is the essence of grandeur. Nobody had heard a score of such proportions devoted to ballet. Never before had such choreography and such dancing been seen. After *The Sleeping Beauty,* ballet could never again sink to its old humdrum form with public approval, for the curious fact emerged that the Maryinsky public which had greeted the new ballet so half-heartedly found itself dissatisfied with its normal ballet fare ever afterwards.

Everybody interested in ballet has seen *The Sleeping Beauty:* everybody interested in music has heard it entire or in Tchaikovsky's suite from the ballet score. Tchaikovsky had approached the work as he approached his symphonies, seriously and imaginatively, and the result was a score of great length in which majesty and poetry interchange with dazzling effect. By that time his vocabulary of musical expression was enormous and is put to full and splendid use. He understood perfectly how to create courtly music, fairy music, the music of youth and of love. As music in itself it is sumptuous, grand, with one noble and ravishing theme after another. As music for dancing it is almost without rival, expressing and often demanding in sound precisely the movements of the dancer. Tchaikovsky had of course been a devotee of the ballet and theater since his youth; he had watched ballet after ballet in Petersburg in the 1860's with the eye of a musician. Even so this faultless collaboration with Petipa still rouses astonishment. Nor does he ever give the impression that he is writing—as he was—to order. The impression is rather that each scene on the stage, every movement, rises inevitably from the marvellous music. At one stroke—in forty days of work—he had created a masterpiece by any musical standard, he had provided ballet dancers with a new standard of music to interpret, had inspired a great choreographer to write his finest work, and had lifted ballet as a whole to the level of great art.

2

Tchaikovsky had not wintered in Italy for eight years. That gives some indication of the change fame had brought; he had never had time to spare from winter concerts and operas since writing the Trio in Florence in 1882. He would have had no time in 1890 if he had not refused every offer to conduct his work in Europe that season, tempting though the offers were. As it was, he could return to Florence at last with the comfortable feeling that his two European tours had done everything he had hoped and more.

He never made up his mind which city he liked best, Florence or Rome, but this time—it was to be his last glimpse of Italy—he chose Florence, probably because he would be less bothered there by society hostesses chasing the great Russian and by composers of every kind soliciting favors. He wanted a rest.

His idea of a rest was not everybody's; he at once began to write an opera. Perhaps a composer could scarcely spend months in Italy without thinking of opera but Tchaikovsky did not need much urging. He had been thinking about this opera for the past two years—on the whole not very favorably—yet in the end it had its way and the world lost an opportunity of seeing what Chekhov would have made of an opera libretto. The opera Tchaikovsky now took up had been suggested by Modest before the meeting with Chekhov and Modest now settled the matter by writing a libretto without waiting for his brother to make up his mind.

The story was taken from Pushkin's *The Queen of Spades*. Modest's libretto was anything but perfect—even the fond Pyotr Ilyich demanded liberal cuts—but it got the composer to work. When Tchaikovsky had the libretto before him he began to see the subject's possibilities. After a few days he was quite converted and wrote the score at a great pace. By the time he moved to Rome for a week or two in April he had sketched the whole thing out and in Rome he orchestrated half the score.

He returned to Russia in a state of great excitement and finished the entire opera at Frolovskoye by the beginning of June. Everything had gone without a hitch and once more, forgetting all that had happened in the past, he announced that he had "unquestionably written my masterpiece." The music was so suggestive of the action, he said, that the scene between Herman and the Countess terrified him when he played it over. Kashkin and Jurgenson, joining him for a few days, were equally taken with the score when they heard it.

Between spells of enthusiastic gardening he at last got to work on the sextet which had been bobbing up and down in his mind for years. He called it "Souvenir of Florence" and by July had completed the draft. This too pleased him, specially the fugue which ends it, and he hastened to tell Nadezhda Filaretovna about it "for I know how much you love chamber music . . . and you can quite easily arrange to hear the sextet well played in your own home." He characteristically began to think more of it than the opera and, to round matters off, to rebuke himself for pride. But nothing could quell his optimism; he had once more thrust down the spectre of a composer who merely repeats himself.

In high good humor he left for Tiflis in August. His spirits were quickly dampened at Kamenka where he called en route. He usually spent a few weeks with his sister each summer but this visit of 1890 was not a success. Everything, he thought, had changed. The deaths of the two elder girls and the absence of the third, Anna, who had married into the von Meck family, had thrown the household into gloom; Alexandra obviously was not well, both she and Lyov looked much older, and their efforts to welcome Pyotr Ilyich with the usual brightness were even more painful than the sight of them sad and silent. The house had gone to the other extreme from the noisy place Tchaikovsky had escaped from years earlier. It was not quiet but dead. Even the village seemed to the sensitive Pyotr Ilyich to have taken its cue from the great house; it had lost all its charm and looked ugly and sordid.

He was glad to be away—he could not rouse his sister—and by the time he reached Tiflis in September had regained enough cheerfulness to respond to the usual warm welcome from everyone. He had grown very fond of his sister-in-law, he loved their little daughter, he admired the way Anatoly was making a good career, and he found a stimulating musical companion in Ippolitov-Ivanov.

He quickly slipped into the half-oriental life of the city—this was his fifth visit—and threw himself into an orgy of music, conducting his own work, listening to concerts and opera, talking music and planning to write more. He was happy and optimistic, reacting as always to kindness and affection from others. In the midst of this happy period, on October 4, he received his last letter from Nadezhda Filaretovna.

3

For some time her letters had been growing shorter and more infrequent—gloomier too. They had troubled Tchaikovsky because much was going wrong in the von Meck household. Her eldest son, whom she adored, was desperately ill with a wasting disease that already showed signs of affecting the brain. Nadezhda Filaretovna's bouts of prostration with splitting headaches had become longer—she often went to bed for days at a time—she had difficulty in throwing off the colds she was forever catching, she had what appeared to be a perpetual cough, and her eyesight was beginning to fail. Finally, a slight paralysis of the right arm almost brought an end to her personal correspondence. She still dictated business letters to one or another of her family but when she wanted to write to Tchaikovsky she had to support her right arm with her left in order to guide her hand over the paper.

All this explained the change in her letters and Tchaikovsky had often grieved that beyond writing fully and affectionately he could not help the woman who had done so much for him. But one change there was not; her letters, brief and wider-spaced though they had become, were still as they had been throughout the past twelve years, affectionate, still hotly possessive, still intensely interested in everything he did and wrote. He was worried for her, he was not hurt for himself; as far as he (or anyone else who reads the letters) could judge the relationship remained as it had always been.

The letter he received at Tiflis on October 4 was not like this; it was not like any letter he had ever had from her. It was short and final. It said that she had lost all her money and could no longer give him an allowance. It ended, "Do not forget me; think of me sometimes."

He did not at all grasp the meaning of this last sentence. He was terribly shocked but his thought was all for her as his reply, written immediately, clearly showed. He begged her not to worry about him; he could do very well without her allowance. What worried him was the thought of her, used to wealth for so many years, being forced to live without it: "I simply can't find the words to tell you how sorry I am for you and how fearful."

Not until he had made plain that all his fears were for her did he speak of the last words of her letter and then he misinterpreted them. Being what he was he could not possibly have taken them in any other sense. "They hurt me a little," he wrote, "but I can't believe you really meant them. Could you really think that I am only able to think of you as long as I am spending your money! How could I possibly forget, even for one moment, all you have done for me and all I owe you? I don't exaggerate when I say that without your friendship and sympathy I should have gone mad and died. You saved me. . . . No, my dear friend, you can be quite sure that I shall remember you and bless you as long as I have a breath left in my body. And now that you have no wealth left to share with me I am glad to think that I can freely demonstrate all the fond and limitless gratitude I feel for you."

He told her that he did not expect her to be able to write for some time but that he looked to Pakhulsky, now her son-in-law, to give him more details and to relieve his anxiety if he could.

No letter had arrived from Pakhulsky by the time Pyotr Ilyich left Tiflis for Moscow at the beginning of November. When he arrived in the capital the first thing he heard was that the von Meck fortune was intact.

Even then, at the height of the fresh shock, he failed to see that her final sentence had been a farewell. He wrote at once to Pakhulsky. Pakhulsky replied after some weeks with the politeness he had always shown but was noncommittal about his mother-in-law. The bewildered Pyotr Ilyich wrote again and again. In due course Pakhulsky sent him a friendly letter but avoided all discussion of Nadezhda Filaretovna who, he said, was ill. His attitude was that all was as usual except that she was too tired to write.

By this time, in spring of the next year, Tchaikovsky was due to go off on a long tour. He wrote again just before leaving. He was mystified, hurt, astonished, but still could not believe that any human being could cut off an intimacy such as theirs so brutally and without giving any reason except a lie that he was bound to discover.

When he returned from his tour in early summer he found another letter from Pakhulsky waiting for him. It was as negative and uncommunicative as the others. Tchaikovsky, angry now, yet still unable to credit such behavior, made a final effort; he sent him a letter which he begged him to show to Nadezhda Filaretovna.

"I have just had your letter," he wrote. "You tell me that Nadezhda Filaretovna is so ill and weak and in such a state of nerves that she can't write to me as she used to. Well, I would not wish for anything in the world to do or say anything that would increase her sufferings. It is not the fact that she does not write to me that hurts and worries and I am bound to say offends me. No, it is the fact that she seems to have lost every scrap of interest in me. It would be quite simple, if she wished to hear about me, to hear through you and Julia Karlovna but she obviously has not once asked either of you to discover how I am or anything about me and my work.

"As you know I have tried to get in touch with N.F. through you but every letter you have written me has politely rebuffed my efforts to preserve, even if only for a short time, some semblance of our former relationship.

"You must know that N.F. wrote to me last September to say that she was ruined and could not help me any longer with money. You must surely have read my reply? It was obvious that my preeminent wish was that my relationship with N.F. should not be changed just because she was not able to support me financially. Incredibly this does not seem possible. Evidently N.F. has lost all her feeling for me. When this idea entered my head I did not write to her again. In other words, for some extraordinary reason the fact that she no longer sent me money had to be the sign for our intimacy to end. This thought is frightfully humiliating for me and I am suffering unbearable worry and agony of mind when I think how I accepted her pension all these years."

It is perhaps unfortunate that he did not stop there. His sufferings were hard to bear precisely because he had never cared for Nadezhda Filaretovna as she had cared for him. Of course the cruelty of the break would have hurt any man—it was stupidly and savagely done—but what Tchaikovsky chiefly felt was humiliation. He knew in his heart that his friendship with her would have taken a very different course if he had not been tempted by the money which made it possible for him to write music fairly free from worry. The position far back in 1877 was a familiar one in the world of art—the artist desperate to give himself wholly to his work, the patron appearing godlike out of the blue. But something is notoriously never given for nothing—the man or woman patron has never been known who could give without any thought of self. Nadezhda Filaretovna had demanded what Tchaikovsky could not give. He had been faced with a terrible temptation and had given way to it. He had, in his eyes in these dark days of 1891, perjured himself for the sake of his music; scarcely one reference to his feeling for her, gratitude apart, had been completely genuine throughout a whole decade of the correspondence. Now, it seemed, she had found him out.

The humiliated man, like the guilty one, tends to go on too long, to lash himself into insincerity. Tchaikovsky did so now. "When I was in the country last autumn I read all N.F.'s letters over again and while I read I thought that the feeling shown in them could not be affected by illness, by worry, or by money troubles. But her feelings have altered nevertheless. It may be that because I never met N.F. I put her on a pedestal. I couldn't imagine treachery from the kind of other-worldly person I imagined her to be. I could sooner imagine the earth giving way under my feet than N.F.'s feelings towards me changing. Yet this is just what has happened, and my faith in mankind, my hope for the world has turned to dust and ashes, my peace of mind has been shattered and the last hope of any happiness I may have been intended by Fate to enjoy has disappeared."

Pakhulsky returned the letter Tchaikovsky had asked him to hand to Nadezhda Filaretovna; he could not show it to her, he said; she was too ill in mind and body. He assured Tchaikovsky that she loved her old friends as before; what seemed like coldness was only the result of her condition; she was very ill.

4

At this point Tchaikovsky abandoned Pakhulsky, though not his hope of discovering why he had been so badly treated. He remained mystified as most of us are to this day. Many explanations

have been put forward. None of them seems adequate. It is improbable that the obvious answer—that Nadezhda Filaretovna had
suddenly discovered that he was a homosexual—is the correct one.
Several of Tchaikovsky's letters to her reveal his homosexuality
so plainly that a woman of her intelligence could not have been
deceived. She was, besides, very well informed about everything
to do with the musical circles in Moscow and could not have
avoided hearing what everybody knew.

Others have suggested that her conscience pricked her unbearably when her son became seriously ill and that she put this down
to her feeling for Tchaikovsky; had she looked after him instead
of devoting most of her thought to Tchaikovsky and his music,
he might have lived to carry on her work. This surmise is given
some confirmation by Alexandra's daughter Anna Lvovna who
had married into the von Meck family. "Her sorest trial," she
says, "was the disease of her eldest, her beloved son. He died
before her eyes after a protracted and agonizing illness and it
seemed to her . . . that her friendship with Pyotr Ilyich had taken
her thoughts away from her family and home and that perhaps
she was even guilty of the horrible death of her gifted son. 'I
must atone for my sin,' she said. She went back to her Faith,
began to pray once more and asked me to order prayers for her
in church. Such a frame of mind naturally affected the correspondence with Pyotr Ilyich; she did not feel it to be such a vital necessity as formerly."

Again it has been thought that Pakhulsky had been intriguing
against Tchaikovsky ever since he succeeded in marrying Julia
von Meck, fearing that Nadezhda Filaretovna might will the bulk
of her fortune away to the composer. The only evidence of this
again comes from Anna Lvovna. "Why Uncle did not give his
letter to Nadezhda Filaretovna to me or to my husband I can't
understand." The interesting point about this is the implication—
which was a fact—that although all the von Meck family lived
together Pakhulsky did not tell Anna Lvovna or her husband
about his correspondence with Tchaikovsky. It must be added

that Anna Lvovna says she thinks Pakhulsky acted "very correctly" in returning the letter—why, she does not explain.

Others suggest that when Nadezhda Filaretovna at last gave up hope of a marriage, when Tchaikovsky refused to divorce Antonina, she began to turn against him.

Yet again, it has been thought that when Tchaikovsky finally became famous, she reacted violently to the very success she had fought for, believing that the last excuse for his dependence on her had disappeared. It is certainly true of possessive natures that they cannot endure sharing their possession.

A final suggestion comes from Anna Lvovna. It must be said that by 1890 this girl had identified herself completely with the von Meck family into which she had married and was obviously under the spell of her strongminded mother-in-law like everyone else in the house. "The changes in Pyotr Ilyich's life," she says, "did not at first affect his relations with my mother-in-law but little by little towards the end of the eighties he began to need her support less and less and did not rely as much as formerly on constant exchange of thoughts with her. In consequence she sometimes began to suspect that his letters to her were written with an effort and that a feeling of reserve was creeping into them."

This solution (one of many attempted by Tchaikovsky's niece) though unlikely to explain the break may well explain what helped to lead up to it. By the end of the 1880's Tchaikovsky was in such demand that his correspondence on all sides was necessarily slackening. As Nadezhda Filaretovna was unable to write as often as in the old days he may have seized the excuse to write less frequently. Her imagination and her intense pride would have done the rest. The tone of his letters, like the tone of hers, however, remained constant; he had never felt for her as she felt for him but his sense of gratitude and of rapport in music was as strong as ever.

However, the truth would seem likely to rest in the simple fact that she was no longer responsible for all her actions. She had always been unbalanced—her manner of life after the death of her

husband was far from normal—and in the past few years she had
become very much more so. "She began to feel extremely ill,"
says Anna Lvovna, "and her dreadful headaches prostrated her
for days. She became very lifeless . . . the tubercular development
in her lungs gained ground and by 1889-90 she was also suffering
from a serious nervous disease which deeply perturbed us all. The
tuberculosis she feared for so long was to kill her three years
later."

Tuberculosis has an extraordinary effect on the sufferer. In
tubercular cases there may be abrupt and senseless likes and dis-
likes which are magnified to the point of insanity—they move
from love to hate in moments and for no observable or analyzable
reason whatever.

Tchaikovsky still had no knowledge of Nadezhda Filaretovna's
true condition; for twelve years he had read accounts of the violent headaches and nerve storms and had inevitably become
largely accustomed to them. He would think, as we would all do,
that if she were really as ill as she thought she would have been
forced to bed and to a doctor long since. Tuberculosis deceives
many; it takes its time.

The truth will never be known. Nadezhda Filaretovna kept
her own counsel in everything. Not until the last year of her life
and the last few months of Tchaikovsky's did she speak, and then
only because the question was put plainly to her. This explanation will be given in its place. It may not convince many readers,
and the probable truth would still seem to rest in her illness.
When it is remembered what this disease does to the most normal
of people, it can be imagined what it could do to a woman already unbalanced and with a son who died showing definite signs
of insanity. And when one comes to think of it, was the last note
of this extraordinary friendship any more remarkable than its
first? Reading again her opening letters to Tchaikovsky, do they
not indicate an emotional and probably abrupt end to the relationship—as abrupt and emotional as its beginning?

CHAPTER 23

The Queen *of* Spades and American Tour
1890-1892

ARTISTS SEEM TO HAVE a capacity for both greater and less good fortune than the ordinary run of men and women. Tchaikovsky now experienced a turn of good fortune. In the autumn of 1890 he was a man struck to the heart by what seemed a wholly unmerited snub to his pride and feelings—and one must admit that he was extraordinarily unfortunate to have had intimate dealings with two unbalanced women. But he was also a composer determined to write music as well as a famous man committed to one engagement after another. However much he would have liked to brood on the insult and the hurt he literally could not do it— neither the world nor his genius would permit it.

At this time he had three items on his schedule, none of which could be ignored. The first was the premiere of *The Queen of Spades,* the second a new ballet, the third a visit to the United States. It cannot be said that he faced any one of them gladly—the wound was fresh and was never to be completely healed—but he faced them and, when the moment came, thought of them only.

The Queen of Spades was presented at the Maryinsky on December 19. Tchaikovsky was well served by the singers (he had been to see some of them months earlier to make sure that they were really enthusiastic about their roles) and by Napravnik as conductor and there was never the slightest doubt that at long last he had written an opera which would command something of the affection given to *Eugene Onegin*, an opera that would not follow the rest on to the scrap heap. The public and critical response to *The Queen of Spades* was virtually unanimous, and Tchaikovsky left the theater believing that the work was safe for posterity.

His confidence has been proved correct. *The Queen of Spades* is not so good an opera as *Eugene Onegin* nor so well suited to the composer's genius but it will always come back into the repertory from time to time because it has what his operas which failed did not, a dramatic situation treated genuinely and dramatically in musical terms and a group of believable characters differentiated skillfully and truthfully.

Tchaikovsky was no doubt fortunate to begin with a superb story by a master of storytelling, but he rose to the challenge. He could understand these people, they were sufficiently close to his time and class to be recreated without difficulty. In general the characters are all musically well observed and with Herman he went further than a character in the round, he really managed to infuse into the music for him something of the psychological subtlety imagined by Pushkin. The music for the fourth act which had so alarmed him when he played it over still grips audiences; it is permissible melodrama extremely well handled, economical and telling.

For those who have not heard this opera it might perhaps be well to say that it is the type of work which needs several hearings if its full impact is to be felt. Unlike so many of the popular operas in the repertory it does not rely on great and immediately appealing arias. The entire work possesses only two arias of moment, Herman's "Three Cards!" and Lisa's "It is almost midnight," and they are scarcely the whistleable variety. At first this lack of great tunes strikes many listeners as disappointing and even flat, but those who persevere discover something better than the obvious attraction of popular melodies, a sterling honesty of purpose throughout and a score which grows on one at every

performance. This score is never brilliant, it is also never cheap—
it is effective because it is truly felt.

A few days after the first night and a party to mark the twenty-
fifth anniversary of his entry into the Petersburg Conservatoire
he went off to Kiev on the way to a New Year stay at Kamenka.
It was a sign of the times that in Kiev he found *The Queen of
Spades* already mounted and was able to hear and watch it re-
laxedly. That put him in a good mood for Kamenka and to his
enormous pleasure he found that the cloud of the summer had
lifted. Alexandra was much more like her old self and if she was
happy he was happy too; it was as simple as that.

Knowing the future, one wonders whether Alexandra had an
instinct that she would never see this dearly loved brother again.
She had the brilliance so often found in those who have reconciled
themselves to death. Such a thought was beyond her brother; a
world without Alexandra was unimaginable to him. He saw only
that, though frail, she seemed to have taken a new hold on life,
deciding to devote herself to the children still left. He rejoiced.
Looking back, he could never recall a happier New Year than
this one of 1891 and he blessed the premonition which had led
him to spend it at Kamenka.

The hint of old and happy times at once reflected itself in his
work. He wanted to write another ballet—the success of *The
Sleeping Beauty* had encouraged Petipa and Vsevolozsky, the
opera house director, to beg for more—and with Lyegoshin's
daughter in mind he thought of *The Nutcracker* from one of
E. T. A. Hoffmann's tales. But the success of *The Queen of Spades*
also made him anxious to write another opera. He read in spurts
in the library at Kamenka which had already provided him with
useful material and came across Zvantsev's translation of Hertz's
King René's Daughter, which had been inspired by Hans Christian
Anderson, liked it, and put Modest to work on a libretto.

Engagements in Moscow and Petersburg drove him away at last.
He wondered for the thousandth time why on earth he submitted

to the treadmill of public life but he went just the same; he was at least cheered to have seen Kamenka in its true colors.

He was so much in demand as conductor, as guest of honor—as at the Guitry *Hamlet* with his incidental music at the Mikhailovsky Theater that February and at Arensky's first opera the month previous—and as encourager of the young talent forever waiting on the doorstep of his hotel, that he did not get back to Frolovskoye and the new ballet until a week or two before he was due to leave for the United States. It was to be his last stay at Frolovskoye. The builders were cutting down the woods he loved and he told Alexei to find another home for them.

He managed to sketch out enough of the ballet to show to Petipa before leaving for Berlin and Paris in the middle of the month. Petipa reacted like the great and practical artist he was; he gave the composer exact details of the music he needed, specifying the number of bars and the kind of emotion needed for each section. This could be taken as an insult or a considerable compliment. The usually touchy Tchaikovsky accepted the directions without loss of face and with absolute faith in the choreographer. It has sometimes been said that he would write to order only for Balakirev, but his response to Petipa is even more astonishing for a man of his pride and fame. Armed with the master's instructions—they were no less—he set off for his most arduous tour. He intended, he said, to spend his many spare moments of travel in completing the ballet.

In Paris he conducted an all-Tchaikovsky concert played by the Colonne orchestra. It was greeted with enthusiasm which he took as an omen of good. He had still two weeks before his ship sailed and once again became the center of attention until, tiring of perpetual soirees and of the bright fulsomeness of his hosts, he decided to spend a few days at Rouen by himself. There was another reason for this sudden flight. He was feeling homesick as he usually did for the first week or two out of Russia and reproached Modest—who had come to see him off—for falling victim to Paris charm and aping the fashionable young Parisians. There was a quarrel.

He had scarcely settled into his Rouen hotel and into a more equable mood than he was joined by Modest. Modest had come to break bad news—soon after Pyotr Ilyich left, a telegram arrived to say that Alexandra had died suddenly at Kamenka—but the moment he saw his brother's contented face he knew that he could not tell him the truth, that he must not ruin the American tour. As Tchaikovsky was amazed to see him and as he had to leave for Kamenka the next day, Modest had a bright idea for explaining both events: he said that Pyotr Ilyich had been quite right to reprimand him for forgetting Russia and aping the French; he had taken the reproof so much to heart that he intended to go straight back where he belonged.

Tchaikovsky, incapable of suspecting such a ruse, accepted the explanation and Modest had to face as best he could an evening of joyousness. He left triumphant, however, and sure that Pyotr Ilyich would reach New York before hearing the news, as he might have done but for a singular chance. He had half intended to go straight from Rouen to Le Havre and his ship, then decided at the last minute to come back to Paris and take the boat train from there so that he could say goodbye to two friends of his, both pianists—the Austrian Sophie Menter and the Russian V. Sapelnikov who had been the soloist in his Second Piano Concerto at the Colonne concert.

Unhappily he was an avid reader of Russian newspapers when out of the country. The day before he was due to leave he went into a reading room in the Passage de l'Opera and settled down to go through the papers. He read every scrap, even the obituaries on the last page and there, in the *Novoye Vremya,* he saw an account of his sister's death.

His first impulse was to rush back to Kamenka. He spent dreadful hours with his friends, talking through the night. He insisted that he had no heart for the tour, he only wanted to be at Kamenka. They urged him to fulfil his obligations to the Americans, pointing out that he could not see Alexandra on her death bed, that he could not even get back in time for the funeral. Why, then, disappoint thousands of music lovers in the new world for no useful purpose? And before morning broke he saw the sense of what they said. A few hours later, utterly wretched, he sailed for New York.

2

It says much for American hospitality and tact that this memorable visit did not collapse before it had properly begun. Tchaikovsky, hating every mile that took him farther from Russia, arrived on April 25 in a black mood, thinking only how soon he could sail back to Europe. He had come to take part in the festivities arranged to mark the opening of what is now Carnegie Hall and thought he could leave in a week or two.

Two days later he was reconciled to an extension of his visit by conducting concerts at Philadelphia and Baltimore. He could never resist genuine kindness and admiration and he found both in New York to a degree that astounded him. He was greeted with heartening warmth by Walter Damrosch and the orchestra he was to conduct, given a luxurious suite in one of Broadway's finest hotels, he was dined by Carnegie, by Damrosch, the Francis Hydes, the Morris Renos in state and in private, taken on tours of the city (the skyscrapers amazed him) taken to Niagara Falls, to Long Island where he spent a night in Ferdinand Mayer's overwhelming summer house, taken to supper at Delmonico's, invited into the Opera House boxes of all New York's great men and discovered with a likable amazement that "I am ten times as famous here as in Europe." He was not given one moment to think or brood. His hotel was besieged by callers, famous and not famous, anxious to talk with Russia's great composer, to get his autograph, his photograph, to invite him out. He was dead tired at the end of each day but undeniably stirred. He could neither complete the ballet score nor feel homesick, there was no time for it. He punctiliously saw everybody and answered every letter in his vast post.

It was all very exhausting but flattering too. He often blessed his steady head—the champagne flowed freely—and he suffered agonies during a three and a half hour dinner at which smoking was not allowed, but by and large he came to admire his generous-hearted hosts who laid themselves out so thoroughly to show him that he was a highly honored guest. He went off to his concerts apprehensive but proud.

Musically, he was immediately struck by the playing of the Symphony Society Orchestra he had to conduct. This gave him immense confidence. All his contributions to the festivities went off triumphantly. At the first, on May 5, he found himself facing a vast audience of close to six thousand in the new hall. He had chosen to conduct his "Coronation March," written for Alexander III's accession ceremonies—an unpretentious work which went well. Three days later, on his fifty-first birthday, he conducted the Third Suite and the next day the First Piano Concerto. He was very moved by his reception: "I was recalled time after time, handkerchiefs were waved, there were shouts and cheers. . . . I've never known such scenes of enthusiasm even in Russia. . . . The Americans had plainly taken me to their hearts." He added typically, "But what moved me most of all was the orchestra's reaction"—for the men he had conducted were on their feet tapping their instruments and offering true homage.

At Baltimore the incessant round of hospitality continued—including a visit to the Knabe piano factory—as well as a successful concert with the Concerto repeated and the "Serenade for Strings" inserted in place of the Suite (the orchestra was short of violins) but Washington pleased Pyotr Ilyich much more. There he could be with Russians in the Embassy and the Metropolitan Club where he was the guest of honor. At the Embassy his Trio was played before the Ambassador (specially returned for the occasion) and all the city diplomats.

Philadelphia's Academy of Music was packed to the doors for

his concert and he left glowing reports behind him as he went back to New York and the final days of his tour. He was desperately tired but game and, surprisingly, glad to be back. His provincial excursion—if one dare use that term of illustrious cities —somehow lacked the glamour of New York. After a few more hectic days he boarded his ship on May 21 worn out but contented. He was loaded with gifts, dazed by all the music he had heard, his hand ached with the autographs he had signed, and his head buzzed with the champagne he had drunk. But it was a good ending and he sailed off urged to return soon and intending to do so—only an unhappy misunderstanding of a cable was to prevent it. Apart from the manners of some journalists who, to his astonishment, were more concerned by a man's appearance than by the worth of his music, he looked back to what seemed a whirlwind tour as the final justification of all his efforts to fit himself to conduct his own music. In the United States, as in Western Europe, he was a celebrity and his music was liked and understood.

By the beginning of June he was in Petersburg and very thankful to be there. Looking back, he thought of the round of parties and dinners and interviews with absolute horror as always. What remained in his mind as entirely pleasurable was the attitude of the American people. He contrasted their openhanded and openhearted welcome with the self-satisfied approval of the Germans on earlier tours, the insincerity of the French, the crudity of the English, and he felt warmly towards this new nation that had taken his music to its heart without reservation. He placed the Americans in his mind with the people of Tiflis, of Prague, people who have never learned the false gospel which confuses nationalism with art.

His happiness to be in Russia again did not live long. Waiting for him was Pakhulsky's final letter and the end of the hopes of a reconciliation with Nadezhda Filaretovna. Waiting too was irritating news from Alexei. His manservant, more luxury-loving than he, never liked the bungalow life of Frolovskoye and always missed the comfort of Maidanovo, and there he transferred the household as soon as Tchaikovsky's back was turned. Tchaikovsky hated suburban life and its endless petty curiosity. He loathed to see trees cut down to make way for yet another rich man's vulgar chalet. Now he was to be plunged into suburbia. He was not pleased and went off to Maidanovo in sombre mood.

The mood exploded on the platform of Klin station a few days later. Tchaikovsky is usually portrayed as a man almost too amiable for this world. The portrait is a truthful one but naturally enough is not the whole truth. He could be roused by many things, by students who made a mock of the subject they were supposed to be studying, by government interference with the arts, and now with a manservant who repaid years of kindness and generosity with an act he knew his master could not approve.

The proverb, he who touches pitch will be defiled, is as true as the day it was written. As ever, these contacts with human stupidity and greed did nothing but soil Tchaikovsky's mind and made him for the moment into a travesty of his kind and just self. He could even forget his manners. And as usual, too, his anger fell on the wrong person.

It so happened that one of the passengers in the train approaching Klin on this particular day was the singer A. V. Panaeva-Kartsova, another pupil of Viardot. Panasha, as he always called her, was married to a distant cousin of Tchaikovsky's. He greatly admired her voice and appearance—"she is the *personification* of my ideal Tatyana"—and was always very glad to see her. He was still hoping to persuade her to play the role.

At Moscow she was joined in her compartment by Modest and he spent the time to Klin telling her about his brother's triumphs in America. "He had a fantastic success," he said—he always tended to exaggerate—"and the Americans simply worship him."

Underneath his chatter she surmised a certain uneasiness and at last it came out: "Petya is expecting me to stay with him for a while and hear the full story of the tour but I'm having to disappoint him, I've very urgent business at Petersburg and must go straight there."

She thought this a little strange; Modest had never had urgent business in his life and might have been expected to spare a day or two for the brother who had been virtually keeping him for years. However she thought no more of it until the train stopped at Klin and Modest got out. She too got out soon afterwards—her little girl had asked for a glass of milk—and saw on the platform a group including Tchaikovsky, Modest, Laroche, and the actor Delazari. She had not realized that Tchaikovsky would actually be at Klin station to greet Modest but, seeing him there, felt that she must speak to him.

As she walked towards him she could see that he was looking angry and resentful and that Modest's face wore an abashed expression. Evidently he had broken the news.

It was not perhaps the best moment to speak but she had begun to walk towards them and could not go back. She went up to Tchaikovsky with her hand flung out. "My dear Pyotr Ilyich, I congratulate you warmly," she cried.

"Congratulate me? What for?" he asked in an irritated voice.

"For your triumphant tour of America, of course."

He looked with angry irony at Modest and shrugged his shoulders petulantly: "I've just had a fine kind of congratulation, I can tell you!" He turned to the rest of his group and cried "I meet with nothing but annoyances and she congratulates me!"

Everybody turned and looked at her reproachfully.

She became angry and burst out *"Si vous le prenez sur ce ton-là . . . !* (If *that's* the tone you're going to take . . .) Good-bye." With that she turned on her heel and walked off quickly.

She soon heard somebody running after her, then the panting voice of Pyotr Ilyich, "Alexandra Valerianovna . . . Tatochka . . . Panasha . . . wait, do wait. Don't be angry."

She walked all the quicker and shouted over her shoulder "No, no. While you're in that kind of mood I don't want to talk to you."

She reached her compartment, jumped in, and slammed the door.

3

That is another side of a great man. If he is great it is a side that never shows itself for long. So it was with Tchaikovsky; having sighed over Maidanovo, its depleted woods and growing cluster of villas, he got down to work. By July he had finished the sketch of *The Nutcracker.* He went straight on to the one-act opera *Yolanta* and completed the draft by the middle of September and, as three months of composition left him unappeased, took up a symphonic poem he had begun in Tiflis the previous year, on *Voivode,* orchestrated it and soon afterwards heard it played for the first time in Moscow. Siloti had blossomed out as a conductor and it was he who directed the symphonic poem in a program including Grieg and Glazunov works.

For once Tchaikovsky reacted promptly. The audience cheered him "passionately." His response was to tear up the score. He understood that a mature man cannot go back to youthful ideas and escape the ludicrous. He was not prepared to be laughed at by posterity for the sake of cheap cheers in the present.

Back again he went somewhat ruffled to Maidanovo and *Yolanta.* He broke off once to visit Anatoly in his new post not far from the Hapsal of happy memories, then returned to finish the opera just before the end of the year.

He ended it in something of a rush; he was booked to conduct two all-Tchaikovsky concerts in Kiev before beginning another short European tour. By the middle of January, 1892, he was breaking fresh ground in Warsaw and earning more "passionate ovations."

From Warsaw he moved to Hamburg to conduct *Eugene Onegin* and there provided another example of his conscientious approach to music. When he understood that the translated libretto would confuse his directions to singers and orchestra he would not go on. He had already heard a possible substitute conductor with admiration the previous evening and listened to his rendering of his own opera in delight. The conductor was the young Gustav Mahler.

That was the whole of the tour—he had decided never again to stay long away from Russia—and after a few days in Paris he was back at Maidanovo by the middle of February making a suite out of his *Nutcracker* score. This suite, so well known to concert audiences, was given its first performance under the composer's baton in Petersburg in March and was immediately hailed as a little masterpiece.

There is good reason for seeing this suite as a disaster. For once Tchaikovsky's taste seems to have deserted him—either that or, working too hurriedly, he took the easy road. In the event almost all the best music in the ballet was left out of the suite. Ever after, up to the present day, thousands of people listen to the suite thinking that they have heard the essence of the ballet. Never was there a greater error; this rather cheap selection does the ballet harm.

An amusing story attaches to this suite. Tchaikovsky, ever searching for novelty, wanted an instrument that would convey the fragility and other-worldliness of the fairies. He was led to the answer by his work the previous autumn on the symphonic poem *Voivode*. That work was a failure but it reminded him that he had used the celesta in the old opera of many years before. The opera had failed and the use of the instrument had passed without notice. He now saw that its exquisite purity of tone would precisely fit his conception of the Sugar Plum Fairy and set about with great stealth to have one brought from the Paris factory. A more generous man than Pyotr Ilyich has rarely existed but when it came to the use of rare or unknown instruments in a symphony orchestra he became the miser in person. He swore everyone concerned to secrecy; he lived in perpetual dread that some other composer—he chiefly feared Rimsky-Korsakov or Glazunov—would manage to hear the celesta, appreciate the unique effects obtainable with it, and use it before he did.

Enormously cheered by getting in first he made a symbolic gesture to his old Law School. It was thirty-three years since he had graduated and gone into the Finance Ministry with the hopeless feeling that his chance of taking up music had slipped away for ever. He left the school to become a government clerk, he returned as Russia's outstanding composer but one would never have guessed it from his manner as he conducted the school orchestra in excerpts from his own works, and one student at least vowed there and then that he would follow in his footsteps. This was a boy by the name of A. B. Khessin.

While in Petersburg, Tchaikovsky received good news. His complaints about Maidanovo—the crowds peering into the garden on the chance of seeing him, the perpetual rings at the bell, the impossibility of taking a walk without running into autograph hunters—had at last melted the stony heart of Alexei. Possibly Alexei had become tired of answering the bell that Tchaikovsky was tired of hearing. He looked about and in the middle of May proudly showed his master into a new home on the outskirts of Klin.

CHAPTER 24

Sixth Symphony
1892-1893

ALEXEI HAD BEEN FEELING for some time that his master was not living in the style befitting a great man and for this last home he did Pyotr Ilyich proud. He was helped in his search for a worthy house for Russia's famous composer by Taneyev's brother who owned a large estate just outside the town. The garden of the house into which Tchaikovsky settled in May, 1892, was bordered on two sides by this estate which ensured him almost complete privacy as well as a sympathetic neighbor who would not sell his land for development.

The Klin house has long been the Tchaikovsky Museum. It is a handsome and substantial building in the fashion of that day, the ground floor brick, the upper floor wood, with a long verandah in front and a pedimented center piece. The rooms are spacious, with high ceilings; the size of the music room can be gauged from the fact that between Tchaikovsky's grand pianoforte, which was placed dead center, and the walls on every side is a space nearly twice the length of the instrument. At right angles to the main window—a double window as everywhere in Russia—he put the long desk on which he did all his composition and behind this again, with its back to the wall, was a couch some seven feet long on which he used to rest between spells of work. Above the couch hung his most prized group of portraits and photographs of his family, specially loved friends, relatives, and musicians. In the center of this group was a large head and shoulder portrait of Mozart.

Although Tchaikovsky was a man of his period—and Alexei even more so—to the extent of filling the house with knickknacks, it was devoid of what is now regarded as essential comfort. There was not an easy chair in the place and his bedroom was monastic to a degree. He did all his work and all his playing—and he was often at the piano by the hour, day after day—on hard upright wooden chairs.

In Tchaikovsky's time the garden was large and heavily wooded, with many flower beds to the front and sides of the house, and though he was only just on the outskirts of Klin, on the Frolov-skoye road, he had the impression of being miles from anywhere. He could not see another house and from some parts of the garden he could obtain the view he most loved, of the flat, apparently illimitable spaces he thought of as Russia at her most character-istic. He was free to walk in the Taneyev woods whenever he pleased.

His difficulty, like that of all famous men, was to make time to compose; the longer he lived the more he was in demand. This explains partly why, having celebrated the entry into his new home by beginning a new symphony, he did not get very far with it. There was another reason too; he was not happy with it. The old dread of having written himself out loomed again and he stopped work abruptly and made a quick series of visits—to see Artot in Berlin and to spend a few days in Paris and Vichy.

Back again, he found himself bogged down by requests from the capitals that he conduct, open festivals, and take part in the direction of the Moscow Musical Society and Conservatoire. He had still to finish the orchestration of *Yolanta* and *The Nutcracker* and by the time he had done this, in September, he had to go off yet again, to Vienna to fulfil a promised concert engagement. In fact he did not fulfil it—the orchestra was so bad that he re-fused to conduct—and it gives the measure of his standing in

Europe that he could make such a gesture and be thought all the more of. He was learning, a little late, that ruthlessness pays.

From the end of October he was up and down between Klin and Petersburg supervising rehearsals of new works, and although he managed to slip in one or two spells of home life before the premieres began in December the new symphony still hung fire.

His opening engagement—after seeing a play by Modest fail—was the first public performance of his Sextet. This work, scored for two violins, two violas, cello, and doublebass, had been written specially for Nadezhda Filaretovna before the break. She had complained that her health did not permit her to get to as many concerts as in earlier years and Tchaikovsky tried to give her at one and the same time a chamber work she could arrange easily to be played in her house and which would give the illusion of a work for small orchestra.

The Sextet was an immediate success in Petersburg and again in Moscow a few days later. It has gradually fallen into disuse but more possibly because of the difficulty of getting the necessary performers together than of any fault in the work itself. It deserves to be played regularly; it is not great music but is very pleasant and extremely cleverly constructed. It is above all suffused with an atmosphere not often associated with this composer, of a calm geniality. One could almost call it an old man's music, serene and resigned. The mood, which is found in other compositions of this final period, has in fact nothing to do with age—he was only fifty when he wrote the Sextet—but a great deal to do with his feeling that he had at last justified his life by his music. To this extent his fame had done nothing but good and in its quiet and unpretentious way the Sextet brings this out most charmingly.

Two days after this Moscow premiere came the Petersburg dress rehearsal of the joint bill of *The Nutcracker* and *Yolanta* in the presence of the Tsar and nobility. It might be forgiven him if, in the midst of a rush of rehearsals, of important first performances, of dinners and of talks with the disciples of the Balakirev group, Tchaikovsky postponed every interview with importunate people of no standing. In fact he would never do this. His answering of every letter written to him in New York is a pointer to his behavior in Petersburg eight months later.

The young student Khessin who had watched Tchaikovsky's visit to his old Law School just after the American tour could never after keep his mind on his studies. One day two students, V. Napravnik, son of the conductor, and Sanya Litke, a distant nephew of Tchaikovsky, came across Khessin in one of the lecture rooms after classes had finished. He seemed to be studying something very earnestly. They walked over to him and looked over his shoulder. Instead of the lecture notes they expected to find, they saw the scores of *Manfred* and *Kamarinskaya*. They scolded him, "I thought you were in the Law School to study law," then left him.

Two weeks later they came up to him with an announcement that took his breath away: "Pyotr Ilyich will see you in his room at the Grand Hotel at eleven o'clock on December 12."

The wretched Khessin scrabbled through the music he had written in spare moments. All of it, he decided, was unfit to show to the great man—"salon trash" he called it. Hurriedly he got to work on a violin and piano sonata, cutting down his law classes to two a week. He persuaded R. Fidelman, pupil of Auer at the Conservatoire, to play the work with him but the music refused to do his bidding: "I was so agitated that all the themes whined away in the minor and I was in absolute despair."

By the twelfth he had "cooked up" the first three movements and feverishly rehearsed them with Fidelman. They did not sound too bad and off they went to the hotel well before eleven o'clock. There he found young Napravnik and Litke and all four went up together and into Tchaikovsky's room. "He seemed in the best of humors. He kissed Volodya and Sanya and affably held out his hand to me. I was struck dumb. I could not say a word. I saw his face light up with an extraordinarily kind smile and affectionately taking me by the hand he guided me into a chair."

It was then that Tchaikovsky showed why he was so much loved. He could see at a glance that young Khessin was in such a state of nervousness that he would not be able to play a note of his work. He no doubt suspected that if he did play it it would be worthless—ninety-nine out of the hundred young men he saw had no talent. But he decided as always to give the boy a chance; he began to talk with the kind of ease he had shown during that noteworthy Balakirev evening, asking questions, telling stories, until Khessin began to feel at home. Then he said, "I hear you have composed a sonata specially for me to hear? That is a great compliment. May I hear it?"

They played the work. Tchaikovsky thanked them and walked up and down the room for a few minutes. Khessin, enraptured by the elegance with which he wore his suit, by his bright eyes, soft voice and expressive use of his hands, waited with little hope.

"Well," said Tchaikovsky at last, "I left the Law for music too."

2

Alexander III was delighted with *Yolanta* and *The Nutcracker* and told the composer so at the end of an evening which rivalled the glories of *The Sleeping Beauty* premiere, with the finest singers and dancers in Russia taking the chief roles. The audience was very appreciative too, both at the dress rehearsal and at the first performance. The critics were not so kind. *Yolanta* has disappeared from the stage except in Russia, but *The Nutcracker* is seen occasionally in performances of the full ballet.

Yolanta is a curious opera. In some respects it could be described as the best opera Tchaikovsky ever wrote. Musicologists have had difficulty in faulting it in construction or in the fittingness of the music. All is smooth and deft, a supreme example of sophisticated writing by a man who obviously has the art of composition at his fingertips. But the whole work is a little too suave, too much like an exhibition of opera making. It has enormous charm, so much so that one has the impression that the characterization has been smothered in it.

There are, of course, many difficulties in the way of a one-act opera reaching the stage. It is a pity that *Yolanta* cannot be heard occasionally for it can give nothing but pleasure, even if the pleasure has the atmosphere of a dream world. Tchaikovsky might well protest that the story demands just such an atmosphere. The answer to this must be left to the individual operagoer.

The Nutcracker is another matter. Tchaikovsky never surpassed this score in his ballet music. What has told heavily against his third great ballet is the last act. This is no more than a series of divertissements for which the composer had to provide music possessing no relation to what had gone before. He did his work well despite a cry of, "How the devil do you expect me to write music to express a kingdom of lollipops!" and in one of the many variegated items of this final act, the grand pas de deux, he wrote what is some of the greatest pas de deux music ever known—constructed with the simplicity of genius from a descending major scale—but in spite of it the act falls to pieces and the music with it.

The last act of *The Sleeping Beauty* is also given over to divertissements which were the curse of ballet in days when leading dancers expected the opportunity to show their paces before admirers and earn curtain calls. *The Sleeping Beauty* last act is just saved by sufficient link with the ballet story—the march of the courtiers, the pas de deux of Aurora and the Prince and the presence of King, Queen and, to wind it up, the fairies. In *The Nutcracker* there is scarcely a pretense of continuing the story.

This is the more lamentable because the opening act is one of the most lively and honest ever devised in ballet—a first-rate story —and Tchaikovsky's handling of the music for children and toys shows a genius for characterization; he loves children but sees their humorous side and does not blink at their unpleasantness. This is a slice of real life expressed with a keen musical irony.

The transformation music is in its very different mood perhaps the most poetical he had ever written. Both here and in the snow-

flakes scene he reverts to and improves on the undeservedly neglected atmospheric music in the first movement of his first symphony. This is the Russia he knows and loves, and every note,
every chord builds up the romantic world of a Kingdom of snow.
If this entrancing scene could have been followed by a fitting
conclusion to the story, which should not be beyond the wit of
man, *The Nutcracker* would now be as worldwide a favorite as
The Sleeping Beauty and *Swan Lake.*

3

Tchaikovsky was roused from disappointment at the tame reception of his work by a message from the past. One month earlier
he had been honored in France; he was elected an associate member of the Academy. The news was read down in the little Alsatian
town of Montbeliard and a letter of congratulation reached him.
It was from Fanny Durbach.

He read it with amazement; he had somehow thought that she
could no longer be alive. "I felt as though I had been told that
my mother had risen from the dead, that the past forty-three years
were nothing but a dream and that I had wakened and found myself back in my little upstairs room at Votkinsk."

He replied at once: was there anything he could do for her?

She replied that the best gift he could make her and the only
one she wanted was to come to see her.

On the first day of the new year, 1893, he was there "in a quiet
street in this little town which itself is so quiet that it might be
one of our Russian 'district' towns."

Fanny opened the door. It was the house in which she and her
sister had been born and which they still owned—a tiny place with
two rooms on each of the three floors. "I knew her at once," he
told Nikolai, moved to write one of his rare letters to this brother.
"She is seventy but does not look it. She has altered amazingly
little, her hair has not gone very grey, she has the old high color
we know and her eyes are still warm and brown. She greeted me

as though we had only been parted for a year or so, joyfully and tenderly but very simply too."

They went upstairs and talked of the past. She had kept all his old copy books and all the letters from him and his mother after she had left the family. He fingered them, read them, and the past rose up so strongly "that it seemed as if the very air I was breathing had the old Votkinsk smell; I could distinctly hear my mother's voice."

He spent the whole of that day and the next with her. At his hotel he discovered that she and her sister, who had also been a governess in Russia, were still teaching locally and were known and loved by the whole town. As he spoke, listened, and looked he could understand why. "It soon became clear to me why we were all so fond of her. She is a remarkably clever and sympathetic woman. She breathes kindness and integrity."

At last he had to go—he had a concert to conduct in Brussels—but promised to come back the next time he visited France. There was to be no next time.

Brussels and Odessa took up the next month—triumphs each of them—and he did not settle down again in Klin until the middle of February. He began work at once on a new symphony. He had torn up the score of the earlier one: "Nothing but meaningless sound patterns," he explained. The new symphony had a program but he did not intend to divulge it: "Let those discover it who can."

He set to at a great rate. In four days he had written the first movement and he could see quite clearly how the rest of the symphony would develop. It was the first time he had ever had such a comprehensive view of a large work.

He was very much excited. "Much of the work will be new in its form. For instance the Finale won't be a great allegro but an adagio of considerable proportions. You simply can't imagine how happy I am to feel that I am not finished yet as a composer."

If he had been left free to write on he would have had the whole thing done in a matter of weeks, he was in a ferment of inspiration, but he was again forced to conduct in Moscow. When he was there the young Sergei Rachmaninov, not long graduated from the Conservatoire, presented him with an autographed copy of the first of his five pieces for piano which Gutheil had just published.

The story behind this offering illustrates unusually well Tchaikovsky's influence on the men of the future. Glazunov, Lyadov, and Arensky, to mention only three of his better known disciples, had all begged him to accept autographed scores, Glazunov more than once. These men offered a heaven-sent chance of what he liked best in social contact, to accept the pleasant without analysis and be pleasant in return; all he had to do was to lean back and bask. His actual response was quite different; a reassuring blend of kindness and good sense. Being super self-critical, he took their praise with a smile and repaid it in the most practical way, by treating their work levelheadedly.

It has, of course, been an established practice from time immemorial for the ambitious young man to flatter the "arrived" older one into helping him, and there is no reason to suppose that this element of calculation was absent from the Tchaikovsky worship of the eighties and nineties. Tchaikovsky, in one comprehensive and civilized gesture, understood this, discounted and forgave. He had not forgotten his own long struggle to get his work played and printed. He did all he could to help every young man whose music he thought well of; he gave introductions to publishers and concert directors and paid them tactful and useful compliments, such as arranging a special private first performance of his Sextet for Glazunov, Lyadov, and their friends.

Above all, he said what he thought and made himself respected as well as liked by the young. He gave good advice, often plain-spoken, believing that if the disciple really wanted to improve his art he would accept well meant criticism. One example was a prophetic letter to Glazunov after he had looked through a new composition. "I often think of you," he wrote. "In some ways you are a puzzle to me. You have genius, that is obvious, but something in you is preventing the broadening of its scope."

Tchaikovsky's handling of Rachmaninov is much more impressive. The story begins in the early summer of 1890, with the four-hand arrangement of *The Sleeping Beauty*. In those days of many pianos, few concerts, and no radio or television sets, two and four hand arrangements of major orchestral works were almost obligatory, since only by playing through such a score at home could most people hope to hear the latest work and enjoy repeat performances. Most of Tchaikovsky's works were arranged in this way. In early days he had to do the arranging himself. Later he paid others to do it.

One of his chosen men for the job was Alexander Ziloti, his favorite Conservatoire pupil, next to Taneyev, in the old days of lecturing, now a well known pianist and professor of pianoforte at the Conservatoire. Ziloti had already made a two hand arrangement of *The Sleeping Beauty* which pleased the composer. In 1890 Tchaikovsky asked him to complete the work by making a four hand arrangement. Ziloti accepted. But in May of this year he wrote to Jurgenson (who was to print the arrangement) and to Tchaikovsky, explaining that his hands were so painful from too much piano practice that he could not do the arrangement. He suggested that his cousin, Rachmaninov, who was staying at the family country estate of Ivanovka with him, should take his place. He asked a fee of one hundred rubles and added a reassuring, "Of course I shall show him how to do it."

Tchaikovsky replied in July, 1890 "I've nothing against Rachmaninov doing the four hand arrangement of the ballet and am confident that, done under your guidance, it will be quite satisfactory. But won't this take him away from his studies?"

The question was pertinent. Rachmaninov was then still a student at the Conservatoire, supposedly cramming for his final year. But he was short of money and the amiable Ziloti tried to do him a double good turn of putting a little cash in his way and at the same time introducing him as a first class arranger and promising composer to the powerful Tchaikovsky. Tchaikovsky had heard all about the brilliant Rachmaninov as a student and remembered hearing him, as a boy, play at Zverev's Sunday evening dinner parties. He gave him the commission.

Less than one month later Tchaikovsky's doubts about the time-table were proved justified. Ziloti wrote to Jurgenson, who was waiting impatiently to print the score, telling the astonished publisher that Rachmaninov had only been able to write the Prologue and First Act and that his hands had become too sore to go on with the work. He added ominously, "Would you like to get someone else to do the Second and Third Acts or wait for Rachmaninov to finish the ballet? He can do it by June first next year when he has wound up all his Conservatoire examinations." He ended with a placatory "You will be very satisfied with the arrangement—it's done with great lightness and ease."

As Tchaikovsky was in Tiflis, Jurgenson agreed on the strength of this assurance to wait until the next year. He proofed the Prologue and First Act arrangements when Ziloti brought them to him and they were still in his office in the middle of June, 1891, when Tchaikovsky asked to see them. As soon as he had gone through the Prologue there was an explosion.

Obviously Ziloti and Rachmaninov had taken advantage of Tchaikovsky's easygoing nature. Both left themselves wide open to the question—How had Rachmaninov's hands so quickly become too tired to go on with the arrangement? "Won't this take him away from his studies?" Tchaikovsky had asked. The answer, which Ziloti was careful not to give, was simple—Rachmaninov never intended the arrangement to take him away from his work for the final year at the Conservatoire. He meant to combine both. Within a few weeks he found this impossible. One had to suffer and that one was the arrangement.

Yet even this might not have mattered if the work he had done was good—Tchaikovsky had patience and would not quibble about a few months delay. But Rachmaninov had discovered from the very beginning that he could only make the arrangement if he did it the shortest possible way. The result was poor. Ziloti and his cousin had plainly forgotten that Tchaikovsky, whose kindness to the young composer was proverbial, was also a hard working and punctilious artist. He had never scamped a job of music in his life and was not prepared to allow others, under cover of his name, to perpetuate a sloppy version of his original score. He looked at the Prologue, flew into a fury and scribbled off a heated rebuke to Ziloti. "I've suffered a lot reading this proof . . . It's not a question of mistakes—the arrangement itself does not please me. The great mistake is not in the proofs but in the fact that we entrusted this work to a boy, however talented he may be."

He then got down to detailed analysis. "Not that it has been done carelessly, on the contrary it's obvious that he considered every detail. But his arrangement has two frightful defects:

1. An absence of boldness and initiative, a too slavish submission to the composer and consequently no strength or brilliance.

2. It is only too obvious that Rachmaninov has made the four hand arrangement from the two hand arrangement and not from the full score."

Then followed a vast list of defects all punctuated with exclamation marks. "In general, inexperience, timidity, make themselves felt at every step. What an odd way he's done the arpeggios for harps! What inconceivable pauses!!!! This is an exercise in a class for elementary theory!!!"

For a moment Tchaikovsky's hatred of causing hurt feelings got the better of his fury at the bungled work. "Justice demands that I say that your cousin took the work seriously and in consequence many parts of the arrangement are light and easy. What are missing are boldness, initiative, creativeness!!!" He added "I'm far too upset to look at the First Act. I feel almost ill and can't sleep at night . . . I wanted the four hand arrangement of the ballet to be done thoroughly, seriously, skilfully, like the arrangements of the symphonies. Now this can't be. The affair is irremediable. But *at least* let it be a little better than it is now!"

What had happened at Ivanovka that summer of 1890 is clear enough. There is very little in common between a two and four hand arrangement—they have to be approached quite differently— and no experienced arranger would dream of making a four hand from a two hand instead of from the original score. Rachmaninov probably knew this. Ziloti certainly did. Yet he allowed his cousin to take the easy way out (it is naturally much quicker to work from a two hand arrangement than from a full score) in the hope that the wool would successfully be pulled over the master's eyes.

The exposure was followed at once by a penitent letter from Ziloti accepting all the blame. Soon afterwards came an equally candid letter from Rachmaninov to some friends in Petersburg. Clearly he had been boasting of his commission from the famous man. "The ballet comes out in autumn. It would have been out earlier but Sasha and I are now altering it a lot because Tchaikovsky abused me up hill and down dale for my arrangement." He added, not without humor, "It's beyond question that of all arrangements in existence mine is the worst. Now, as I said, we're improving it and it will at least resemble something, it will resemble an arrangement, though God knows that's not much to crow about."

But he had learned his lesson. More notably, Tchaikovsky bore no malice. He could with reason have wiped the boy off as lazy and irresponsible (he had been the cause of a delay of many months in the publication of the arrangement) and have left him to get on in the world of music as best he could. But it was here that Tchaikovsky showed his greatness; what he actually did was revealed in an ecstatic if irreverent letter from Rachmaninov at the end of 1892.

Between the rebuke of 1891 and this letter Rachmaninov had worked hard and well, and Tchaikovsky had noticed it. The day after the first performance of *Yolanta* on December 18, 1892, a newspaper reporter asked the composer what he proposed to write next. The matter is taken up from there by Rachmaninov:

"Tchaikovsky told the reporter that he thought it time he stopped writing and gave way to young blood. To the reporter's question, Is there any worthy new blood in Russia? Tchaikovsky said Yes, and named Glazunov in Petersburg and Arensky and *myself* in Moscow. How I thanked the old man for not forgetting me! The moment I read this report I sat down and composed one of my five pieces as a kind of thanksgiving."

It was this piece that he offered to Tchaikovsky in the early spring of 1893 with a handwritten dedication "from its deeply respectful composer." Tchaikovsky accepted it, though ironically enough he preferred, of the five pieces, two that their composer had not thought good enough to dedicate to him. But he did not forget Rachmaninov. When he heard from him that his first opera *Aleko* was to be produced at the Bolshoi in May he came up specially from Klin. He did not come only for the first performance, he attended the dress rehearsal and there was able to provide the kind of unobtrusive but valuable help men loved him for. He walked into the theater, sat himself down by Rachmaninov, listened for a while, then whispered "Aren't they taking it a bit slowly?"

Rachmaninov agreed. He added, apologetically, that he could not bring himself to interfere with a conductor whose reputation was so much greater than his own.

Tchaikovsky's own youthful deprecatory manner rose up before him. Another Pyotr Ilyich! Without saying more he got up, walked to the conductor and said "Mr. Rachmaninov and I think the tempo ought to be taken a little quicker." The tempo was immediately changed.

But this was only the beginning of his kindness to the young man who had botched an arrangement for him. After the rehearsal of the opera, which Tchaikovsky thought "charming," he asked Vsevolozhsky, the Director of the Imperial Theatres, to come down from Petersburg for the first performance, shared a box with him and, when the curtain was finally lowered, leaned forward in full view of the entire audience and clapped vigorously. As Rachmaninov was to say years later *"Aleko* succeeded more because of the great kindness of Tchaikovsky than because of the actual music."

Before he and Tchaikovsky parted on the night of the first performance the master had paid him two great compliments: he agreed to conduct in Petersburg the following January the first performance of Rachmaninov's symphonic fantasy *The Rock* which was to be completed that summer, and he said to the youthful composer in his easy way: "You know I've just finished *Yolanta?* It doesn't fill an entire evening. Would you object if it were performed with *Aleko?"*

Neither plan was to come to anything—Tchaikovsky died before they could be carried out—but Rachmaninov remembered his kindness to the end of his life and the tactful manner in which it was offered as if by agreeing the younger man would confer a great favor on Tchaikovsky. Long afterwards Rachmaninov told the story, ending it always with "And he actually used those words —'Would you object?'!"

4

After another short stay at Klin Tchaikovsky had to go off again with the new symphony still unfinished, this time to England where he had been offered the honorary degree of Doctor of Music at Cambridge University. He broke his journey at Petersburg to attend a party at the Rimsky-Korsakovs and was asked by his host, supported by Lyadov and Glazunov, if he would conduct the Musical Society concerts that winter. He accepted.

The invitation to conduct the orchestra made famous by Rubinstein and Balakirev must have delighted him; certainly it set the seal on his lifelong refusal to take sides; at long last the revolutionaries had accepted him as a nationalist composer in the best sense of the word. He had never given way to the years of pressure to tie himself to a group and had abstained from controversy; his music had done the arguing and at last had won a bloodless victory.

By the end of May he was in London for an honor he could not rate in the same category. It is a little difficult to know why he accepted the invitation from a country which he had described as "only just made tolerable by Shakespeare and Dickens." The explanation seems to be the hope of meeting Grieg again, for the Norwegian was one of the group of eminent European musicians to receive a doctorate. In fact he was too unwell to attend and Tchaikovsky had to make do with Saint-Saëns and Boïto; Max Bruch he did not like at all.

Nor did he like London, appalled by its dirt and tastelessness, though the sheer volume of traffic and the sense of a great business city impressed him. He conducted the London Philharmonic in the Fourth Symphony and was gratified to find the audience forgetting their famed English reticence to such an extent that Saint-Saëns, following with one of his works, played to a hall rather drained of enthusiasm.

This triumph was repeated at the mixed concert by the University Musical Society; *Francesca,* conducted by Tchaikovsky, had an uproarious welcome which threw into the shade the reception given to Bruch, Boïto, Grieg, and the rest.

The day after the awarding of the doctorates, on June 13, Tchaikovsky thankfully departed for Paris and Moscow, taking in a visit to Sophie Menter in Vienna en route. He came back to Klin and to news of the loss of more old friends, particularly of Albrecht, his colleague at the Conservatoire from his arrival there nearly thirty years earlier.

Modest, like everyone who has followed him, comments on Tchaikovsky's calm acceptance of these deaths which a few years before would have thrown him into a long fit of melancholy. The reason for this change of attitude is unquestionably the symphony which he took up the moment he reached home—the symphony and all that it stood for. This third attempt to provide an answer to the problem of the workings of fate in men's lives, above all

of fate's final stroke—death—was significantly free from the struggles attending the composition of the two earlier symphonies.
With this Sixth Symphony he never hesitated; the whole work
took only twelve days to sketch out and not much more than
twice that time to orchestrate. It was a remarkable feat which
made nonsense of his complaints that he was beginning to lose his
facility; the score shows no sign of effort.

This summer at Klin was one of his most productive for he
not only finished the Sixth Symphony before the end of August
but went far to complete a Third Piano Concerto. The history
of this concerto is instructive. Like all composers Tchaikovsky
was thrifty. He disliked wasting material. He soon regretted having torn up the beginnings of the previous symphony. He had
done so because it was impersonal music, wholly extrovert, and
for that reason unsuitable for a symphony. He thought of a symphony as essentially an expression of the writer's feelings, of his
philosophy of life; lacking that, he had no wish to go on with it,
to make, as he said, "meaningless harmonies and modulations and
a rhythmical scheme expressive of nothing."

However these formed music of a kind that also had a place in
the world, particularly when written by a composer whose very
handling of a theme was a delight to hear and, for the musicologist, to analyze. The main theme he had used for the abortive
symphony might have meant nothing to him personally but as a
theme it was highly attractive and, as usual, skillfully worked out.

In this summer of 1893 he realized that the material might be
used as the opening movement of a piano concerto which did not
demand the introversive mood of a symphony. He remembered
what he had written and at once began to reconstruct it from
memory in concerto form. He finished the first movement and
orchestrated it and sketched out a slow movement and Finale
before he had to break off to conduct at Petersburg and Hamburg.

As he did not live to finish this work its future career had best
be dealt with here. After his death Taneyev orchestrated the
slow movement and the Finale. The completed concerto was often

played and has been heard outside Russia several times. Taneyev unhappily was not a Tchaikovsky and the movements he orchestrated are a sad falling away from the first.

Recently another Russian musicologist, Semyon Bogatyrev, has reverted to Tchaikovsky's original idea and has reconstructed the entire work—to which he added a scherzo from a piano piece of 1893—and put it out as Tchaikovsky's Seventh Symphony. This work has also been played in the West.

It must be said that this devotion to the composer is labor thrown away. Tchaikovsky decided that the work would not make a satisfactory symphony. How right he is Bogotyrev has now demonstrated and it may be hoped that this piece of mistaken idolatry, perpetrated only by defying Tchaikovsky's wishes, may now be forgotten. The first movement of the concerto as Tchaikovsky wrote it is sometimes played alone. It is very well worth playing and should be kept in the repertory. Anything Tchaikovsky had to say about the use of pianoforte and orchestra is far too valuable and attractive to be lost.

While he was at work on it in the midst of a summer of gardening, entertaining, and composing he received his last letter from Fanny. It contained his last command too; once a governess always a governess and Fanny's reaction to their reunion after the first joy had subsided was in character—she set him a task. Taking up where she had left off forty-five years earlier her instinct to bend the intensely romantic to the service of the intensely practical got to work on the man she still saw as her young Petya. He had not turned out to be the great literary genius she had fondly hoped; that was a pity, but to be a great composer was an honor too and a responsibility. Seeing him again she saw Russia again and this, to the undying pedagogue in her, was merely the starting point for a new educational scheme.

"I never saw such beautiful sunsets as in Russia," she wrote, "when the sky was covered with amazingly bright colors. I particularly liked the calm, mild evenings at the end of summer. The canoes of the men fishing rocked on the lake when they cast their lines. The water was smooth and like a mirror in which the dying sun was reflected. I shall never forget these evenings and the view from the balcony. From there too we heard tender, sad songs sung by the peasants and they alone disturbed the silence of those wonderful nights. Do you remember them? You ought to, for neither you nor any other of the children ever wanted to go to bed on such evenings."

Then came the task. He knew the method well and must have smiled as he read, for this was the Fanny of old, approaching the horse she intended to ride, a tempting piece of sugar in her hand. "If you do remember those songs at Votkinsk, set them to music. Then you will bring your Russia to those who cannot be there to enjoy them. Pushkin, that noble poet of yours, used to say that he wanted his poems to be known and loved wherever Russian was spoken, down to the meanest peasant's hut. Splendid aspiration! But yours can and should be greater still, for the language in which you speak is universal."

To Fanny in Montbeliard he remained her pupil at the age of fifty-three and to any children lucky enough to live near the Klin house he remained an ageless playmate, devising the kind of games that had thrilled the twins forty years earlier. Fanny was not mistaken nor were his child friends of Klin; on occasion he was nothing but a child—or, since that can sound condescending, he had preserved a childlike heart. An incident this summer provides a refreshing sidelight on the great man who had so recently marched solemnly and impressively in his red and white robes at Cambridge, the essence of dignity, the world-famous composer who was so soon to give mankind yet another imperishable masterpiece.

Like so many Russians, he was a madly keen collector of mushrooms and could indulge his passion freely at Klin; the woods and fields round his house were filled with them. However, as anyone will know who has taken to the sport there are mushroom collectors and mushroom collectors; some have the eye for it, others have not. Tchaikovsky was of the latter persuasion, Kashkin of the former.

Kashkin came over for a weekend during the summer and Tchaikovsky at once—he could never believe that his bad luck would last—insisted that they go out mushrooming. When they reached the wood in which the best kind grew (they called them the white ones as distinct from the dark) Kashkin spotted them first as usual, gathering them at times from under Tchaikovsky's very nose.

Tchaikovsky stood this for a time in silence, then looked from his friend's half filled basket of white mushrooms to his measly collection of dark ones and burst out irritably "Let's split up. You'll only pinch my mushrooms again if we stay together."

Kashkin agreed and each went to different parts of the wood. For once Tchaikovsky was in luck; after walking some way he stumbled on a colony of white mushrooms, a colony so thick that even he could not miss them. He stared for a moment, speechless before the sight of such riches. When the truth dawned he "let out a fearful yell."

It was a cry of triumph but to Kashkin, out of sight, it sounded like a cry for help. He hurried through the trees in the direction of the cries—for they were still going on. When he discovered Tchaikovsky at last he saw him standing in the midst of his colony of mushrooms like one possessed, crowing with joy.

Tchaikovsky heard his footsteps cracking the twigs. He looked back, his face changed and so did his cry; from a yell of triumph it turned to a scream of fear. He waved one hand violently at him. "They're mine!" he shouted, "all mine!"

As Kashkin still continued to approach Tchaikovsky suddenly threw himself headlong into the heart of the colony. He lay there spreadeagled, his wide-stretched arms covering as many of the precious mushrooms as possible. "Don't you dare come nearer, Nikolai!" he shouted, his face red and excited. "They're mine, d'you hear! *I* found them. You aren't going to pinch these. Don't you dare move! Go away, go right away!"

5

In September, with the symphony ready for its first performance in Petersburg, Tchaikovsky went off to see Anatoly in the country at Mikhailovskoe. He loved it and took the train for Hamburg with reluctance. He stayed there only long enough to conduct *Yolanta* successfully, then went back to Klin to try to tidy up the piano concerto.

This short last visit ended as usual with music and, after the music, with a good story—involuntary on Tchaikovsky's part. He had with him two former students, the cellists A. A. Brandukov (the "Pezzo capriccio" had been dedicated to him) and Y. I. Poplavsky. On their final evening they played Saint-Saëns' cello concerto with Tchaikovsky at the piano and both cellists taking the solo part. When the concerto was finished Tchaikovsky stayed at the piano strumming idly. After a time he found himself playing something that seemed vaguely familiar. He played to the end, swung round on the stool, and said "That's a pleasant little thing. Who's it by?"

"Tchaikovsky," said Poplavsky, and all three howled with laughter, the absentminded composer most of all.

The next morning, October 7, the three of them travelled back to Moscow. Two more of Tchaikovsky's old friends had died— Apukhtin in Petersburg, Zverev in Moscow—and he was on his way to attend the memorial service for his colleague.

At a gathering of still-living friends the day after the service, they talked about Zverev as surviviors usually do and about their own chances of survival. Kashkin decided to keep the subject light and turned to Tchaikovsky with a "You'll outlive us all, Petya." He believed it, he said afterwards; he had never seen his friend look so calm and strong. Tchaikovsky smiled and said he thought it unlikely but admitted that he couldn't remember feeling so well or so contented.

This contentment could have come wholly from his feeling that in the new symphony he had at last expressed himself adequately on the subject of Fate which had haunted him all his adult life. But there was another possible reason why his friends found him in such excellent form; he heard that Anna Lvovna was in Moscow and went to see her.

He had met his niece for tea at the new von Meck house in Prechistensky Avenue a few months earlier, when she was on her way to Wiesbaden with Nadezhda Filaretovna in a final attempt to arrest the rapid spread of her mother-in-law's tuberculosis, and had begged her to try to find out the cause of the break. Anna Lvovna was astounded by the feeling he displayed—"I only knew then how deeply he had taken the rupture to heart"—which gives some idea of the secrecy of life in the von Meck household.

At that first meeting she promised to do her best. At this second meeting, in October, 1893, she had just come back from Wiesbaden. The cure had failed—the disease had already reached the throat—but she had persuaded Nadezhda Filaretovna to break her long silence at last; in painful whispers—she could scarcely speak —she told her daughter-in-law: "I knew I was no longer necessary to him, that I could no longer give him anything he wanted. Our correspondence was still a joy to me but I didn't feel I had any right to please myself alone if it had become a burden to him. It is true I refused to give him any further material assistance but could that really have been important to him? If he didn't understand why I had done it and he still felt that I was necessary to him, why didn't he write again?"

What Tchaikovsky thought of this explanation we shall never know. To an outsider it might seem inadequate and even misleading; his instant reply to Nadezhda Filaretovna's curt note, both the speed and the contents of it, put him firmly in the right, and he had made clear that he would write to Pakulsky in full only to save her the trouble of replying at such a painful time—for she had led him to believe that she was financially ruined. How any woman could resist replying at once to such a demonstration of sympathy is difficult to understand.

But Tchaikovsky was not an outsider and he was not calculating. He probably thought with immense relief that everything had been the result of the kind of misunderstanding that can happen between correspondents, each waiting for the other to write. This would not lessen the sadness of the break, would probably accentuate it. The one positive thing his niece's explanation did for him was to wipe out the supposed insult of Nadezhda's final note and reduce it to the tactless action of a sick but still fond woman.

"I did not have time to speak to him fully," said Anna Lvovna afterwards, "but I should like to believe that the little I did say was partly the cause of the particularly brilliant mood of his last days, a mood noticed by everyone who met him."

As against this theory we have Modest's report that in his final hours the unconscious Pyotr Ilyich several times murmured Nadezhda Filaretovna's name in tones of deep reproach. Modest's report is suspect—he disliked the connection and was furious at the way his brother had been treated—but even if it were true the two statements are not necessarily incompatible: Tchaikovsky had suffered deeply, and as we know by our own dreams these scars never disappear from the unconscious. Certainly Tchaikovsky's cheerfulness and confidence were marked by all at that gathering of old friends in Moscow the day after Zverev's funeral, and by that time he had seen and spoken to Anna Lvovna.

That night he took the train to Petersburg for the last time—none of them was to see him again. For months he had thought of little but this new symphony into which he had put all the concentrated wisdom of the years, musical wisdom and moral wisdom too. He was excited by the prospect of conducting it for the first time. Yet when the young Rachmaninov called on him with a new suite for two pianos in his hands and begged to be allowed to dedicate it to him if he thought well of it, Pyotr Ilyich at once sat down and played it with him. He did more; liking the work, he insisted that Taneyev must hear it.

An appointment was made and at the fixed time they met in Taneyev's music room and played the work over again together.

When they had finished, Tchaikovsky got up and gestured to Taneyev and—as Rachmaninov tells the story—"said with that kind and attractive smile of his, 'Isn't it good? And that's not all. Young Seryozha here has written a concerto this summer, and six songs *and* The Rock as well as this Suite.' He laughed again with a grimace 'And I think *I* work hard! And all I've done is to write one symphony!' "

At this time too he met Vasily Sapelnikov, the soloist in his B Flat Minor Concerto at Hamburg five years earlier and of the G Major Concerto in Paris just before the American visit. Sapelnikov congratulated him on the completion of a new symphony.

"Ah, yes," said Tchaikovsky with his rueful grin. "But what I really want to do, Vasily Lvovich, is to write a thoroughly good opera."

That is Tchaikovsky, the Tchaikovsky of the mushrooms, the Tchaikovsky who a few days later, on October 28, ascended the podium at the first concert of the season given by the Musical Society at Petersburg, elegant, assured, handsomer than ever and, if his face was allowed as evidence, a man at last at peace with himself.

The audience gave far more of their applause to a performance of the B Flat Minor Concerto that evening than to the premiere of the Sixth Symphony. This is understandable; the mood and construction of the work demanded a degree of reflection that no contemporary audience could possibly give to a single performance. The Finale alone, that movement of supreme genius, was so original that musicians were to ponder it for years to come. It cannot be improved, it is unique, and sums up the composer's thought and feelings with such beauty and sincerity that one has the sense that there is no more for him to say.

Tchaikovsky perhaps felt this. It is noteworthy that the indifferent reception of the work did not disturb him. He saw that audience and critics were puzzled and understood that they must be puzzled. He trusted to time. "I have never felt so proud of anything I've written."

Tchaikovsky was an artist. So too was the fate of which he had thought and written so much. He had composed his requiem and fate acted for the last time. Five days after the concert, on November 2, he was not at breakfast. Modest looked into his room; he was unwell, he said. He got up nevertheless and paid a promised call on Napravnik. He was feeling no better when he came back but laughed at Modest's suggestion that he call a doctor. At lunch he felt thirsty and before he could be stopped had filled and drunk a tumblerful of unboiled water.

When Glazunov looked in during the afternoon Tchaikovsky still felt ill but brushed aside every attempt of the alarmed young man to take it seriously.

That evening Modest fetched a doctor without telling Pyotr Ilyich. The doctor at once called in his brother, the famous Leo Bertenson. They diagnosed cholera. Tchaikovsky whispered to Modest, "This is death."

He spent a night of agonizing pain, and of courage too, for he refused to be nursed and sent everyone to their beds. The next morning, Friday, he seemed to have recovered and, like his mother so many years ago, thought he had got the better of the disease. By the early hours of Saturday morning the cramps had come back so piercingly that he gave up hope. He told the doctors to go and attend to the living: "I shan't get better," he said.

The group about the bedside grew larger on Sunday, his brother Nikolai was there, Alexei had hurried up from Klin. Tchaikovsky did not recognize them.

The final remedy, the hot bath, was tried.

Early the next morning, November 6, 1893, he died peacefully.

Catalogue of Works

(Restricted to opus numbers except when work is discussed in text)

TITLE	COMPOSED	FIRST PERFORMED	OPUS
Orchestral Works			
Overture to The Storm	1864		76(posthumous)
Symphony No. 1 in G Minor ("Winter Daydreams")	1866 (revised 1874)	Moscow 1868	13
Festival Overture on Danish National Anthem	1866		15
Symphonic Poem Fatum	1868	Moscow 1869	77(posthumous)
Fantasy Overture Romeo and Juliet	1869 (revised 1870, 1880)	Moscow 1870	
Symphony No. 2 in C Minor	1872 (revised 1879)	Moscow 1873	17
Fantasy Overture The Tempest	1873	Moscow 1873	18
Symphony No. 3 in D Minor	1875	Moscow 1875	29
Marche Slave	1876	Moscow 1876	31
Fantasy Francesca da Rimini	1876	Moscow 1877	32
Symphony No. 4 in F Minor	1877	Moscow 1878	36
Suite No. 1 in D Minor	1878-79	Moscow 1879	43
Capriccio Italien	1880	Moscow 1880	45
Overture 1812	1880	Moscow 1882	49
Coronation March	1883	Moscow 1883	
Suite No. 2 in C Major	1883	Moscow 1884	53
Suite No. 3 in G Major	1884	St. Petersburg 1885	55
Manfred Symphony	1884-85	Moscow 1886	58
Suite No. 4	1887	Moscow 1887	61
Symphony No. 5 in E Minor	1888	St. Petersburg 1888	64
Fantasy Overture Hamlet	1888	St. Petersburg 1888	67a
Symphonic Poem Voivode	1890-91	Moscow 1891	78
Nutcracker Ballet Suite	1892	St. Petersburg 1892	71a
Symphony No. 6 in B Minor	1893	St. Petersburg 1893	74

TITLE	COMPOSED	FIRST PERFORMED	OPUS
Ballets			
Swan Lake	1875-76	Moscow 1877	20
The Sleeping Beauty	1888-89	St. Petersburg 1890	66
The Nutcracker (Casse Noisette)	1891-92	St. Petersburg 1892	71
Incidental Music			
Synegurochka	1873	Moscow 1873	12
Hamlet	1891	St. Petersburg 1891	67b
String Orchestra			
Serenade For Strings in C Major	1880	Moscow 1882	48
Solo Instruments with Orchestra			
Concerto in B Flat Minor for pianoforte	1874-75	Boston 1875	23
Sérénade Mélancolique for violin	1875	Moscow 1876	26
Variations on a Rococo Theme for cello	1876	Moscow 1877	33
Valse-Scherzo for violin	1877	Paris 1878	34
Concerto in D Major for violin	1877-78	Vienna 1881	35
Concerto in G Major for pianoforte	1879-80	Moscow 1882	44
Concert Fantasy for pianoforte	1884	Moscow 1885	56
Pezzo capriccioso for cello	1887	Moscow 1889	62
Concerto in E Flat Major for pianoforte (first movement only)	1893	St. Petersburg 1895	75 (posthumous)
Concerto in E Flat Major for pianoforte (Andante and Finale with Taneyev's orchestration)	1893 (sketch)	St. Petersburg 1896	79 (posthumous)
Chamber Music			
String Quartet in D Major	1871	Moscow 1871	11
String Quartet in F Major	1874	Moscow 1874	22
String Quartet in E Flat Minor	1876	Moscow 1876	30
Trio for violin, pianoforte, and cello in A Minor	1881-82	Moscow 1882	50
String Sextet in D Minor	1887-92	St. Petersburg 1892	70
Violin and Pianoforte			
Souvenir d'un lieu cher	1878		42

TITLE	COMPOSED	FIRST PERFORMED	OPUS
Pianoforte			
Sonata in C Sharp Minor	1865		80(posthumous)
Scherzo à la russe and Impromptu in E Flat Minor	1867		1
Souvenir de Hapsal	1867		2
Valse-Caprice in D Major	1868		4
Romance in F Minor	1868		5
Valse-Scherzo in A Major	1870		7
Capriccio in G Flat Major	1870		8
Three Pieces	1870		9
Nocturne and Humoresque	1871		10
Six Pieces	1873		19
Six Pieces on a Single Theme	1873		21
The Seasons: Twelve Pieces	1875-76		37b
Twelve Pieces of Moderate Difficulty	1876-78		40
Sonata in G Major	1878		37
Children's Album: 24 Easy Pieces	1878		39
Six Pieces	1882		51
Dumka	1886		59
Eighteen Pieces	1893		72
Operas			
Voivode	1867-68	Moscow 1869	3
Undine	1869		
Oprichnik	1870-72	St. Petersburg 1874	
Vakula The Smith	1874	St. Petersburg 1876	14
Cherevichki (Vakula revised and renamed)	1885	Moscow 1887	
Eugene Onegin	1877-78	Moscow 1879	24
The Maid of Orleans	1878-79	St. Petersburg 1881	
Mazeppa	1881-83	Moscow 1884	
The Sorceress	1885-87	St. Petersburg 1887	
The Queen of Spades	1890	St. Petersburg 1890	68
Yolanta	1891	St. Petersburg 1892	69
Choral Works			
Cantata Ode to Joy for four solo voices, chorus, and orchestra	1865		
Cantata for the opening of the Moscow Polytechnic Exhibition for tenor, chorus, and orchestra	1872		

TITLE	COMPOSED	FIRST PERFORMED	OPUS
Choral Works			
Coronation Cantata Moscow for mezzo- soprano, baritone, chorus, and orchestra	1883		
Greetings to Anton Rubinstein Cantata for unaccompanied mixed chorus	1889		
Church Music			
Liturgy of St. John Chrysostom for four-part mixed chorus	1878		41
Vesper Mass Eighteen harmonized liturgical songs for mixed chorus	1881-82		52

TITLE	COMPOSED	DEDICATION	OPUS
Songs		*Dedication*	
Six Songs	1869	Various	6
Six Songs	1872	Various	16
Six Songs	1875	Various	25
Six Songs	1875	Princess E. A. Tsertelevaya	27
Six Songs	1875	Various	28
Six Songs	1878	A. I. Tchaikovsky	38
Seven Songs	1880	A. V. Panayeva	47
Sixteen Songs for Children	1881-83	—	54
Songs			
Six Songs	1884	Various	57
Twelve Songs	1886	—	60
Six Songs	1887	—	63
Six French Songs	1888	Désirée Artot-Padilla	65
Six Songs	1893	N. N. Figner	73
Vocal Duet			
Six Duets	1880	T. L. Davidova	46

Bibliography

NOTE: In view of the enormous Tchaikovsky bibliography the following list has been confined to primary sources in Russian with the addition of a few general titles which have been found helpful.

Most of the manuscript material referred to in this book (autograph manuscripts and copies of lost originals) will be found in the:

> Archives of the Tchaikovsky Museum, Klin
> Philharmonic Museum, Leningrad
> State Public Library, Leningrad
> Conservatory Library, Leningrad
> Conservatory Library, Moscow
> Central State Archives of Literature and Art
> Glinka Central Museum of Musical Culture
> State Historical Archives of Leningrad Oblast
> Library of Congress, Washington

Letters, articles, diaries, and reminiscences, printed and unprinted

Perepiska M. A. Balakireva s P. I. Chaikovskim (Correspondence of M. A. Balakirev with P. I. Tchaikovsky). St. Petersburg, 1912

Perepiska Chaikovskogo s Besselem (Correspondence of Tchaikovsky with Bessel). Moscow, 1923

Perepiska s P. I. Jurgensonom (Correspondence with P. I. Jurgenson) Ed. V. A. Zhdanov and N. T. Zhegin. Moscow, n.d.

Perepiska s N. F. fon Mekk (Correspondence with N. F. von Meck) Ed. V. A. Zhdanov and N. T. Zhegin. 3 vols. Moscow, 1934-36

Perepiska P. I. Chaikovskogo i E. F. Napravnik, 1872-93 (Correspondence of P. I. Tchaikovsky and E. F. Napravnik, 1872-93). Moscow, n.d.

Pisma P. I. Chaikovskogo i S. I. Taneyeva (Letters of P. I. Tchaikovsky and S. I. Taneyev). Ed. M. I. Tchaikovsky. Petrograd, 1916

Ostrovsky i russkie kompozitory: pisma (Ostrovsky and Russian Composers: Letters). Ed. E. M. Kolosova and V. Filippov. Moscow-Leningrad, 1937

P. I. Chaikovsky. Pisma k rodnym (P. I. Tchaikovsky. Letters to Relatives). Ed. V. A. Zhdanov. Moscow, 1940

P. I. Chaikovsky. Pisma k blizkim (P. I. Tchaikovsky. Letters to Intimates). Moscow, 1955

Dyevniki P. I. Chaikovskogo 1873-91 (Diaries of P. I. Tchaikovsky 1873-91). Ed. I. I. Tchaikovsky. Moscow, 1923 (Eng. trans., New York, 1945)

*Literaturnie proizvedenia i perepiska (Literary Works and Correspondence). Vols. 1-7. Moscow, 1944-64 (Vols. 8-10 not yet published)

Rukovodstvo k prakticheskomu izucheniu harmonii: uchebnik sostavlenny professorom moskovskoi konservatorii P. Chaikovskim (Guide to the Practical Study of Harmony: A Manual Compiled by the Professor of the Moscow Conservatoire, P. Tchaikovsky). Moscow, 1871

Proshloe russkoi muzyki: materyali i issledovania (A History of Russian Music: Materials and Sources) by B. V. Asafyev. Petrograd, 1920

Vospominania i pisma (Recollections and Letters). Ed. Igor Glebov (B. V. Asafyev). Leningrad, 1924

50 lyet russkoi muzyki v moikh vospominaniakh (My Recollections of 50 Years of Russian music) by M. M. Ippolitov-Ivanov. Moscow, 1934

Iz moikh vospominany o P. I. Chaikovsky (Recollections of P. I. Tchaikovsky) by V. V. Bessel. Imperial Theaters Yearbook, 1896-97

Muzykalnie felyetoni i zametki Petra Ilicha Chaikovskogo, s prilozheniem portreta, avtobiograficheskogo opisania puteshestvia zagranitsu v 1888 godu i predislovia G. A. Larosha (Musical Articles and Notes of Pyotr Ilyich Tchaikovsky, Including a Portrait, an Autobiographical Account of His Tour Abroad in 1888 and a Foreword by H. A. Laroche). Moscow, 1898

Iz moikh vospominany o P. I. Chaikovskom (Recollections of P. I. Tchaikovsky) by H. A. Laroche. Severny Vestnik, St. Petersburg, 1893, 1894

Na pamyat o P. I. Chaikovskom (In Memory of P. I. Tchaikovsky) by H. A. Laroche and N. D. Kashkin. Moscow, 1894

Sobranie muzykalno-kriticheskikh statei (Collected Music Criticism Articles) by H. A. Laroche. Moscow, 1922

Vospominania o P. I. Chaikovskom (Recollections of P. I. Tchaikovsky) by N. D. Kashkin. Moscow, 1896, 1954

Vospominania o P. I. Chaikovskom (Recollections of P. I. Tchaikovsky) by K. N. de Lazari (Konstantinov). Rossia, 1900

Moi vospominania o P. I. Chaikovskom (My recollections of P. I. Tchaikovsky) by I. A. Klimenko. Ryazan, 1908

* This collection will include everything written by Tchaikovsky. It contains many articles long since overlooked and many letters never before printed and in some cases only recently discovered. Students must be warned, however, that the editors have deliberately excised passages which in their opinion reflect unfavorably on the subject personally or politically. The omissions are not concealed and can be added by reference to the autograph manuscripts.

Lyetopis moei muzykalnoi zhizni (Annals of My Musical Life) by N. A. Rimsky-Korsakov. 3rd and 4th ed., Ed. A. N. Rimsky-Korsakov. Moscow-Leningrad, 1928, 1932. Reprinted in *Complete Works,* Moscow, 1955. (Eng. trans. 3rd ed., New York, 1942)

P. I. Chaikovsky kak dirizhor (P. I. Tchaikovsky as conductor) by I. P. Pryanishnikov. *Russkaya muzykalnaya gazeta.* Petrograd, 1918

P. I. Chaikovsky v roli muzykalnogo kritika (P. I. Tchaikovsky as Music Critic) by G. Timofeyev. *Russkaya muzykalnaya gazeta* St. Petersburg, 1899

Moyo znakomstvo c Chaikovskim (My Friendship with Tchaikovsky) From *Letters, Articles, and Recollections* by A. K. Glazunov. Moscow, 1958

Vstrecha c Chaikovskim (A Meeting with Tchaikovsky) from *My Recollections* by A. B. Khessin, Moscow, 1960

Zavyet khudozhnika (An Artist's Advice) by I. E. Grabar. *Ogonyok,* 1940

Vospominania o P. I. Chaikovskom (Recollections of P. I. Tchaikovsky) from *Letters and Recollections* by V. P. Pogozhev, Ed. Igor Glebov. Leningrad, 1924

Iz vospominany ob avtore Pikovoi damy (My Recollections of the Composer of *The Queen of Spades*) by N. N. Vilde. *Teatralnaya gazeta.* Moscow, 1915

Iz konservatorskikh vospominany 1871-79 (My Conservatoire Recollections 1871-79) by R. V. Genika. *Russkaya musykalnaya gazeta.* Moscow, 1916

Chaikovsky na Ukraine (Tchaikovsky in the Ukraine) by A. V. Khimichenko. Mistetstvo, 1940

Vospominania o P. I. Chaikovskom (Recollections of P. I. Tchaikovsky) by Bemol (pseudonym, author not established). *Novoe vremya,* 1893

Pamyatnie vstrechi (Memorable Meetings) by L. P. Steinberg. *Komsomolskaya pravda,* 1940

Iz vospominany artista-muzykanta (Recollections of an Artist-Musician) by I. V. Lipaev. *Russkaya starina,* 1896

Moi vospominania o velikom kompozitore (My Recollections of a Great Composer) by S. I. Levin. *Bolshevistskoe znamya.* Odessa, 1940

Vystuplenia P. I. Chaikovskogo v Parizhe (Tchaikovsky's Performances in Paris) by D. A. Chernomordikov. *Sovyetskaya muzyka,* 1940

Iz moikh vospominany o P. I. Chaikovskom (My Recollections of P. I. Tchaikovsky) by V. V. Yastrebtsev. *Russkaya muzykalnaya gazeta,* 1899

Moi vospominania o Chaikovskom (My Recollections of Tchaikovsky) by V. E. Napravnik. *Sovyetskaya muzyka,* 1949

Posledny dyen P. I. Chaikovskogo v Klinu (Tchaikovsky's Last Day at Klin) by Y. I. Poplavsky. *Artist,* 1894

Klochki zhizni c beregov Nevy, 25 oktyabr (Glimpses of Life on the Banks of the Neva, 25 October) by Skitalyets (S. G. Petrov). *Ranneye,* 1913

Vospominania opernoi artistki (Recollections of an Opera Artist) by E. K. Pavlovskaya. Ms. Tchaikovsky Museum

Vospominania (Recollections) and Vospominania o vstrechakh c Chaikovskim v Tiflise (Recollections of Meetings with Tchaikovsky at Tiflis) by A. N. Amfiteatrova-Levitskaya. Mss. Tchaikovsky and Glinka Museums

O moikh vstrechakh c P. I. Chaikovskim (My Meetings with Tchaikovsky) by L. V. Nikolaev. Ms. Glinka Museum

Vospominania o prebyvanii Chaikovskogo v Taganroge i Odesse (Recollections of Tchaikovsky at Taganrog and Odessa) by I. I. Tchaikovsky. Ms. Tchaikovsky Museum

Kontserty P. I. Chaikovskogo v Kharkove—po lichnym vospominaniam (P. I. Tchaikovsky's Concerts at Kharkov—Personal Recollections) by I. E. Bukinik, 1943. Ms. Tchaikovsky Museum

Meetings with Tchaikovsky in America and England by Walter U. Damrosch, 1946. With a photograph of letter from Tchaikovsky to Damrosch. Ms. Tchaikovsky Museum

O Chaikovskom—vospominania svoi i chuzhie (Recollections of Tchaikovsky by Myself and Others) by S. N. Neuberg-Kashkina, 1959. Ms. Tchaikovsky Museum

Vospominania o P. I. Chaikovskom (Recollections of P. I. Tchaikovsky) from Chetyre pyatykh vyeka (Four-Fifths of a Century) by A. I. Bryullova, 1929. Ms. Glinka Museum

Vospominania o P. I. Chaikovskom (Recollections of P. I. Tchaikovsky) by N. N. Kondratyeva 1940. Ms. Tchaikovsky Museum

Iz moikh vospominany o P. I. Chaikovskom (My Recollections of P. I. Tchaikovsky) Talk given at Moscow State Conservatoire 11 May 1940 by A. L. Meck-Davidova. Ms. Tchaikovsky Museum

Moi vstrechi c P. I. Chaikovskim (My Meetings with P. I. Tchaikovsky) by Y. M. Yurev. Ms. Tchaikovsky Museum. Part published in Zapiski (Memoirs). Leningrad-Moscow, 1948

Souvenirs de P. I. Tchaikovski by Fanny Durbach, 1895. Ms. Tchaikovsky Museum

Avtobiograficheskie zametki M. I. Chaikovskogo (Autobiographical Notes by M. I. Tchaikovsky). Ms. Tchaikovsky Museum

Letters from Fanny Durbach to P. I. and M. I. Tchaikovsky and from A. A., P. I. and M. I. Tchaikovsky and A. V. Popova to Fanny Durbach. Tchaikovsky Museum

Extracts from letters and articles in: Vospominania o P. I. Chaikovskom (Recollections of P. I. Tchaikovsky) ed. V. V. Protopopov. Moscow, 1962 and in the Annual Report of the Tchaikovsky Museum

Dni i gody P. I. Chaikovskogo: lyetopis zhizni i tvorchestva (Days and Years of P. I. Tchaikovsky: Annals of His Life and Work) Ed. V. Yakovlev. Moscow-Leningrad, 1940

GENERAL TITLES

Correspondence between M. A. Balakirev and N. A. Rimsky-Korsakov. *Musical Contemporary,* Petersburg, 1915-16, 1916-17

Correspondence between M. A. Balakirev and V. V. Stasov. Moscow, 1935

Correspondence between N. A. Rimsky-Korsakov and V. V. Stasov. *Russian Thought,* Petersburg, 1910

A. P. Borodin's Letters. Ed. S. A. Dyanin. 3 vols., Moscow, 1928, 1936, 1949

V. V. Stasov, A. P. Borodin: Life, Letters and Musical Articles. Petersburg, 1889
V. V. Stasov. Pisma k rodnym (Letters to Relatives). Moscow, 1958
S. A. Dyanin, Borodin. Moscow, 1962 (Eng. trans. 1963)
V. V. Stasov, Collected Works. Petersburg, 4 vols., 1894, 1905
V. V. Stasov, The 25th Anniversary of the Free Music School. Petersburg, 1887
V. Karenin, Vladimir Stasov. 2 vols., Leningrad, 1926
C. Cui, Musico-critical Articles. 4 vols., Petersburg, 1892-95
D. Lobanov, Serov and His Contemporaries. Petersburg, 1889
V. S. Serova, Alexander Nikolayevich Serov. Petersburg, 1914
A. S. Dargomijhsky, Autobiography, Letters and Reminiscences of My Contemporaries. Leningrad, 1922
N. F. Findeisen, Dargomijhsky. Moscow, 1904
N. N. Rimskaya-Korsakova, My Reminiscences of A. S. Dargomijhsky. Russian Tatler, 1913
N. N. Rimskaya-Korsakova, N. A. Rimsky-Korsakov: Life and Creative Work. 2 vols., Moscow, 1933-35
A. Famintsyn, The Recitals of Hans von Bülow. *Musical Leaflet*, Petersburg, 1873-74
G. Fedorova, A. K. Glazunov. Moscow and Leningrad, 1947
N. D. Kashkin, A History of Russian Music. Moscow, 1908
Rosa Newmarch, The Russian Opera. London, 1913
M. Cooper, Russian Opera. London, 1952
Rostislav Hofmann, Un Siècle d'Opéra Russe. Paris, 1946
Tchaikovsky: A Symposium. Ed. Gerald Abraham. London, 1946
S. I. Taneyev. Diaries, unprinted. Glinka Central Museum of Musical Culture, Materiali i dokumenti, Moscow, 1952

BIOGRAPHIES

Modest Tchaikovsky, Life and Letters of Pyotr Ilyich Tchaikovsky, 3 vols., Moscow, 1900-02
(Eng. trans. abridged by Rosa Newmarch, London, 1906)
Rosa Newmarch, Tchaikovsky: His Life and Works. London, 1900 (Revised ed., 1907)
M. D. Calvocoressi, and Gerald Abraham. Masters of Russian Music. London, 1936
H. Weinstock, Tchaikovsky. New York, 1943

Index